T0335898

Managing and Processing Big Data in Cloud Computing

Rajkumar Kannan
King Faisal University, Saudi Arabia

Raihan Ur Rasool
King Faisal University, Saudi Arabia

Hai Jin
Huazhong University of Science and Technology, China

S.R. Balasundaram
National Institute of Technology, Tiruchirappalli, India

A volume in the Advances in Data Mining and
Database Management (ADMDM) Book Series

Published in the United States of America by
      Information Science Reference (an imprint of IGI Global)
      701 E. Chocolate Avenue
      Hershey PA, USA 17033
      Tel: 717-533-8845
      Fax: 717-533-8661
      E-mail: cust@igi-global.com
      Web site: http://www.igi-global.com

Copyright © 2016 by IGI Global. All rights reserved. No part of this publication may be reproduced, stored or distributed in any form or by any means, electronic or mechanical, including photocopying, without written permission from the publisher. Product or company names used in this set are for identification purposes only. Inclusion of the names of the products or companies does not indicate a claim of ownership by IGI Global of the trademark or registered trademark.

Library of Congress Cataloging-in-Publication Data

Names: Kannan, Rajkumar.
Title: Managing and processing big data in cloud computing / Rajkumar Kannan,
  Raihan Ur Sool, Hai Jin, and S.R. Balasundaram, editors.
Description: Hershey, PA : Information Science Reference, [2016] | Includes
  bibliographical references and index.
Identifiers: LCCN 2015041973| ISBN 9781466697676 (hardcover) | ISBN
  9781466697683 (ebook)
Subjects: LCSH: Database management. | Big data. | Cloud computing.
Classification: LCC QA76.9.D3 M33664 2016 | DDC 005.7--dc23 LC record available at http://lccn.loc.gov/2015041973

This book is published in the IGI Global book series Advances in Data Mining and Database Management (ADMDM)
(ISSN: 2327-1981; eISSN: 2327-199X)

British Cataloguing in Publication Data
A Cataloguing in Publication record for this book is available from the British Library.

All work contributed to this book is new, previously-unpublished material. The views expressed in this book are those of the authors, but not necessarily of the publisher.

For electronic access to this publication, please contact: eresources@igi-global.com.

Advances in Data Mining and Database Management (ADMDM) Book Series

David Taniar
Monash University, Australia

ISSN: 2327-1981
EISSN: 2327-199X

Mission

With the large amounts of information available to organizations in today's digital world, there is a need for continual research surrounding emerging methods and tools for collecting, analyzing, and storing data.

The **Advances in Data Mining & Database Management (ADMDM)** series aims to bring together research in information retrieval, data analysis, data warehousing, and related areas in order to become an ideal resource for those working and studying in these fields. IT professionals, software engineers, academicians and upper-level students will find titles within the ADMDM book series particularly useful for staying up-to-date on emerging research, theories, and applications in the fields of data mining and database management.

Coverage
- Neural Networks
- Customer Analytics
- Decision Support Systems
- Profiling Practices
- Quantitative Structure–Activity Relationship
- Educational Data Mining
- Cluster Analysis
- Information Extraction
- Association Rule Learning
- Text Mining

IGI Global is currently accepting manuscripts for publication within this series. To submit a proposal for a volume in this series, please contact our Acquisition Editors at Acquisitions@igi-global.com or visit: http://www.igi-global.com/publish/.

The Advances in Data Mining and Database Management (ADMDM) Book Series (ISSN 2327-1981) is published by IGI Global, 701 E. Chocolate Avenue, Hershey, PA 17033-1240, USA, www.igi-global.com. This series is composed of titles available for purchase individually; each title is edited to be contextually exclusive from any other title within the series. For pricing and ordering information please visit http://www.igi-global.com/book-series/advances-data-mining-database-management/37146. Postmaster: Send all address changes to above address. Copyright © 2016 IGI Global. All rights, including translation in other languages reserved by the publisher. No part of this series may be reproduced or used in any form or by any means – graphics, electronic, or mechanical, including photocopying, recording, taping, or information and retrieval systems – without written permission from the publisher, except for non commercial, educational use, including classroom teaching purposes. The views expressed in this series are those of the authors, but not necessarily of IGI Global.

Titles in this Series

For a list of additional titles in this series, please visit: www.igi-global.com

Handbook of Research on Innovative Database Query Processing Techniques
Li Yan (Nanjing University of Aeronautics and Astronautics, China)
Information Science Reference • copyright 2016 • 625pp • H/C (ISBN: 9781466687677) • US $335.00 (our price)

Handbook of Research on Trends and Future Directions in Big Data and Web Intelligence
Noor Zaman (King Faisal University, Saudi Arabia) Mohamed Elhassan Seliaman (King Faisal University, Saudi Arabia) Mohd Fadzil Hassan (Universiti Teknologi PETRONAS, Malaysia) and Fausto Pedro Garcia Marquez (Campus Universitario s/n ETSII of Ciudad Real, Spain)
Information Science Reference • copyright 2015 • 500pp • H/C (ISBN: 9781466685055) • US $285.00 (our price)

Improving Knowledge Discovery through the Integration of Data Mining Techniques
Muhammad Usman (Shaheed Zulfikar Ali Bhutto Institute of Science and Technology, Pakistan)
Information Science Reference • copyright 2015 • 391pp • H/C (ISBN: 9781466685130) • US $225.00 (our price)

Modern Computational Models of Semantic Discovery in Natural Language
Jan Žižka (Mendel University in Brno, Czech Republic) and František Dařena (Mendel University in Brno, Czech Republic)
Information Science Reference • copyright 2015 • 335pp • H/C (ISBN: 9781466686908) • US $215.00 (our price)

Mobile Technologies for Activity-Travel Data Collection and Analysis
Soora Rasouli (Eindhoven University of Technology, The Netherlands) and Harry Timmermans (Eindhoven University of Technology, The Netherlands)
Information Science Reference • copyright 2014 • 325pp • H/C (ISBN: 9781466661707) • US $225.00 (our price)

Biologically-Inspired Techniques for Knowledge Discovery and Data Mining
Shafiq Alam (University of Auckland, New Zealand) Gillian Dobbie (University of Auckland, New Zealand) Yun Sing Koh (University of Auckland, New Zealand) and Saeed ur Rehman (Unitec Institute of Technology, New Zealand)
Information Science Reference • copyright 2014 • 375pp • H/C (ISBN: 9781466660786) • US $265.00 (our price)

Data Mining and Analysis in the Engineering Field
Vishal Bhatnagar (Ambedkar Institute of Advanced Communication Technologies and Research, India)
Information Science Reference • copyright 2014 • 405pp • H/C (ISBN: 9781466660861) • US $225.00 (our price)

Handbook of Research on Cloud Infrastructures for Big Data Analytics
Pethuru Raj (IBM India Pvt Ltd, India) and Ganesh Chandra Deka (Ministry of Labour and Employment, India)
Information Science Reference • copyright 2014 • 570pp • H/C (ISBN: 9781466658646) • US $345.00 (our price)

www.igi-global.com

701 E. Chocolate Ave., Hershey, PA 17033
Order online at www.igi-global.com or call 717-533-8845 x100
To place a standing order for titles released in this series, contact: cust@igi-global.com
Mon-Fri 8:00 am - 5:00 pm (est) or fax 24 hours a day 717-533-8661

Editorial Advisory Board

Rajeev Agrawal, *North Carolina A&T State University, USA*
Kalaiarasi Anbananthen, *Multimedia University, Malaysia*
Frederic Andres, *National Institute of Informatics, Japan*
Peter Bloodsworth, *National University of Science and Technology (NUST), Pakistan*
George Ghinea, *Brunel University, UK*
Pierre Gouton, *University of Burgundy, France*
Asanee Kawtrakul, *Kasetsart University, Thailand*
Hammad Majeed, *National University of Computer and Emerging Sciences (FAST-NU), Pakistan*
Kamran Munir, *University of West of England, UK*
Manjeet Rege, *St. Thomas University, USA*
Qiang Sun, *Shanghai Dianji University, China*

Table of Contents

Detailed Table of Contents

Chapter 1
Bunjamin Memishi, Universidad Politecnica de Madrid, Spain
Shadi Ibrahim, Inria, France
Maria S. Perez, Universidad Politecnica de Madrid, Spain
Gabriel Antoniu, Inria, France

MapReduce has become a relevant framework for Big Data processing in the cloud. At large-scale clouds, failures do occur and may incur unwanted performance degradation to Big Data applications. As the reliability of MapReduce depends on how well they detect and handle failures, this book chapter investigates the problem of failure detection in the MapReduce framework. The case studies of this contribution reveal that the current static timeout value is not adequate and demonstrate significant variations in the application's response time with different timeout values. While arguing that comparatively little attention has been devoted to the failure detection in the framework, the chapter presents design ideas for a new adaptive timeout.

Chapter 2
Hammad Majeed, National University of Computer and Emerging Sciences (NUCES),
Pakistan
Firoza Erum, National University of Computer and Emerging Sciences (NUCES), Pakistan

Internet is growing fast with millions of web pages containing information on every topic. The data placed on Internet is not organized which makes the search process difficult. Classification of the web pages in some predefined classes can improve the organization of this data. In this chapter a semantic based technique is presented to classify text corpus with high accuracy. This technique uses some well-known pre-processing techniques like word stemming, term frequency, and degree of uniqueness. In addition to this a new semantic similarity measure is computed between different terms. The authors believe that semantic similarity based comparison in addition to syntactic matching makes the classification process significantly accurate. The proposed technique is tested on a benchmark dataset and results are compared with already published results. The obtained results are significantly better and that too by using quite small sized highly relevant feature set.

Maryam Qamar, National University of Sciences and Technology, Pakistan
Mehwish Malik, National University of Sciences and Technology, Pakistan
Saadia Batool, National University of Sciences and Technology, Pakistan
Sidra Mehmood, National University of Sciences and Technology, Pakistan
Asad W. Malik, National University of Sciences and Technology, Pakistan
Anis Rahman, National University of Sciences and Technology, Pakistan

This work covers the research work on decentralization of Online Social Networks (OSNs), issues with centralized design are studied with possible decentralized solutions. Centralized architecture is prone to privacy breach, p2p architecture for data and thus authority decentralization with encryption seems a possible solution. OSNs' users grow exponentially causing scalability issue, a natural solution is decentralization where users bring resources with them via personal machines or paid services. Also centralized services are not available unremittingly, to this end decentralization proposes replication. Decentralized solutions are also proposed for reliability issues arising in centralized systems and the potential threat of a central authority. Yet key to all problems isn't found, metadata may be enough for inferences about data and network traffic flow can lead to information on users' relationships. First issue can be mitigated by data padding or splitting in uniform blocks. Caching, dummy traffic or routing through a mix of nodes can be some possible solutions to the second.

Kiran Fatima, National University of Computer and Emerging Sciences (NUCES), Pakistan
Hammad Majeed, National University of Computer and Emerging Sciences (NUCES),
    Pakistan

Real-world histology tissue textures owing to non-homogeneous nature and unorganized spatial intensity variations are complex to analyze and classify. The major challenge in solving pathological problems is inherent complexity due to high intra-class variability and low inter-class variation in texture of histology samples. The development of computational methods to assists pathologists in characterization of these tissue samples would have great diagnostic and prognostic value. In this chapter, an optimized texture-based evolutionary framework is proposed to provide assistance to pathologists for classification of benign and pre-malignant tumors. The proposed framework investigates the imperative role of RGB color channels for discrimination of cancer grades or subtypes, explores higher-order statistical features at image-level, and implements an evolution-based optimization scheme for feature selection and classification. The highest classification accuracy of 99.06% is achieved on meningioma dataset and 90% on breast cancer dataset through Quadratic SVM classifier.

Chapter 5

Shahid Nawaz, National University of Sciences and Technology, Pakistan
Asad Waqar Malik, National University of Sciences and Technology, Pakistan
Raihan ur Rasool, National University of Sciences and Technology, Pakistan

Cloud computing is modus operandi of manipulating server clusters hosted at secluded sites on Internet for storage, processing, and retrieval of data. It tenders suppleness, disaster recovery, competitiveness, and cutback in capital and operational cost for ventures, principally small and medium ones, which hold meager resource base. Virtualization at plinth of cloud computing sanctions utilizing physical hardware stratum to frame and administer virtualized infrastructure, storage areas, and network interfaces. Virtual machines, administered on clouds to seize inherent advantages of virtualization, are fabricated on storage area networks (Armbrust et al., 2009). But whenever user endeavors to access them from remote location it resulted in hundreds of megabytes of data reads and ensuing congestion in network. Question is how to instigate virtual machines and load their applications in minimal time. The ingenious Ceaseless Virtual Appliance Streaming system assures virtual machine's streaming just like video on demand. It trims down burden over existing resources and offers improved network utilization.

Chapter 6

Usman Ashraf, King Faisal University, Saudi Arabia
Syed Salman Haider Rizvi, Air University, Pakistan
Mohammad Faisal Azeem, Air University, Pakistan

In the world of wireless communication technologies, the new standard IEEE 802.11n (MIMO) has revolutionized the available wireless bandwidth. Significant industrial and academic research has been initiated on this new technology around the world. Moreover, international as well as local manufacturers are highly interested in commercialization and performance improvement of this new technology. This is a research project in which we will perform comprehensive benchmarking of IEEE 802.11n in wireless multi-hop environments. In this project we evaluate the performance of routing metrics: Hop Count (HC) and Expected Transmission Count (ETX) on a test bed at A-Block Air University.

Chapter 7

Sajid Umair, National University of Sciences and Technology, Pakistan
Umair Muneer, National University of Sciences and Technology, Pakistan
Muhammad Nauman Zahoor, National University of Sciences and Technology, Pakistan
Asad W. Malik, National University of Sciences and Technology, Pakistan

Due to wide variety of smart phones and capability of supporting heavy applications their demand is increasing day by day. Increase of computation capability and processing power Mobile cloud computing (MCC) becomes an emerging field. After cloud computing mobile cloud provide significant advantage and usage with reliability and portability. Challenges involved in mobile cloud computing are energy consumption, computation power and processing ability. Mobile cloud provides a way to use cloud resources on mobile but traditional models of smart phones does not support cloud so researchers introduce new models for the development of MCC. There are certain phases that still need improvement and this field attracts many researchers. Purpose of this chapter is to analyze and summarize the challenges involved in this field and work done so far.

S. ZerAfshan Goher, National University of Sciences and Technology, Pakistan
Barkha Javed, National University of Sciences and Technology, Pakistan
Peter Bloodsworth, National University of Sciences and Technology, Pakistan

Due to the growing interest in harnessing the hidden significance of data, more and more enterprises are moving to data analytics. Data analytics require the analysis and management of large-scale data to find the hidden patterns among various data components to gain useful insight. The derived information is then used to predict the future trends that can be advantageous for a business to flourish such as customers' likes/dislikes, reasons behind customers' churn and more. In this paper, several techniques for the big data analysis have been investigated along with their advantages and disadvantages. The significance of cloud computing for big data storage has also been discussed. Finally, the techniques to make the robust and efficient usage of big data have also been discussed.

Manjunath Thimmasandra Narayanapppa, BMS Institute of Technology, India
A. Channabasamma, Acharya Institute of Technology, India
Ravindra S. Hegadi, Solapur University, India

The amount of data around us in three sixty degrees getting increased second on second and the world is exploding as a result the size of the database used in today's enterprises, which is growing at an exponential rate day by day. At the same time, the need to process and analyze the bulky data for business decision making has also increased. Several business and scientific applications generate terabytes of data which have to be processed in efficient manner on daily bases. Data gets collected and stored at unprecedented rates. Moreover the challenge here is not only to store and manage the huge amount of data, but even to analyze and extract meaningful values from it. This has contributed to the problem of big data faced by the industry due to the inability of usual software tools and database systems to manage and process the big data sets within reasonable time limits. The main focus of the chapter is on unstructured data analysis.

Farid Ahmad, Adama Science and Technology University, Ethiopia

Data virtualization is the procedure of combining data from different sources of information to develop a solo, logical and virtual view of facts so that it can be accessed by front-end resolutions such as applications, dashboards and portals without having to know the data's exact storingsite. Several organizations ride multiple types of database management systems, such as Oracle and SQL servers, which do not work fine with one another. Therefore, enterprises face new challenges in data integration and storage of huge amounts of data. With data virtualization, commercial handlers are able to get real time and consistent information speedily, which supports them to take foremost corporate decisions. The process of data virtualization involves abstracting, transforming, federating and delivering data from unequal sources. The key objective of data virtualization technology is to deliver a single point of access to the data by aggregating it from a wide range of data sources.

Chapter 11
Manjunath Thimmasandra Narayanapppa, BMS Institute of Technology, India
T. P. Puneeth Kumar, Acharya Institute of Technology, India
Ravindra S. Hegadi, Solapur University, India

Recent technological advancements have led to generation of huge volume of data from distinctive domains (scientific sensors, health care, user-generated data, finical companies and internet and supply chain systems) over the past decade. To capture the meaning of this emerging trend the term big data was coined. In addition to its huge volume, big data also exhibits several unique characteristics as compared with traditional data. For instance, big data is generally unstructured and require more real-time analysis. This development calls for new system platforms for data acquisition, storage, transmission and large-scale data processing mechanisms. In recent years analytics industries interest expanding towards the big data analytics to uncover potentials concealed in big data, such as hidden patterns or unknown correlations. The main goal of this chapter is to explore the importance of machine learning algorithms and computational environment including hardware and software that is required to perform analytics on big data.

Chapter 12
Muhammad Adeel, International Islamic University, Pakistan

With the recent explosion of internet usage as well as more and more devices are being hooked up with the cloud, big data is becoming a phenomena to tackle with. Big data management was initially a question of concern for only the big commercial players such as Google, Yahoo, Microsoft and others. But it has now become a concern for others, too. According to recent estimates, big data will continue to grow from terabytes into exabytes and beyond. This data needs to be made available for an organization's own use as well can be made available for scientific and commercial needs to the interested entities. This can include different user segments such as academia, industry etc. Academic use of big data is for further research and enablement of big data over cloud, working with it in containers, usage in virtualized environments etc. This generates a need for a sustainable infrastructure which can hold and maintain big data with opportunities for extended processing.

Cloud computing is based on the concepts of distributed computing, grid computing, utility computing and virtualization. It is a virtual pool of resources which are provided to users via Internet. It gives users virtually unlimited pay-per-use computing resources without the burden of managing the underlying infrastructure. Cloud computing service providers' one of the goals is to use the resources efficiently and gain maximum profit. This leads to task scheduling as a core and challenging issue in cloud computing. This paper gives different scheduling strategies and algorithms in cloud computing.

Chapter 14

Sustainability creates and maintains the conditions under which humans and nature can exist in productive accord, that permit fulfilling the social, economic and other requirements of present and future generations. There is a debate that cloud computing is green contributing to sustainability or a risk of climate change. Cloud computing if compared to traditional on-premise computing, is a cost effective, energy-efficient, scalable and on-demand computing. There is no doubt that the expansive power of computing can help us address sustainability challenges, but this technology also draws from the Earth's finite environmental stocks and biosphere which results in risk of climate change.

Chapter 15

This chapter introduces the concept of heterogeneity as a perspective in the architecture of big data systems targeted to both vertical and generic workloads and discusses how this can be linked with the existing Hadoop ecosystem (as of 2015). The case of the cost factor of a big data solution and its characteristics can influence its architectural patterns and capabilities and as such an extended model based on the 3V paradigm is introduced (Extended 3V). This is examined on a hierarchical set of four layers (Hardware, Management, Platform and Application). A list of components is provided on each layer as well as a classification of their role in a big data solution.

Foreword

Growth of technology is too rapid in all direction now days and that growth increases the datasets too in huge, that huge collection of datasets is known as Big data. Big data's are huge in size and complex to handle by commonly used data processing tools and applications. These datasets are unstructured and often come from various sources such as social media, social sensors, scientific applications, archives, web documents, electronic health records, business applications, web logs etc. They are larger in size with fast data in/out. Further, big data should have high value and ensure trust for decision making. Also, these data come from heterogeneous sources and heterogeneity is another important property besides variety, volume, velocity, value and veracity.

Currently there are several available technologies which can support handling big data including parallel processing, distributed computing, cloud computing platforms, large storage systems and MapReduce. Based on current estimation by International Data Corporation (IDC) related to the global data is that approximately close to 50% of data is handled through Cloud Computing. Further, cloud computing supports massive storage and computation facility to support big data processing. Therefore, there is an urgent need to investigate the challenges of big data computing by leveraging the potential of cloud computing. This book focuses that how to will address the challenges of both big data and cloud computing.

This book provides window to academic and industrial communities with recent advances in development, application and impact of new big-data platforms and technologies for exploiting floods of big data sources. In addition this book encourages more research in big data and cloud computing technologies.

Noor Zaman
King Faisal University, Saudi Arabia

Preface

This edited book aims to present the state-of-the-art research and development of big data computing on the cloud.

There are many technologies that support handling big data including *parallel processing, distributed computing* and *cloud computing*. Cloud computing supports massive storage and computation facility to support big data processing. Therefore, there is an urgent need to investigate the challenges of big data computing by leveraging the potential of cloud computing and this edited book exactly will address the real-world applications, challenges and complexities of both big data and cloud computing.

The objective of this edited book is to provide academics and practitioners the recent advances and trends in the development, application and impact of the big-data technologies for the cloud. In particular, this book will explore the challenges of supporting big data processing by exploiting the potential of cloud computing.

This edited book has attracted potential chapters in wide areas including text classification, social networks, big data, map reduce, Hadoop, virtual packet streaming, wireless multi-hop networks, mobile cloud computing, big data virtualization, machine learning, resource scheduling for big data, green and energy-efficiency issues in cloud and big data architectures.

We believe that this book would serve a broad audience including academics, researchers, students and practitioners in the field of business, data science, health, environmental services, government, defense, manufacturing and networking industries.

Rajkumar Kannan
King Faisal University, Saudi Arabia

Raihan Ur Rasool
King Faisal University, Saudi Arabia

Hai Jin
Huazhong University of Science and Technology, China

S.R. Balasundaram
National Institute of Technology, India

Acknowledgment

We thank and appreciate all contributors including the authors of accepted chapters, and many other participants who submitted their chapters that cannot be included in the book due to space limits.

Our special thanks to IGI team for their kind support and great efforts in bringing the book to fruition. In addition, we also appreciate all editorial advisory board and the reviewers who have helped us to review the submissions on time and to give valuable feedbacks to the submitting authors.

Chapter 1
On the Dynamic Shifting of the MapReduce Timeout

Bunjamin Memishi
Universidad Politecnica de Madrid, Spain

Maria S. Perez
Universidad Politecnica de Madrid, Spain

Shadi Ibrahim
Inria, France

Gabriel Antoniu
Inria, France

ABSTRACT

MapReduce has become a relevant framework for Big Data processing in the cloud. At large-scale clouds, failures do occur and may incur unwanted performance degradation to Big Data applications. As the reliability of MapReduce depends on how well they detect and handle failures, this book chapter investigates the problem of failure detection in the MapReduce framework. The case studies of this contribution reveal that the current static timeout value is not adequate and demonstrate significant variations in the application's response time with different timeout values. While arguing that comparatively little attention has been devoted to the failure detection in the framework, the chapter presents design ideas for a new adaptive timeout.

INTRODUCTION

The ever growing size of data (i.e., Big Data) has motivated the development of data intensive processing frameworks and tools. In this context, MapReduce (Dean & Ghemawat, 2004; Jin et al., 2011) has become a relevant framework for Big Data processing in the clouds, thanks to its remarkable features including simplicity, fault tolerance, and scalability. The popular open source implementation of MapReduce, Hadoop (*Apache Hadoop Project*, 2015), was developed primarily by Yahoo!, where it processes hundreds of Terabytes of data on at least 10,000 cores, and is now used by other companies, including Facebook, Amazon, Last.fm, and the New York Times (*Powered By Hadoop*, 2015).

Undoubtedly, failure is a part of everyday life, especially in current data-centers which comprise thousands of commodity hardware and software (Chandra, Prinja, Jain, & Zhang, 2008; Oppenheimer, Ganapathi, & Patterson, 2003; Pinheiro, Weber, & Barroso, 2007). Consequently, MapReduce was designed with hardware failure in mind. In particular, Hadoop tolerates machine failures (crash failures)

DOI: 10.4018/978-1-4666-9767-6.ch001

Copyright © 2016, IGI Global. Copying or distributing in print or electronic forms without written permission of IGI Global is prohibited.

by re-executing all the tasks of the failed machine by the virtue of data replication. Furthermore, in order to mask temporary failures caused by network or machine overload (timing failure) where some tasks are performing relatively slower than other tasks, Hadoop re-launches other copies of these tasks on other machines.

Foreseeing MapReduce usage in the next generation Internet (Mone, 2013), a particular concern is the aim of improving the MapReduce's reliability by providing better fault tolerance mechanisms. While the handling and recovery in MapReduce fault-tolerance via data replication and task re-execution seem to work well even at large scale (Ko, Hoque, Cho, & Gupta, 2010; Ananthanarayanan et al., 2011; Zaharia, Konwinski, Joseph, Katz, & Stoica, 2008), there is relatively little work on detecting failures in MapReduce. Accurate detection of failures is as important as failures recovery, in order to improve applications' latencies and minimize resource waste.

At the core of failure detection mechanism is the concept of heartbeat. Any kind of failure that is detected in MapReduce has to fulfill some preconditions, in this case to miss a certain number of heartbeats, so that other entities in the system detect the failure. Currently, a static timeout based mechanism is applied for detecting fail-stop failure by checking the expiry time of the last received heartbeat from a certain machine. In Hadoop, each TaskTracker sends a heartbeat every 3s, the JobTracker checks every 200s the expiry time of the last reported heartbeat. If no heartbeat is received from a machine for 600s, then this machine will be labeled as a failed machine and therefore the JobTracker will trigger the failure handling and recovery process. However, some studies have reported that the current static timeout detector is not effective and may cause long and unpredictable latency (Dinu & Ng, 2011, 2012).

An accurate timeout detector is important not only to improve application's latency but also to improve resource utilization, especially in the cloud where you pay for the resources you use. Accordingly, a series of experiments is conducted to measure the performance of Hadoop with different timeout values while varying the application input sizes and the failure injection times. The authors find that, in the presence of single machine failure the applications' latencies vary not only in accordance to the occurrence time of the failure, similar to (Dinu & Ng, 2012), but also vary with the job length (short or long). Furthermore, the experimental results report not only a noticeable variation of the application's latency with different timeout value, but also demonstrate the opportunity to achieve better performance. For example, when using a small timeout value of 10s, it is achieved a 3X performance improvement for the sort benchmark compared to the default one. Thus, a significant potential exists for performance improvement in MapReduce applications, when choosing the appropriate timeout failure detector. The authors believe that a new methodology to adaptively tune the timeout detector, at runtime and according to the job progress, can significantly improve the overall performance of MapReduce applications under failure. Therefore, they discuss three potential fine-tuning approaches that could be used towards an optimal timeout failure detector in MapReduce.

In order to clarify some preliminary knowledge, the background section comes first. Then, it follows the section of general fault tolerance in Hadoop. The timeout problem is described in details after this. The methodology overview comes next, which is closely linked with experimental analysis section. There are given open challenges in the following section. A related work on improving fault-tolerance mechanism in MapReduce is presented after, before concluding the chapter with the summary section.

BACKGROUND

This section gives the essential theoretical preliminaries in order to easily follow the ongoing part of the chapter. It explains the MapReduce framework first. After this, briefly it mentions its wide-spread implementation, Apache Hadoop, and its next-generation MapReduce implementation, commonly known as Hadoop YARN (Yet Another Resource Negotiator), which are classified as MapReduce *1.0* and MapReduce *2.0*, respectively.

MapReduce

MapReduce is an important framework in data-intensive computing. It represents a programming model for processing large data sets (Dean et al., 2004). It has been more than a decade that MapReduce has been discussed by researchers, including the database community. Even though its benefits have been questioned when compared with parallel databases, some authors suggest that both approaches have their own advantages, and there is not a risk that one could become *obsolete* (Stonebraker et al., 2010). MapReduce's advantages over parallel databases include storage-system independence and fine-grain fault tolerance for large jobs. Its simple philosophy around implementation and usage, and automatic parallelism while keeping strong scalability, have created a huge community interest for exploring MapReduce, especially in environments where data-intensive applications are a major concern. Due to this, MapReduce is becoming more and more popular, and is used for different large-scale computing environments, such as in Facebook Inc. (*Facebook, Inc.*, 2015), Yahoo! Inc. (*Yahoo! Inc.*, 2015), and Microsoft Corporation (*Microsoft, Inc.*, 2015).

By default, every MapReduce execution needs a special node, called *master*; the other nodes are called *workers*. The master keeps several data structures, like the state and the identity of the worker machines, and the worker nodes are assigned different tasks by the master. Depending on the phase, tasks may have two different roles: map or reduce. As explained in (Dean et al., 2004), users have to specify a map function that processes a *key/value* pair to generate a set of intermediate *key/value* pairs, and a reduce function that merges all intermediate values associated with the same intermediate key. In this way, many real world problems can be expressed by means of the MapReduce model.

A simple MapReduce data workflow is shown in Figure 1. This figure represents a MapReduce workflow scenario, from the time of taking the input data until the stage when the output data is being produced. The most common implementations keep the input and output data in a reliable distributed file system, while the intermediate data is kept in the local file system at the worker nodes.

Apache Hadoop

The most common implementation of MapReduce comes as a part of the Apache Hadoop open-source framework (*Apache Hadoop Project*, 2015). Hadoop uses the Hadoop Distributed File System (HDFS) as the underlying storage backend, but it is designed to work on many other distributed file systems as well. Additional add-ons, such as network striping module for HDFS, created by Facebook, are also available (Rutman, 2011).

Figure 1. MapReduce logical workflow

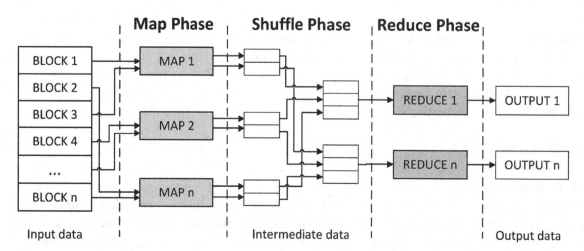

The MapReduce master/worker philosophy is present in Hadoop iterations including those between the MapReduce 1.0 and MapReduce 2.0, widely known as Apache Hadoop and Hadoop YARN, respectively.

In Apache Hadoop, the main components are MapReduce and HDFS. Together, they are assumed to maintain any cluster infrastructure. Hadoop MapReduce consists of a JobTracker and many TaskTrackers, which are synonyms for the processing master and workers. TaskTrackers consist of a limited number of slots for running map or reduce tasks. The MapReduce workflow is managed by the JobTracker, whose responsibility goes beyond the MapReduce process that among others includes resource management. Hadoop HDFS consists of a NameNode and many DataNodes, which are synonyms for the storage master and workers. Whereas the NameNode manages the file system metadata, DataNodes hold a portion of data in blocks.

Due to many limitations, primarily scalability issues, the Hadoop community, leaded by Yahoo! researchers, represented Hadoop YARN (*Apache Hadoop NextGen MapReduce (YARN)*, 2015; Vavila-palli et al., 2013).

In Hadoop YARN, the basic idea behind the framework is the separation between the two main operations of the classic Hadoop JobTracker, resource management and job scheduling/monitoring, into separate entities or daemons. Nevertheless, the MapReduce process has remained the same, with the main difference that now, each job request consists of its own master, called Application Master.

GENERAL DESCRIPTION OF FAULT-TOLERANCE IN HADOOP

Figure 2 shows a big picture of the default fault-tolerant concepts and their mechanisms in Hadoop's MapReduce. At the core of failure detection mechanism is the concept of heartbeat. Any kind of failure that is detected in MapReduce has to fulfill some preconditions, in this case to miss a certain number of heartbeats, so that the other entities in the system detect the failure. The classic implementation of MapReduce has no mechanism for dealing with failure of the master, thus in this case, the complete job also fails. The MapReduce cluster administrators must first detect this situation, and then manually

Figure 2. Fault tolerance in MapReduce: The basic fault tolerance definitions (detection, handling and recovery) with their corresponding implementations.

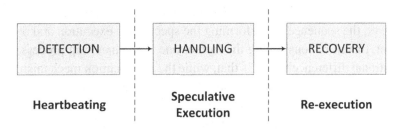

restart the master. The heartbeat mechanism does not apply to detecting the failure of the master. This is because every other entity sends a heartbeat report to the master, but the master's health is monitored by the administrator who monitors MapReduce cluster.

Because the worker sends heartbeats to the master, its failure will stop these heartbeat notifications. From the worker side, there is a simple loop that periodically sends heartbeat method calls to the master; by default, this period has been adjusted to 3s in most of the implementations. The master makes a checking point every 200s, as to whether it has missed any heartbeats from a worker for a period of 600s, which is 10 minutes. If this condition is fulfilled, then a worker is declared as dead and removed from the master's pool of workers upon which can schedule tasks on. After the master declares the worker as dead, the tasks running on a failed worker are restarted on other workers. Because the map tasks that are completed were keeping their output on the dead worker, they have to be restarted as well. Differently, reduce tasks that were not completed, need to be executed in different workers, but since completed reduce tasks have saved their outputs in HDFS, their re-execution is not necessary. However, it is important to mention that some ongoing tasks may get re-executed before the worker is declared as a failed worker if they are detected as stragglers, thanks to the speculative execution mechanism.

Apart from telling the master that a worker is alive, heartbeats also double as a channel for messages. As a part of the heartbeat, a worker will indicate whether it is ready to run a new task, and if it is, the master will allocate a task, which is used to communicate to the worker using the heartbeat return value (White, 2012; Huang et al., 2010).

The heartbeat also works in a finer-grain case, the one between a particular task and its worker where it has been executed on. If the worker notices that it did not receive a progress update for a while, it proceeds to mark the task as failed. Including here, the timeout period after which a task is considered failed is by default 600s. After this, the worker's duty is to notify the master that a task attempt has failed; with this, master reschedules a different execution of the task, while trying to avoid rescheduling the task on the same worker where it has previously failed.

An interesting dilemma is how to differentiate the handling and recovery mechanisms. A simple question arises: Does MapReduce differentiate between handling and recovery?

The speculative execution is meant to be a method of launching another equivalent task as a backup, but only after all the normal tasks have been launched, and after the average running time of the other tasks. In other words, a speculative task basically runs for map and reduce task that has its progress rate below a certain percentage of the progress rate of the majority of running tasks.

In some sense, both, speculative execution and re-execution try to complete a MapReduce job as soon as possible, with the least processing time, while executing its tasks on minimal resources (e.g., to avoid long occupation of resources by some tasks). This is not particularly true, since even speculative execution has proven to exhaust a considerable amount of resources, when executed on heterogeneous environments (Zaharia et al., 2008; Lin et al., 2010) or when the system is going under failures (Dinu & Ng, 2012). However, the sequence of performing the speculative execution and re-execution is what makes them different, therefore considering the former one in the handling process, and the latter one in recovery. An additional difference to this is that, while the re-execution mechanism tries to react after the heartbeat mechanism has declared that an entity has failed, the speculative execution does not need the same timeout condition in order to take place; it reacts sooner.

Failures may have variations also in MapReduce framework; since the beginning and until now, its nomenclature has not been unanimous and generalized so as to be uniquely used by different communities. Additionally, the authors have not seen even a single description which separates faults, errors, and failures inside MapReduce, even though this is possible. For instance, you may consider two cases when these distinctions can take place also in the MapReduce framework:

- **Job Failure:** Herein, it is considered a failure when the job does not complete successfully. In this case, the first task that fails can be considered as an error, because it will request its speculation or re-execution from the master.
- **Task Failure:** Herein, this failure is considered a finer grain case. This can happen because the network is overloaded (which in this case represents an error, because the network fault is active and loses some deliveries). Since the worker cannot deliver an acknowledgment to the master that a task has finished its processing, the master considers the task as failed.

It is therefore better to assume that in MapReduce, a task or any other entity is facing a failure, whenever it does not fulfill its intended function.

During a map phase, if a map task crashes, then Hadoop tries to re-compute it in a different Task-Tracker. In order to make sure that this computation takes place, the majority of reducers should complain for not receiving the map task output or the number of notifications which are bigger or equal to three (Roy, Setty, Kilzer, Shmatikov, & Witchel, 2010). The failed tasks have a higher priority to be executed from the other ones; this is done to detect when a task fails repeatedly due to a bug and stop the job. In a reduce phase, a reduce task failure will have to be executed in a different TaskTracker, having in mind that the three reduce phases should start from the beginning. The reduce task is considered as failed, if the majority of its shuffle attempts fail, the shuffle phase does not succeed to get five map outputs, or its progress stops for a long time. During the shuffle phase, a failure may also happen (in this case, a network failure), because two processes (in our case two daemons) can be in a working state, but a network failure may stop any data interchange between them. MapReduce implementations have seen its security improvement through Kerberos authentication system, preventing a malicious reduce task from requesting another user's map output.

THE TIMEOUT PROBLEM

Herein the section, the authors try to describe the reasons which served as a motivation to this work. The timeout problem and its limitations are captured from theoretical assumptions. Next, they analyze its impact in multiple jobs cluster.

Break Down Assumptions

Any framework may choose to implement a static or dynamic timeout. The static way is understood as tuning the timeout parameter when starting the job and not changing it until the job execution completes. It is well known that a static timeout value which is applicable to any application, infrastructure or networking environment does not exist (Plank, Allen, & Wolski, 2001). This is due to its limitations: firstly, that value is not applicable to all the scenarios, and secondly, even if the timeout value would have been chosen well at the beginning, the application, infrastructure and the networking environment may suffer changes (e.g., failures, delays, etc.). This is the case of Hadoop, which has a static timeout value (*Apache Hadoop Project*, 2015), not being a solution for every Hadoop job; at least this is impossible with the today's Hadoop failure detection mechanism. The failure timeout problem is explained with examples shown in Figure 3.

- **First Case:** 30 min job (*J*1). The timeout is fine here, but if only the failure is assumed to happen during the first 20 min. Otherwise, if the failure is happening in the last minutes, it may force the job to complete later, even though with a smaller performance degradation.
- **Second Case:** 15 min job (*J*2). It is assumed that a job that has a big workload needs around 15-16 min to complete. In this case, the 10 min timeout is fine, only if the failure happens during the first 5-6 min. This, because the lost worker interval will be equal to the job completion time, and in case the failure happens before, the job completion time will not vary from the default job completion time.

Figure 3. Assumed timeout reaction to different jobs

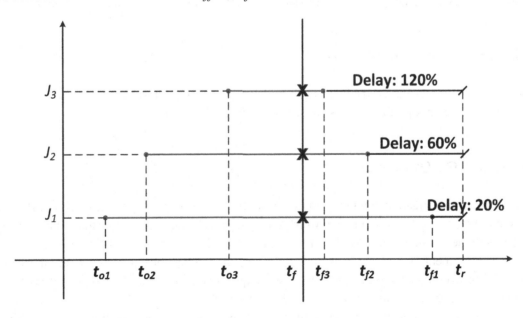

Ji : job	toi : time of origin	tfi : time estimated
tf : time of failure	tr : time completed	

- **Third Case:** 7 min job (*J*3). This type of jobs has a workload that should finish running for about 7 min. The default timeout is already long for this type of jobs; hence the performance degradation reaches about 120%.

One static timeout is not appropriate for the three cases. Moreover, within the same job the occurrence time of failure may significantly affect the performance, thus it is important to re-adjust the timeout value according to the current progress of the running job.

Real World Numbers

According to the declarations of major industry leaders (such as Google's Jeff Dean (Dean, 2006, 2010)) there are 5 failures in average for each MapReduce job in their clusters. Since each failure in Hadoop's MapReduce needs 10 min to be affirmed, this means that if those failures happen in different time periods, they would prolong job completion time for 50 min.

Assume a cluster upon which are being executed million jobs per day. If the 5 failures mentioned above result in a delay of only 5 minutes in total of each job, this leads to a delay of 3,472.22 days, meaning, 3,472.22 days of additional resource utilization:

$$1,000,000 \, jobs * 5 \, min = 5,000,000 \, min = 83,333.33 \, hours = 3,472.22 \, days$$

In the case that the situation gets worse, and assuming those failures to cause 10 min of delay, then the hardware resources will be misused for 6,944.44 days.

Finally, the worse case assumption is to calculate those failures in a different time period that is 50 min of delay for each job. Then, hardware resources are misused for 34,722.22 days, which is an astonishing number:

$$1,000,000 \, jobs * 50 \, min = 50,000,000 \, min = 833,333.33 \, hours = 34,722.22 \, days$$

Undoubtedly, this calculation frightens everybody who looks upon these numbers, and is willing to execute MapReduce on top of a cluster/s consisting of unreliable resources.

METHODOLOGY OVERVIEW

The experimental investigation conducted in this paper focuses on exploring the impact of different parameters into the Hadoop timeout, in other words the authors try to address the question of how different parameters and their combination do impact the failure detection mechanism of Hadoop.

The first experiments are related to analyzing the default Hadoop configuration under failures while having different workloads as input; basically, these experiments do work under a default Hadoop environment, without changing any parameter inside Hadoop. The second kind of experiments, which are the most extensive experiments at the same time, is related to failure injection but while changing the TaskTracker's timeouts. Below the authors describe the experimental environment, such as the platform, deployment setup and used tools.

Platform

All the experiments were carried out in Grid'5000 experimental testbed (J´egou et al., 2006). Grid'5000 is a scientific instrument for the study of large scale parallel and distributed systems. It aims at providing a highly reconfigurable, controllable and monitorable experimental platform to its users. The infrastructure of Grid'5000 is geographically distributed on different sites hosting the instrument, initially 9 sites in France (10 since 2011). For the sake of accuracy, there are used nodes of the same site Sophia and even from the same cluster *Sol*. The complete deployment contains 23 machines from the cluster *Sol* that are built from Sun Fire X2200 M2 family, with AMD Opteron Dual-Core 2218 2.6GHz Processors, while using Linux 2.6.32-5-xen-amd64 x86 64 of Debian GNU/Linux. The *Sol*'s cluster network is Ethernet network that provides an intra-cluster communication speed of 1 Gbps. The experimental setup is summarized in Table 1.

Benchmark

MapReduce applications are typically categorized as CPU-intensive, I/O bound, or both. For the analysis, there it is chosen the sort application that is commonly used for benchmarking MapReduce frameworks, preferred application in other relevant MapReduce papers (Dean et al., 2004; Zaharia et al., 2008; Ibrahim et al., 2012) and day to day testing of Hadoop, including at Yahoo (*Scaling Hadoop to 4000 nodes at Yahoo!*, 2014).

The sort application consists in sorting *key/value* records based on key. In Hadoop, the sort application simply uses the map/reduce framework to sort the input directory into the output directory. The inputs and outputs must be Sequence files where the keys and values are BytesWritable. The sort MapReduce implementation takes advantage of the default optimizations performed by the framework that implicitly sorts both intermediate data and output data. In the following experiments, differently from Hadoop that generates random data using RandomWriter, it has been generated a random data in advance, in order to only sort the data using the sort example.

Hadoop Deployment

The Hadoop version that has been deployed in the testbed is Hadoop-1.0.1, and when not mentioned otherwise, the default configurations of it are used. The Hadoop instance consists of the NameNode, the JobTracker and the Hadoop client, each deployed on a dedicated machine, leaving 20 nodes to serve as both DataNodes and TaskTrackers.

Table 1. Environmental setup

Platform	Grid'5000 testbed
Site	Sophia
Network bandwidth	Ethernet 1 Gbps
Number of nodes	23
Hadoop	1.0.1
Input data	20 GB (if not stated otherwise)
Application	Sort

TaskTrackers were configured with 2 slots to run up to 2 map tasks and 2 slots to run up to 2 reduce tasks. The Hadoop Distributed File System (HDFS) is having its default configuration of maintaining a chunk size of 64 MB, and the default replication factor of 3 for the input and output data.

Failure Injection Pattern

The failure injection pattern works on the principle of the job progress score. In this case, the progress score of a job is based on the progress of the map and reduce phase; both of them, map and reduce phase have been divided into 11 progress phases or intervals that would contain failure injection. These failure injection phases are given in Table 2. According to the interval, exactly one particular failure has been injected to a MapReduce job. This means, after each run of the Hadoop job, Hadoop was restarted to inject the failure in another progress phase, but under the same environment conditions of the previous jobs. For accuracy concerns, each progress phase has been running at least three rounds.

As it could be noticed from the table, some of the experiments are clearly redundant. When you execute the experiments according to the map progress phase, for example the map phase that circles from (81-85)%, this phase is basically repeated when you execute the reduce phase that circles at about (21-25)%. However, it was not excluded from any of the rounds; this redundancy has proven to be beneficial later on, because it ensures the accuracy of the experiments.

In the next section, the authors present experimental analyses that support the previous observations of the timeout problem subsections.

EXPERIMENTAL ANALYSIS

Below, it is discussed the main analysis, whose importance is strongly related to the timeout problem.

Table 2. Map and Reduce progress phases when failure is injected

MapReduce Phase	
Map Progress Phase	**Reduce Progress Phase**
[01-05]	[01-05]
[11-15]	[11-15]
[21-25]	[21-25]
[31-35]	[31-35]
[41-45]	[41-45]
[51-55]	[51-55]
[61-65]	[61-65]
[71-75]	[71-75]
[81-85]	[81-85]
[91-95]	[91-95]
[100]	[96-99]

Impact of Fail-Stop on Different Application Length

The failure occurrence plays a very important role in the delays of the job response times under failures, as mentioned in (Dinu & Ng, 2012). However, the job length itself, contributes strongly to this delay: shorter jobs will extremely suffer long response time while long jobs may experience a little overhead which depends on the failure detector as well. In this set of experiments, the aim to see the co-relation between the job length and failure detector in Hadoop and provide a big picture on the impact of the current static failure detector in Hadoop on different application length (i.e., these applications vary in their expected running times without failure). Accordingly, it is run the distributed *Sort* application while varying the input sizes (from 2GB to 60GB). To ensure consistent failure injunction pattern, it has been injected a single failure with respect to the job progress: the authors monitor the job progress of the application and inject the fail-stop failure after 30% of the job is accomplished.

Figure 4 presents the ratio between the completion times of different workloads. Basically, as the workload gets smaller, the performance degradation is higher. This is the opposite, in meaning that the degradation of job completion time lowers with bigger workloads. The response to this is the following: as the job completion time to the smaller workloads is short, the default timeout that is present in Hadoop prolongs the job completion time in these cases. This is the default time needed so that the JobTracker declares a specific TaskTracker as dead and tries to re-execute its completed tasks in other TaskTrackers. A job with only 2 GB of input data that needs to complete in almost 57s in normal circumstances, when having a single failure, its completion time will jump to approximately 600s more. In these experiments,

Figure 4. An example explaining the timeout problems when having to face jobs with different workloads. The X axis represents different input sizes for sort application and the corresponding completion time in normal runs, without failure.

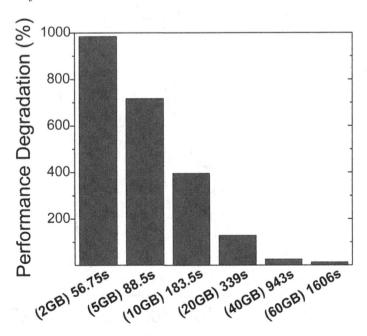

this completion time is 615s, because the injected failure happens after the first 10s of job execution, in other words, after the map phase accomplishes around 30-40% of its completion. As a consequence, the performance degradation gets astonishingly high value that circles around 1000%.

In a bigger workload, as it is the last workload in the experiments consisting of 60 GB of data, the performance degradation is obviously smaller. Herein, as the job completion time without failure is around 1606s, the job completion time when the failure was injected goes to 1825s. So, 600s of timeout is a very high number, but its impact on this workload is relatively low comparing to the first case, as you may notice that the performance degradation circles around 13% now.

Co-Relation between Job Length and Failure Detector in Hadoop

In Figure 5, it is given another approach of looking into the ratio between the response time and the timeout, when failures are injected in different phases of the job progress. To ensure consistent and comparable results when discussing the co-relation between the job length and failure timeout, the au-

Figure 5. An example explaining the different timeouts when having to face different failure injections

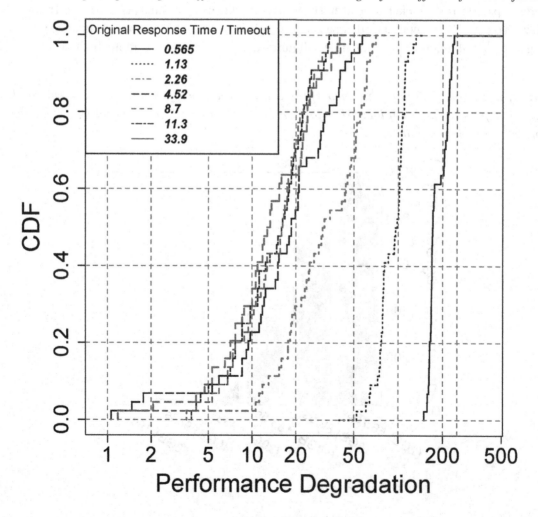

thors fix both the cluster size and the data size (here the input data size is 20GB) and they just vary in the timeout. Thus, they get different ratios of (*Original Response Time/Timeout*). Where the *Original Response* Time is the completion time of the sort application without failure (339s in present experiments) and the *timeout* is set to one of the following values: 600s, 300s, 150s, 75s, 39s, 30s, and 10s.

As it can be noticed, the performance degradation to the default Hadoop timeout, shown with the right most line, is clearly distinguished from the other timeouts, no matter the failure injection time. When the timeout decreases in the other cases, the performance degradation gets smaller too, until a point when different timeouts give the same performance degradation, as shown in figure 5.

This means that for each workload, there is some response time which is the optimum in practice, no matter if you continue to lower the timeout after this point. In contrary, it may only increase the bandwidth of passing messages in the system, or wrongly declare TaskTrackers as lost. In the current experiments, it can easily be shown that for a workload of 20 GB of data, the sample timeout which reacts the best, after which no improvement are being made, is the timeout of 39s.

Is summary, at coarse-grained level, the authors observe that the failure recovery is strongly dependent on both the job length (i.e., completion time without failure) and the timeout (i.e., the ratio *Original Response Time/Timeout*). Hereafter this ratio is called "Correlated failure detection ratio (CFDR)".

A smaller ratio always indicates long response time under failure (*f*) while bigger value indicates shorter response time. Here, the following naive equation of the maximum performance degradation under failure is derived:

$$\text{Max(Performance degradation}_f) = \frac{1}{\text{CFDR}} + C \tag{1}$$

where C is the overhead of re-executing the tasks which have already been executed on the failed node.

At fine-grained level, it was observed that the failure recovery depends on the occurrence time of failure: here the performance varies according to the time left to the job to be completed (when to start re-executing the completed tasks), and the ongoing tasks (whether they are speculated or not). For example, analyzing the timeout value of 39s, it could be seen that the performance degradation to the default Hadoop timeout varies between 1% and 40%. Here, launching speculative reduce tasks of the failed nodes (before it is declared as failed) is beneficial as it decreases the waiting time of re-fetching the reduce input data of these reducers (reduce tasks on the failed machine) and the failure overhead is contributed to by re-executing map tasks on the failed machine and re-fetching their output by other reducers.

ONGOING WORK AND CHALLENGES

The issue being addressed here is towards an optimal timeout in the open source Hadoop, which satisfies the requirements of different jobs coming from different MapReduce applications. In this section, the authors discuss an estimation module as an important component towards optimal timeout value and three fine-tuning approaches that they propose: (1) timeout based on the progress score, (2) an application based timeout, and (3) accuracy timeout, based on monitoring system information.

Estimation Comes First

In order to build a dynamic timeout, it is required to know how to estimate a basic process completion time. MapReduce framework can be divided in many execution components, and look into them from bottom-up or top-down. In order to estimate time completion, it is important to know what it is meant for. Estimation may be adjusted for different concepts, including an entire dataflow execution, individual job or task, etc. Estimating task duration is the most fundamental issue. This, because a task can delay its phase (map or reduce), consequently delays the overall job to whom it belongs and so on. Therefore an adaptive timeout model is circled around a task, more than a phase and a job. It is assumed that all tasks of a particular phase are started by the JobTracker that divides an equal input data to each of them. The JobTracker's duty is to additionally send a heartbeat to each of them, and watch out whether each task is respecting the given timeout.

Estimating a task completion may be performed by a comparison of an expected value to an actual, measured value. The expected value is computed from a system model of normal behavior, as demonstrated in (Salfner, Lenk, & Malek, 2010). In other words, the expected value is either computed from previous (buffered) monitoring values or from other monitoring variables measured at the same time. As the number of buffered values increases, the learning curve gets higher and more accurate in future estimations.

Shifting Methods

After a proper estimation of the completion time, the next step is to define different strategies for dynamic shifting of the timeout. Herein three techniques are explored.

Progress Score Timeout

A dynamic timeout can easily rely on the progress score, which is an already built-in feature in MapReduce. By using an estimation derived from the Estimation Comes First section, this calculation is done according to the estimated time left for each of the tasks, that is a function of cluster availability, application type, network, and the data size (Ananthanarayanan et al., 2010), adding the x parameter for the standard deviation error. A double x has proven to give very accurate results in wide area collective operations (Plank et al., 2001).

Last, but not least, is the heartbeat period: the authors believe that real time estimation, and informing each worker node about the new timeout will cause higher bandwidth utilization. Therefore, they argue that a heartbeat return value needs to be tuned into a bigger value than 1-3s at some scenarios, so as to optimize the network utilization.

Application Based Timeout

There are cases when the system is willing to offer a prior adjustment, but without any additional interference during the job execution. In this step, it is possible to offer a different timeout tuning, depending on the application and the workload. Applications will be clustered in different groups according to their behavior. Each job is part of a particular application (e.g. sort, grep, etc.), and according to the input data, the timeout can be fine-tuned so as to be fair executed upon the application's job.

In the Hadoop mailing list (*Apache Hadoop Project*, 2015), there have been identified many threads with request for fine-tuning a longer and shorter timeout. Longer lasting jobs were facing difficulties, because of the high risk that the default timeout of 10min was declaring false failures when missing response heartbeats. On the other side, small clusters were facing the opposite; their jobs needed shorter timeout, because only in that way they could optimize the resource utilization. An application based timeout is the perfect match to these scenarios.

Accuracy Based Timeout

MapReduce framework is also gaining an impressive ground in critical infrastructures, where a MapReduce application is assumed to be reliable in most of the cases. For this issue, the plan is on investigating the idea of accurately detecting a failure while being informed from two sources: (I) the MapReduce heartbeat mechanism itself, (II) another system monitoring tool. Basically, the idea consists in trying to benefit from the monitoring system information, in order to use it as input to our failure detection mechanism. While having two observers, every time when a change happens that is detected from the two entities, you may detect relationships between correlations, and react in advance based on our pre-defined conditions.

The three techniques can function as individual components or be combined for different infrastructures requirements. The authors are exploring their correlation, in order to draw the optimal relationships between them, not excluding also their relationship with the default heartbeat mechanism of Hadoop itself. They argue that such an approach is applicable to all Hadoop releases, since the problem seems to be present in every consequent release.

RELATED WORK

The MapReduce framework has gathered huge interest in the last few years. Some research has been dedicated to adopting MapReduce in different environments such as graphics processing unit (He, Fang, Luo, Govindaraju, & Wang, 2008) and virtual machines (Ibrahim et al., 2009). Many works on improving MapReduce performance have been introduced through locality-execution in the map phase (Zaharia et al., 2010), mitigating data skew (Ibrahim et al., 2010; Kwon, Balazinska, Howe, & Rolia, 2013; Ibrahim et al., 2013), tuning the schedulers at OS-kernel (Ibrahim, Jin, Lu, He, & Wu, 2011). The fault-tolerant aspect has not remained intact either. Many extensions have been introduced also in this direction, knowing that repeated failures would especially miss perform large scale computing clusters.

Large-scale study of failures. In (Dinu & Ng, 2012), the authors have evaluated Hadoop, demonstrating a large variation in Hadoop job completion time in the presence of failures. According to the authors, this is because Hadoop uses the same functionality to recover from worker failure, independently of what is the cause or failure type. Since Hadoop couples failure detection and recovery with overload handling into a conservative design with conservative parameter choices, it is often slow in reacting to failures and also exhibits large variations in response time under failure. The authors conclude that Hadoop makes unrealistic assumptions about task progress rates, re-discovers failures individually by each task at the cost of great degradation in job running time, and does not consider the causes of connection failures between its tasks which leads to failure propagation to healthy tasks. In (Bressoud & Kozuch, 2009), the authors have evaluated the performance and overhead of both the checkpointing-based fault-tolerance and the re-execution based fault tolerance in MapReduce through event simulation driven by Los Alamos National Labs (LANL) data. Regarding MapReduce, the fault tolerance mechanism which was explored is re-execution, where all map or reduce tasks from a failed core are reallocated dynamically to operational cores whether the tasks had completed or not (i.e., partial results are stored locally), and execution is repeated in its entirety. While evaluating the performance of MapReduce in the context of real-world failure data, it was identified that there is pressure to decrease the size of individual map tasks as the cluster size increases. In (Jin & Sun, 2013), the authors have introduced an analytical study of MapReduce performance under failures, comparing it to MPI. This research is HPC oriented and proposes an analytical approach to measure the capabilities of the two programming models to tolerate failures. In the MapReduce case, they have started with the principle that any kind of failure is isolated in one process only (e.g., map task). Due to this, the performance modeling of MapReduce was built on the analysis of each single process. The model consists of introducing "an upper bound of the MapReduce execution time when no migration/replica is utilized, followed by an algorithm to derive the best performance when replica based balance is adopted". According to the evaluation results, MapReduce achieves better performance then MPI on less reliable commodity systems.

Single point of failure. In being single point of failure, the MapReduce master is especially challenging for any contribution whatsoever. An important proposal to the high availability of the MapReduce master comes from IBM researchers (Wang et al., 2009). Their main idea consists in a metadata replication based solution to enable high availability of the Hadoop cluster, by removing the single point of failure in Hadoop. This approach is viable for both, NameNode and JobTracker, and involves three major steps: (i) Initialization phase, where each standby/slave node is first registered to active/primary node and its initial metadata are caught up with those of active/primary node; (ii) Replication phase, when the runtime metadata for a future failover are replicated; and (iii) Failover phase, when standby/ new elected primary node takes over all communications. An implementation of this contribution has been done by Facebook (Borthakur et al., 2011), by creating the active and standby AvatarNode. The AvatarNode node was simply wrapped to the NameNode, and the standby AvatarNode takes the role of the active AvatarNode in less than a minute. In (Okorafor & Patrick, 2012), the authors propose an automatic failover solution for the MapReduce JobTracker, which could possibly solve the single point of failure. This approach is based on the Leader Election Framework (Cachin, Guerraoui, & Rodrigues, 2011), by using Apache Zookeper (*Apache* Zookeeper, 2015). The approach works by enabling multiple JobTrackers (at least three) that start together, but only one of them is the JobTracker leader at a particular time. The leader does not serve any user, but receives periodical checkpoints from the remaining JobTrackers. If one of the NameNodes fails, the leader recovers its availability from the most recent checkpointed data. However, this solution within Yarn has not been explored for job masters (Vavilapalli et al., 2013) and only addresses other single points of failure, such as the resource manager daemon. For unstable environments, some other works (Lin, Ma, & Feng, 2012), (Chohan et al., 2010), (Liu, 2011) introduce dedicated nodes for the main daemons, including the master daemon.

Failure Detection in MapReduce. In (Zhu & Chen, 2011), the authors have proposed two mechanisms to improve the failure detection in Hadoop via heartbeat, but only in the worker side which is the TaskTracker. While the adaptive interval mechanism adjusts the TaskTracker timeout according to the estimated job running time in a dynamic way, the reputation-based detector compares the number of fetch-errors reported when copying intermediate data from the mapper and when any of the Task-

Trackers reaches a specific threshold that TaskTracker will be announced as a failed one. As the authors explain, the adaptive interval is advantageous to the small jobs while the reputation-based detector is mainly dedicated for the case of longer jobs. However, adjusting the timeout according to the estimated job running time cannot always provide the best solution. Furthermore, this approach is still using one static timeout for the whole run of the application which in turn leads to variation in the application's performance under failure.

Failure Handling in Mapreduce. Upon failure, intermediate map output that is stored on the failed machine becomes inaccessible for unfinished reduce tasks, and those tasks need to be re-executed. In (Ko, Hoque, Cho, & Gupta, 2010), the authors propose an Intermediate Storage System (ISS) that incorporates three replication techniques (i.e., asynchronous replication, rack-level replication, and selective replication) to keep intermediate data safe under failures while minimizing the performance overhead of replication. In a recent study (Memishi, Perez, & Antoniu, 2015), the authors propose Diarchy, a novel approach for management of masters, whose aim is to increase the reliability of YARN, based on the sharing and backup of responsibilities between two masters working as peers. Despite the fact that Diarchy seems only to improve the reliability of failure handling between masters, its functioning also puts a lower boundary in the worst case assumption, with the number of Diarchy failed tasks not surpassing the half number of failed tasks of Hadoop YARN.

Stragglers in MapReduce. The concept of stragglers is very important in the MapReduce community. Most of the state-of-the-art in this direction has intended to improve the job execution time, by means of doubling the overall small jobs (Ananthanarayanan, Ghodsi, Shenker, & Stoica, 2013), or just by doubling the suspected tasks (stragglers) through different speculative execution optimizations (Dean et al., 2004; Isard, Budiu, Yu, Birrell, & Fetterly, 2007; Zaharia et al., 2008; Ananthanarayanan et al., 2010; Chen, Liu, & Xiao, 2014; Xu & Lau, 2014). In (Zaharia et al., 2008), the authors have also proposed a new scheduling algorithm called Longest Approximate Time to End (LATE) to improve the performance of Hadoop in a heterogeneous environment, brought by the variation of VM consolidation amongst different physical machines, by preventing the incorrect execution of "speculative tasks".

There were also contributions related to byzantine failures. In (Costa, Pasin, Bessani, & Correia, 2010), the authors present a byzantine fault-tolerant (BFT) MapReduce runtime system that is capable of tolerating faults that involve the results of computation of tasks, primarily cases such as of DRAM and CPU errors/faults. This BFT MapReduce follows the principle of executing each task more than once, and even more, depending on the particular scenarios. For efficiency, it uses several mechanisms to minimize both the number of copies of tasks executed and the time needed to execute them. The same proposal has also been adapted to multi-cloud environments in (Correia et al., 2012).

SUMMARY

To summarize, the authors have discussed the inefficiencies of the default failure detection mechanism in Hadoop's MapReduce. They argue that an additional effort is necessary to represent a dynamic shifting of the MapReduce timeout in realtime, so that MapReduce clusters can perform better resource utilization. After observing the problem from different points of view, the authors have described out ideas behind the design and implementation of an adaptable timeout, applicable to different scenarios.

REFERENCES

Ananthanarayanan, G., Agarwal, S., Kandula, S., Greenberg, A., Stoica, I., Harlan, D., ... (2011). Scarlett: coping with skewed content popularity in mapreduce clusters. In *Proceedings of the sixth conference on computer systems* (pp. 287–300). New York, NY, USA: ACM; Available from http://doi. acm.org/10.1145/1966445.1966472 doi:10.1145/1966445.1966472

Ananthanarayanan, G., Ghodsi, A., Shenker, S., & Stoica, I. (2013). Effective straggler mitigation: Attack of the clones. In *Proceedings of the 10th usenix conference on networked systems design and implementation* (pp. 185–198). Berkeley, CA, USA: USENIX Association; Available from http://dl.acm. org/citation.cfm?id=2482626.2482645

Ananthanarayanan, G., Kandula, S., Greenberg, A., Stoica, I., Lu, Y., Saha, B., ... (2010). Reining in the outliers in map-reduce clusters using Mantri. In *Proceedings of the 9th usenix conference on operating systems design and implementation* (pp. 1–16). Berkeley, CA, USA: USENIX Association; Available from http://dl.acm.org/ citation.cfm?id=1924943.1924962

Apache Hadoop NextGen MapReduce (YARN). (2015). http://hadoop.apache.org/docs/ current/hadoop-yarn/hadoop-yarn-site/YARN.html

Apache Hadoop Project. (2015). http://hadoop.apache.org/

Apache Zookeeper. (2015). http://zookeeper.apache.org/

Borthakur, D., Gray, J., Sarma, J. S., Muthukkaruppan, K., Spiegelberg, N., Kuang, H., ... (2011). Apache Hadoop goes realtime at Facebook. In *Proceedings of the 2011 acm sigmod international conference on management of data* (pp. 1071–1080). New York, NY, USA: ACM; Available from http://doi.acm.org/10.1145/1989323.1989438 doi:10.1145/1989323.1989438

Bressoud, T. C., & Kozuch, M. A. (2009). Cluster fault-tolerance: An experimental evaluation of checkpointing and MapReduce through simulation. In *Proceedings of the 2009 IEEE International Conference on Cluster Computing and Workshops (CLUSTER'09)* (pp. 1–10). New York, NY, USA: IEEE. Available from doi:10.1109/CLUSTR.2009.5289185

Cachin, C., Guerraoui, R., & Rodrigues, L. (2011). *Introduction to Reliable and Secure Distributed Programming* (2. ed.). Springer.

Chandra, A., Prinja, R., Jain, S., & Zhang, Z. (2008, August). Co-designing the failure analysis and monitoring of large-scale systems. S*IGMETRICS Perform. Eval. Rev.*, 36, 10–15. Available from http://doi.acm.org/10.1145/1453175.1453178

Chen, Q., Liu, C., & Xiao, Z. (2014, April). Improving mapreduce performance using smart speculative execution strategy. Computers. *IEEE Transactions on*, *63*(4), 954–967.

Chohan, N., Castillo, C., Spreitzer, M., Steinder, M., Tantawi, A., & Krintz, C. (2010). See Spot Run: Using Spot Instances for MapReduce Workflows. In *Proceedings of the 2nd usenix conference on hot topics in cloud computing* (pp. 7–7). Berkeley, CA, USA: USENIX Association. Available from http://dl.acm.org/citation.cfm?id= 1863103.1863110

Correia, M., Costa, P., Pasin, M., Bessani, A., Ramos, F., & Verissimo, P. (2012, Oct). On the feasibility of byzantine fault-tolerant mapreduce in clouds-of-clouds. In *Reliable distributed systems (srds), 2012 ieee 31st symposium on* (p. 448-453). doi:10.1109/SRDS.2012.46

Costa, P., Pasin, M., Bessani, A., & Correia, M. (2010). Byzantine Fault-Tolerant MapReduce: Faults are Not Just Crashes. In *Proceedings of the 3rd ieee second international conference on cloud computing technology and science* (pp. 17–24). Washington, DC, USA: IEEE Computer Society. Available from doi:10.1109/CloudCom.2010.25

Dean, J. (2006). Experiences with MapReduce, an abstraction for large-scale computation. In *Proceedings of the 15th international conference on parallel architectures and compilation techniques* (pp. 1–1). New York, NY, USA: ACM; Available from http://doi.acm.org/10.1145/1152154.1152155 doi:10.1145/1152154.1152155

Dean, J. (2010). Building Software Systems at Google and Lessons Learned. *Stanford EE Computer Systems Colloquium.* Available at http://www.stanford.edu/class/ ee380/Abstracts/101110-slides.pdf)

Dean, J., & Ghemawat, S. (2004). MapReduce: simplified data processing on large clusters. In *Proceedings of the 6th conference on symposium on operating systems design & implementation.* USENIX Association. doi:10.1145/1327452.1327492

Dinu, F., & Ng, T. E. (2012). Understanding the effects and implications of compute node related failures in Hadoop. In *Hpdc '12: Proceedings of the 21st international symposium on high-performance parallel and distributed computing* (pp. 187–198). New York, NY, USA: ACM.

Dinu, F., & Ng, T. S. E. (2011). Hadoop's Overload Tolerant Design Exacerbates Failure Detection and Recovery. In *Proceedings of the 9th usenix conference on operating systems design and implementation* (pp. 1–7). New York, NY, USA: ACM.

Facebook, Inc. (2015). https://www.facebook.com/

Grid5000:Home. (2015). https://www.grid5000.fr/

He, B., Fang, W., Luo, Q., Govindaraju, N. K., & Wang, T. (2008). Mars: a MapReduce framework on graphics processors. In *Proceedings of the 17th international conference on Parallel architectures and compilation techniques (PACT'08)* (pp. 260–269). New York, NY, USA: ACM; Available from http://doi.acm.org/10.1145/1454115.1454152 doi:10.1145/1454115.1454152

Huang, D., Shi, X., Ibrahim, S., Lu, L., Liu, H., Wu, S., ... (2010). MR-scope: a real-time tracing tool for MapReduce. In *Proceedings of the 19th ACM International Symposium on High Performance Distributed Computing (HPDC'10)* (pp. 849–855). New York, NY, USA: ACM; Available from http://doi.acm.org/10.1145/1851476.1851598 doi:10.1145/1851476.1851598

Ibrahim, S., Jin, H., Lu, L., He, B., Antoniu, G., & Wu, S. (2012). Maestro: Replica-Aware Map Scheduling for MapReduce. In *Proceedings of the 2012 12th ieee/acm international symposium on cluster, cloud and grid computing (ccgrid 2012)* (pp. 435– 442). Washington, DC, USA: IEEE Computer Society. Available from doi:10.1109/CCGrid.2012.122

Ibrahim, S., Jin, H., Lu, L., He, B., Antoniu, G., & Wu, S. (2013). Handling partitioning skew in MapReduce using LEEN. *Peer-to-Peer Networking and Applications*, 6(4), 409–424. doi:10.1007/s12083-013-0213-7

Ibrahim, S., Jin, H., Lu, L., He, B., & Wu, S. (2011). Adaptive Disk I/O Scheduling for MapReduce in Virtualized Environment. In *Proceedings of the 2011 International Conference on Parallel Processing (ICPP 2011)* (pp.335–344). Washington, DC, USA: IEEE Computer Society. Available from doi:10.1109/ICPP.2011.86

Ibrahim, S., Jin, H., Lu, L., Qi, L., Wu, S., & Shi, X. (2009). Evaluating mapreduce on virtual machines: The hadoop case. In *Proceedings of the 1st International Conference on Cloud Computing (cloudcom'09)* (pp. 519–528). Springer Berlin Heidelberg: Springer Berlin Heidelberg. Available from doi:10.1007/978-3-642-10665-1_47

Ibrahim, S., Jin, H., Lu, L., Wu, S., He, B., & Li, Q. (2010). LEEN: Locality/Fairness-Aware Key Partitioning for MapReduce in the Cloud. In *Proceedings of the 2010 IEEE Second International Conference on Cloud Computing Technology and Science (cloudcom 2010)* (pp. 17–24). Washington, DC, USA: IEEE Computer Society. Available from doi:10.1109/CloudCom.2010.25

Isard, M., Budiu, M., Yu, Y., Birrell, A., & Fetterly, D. (2007). Dryad: distributed data-parallel programs from sequential building blocks. In *Proceedings of the 2nd acm sigops/eurosys 2007* (pp. 59–72). New York, NY, USA: ACM; Available from http://doi.acm.org/10.1145/1272996.1273005 doi:10.1145/1272996.1273005

J'egou, Y., Lant'eri, S., Leduc, J., Melab, N., Mornet, G., & Namyst, R. et al.. (2006, November). Grid'5000: A large scale and highly reconfigurable experimental Grid testbed. *International Journal of High Performance Computing Applications*, 20(4), 481–494. doi:10.1177/1094342006070078

Jin, H., Ibrahim, S., Li, Q., Cao, H., Wu, S., & Shi, X. (2011). *The mapreduce programming model and implementations. Cloud computing: Principles and Paradigms* (pp. 373–390). John Wiley & Sons, Inc. doi:10.1002/9780470940105.ch14

Jin, H., & Sun, X.-H. (2013). Performance comparison under failures of MPI and MapReduce: An analytical approach. In *Future Generation Computer Systems 29 (7)* (pp. 1808–1815). Available from; doi:10.1016/j.future.2013.01.013

Ko, S. Y., Hoque, I., Cho, B., & Gupta, I. (2010). Making cloud intermediate data fault-tolerant. In *Proceedings of the 1st acm symposium on cloud computing* (pp. 181– 192). New York, NY, USA: ACM. Available from http://doi.acm.org/10.1145/ 1807128.1807160

Kwon, Y. C., Balazinska, M., Howe, B., & Rolia, J. (2012). SkewTune: mitigating skew in mapreduce applications. In *Proceedings of the 2012 ACM SIGMOD International Conference on Management of Data (SIGMOD'12)* (pp. 25–36). New York, NY, USA: ACM; Available from http://doi.acm.org/10.1145/2213836.2213840 doi:10.1145/2213836.2213840

Lin, H., Ma, X., Archuleta, J., Feng, W.-c., Gardner, M., & Zhang, Z. (2010). MOON: MapReduce On Opportunistic eNvironments. In *Proceedings of the 19th acm international symposium on high performance distributed computing* (pp. 95–106). New York, NY, USA: ACM; Available from http://doi.acm.org/10.1145/1851476.1851489

Lin, H., Ma, X., & Feng, W.-C. (2012, June). Reliable MapReduce Computing on Opportunistic Resources. *Cluster Computing, 15* (2), 145–161. Available from10.1007/s10586-011-0158-7

Liu, H. (2011). Cutting MapReduce Cost with Spot Market. In *Proceedings of the 3rd usenix conference on hot topics in cloud computing* (pp. 5–5). Berkeley, CA, USA: USENIX Association. Available from http://dl.acm.org/citation.cfm?id= 1863103.1863110

Memishi, B., Perez, M. S., & Antoniu, G. (2015). Diarchy: An optimized management approach for mapreduce masters. *Procedia Computer Science, 51*, 9 - 18. Available from http://www.sciencedirect.com/science/article/pii/S1877050915009874 (International Conference on Computational Science, {ICCS} 2015 Computational Science at the Gates of Nature)

Microsoft, Inc. (2015). http://www.microsoft.com/

Mone, G. (2013, January). Beyond Hadoop. *Communications of the ACM, 56*(1), 22–24. http://doi.acm.org/10.1145/2398356.2398364 doi:10.1145/2398356.2398364

Okorafor, E., & Patrick, M. K. (2012, May). Availability of JobTracker machine in Hadoop/MapReduce Zookeeper coordinated clusters. *Advanced Computing: An International Journal, 3* (3), 19–30. Available from http://www.chinacloud.cn/upload/ 2012-07/12072600543782.pdf

Oppenheimer, D., Ganapathi, A., & Patterson, D. A. (2003). Why do Internet services fail, and what can be done about it? In *Proceedings of the 4th conference on usenix symposium on internet technologies and systems* -volume 4 (pp. 1–1). Berkeley, CA, USA: USENIX Association. Available from http://dl.acm.org/citation.cfm?id= 1251460.1251461

Pinheiro, E., Weber, W.-D., & Barroso, L. A. (2007). Failure trends in a large disk drive population. In *Proceedings of the 5th usenix conference on file and storage technologies* (pp. 2–2). Berkeley, CA, USA: USENIX Association; Available from http://dl.acm.org/citation.cfm?id=1267903.1267905

Plank, J. S., Allen, M., & Wolski, R. (2001). The Effect of Timeout Prediction and Selection on Wide Area Collective Operations. In P*roceedings of the ieee international symposium on network computing and applications (nca'01)* (pp. 320–329). Washington, DC, USA: IEEE Computer Society; Available from http://dl.acm.org/citation.cfm?id=580585.883098

PoweredBy Hadoop. (2015). http://wiki.apache.org/hadoop/PoweredBy

Roy, I., Setty, S. T. V., Kilzer, A., Shmatikov, V., & Witchel, E. (2010). Airavat: security and privacy for MapReduce. In *Proceedings of the 7th USENIX conference on Networked systems design and implementation* (pp. 20–20). Berkeley, CA, USA: USENIX Association. Available from http://dl.acm.org/citation.cfm?id= 1855711.1855731

Rutman, N. (2011). Map/Reduce on Lustre -Hadoop Performance in HPC Environments (Tech. Rep.). Langstone Road, Havant, Hampshire, PO9 1SA, England. Available from http://doi.acm.org/10.1145/1629175.1629197

Salfner, F., Lenk, M., & Malek, M. (2010). A survey of online failure prediction methods. *ACM Computing Surveys, 42*(3), 1–42. doi:10.1145/1670679.1670680

Scaling Hadoop to 4000 nodes at Yahoo! (2014). http://developer.yahoo.com/blogs/hadoop/posts/2008/09/ scaling\ hadoop\ to\ 4000 nodes\ a/.

Stonebraker, M., Abadi, D., DeWitt, D. J., Madden, S., Paulson, E., Pavlo, A., & Rasin, A. (2010, January). MapReduce and parallel DBMSs: Friends or foes? *Communications of the ACM, 53*(1), 64–71. http://doi.acm.org/10.1145/1629175.1629197 doi:10.1145/1629175.1629197

Vavilapalli, V. K., Murthy, A. C., Douglas, C., Agarwal, S., Konar, M., Evans, R., ... (2013). Apache Hadoop YARN: Yet Another Resource Negotiator. In *Proceedings of the 4th annual symposium on cloud computing* (pp. 5:1–5:16). New York, NY, USA: ACM. Available from http://doi.acm. org/10.1145/2523616.2523633

Wang, F., Qiu, J., Yang, J., Dong, B., Li, X., & Li, Y. (2009). Hadoop high availability through metadata replication. In *Proceedings of the first international workshop on cloud data management* (pp. 37–44). New York, NY, USA: ACM; Available from http://doi.acm.org/10.1145/1651263.1651271 doi:10.1145/1651263.1651271

White, T. (2012). *Hadoop -The Definitive Guide: Storage and Analysis at Internet Scale* (3. ed., revised and updated). O'Reilly.

Xu, H., & Lau, W. C. (2014, June). Speculative execution for a single job in a mapreducelike system. In *Cloud computing (cloud), 2014 ieee 7th international conference on* (p. 586-593).

Yahoo. Inc. (2015). http://www.yahoo.com/

Zaharia, M., Borthakur, D., Sarma, J. S., Elmeleegy, K., Shenker, S., ... (2010). Delay scheduling: a simple technique for achieving locality and fairness in cluster scheduling. In *Proceedings of the 5th European conference on Computer systems (EuroSys'10)* (pp. 265–278). New York, NY, USA: ACM; Available from http://doi.acm.org/10.1145/1755913.1755940 doi:10.1145/1755913.1755940

Zaharia, M., Konwinski, A., Joseph, A. D., Katz, R., & Stoica, I. (2008). Improving MapReduce performance in heterogeneous environments. In *Proceedings of the 8th USENIX conference on Operating systems design and implementation* (pp. 29–42). Berkeley, CA, USA: USENIX Association; Available from http://dl.acm.org/ citation.cfm?id=1855741.185574

Zhu, H., & Chen, H. (2011). Adaptive failure detection via heartbeat under Hadoop. In *Proceedings of the 2011 IEEE Asia-Pacific Services Computing Conference (ApSCC'11)* (pp. 231–238). New York, NY, USA: IEEE. Available from doi:10.1109/APSCC.2011.46

Chapter 2
Exploiting Semantics to Improve Classification of Text Corpus

Hammad Majeed
National University of Computer and Emerging Sciences (NUCES), Pakistan

Firoza Erum
National University of Computer and Emerging Sciences (NUCES), Pakistan

ABSTRACT

Internet is growing fast with millions of web pages containing information on every topic. The data placed on Internet is not organized which makes the search process difficult. Classification of the web pages in some predefined classes can improve the organization of this data. In this chapter a semantic based technique is presented to classify text corpus with high accuracy. This technique uses some well-known pre-processing techniques like word stemming, term frequency, and degree of uniqueness. In addition to this a new semantic similarity measure is computed between different terms. The authors believe that semantic similarity based comparison in addition to syntactic matching makes the classification process significantly accurate. The proposed technique is tested on a benchmark dataset and results are compared with already published results. The obtained results are significantly better and that too by using quite small sized highly relevant feature set.

INTRODUCTION

Web page classification (WPC) also known as web page categorization is the identification of membership of a web page. Choi and Yao (Choi & Yao, 2005) defined it mathematically as:

Let C represents predefined categories C = {c_1, c_2, ..., c_k} and D = {d_1, d_2, ..., d_n} represents the number of web pages or documents need to be classified. The decision matrix be Z=DxC where each entry represents either belonging to a set {0, 1} where 1 indicates the document d_i belonging to category c_i, and 0 indicates not belonging to the category. A document can belong to more than one category. Web page classification means approximating function f: DxC → {0, 1} by a learned function called a classifier f': DxC → {0,1} both the functions closely match each other. The f' is acquired by machine

DOI: 10.4018/978-1-4666-9767-6.ch002

Copyright © 2016, IGI Global. Copying or distributing in print or electronic forms without written permission of IGI Global is prohibited.

learning over training examples; each training example has a label of category to which it belongs. The function f' is used during training and the classification of web pages. The decision matrix is given in *Table 1*.

BASIC APPROACHES OF WEB PAGE CLASSIFICATION

Web page classification is a supervised machine-learning problem in which a web page is categorized using a trained classifier. The web pages are written in HTML and are semi structured in nature. They are connected through hyperlinks forming a directed graph. The data on web is frequent, non-homogeneous and vigorously changing.

Basic approaches of web page classification are *subject classification*, (also known topic-based classification), *functional classification* (also known genre-based or style-based classification), *sentiment classification, binary classification, multi class classification, hard classification, soft classification, flat classification* and *hierarchical classification.*

In subject classification, web pages are classified on the basis of subject or content of web page. This means a page can belong to many categories, for example the "news" domain in yahoo.com is world, business, entertainment, sports, tech, politics etc.

Functional or genre-based classification considers the role of web page based on the content. For example it decides whether the page is a "homepage", "product catalogue" or an "advertisement page".

Sentiment classification takes into account the opinion of the author of the page, i.e. how has author presented his views on a given topic. It deals with the emotions of the writer of the web page.

If there are exactly two categories in a given problem then binary classification is used to classify the pages. For example 0 represents not belonging to a class and 1 represents belonging to it. Multiclass classification has many class labels, and it decides the class of the web page. For example, in case of yahoo pages the classifier has multi-labels business, sports, entertainment etc.

On the basis of type of class assignment, classification can be divided into hard and soft classification. Hard classification means a page exclusively belongs to one class or not and has no transitional state, whereas soft classification classifies a page probabilistically.

Organization of categories leads to two types of classification, flat and hierarchical classification. The categories in flat classification are parallel i.e. no category surpasses other. For example in yahoo news domain entertainment, sports, business are alike categories. While in entertainment category movies, television, celebs are sub categories.

Table 1. Decision matrix for classifying n documents in k classes

	C_1	C_2	...	C_k
D_1	Z_{11}	Z_{12}	...	Z_{1k}
D_2	Z_{21}	Z_{22}	...	Z_{2k}
...	...	...	...	...
D_n	Z_{n1}	Z_{n2}	...	Z_{nk}

WEB PAGE REPRESENTATION AND FEATURE EXTRACTION

A web page is a document written in HTML (hyper text markup language), it contains strings of characters, tables, HTML tags, and hyperlinks and images. For classification purpose, the information from web page is extracted and a feature vector is constructed to extract useful information of a web page.

A web page contains rich text, which is preprocessed to extract useful information. The data is written between the pair of HTML tags <title> my page </title> the importance of strings of characters is guessed by the tag they are written inside. The tags are removed for the classification. Stop words are prepositions, pronouns and conjunctions, which are removed because they appear frequently in text but give no information about the subject of the web page. The words that appear rarely in text are removed because their contribution to the text is minimal. *Word stemming* is performed to bring uniformity in the text. Word Stemming means removing the suffix or prefix of a word for example borrow, borrowing or borrowed.

One of the web page representations is *bag of words*, where the words in the document d_i are assigned weights. The assigned weights show the importance of the word.

Most simple method of assignment of weight is binary assignment. If a word exists in the web page then it is assigned 1 otherwise 0.

$$W_j = 1 \quad if term \in webpage$$
$$\quad\quad 0 \quad\quad\quad Otherwise$$

Another popular weighting scheme is *tf-idf* Term Frequency Inverse Document Frequency. *tf* is the term frequency in current page and *idf* is global frequency of the term. The *idf* is the inverse document frequency calculated by the formula given below.

$$idf\left(t_i\right) = log\left(\frac{N}{df\left(t_j\right)}\right)$$

tf-idf shows the importance of terms/words in a web page. The value of *idf* shows how frequently the term occurred in the document, if the value is low it means the term is frequently occurring in many documents and vice versa.

IMPORTANCE OF SEMANTICS IN CLASSIFICATION

Most of the classification systems use bag of words or its variants for finding relevant features. Few are using *correlation* and *collocation* of terms for classification. Very few techniques use semantics of words for classification. The authors believe that semantics of text is very important in classification and must be part of it.

The main reason for this is that languages (for example English) are very ambiguous. English nouns have on average 5-8 close synonyms. There are words – example "strike" – that have more than 30 common meanings (strike a baseball, strike price buying stock, going on strike as an employee etc.). Now if you use a simple bag of words as features the software will never be able to make a clear distinction between an important fact (strike = work stoppage) and irrelevant information (baseball). Hence the classification result is also ambiguous and not very precise.

In the following section WordNet lexical database (Princeton University, 2010) (Simpson & Dao, 2010) will be discussed in detail. This is a widely used tool for calculating semantic similarity of words/phrases. The proposed technique is also based on this database.

WORDNET

WordNet (Simpson & Dao, 2010) is designed to establish connections between four types of Parts of Speech (PoS) - noun, verb, adjective, and adverb. The smallest unit in a WordNet is *synset*, which represents a specific meaning of a word. It includes the word, its explanation, and its synonyms. The specific meaning of one word under one type of PoS is called a *sense*. Each synset has a gloss that defines the concept it represents. For example, the words night, nighttime, and dark constitute a single synset that has the following gloss: the time after sunset and before sunrise while it is dark outside. Synsets are connected to one another through explicit semantic relations. Some of these relations (hypernym, hyponym for nouns, and hypernym and troponym for verbs) constitute is-a-kind-of (holonymy) and is-a-part-of (meronymy for nouns) hierarchies.

For example, tree is a kind of plant, tree is a hyponym of plant, and plant is a hypernym of tree. Analogously, trunk is a part of a tree, and we have trunk as a meronym of tree, and tree is a holonym of trunk. For one word and one type of PoS, if there is more than one sense, WordNet organizes them in the order of the most frequently used to the least frequently used.

SEMANTIC SIMILARITY BETWEEN WORDS

Given two words, semantic similarity determines how similar two words are. The higher the score, the more similar the meaning of the two words.

The steps for computing semantic similarity between two words are as follows:

- Part-of-speech disambiguation (or tagging).
- Stemming words.
- Find the most appropriate sense for every word in a sentence (Word Sense Disambiguation).
- Finally, compute the similarity of the sentences based on the similarity of the pairs of words.

PoS Disambiguation

During PoS disambiguation, correct part of speech (PoS - like noun, verb, pronoun, adverb) is identified of the word. The algorithm takes a word as input. The output is a single best POS tag for the word. Brill Tagger PoS disambiguation is commonly used tagger by research community. Brill Tagger is an error-driven transformation-based learning. It guesses the tag of each word and then fixes the mistakes.

Stemming Word

Porter stemming (Porter, 2006) is a process of removing the common morphological and in flexional endings of words. It can be thought of as a lexicon finite state transducer with the following steps: Surface form -> split word into possible morphemes -> getting intermediate form -> map stems to categories and affixes to meaning -> underlying form. i.e.: foxes -> fox + s -> fox.

Word Sense Disambiguation (WSD)

Disambiguation is the process of finding out the most appropriate sense of a word. The Lesk algorithm is a commonly used for this purpose [13]. Lesk algorithm uses dictionary definitions (gloss) to disambiguate a polysemous word in a sentence context. The major objective of its idea is to count the number of words that are shared between two glosses. The more overlapping the words, the more related the senses are.

To disambiguate a word, the gloss of each of its senses is compared to the gloss of other word. Word is assigned to the sense whose gloss shares the largest number of words with the glosses of the other word.

SEMANTIC SIMILARITY BETWEEN TWO SYNSETS

The similarity between two words is computed by calculating the semantic similarity between word senses. Semantic similarity between two word senses is based on the path length similarity.

Figure 1 shows an example of the hyponym taxonomy in WordNet used for path length similarity measurement.

In Figure 1, the length between car and auto is 1, car and truck is 3, car and bicycle is 4, car and fork is 12.

Figure 1. Hierarchy structure used by WordNet for calculating path length similarity (Simpson & Dao, 2010)

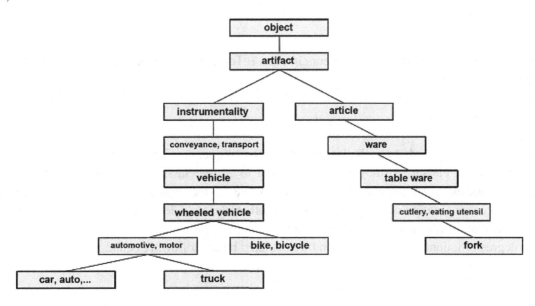

PROPOSED TECHNIQUE

Our proposed technique is divided into two parts: 1) preprocessing of web pages to extract useful information 2) Classification. The preprocessing step includes extracting information from headings, calculating term frequencies, degree of uniqueness and semantic similarity between terms. After this words are semantically grouped together. These groups form the set of most relevant features for classification.

Preprocessing

A web page is composed of content, images, HTML tags, hyperlinks and other media. Pre-processing of web pages reduce the problem dimension and makes the problem tractable.

Extracting Words from HTML Pages

It has been observed that important information about a web page is present in the headings. Therefore, content is extracted from the *<title>*, *<h1>*, *<h2>*, *<h3>*, *<h4>*, *<h5>* and *<h6>* tags.

Stop words are removed from data, which are frequently occurring words such as prepositions, pronouns and conjunctions. Stop words are removed from the data. Moreover, symbols such as comma, dollar sign, percentage and other symbols are also removed as they are useless for classification. Similarly, names of months and days do not provide any information so they are also removed from pages. Numbers and digits are also discarded. Rest of the data is compared with words from dictionary so that names, abbreviations, and slang words are removed from the data.

Term Frequency (tf)

Term frequency is the number of occurrences of a term in a corpus. Terms which occur frequently in a class are representatives of that class. Frequencies of words selected from the previous stages are calculated in the corpus

$$tf(t_i) = n$$

where n is the number of times term t occurs in class i. Term frequency of each term is calculated for each class in the corpus.

Degree of Uniqueness

Frequently occurring words of each class are tested for uniqueness. This value shows the occurrence of a term in all the classes. At most a term can occur in all the classes of the corpus. At least a term can occur in one class. Value one is an ideal value for the degree of uniqueness. This means a term is frequently occurring within a class but is absent in other classes. Clearly this fact makes the term an exclusive feature for the member ship of the class.

The degree of uniqueness for term t can be calculated by the following equation.

$$D(t) = \sum_{j=1}^{n} \begin{matrix} 1 & if\, term\, is \in class\, j \\ 0 & otherwise \end{matrix}$$

where n is the total number of classes in the dataset. The lower the value of $D(t)$, means that the term t is unique among different classes. Similarly, the higher value of $D(t)$ shows that the term t is present in multiple classes.

Semantic Similarity among Terms

Semantic similarity is a measurement of semantic relation between the meanings of two terms. A word may have different meanings depending upon the context. These different meanings are senses of that word. For example, the word "interest" can have different meanings depending upon the sentence. In the phrases, "interest from a bank" and "interest in music" the word interest has two different senses. In this work, WordNet based semantic similarity measurement is used to calculate similarity of two terms.

Algorithm for computing semantic similarity of the extracted words from html page with all the terms of each class is shown in Table 2.

Similarity score is calculated for each term. A list of similar terms is maintained for each term. This list contains terms with similarity score greater than the threshold value. For this study, threshold was set to 0.9 so that the words that are highly similar are grouped together.

Table 3 shows some of the groups created by **Error! Reference source not found.** All the groups show a high level of semantic similarity, hence an efficient feature selection.

Dimension Reduction by Group Merging

Groups sharing one or more same words are merged by taking union of these groups. Rationale behind this is the fact that the group containing semantically similar and relevant words must also be relevant, therefore can be merged. Groups having "frequently occurring" and "unique" terms are the best attributes to describe the document unambiguously. This step greatly reduces the problem dimension by selecting the most relevant features. Figure 2 shows the pictorial representation of group creation and merging.

Table 2. Pseudo code to generate semantically similar groups. Function returns a list of semantically similar words to the word passed as an input.

```
1: function SEMENTICSIMILARITY(word; Terms)
2: similarWordsList = {}
3: threshold = 0.9
4: for all t in Terms do
5: score = findSim(word; t) . WordNet Call
6: if score > threshold then
7: Add t to similarWordsList
8: end if
9: end for
10: return similarWordsList
11: end function
```

Table 3. Semantically similar groups

S. No.	Semantically Similar Terms
1.	Credit, credits, reference, references
2.	Alumni, graduate
3.	Affiliations, associations
4.	Reference, references
5.	Data, information
6.	Associated, links, related
7.	Education, teaching
8.	Awards, honors
9.	Assignments, awards, grant, grants
10.	Document, papers
11.	Curriculum, programs, program
12.	Issue, issues, publication, subject
13.	Class, classes, family

Figure 2. Graphical representation of group creation and merging. Each box is a group of semantically similar terms. Term frequency of each word is mentioned in parenthesis. Group frequency (gf) is the cumulative of term frequencies. Bottom left two groups are similar as they share same words. These groups will be merged together by taking union. After merging, gf of the merged groups is calculated (shown in the top row). Top groups are the finally selected groups (attributes) for classification.

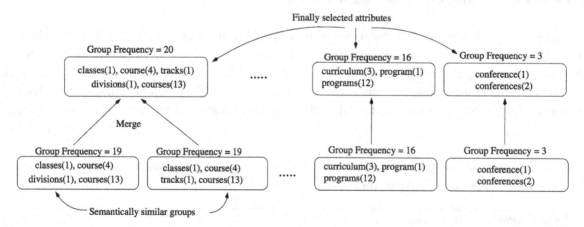

Classification

Classification of a test web page starts by removing HTML tags, stop words, punctuation marks, dates, numeric values, symbols and words that do not exist in dictionary such as names, abbreviations.

For the test page match-counts for all the classes are maintained. Initially all the counts are set to zero. Each term from the pre-processed web page is searched in the group lists of all the classes. If the word exists in a class, the match-count for the matched class is incremented and no more matching is done.

However, in case of failure the term is semantically matched with the terms of groups of each class. If the semantic similarity is greater than the threshold a hit is declared and match-count of the matched class is incremented. The term is added to the group to improve the performance of the classifier in the subsequent searches.

The highest match-count is declared class label for the web page. Classification algorithm is shown as Table 4.

EXPERIMENTAL SETUP

All the experiments are performed for binary classification. For the experiments all the classes and all the web pages of a class are used for classification. 10-folds cross validation is performed and average results are mentioned here. The accuracy is calculated by the following equation:

$$Accuracy = \frac{True\_Positives + True\_Negatives}{Positives + Negatives}$$

where True_Positives are the instances belonging to the class, which were classified correctly, True_Negatives are the negative examples correctly classified, Positives are all the pages belonging to the class and Negatives are all the pages not belonging to the class.

Dataset Used

WebKB data set was used to test the efficiency of the proposed technique. The data set was collected by CMU text learning group in 1997. It contains web pages of computer science department of four uni-

Table 4. Classification algorithm

```
function CLASSIFICATION(doc)
pageTermList ← filtered words from doc
numberOfClass ← C
match_count[numberofClass] ← 0
for all t in pageTermList do
      for i: 1 to numberOfClass do
            for j: 1 to numberOfGroups[i] do
                  if t exists in group j then
                          ++match count[i];
                          break;
                  else if t exists in synonym list of group j then
                          ++match count[i]
                          Add t in group j
                          break;
                  end if
            end for
      end for
end for
return class with highest match count
end function
```

versities. The data was manually classified into 7 classes and total number of pages is 8282. The classes are Course (930 pages), Department (182 pages), Faculty (1124 pages), Project (504 pages), Staff (137 pages), Student (1641 pages), and Other (3764 pages). The class other contains all the pages, which are not homepages. The data is organized in directories, one directory for each class. Table 5 shows the number of pages divided among different universities.

WebKB has highly unbalanced data making the classification of pages challenging. For instance, the class "department" contains only 184 pages whereas the class "student" contains 1641 web pages. Unbalanced data can misguide the classification process. For example, if term frequency of a word is calculated for the pages then the words in the "department" pages will be quite small as compared to the words in the "student" pages. Some researchers normalized these frequencies to address this issue.

The classes in this dataset are highly related with each other as the data is collected from university domain. For example, the classes "staff" and "faculty" consists of a large number of words, which are similar. There exists high inter-class and low intra-class similarity between the classes. This is the main cause of miss-classification. For this reason most of the research work did not classify all the data rather focused on two-three selected classes. Whereas, this work presents a technique which has the ability to classify all the classes with high accuracy. Table 6 shows the number of pages divided among different categories.

Use of this data set gives an idea of the efficiency of the proposed technique on unbalanced data with high inter class and low intra class association. Furthermore, the large number of pages and diverse collection sources makes this study comprehensive and generic.

Table 5. Number of webpage distribution per university

Sr. No.	University	Number of Pages
1.	Cornell	867
2.	Texas	827
3.	Washington	1205
4.	Wisconsin	1263
5.	Miscellaneous	4120

Table 6. Number of webpage distribution per class

Sr. No.	Category	Number of Pages
1.	Course	930
2.	Department	182
3.	Faculty	1124
4.	Project	504
5.	Staff	137
6.	Student	1641
7.	Other	3764

Related Work Using WebKB Dataset

J. Alamelu Mangai et al (Mangai, Kothari, & Kumar, 2012) have performed binary classification of WebKB data set. They have considered only course class by taking the web pages of course class as positive examples and considering the pages of other classes as a negative class. 10-fold cross-validated results of different combinations of positive and negative examples have reported. They have experimented with five different classifiers including Naïve Bayes, K Star, J48, ID3 and OneR.

In (Ozel S. A., 2011b), Selma Ayse Ozel has used Genetic Algorithm for classifying web pages. Experiments were performed on two classes of WebKB i.e. course and student. The distribution of pages for the purpose of training and testing is such that 158 pages from course category were taken for training and 72 pages from course category were taken as test pages. 575 pages from non-course category were taken for training and 246 pages were taken for testing purpose. In the second experiment, 1485 web pages were taken from student class for training and 156 web pages for testing. 2822 web pages were taken for training from non-student category and 942 web pages for testing.

Selma Ayse Ozel (Ozel S. A., 2011a) has proposed another Genetic Algorithm based technique for selecting features for web page classification. Binary web page classification experiments were performed on four classes of the WebKB data set including course, project, faculty and student classes. The training and test sets were created such that the pages belonging to Cornell, Texas, and Washington universities were used for training and pages from Wisconsin university are used in the test phase. For the course class, 883 pages are taken as positive examples whereas 3764 pages are taken as negative examples. The faculty dataset contains 1028 pages as positive examples and 3764 pages as negative examples.

Hwanjo Yu et al in (H. yu & Chuan, 2002), have performed web page classification using positive example based learning for the classifier. Three classes of WebKB dataset were used in the experiments; they were student, project and faculty classes. The total web pages in the student category are 1641. Out of these 1052 web pages were used for training and 589 web pages were used for testing. 662 non-student web pages were selected randomly for testing. Similarly, for the project category, out of total 504 web pages, 339 web pages were used for training and 165 web pages were used for testing. 753 non-project pages were used for testing of negative pages. For the faculty class, there are a total of 1124 pages. 741 of these were used for training and 383 were used for testing. For the testing of negative pages for the faculty class, 729 non-faculty pages were used.

M. Indra Devi et al in (Devi, Rajaram, & Selvakuberan, 2008), have classified web pages by generating best features. Experiments were performed on two classes of WebKB dataset i.e. course and student. All the pages from course category were used as positive examples and 66 pages from non-course category were used as negative examples. All the pages from the student category were used as positive examples and 229 pages from non-student category were used as negative examples.

Summary of the results of the above-mentioned techniques for WebKB data set is mentioned in Table 7.

RESULTS AND DISCUSSION

Results of binary classification of WebKB dataset are shown in Table 8. Our technique has shown high accuracy for all the categories barring Faculty and Student. The authors believe that this is due to imbalance of data set. These two classes have significantly high number of web pages as compared to other classes.

Table 7. Summary of results of different techniques using WebKB data set

Approach	Classes	Accuracy	Classifier
(Mangai, Kothari, & Kumar, 2012)	1	Course (97%)	OneR, ID3,J48, NB, Kstar
(Ozel S. A., 2011b)	2	Student (89%) Course (95%)	GA
(Ozel S. A., 2011a)	4	Student (91%) Course(93%) Faculty(94%) Project(95%)	KNN, Decision tree, Bayes
(H. yu & Chuan, 2002)	3	Student (94%) Project (86%) Faculty (91%)	A modified SVM

Table 8. Result of classification for WebKB dataset using proposed technique

S. No.	Category	Accuracy
1.	Course	97.3%
2.	Department	96%
3.	Faculty	82%
4.	Project	99%
5.	Staff	97%
6.	Student	78%

Table 9 shows class wise accuracies of WebKB data set for different binary classifiers. It can be observed that no technique has performed binary classification for all the classes except our proposed technique. Most of the techniques have performed experiments for only two classes i.e. course and student. However, one technique has performed classification for four classes leaving out department and staff.

The proposed technique has resulted in the highest accuracies for course, department, project and staff classes. The accuracies for the other two classes are 82% and 78%. However, the proposed technique has used less number of features than the other mentioned techniques. Table 10 shows the number of features used by each classifier. It can be seen that there is a major difference in our number of features than that of other techniques.

Table 9. Comparison of accuracy with other published techniques

Technique	Classifier	Course	Department	Faculty	Project	Staff	Student
Supervised Discretization Algorithm (Mangai, Kothari, & Kumar, 2012)	OneR, ID3,J48, NB, Kstar	97.09%	-	-	-	-	-
Genetic Algorithm using tagged terms as features (Ozel S. A., 2011a)	GA	95%	-	-	-	-	89%
Genetic Algorithm based optimal feature selection (Ozel S. A., 2011b)	GA, KNN, Decision tree, Bayes	93%	-	**94%**	95%	-	**91%**
Our Proposed Technique		**97.3%**	**96%**	82%	**99%**	**97%**	78%

Table 10. Comparison of number of features used by each technique

Technique	Course	Department	Faculty	Project	Staff	Student
Genetic Algorithm using tagged terms as features	3700	-	-	-	-	15605
Genetic Algorithm based optimal feature selection	33519	-	47376	30856	-	49452
Our Proposed Technique	**19**	**21**	**15**	**30**	**7**	**63**

An accuracy of 97.3% is achieved for course folder using only 19 features. The accuracy for department is 96% using 21 features. Only 15 features were used for the classification of faculty class achieving an accuracy of 82%. For the project category, an accuracy of 99% has been achieved using 30 features. The accuracy for staff class is 97% using only 7 attributes. An accuracy of 78% has been achieved using 63 features. Recall, that over here features means the number of terms semantically grouped together.

CONCLUSION

This chapter discusses a semantic based approach for classification of text corpus. The proposed technique not only captures the syntactic similarity of the features (words) but also the semantic similarity. Semantically+Syntactic similarity has improved the classification accuracy many folds by using small but highly relevant number of feature set. The chapter also discusses the technique of merging semantically similar groups to reduce the number of features, which helps in making the classification process efficient.

REFERENCES

Choi, B., & Yao, Z. (2005). Web Page Classification. [Springer.]. *Studies in Fuzziness and Soft Computing.*, *180*, 221–274. doi:10.1007/11362197_9

Devi, M. I., Rajaram, R., & Selvakuberan, K. (2008, March 1). *Generating best features for web page classification.* Retrieved Jul 15, 2015, from Generating best features for web page classification: http://www.webology.org/2008/v5n1/a52.html

H. yu, J. H., & Chuan, K. (2002). PEBL: positive example based Learning for web page classification using SVM . *ACM SIGKDD international conference on knowledge discovery and data mining* (pp. 239-248). ACM.

Mangai, J., Kothari, D., & Kumar, V. (2012). *A supervised discretization algorithm for web page classification. Innovations in Information Technology (IIT)* (pp. 226–231). Dubai: IEEE.

Ozel, S. A. (2011a). A web page classification system based on a genetic algorithm using tagged-terms as features. *Expert Systems with Applications*, *38*(4), 3407–3415. doi:10.1016/j.eswa.2010.08.126

Ozel, S. A. (2011b). *A genetic algorithm based optimal feature selection for Web page classification. Innovations in Intelligent Systems and Applications (INISTA)* (pp. 1–5). Istanbul: IEEE.

Porter, M. (2006). An algorithm for suffix stripping. *Program*, *40*(3), 211–218. doi:10.1108/00330330610681286

Princeton University. (2010, January 1). *About WordNet. Princeton University. 2010*. Retrieved July 14, 2015, from http://wordnet.princeton.edu

Simpson, T., & Dao, T. (2010, Feb 8). *WordNet-based semantic similarity measurement*. Retrieved July 14, 2015, from http://www.codeproject.com/Articles/11835/WordNet-based-semantic-similarity-measurement

Chapter 3
Centralized to Decentralized Social Networks:
Factors that Matter

Maryam Qamar
National University of Sciences and Technology, Pakistan

Sidra Mehmood
National University of Sciences and Technology, Pakistan

Mehwish Malik
National University of Sciences and Technology, Pakistan

Asad W. Malik
National University of Sciences and Technology, Pakistan

Saadia Batool
National University of Sciences and Technology, Pakistan

Anis Rahman
National University of Sciences and Technology, Pakistan

ABSTRACT

This work covers the research work on decentralization of Online Social Networks (OSNs), issues with centralized design are studied with possible decentralized solutions. Centralized architecture is prone to privacy breach, p2p architecture for data and thus authority decentralization with encryption seems a possible solution. OSNs' users grow exponentially causing scalability issue, a natural solution is decentralization where users bring resources with them via personal machines or paid services. Also centralized services are not available unremittingly, to this end decentralization proposes replication. Decentralized solutions are also proposed for reliability issues arising in centralized systems and the potential threat of a central authority. Yet key to all problems isn't found, metadata may be enough for inferences about data and network traffic flow can lead to information on users' relationships. First issue can be mitigated by data padding or splitting in uniform blocks. Caching, dummy traffic or routing through a mix of nodes can be some possible solutions to the second.

DOI: 10.4018/978-1-4666-9767-6.ch003

Copyright © 2016, IGI Global. Copying or distributing in print or electronic forms without written permission of IGI Global is prohibited.

OSN INTRODUCTION AND MOTIVATION TOWARDS DOSN

Online social networks (OSNs) result from online interactions between people and communities (groups), for example Facebook, Twitter etc. In the current centralized paradigm, most of the OSN providers grant free services to its users and in exchange reserve the rights to use the data shared/published by users in any possible way. This raises serious privacy and content ownership concerns and requires a strong trust in the OSN providers. Also OSNs need to be highly scalable to incorporate exponentially growing number of users which is difficult for a centralized architecture. Availability of data might also become an issue in terms of servers' downtime and service shut down. Moreover there is a severe lack of interoperability between different OSN sites, so users wanting to share same data on different OSNs need to upload it separately and developers are compelled to develop same social applications using different APIs to deploy on different OSNs.

These issues being faced by centralized OSNs motivated the research for decentralizing the OSNs, the work in this field addresses privacy and access control, availability of data, scalability, usage of data under different administrative domains by social applications etc.

Section II introduces Decentralized OSN (DOSN) and defines an abstract architecture model. Section III talks about the issues of centralized OSNs as motivational factors for seeking peer-to-peer (p2p) solutions. In section III we elaborate the work with respect to specific factors. Section IV concludes the paper.

DOSN ARCHITECTURE

In simple words DOSN can be defined as an online social service with an underlying distributed network layout which lets users communicate and share. A general architecture layout for DOSN inspired by the work of Paul et al. (2014) is shown in figure 1. It comprises of a lowest Network layer, a middle layer consisting of DOSN's core functionality and an upper layer subdivide in two layers with upper most being a user interface and the lower one hidden from users providing services to upper layer.

Figure 1. DOSN Architecture1

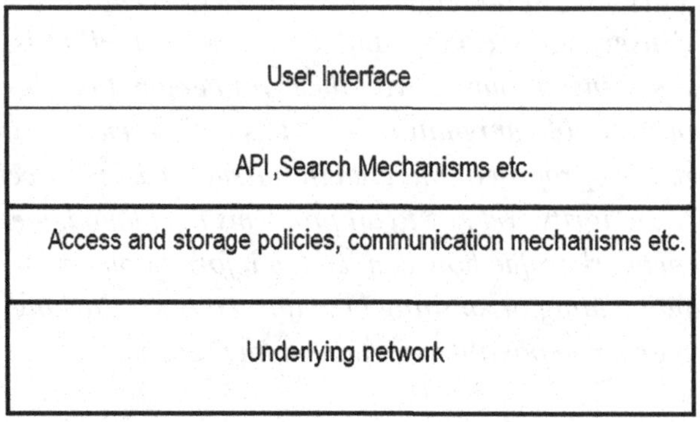

User Interface
API,Search Mechanisms etc.
Access and storage policies, communication mechanisms etc.
Underlying network

DECENTRALIZATION

A lot of factors motivate and control a big move like decentralizing online social networks, in this paper focus is on some primary ones, that is, privacy control, availability, scalability, security and reliability of data. Some basic research in this field is discussed first then more focused work regarding each issue is discussed in its relevant sub-section.

Buchegger and Datta (2009) did a case study to put forward the opportunities and challenges, a p2p social network comes with. It is speculated that the removal of a central entity with unequal power over users' data is a base opportunity and motivation for users' to adopt decentralized architecture, where their privacy can be protected via a combination of encryption techniques and inherent capabilities of p2p architecture, on the other side the service providers of central OSNs will look at the paradigm shift regrettably as they will possibly lose business opportunities. The challenge of realizing decentralized social networks lies in the nature of social networking, DOSNs should make data available even when individual peers are down, grant authorized access and tackle security issues.

PAPEER by Frey et al. (2009) is a decentralized p2p architecture that provides an interface to search for research papers and researchers, with a desired interest field, in standard repositories and shared local repositories of other researchers. Its users can associate tags and comments with papers, which are used for retrieving work of interest or recommend people interested in the same field. A concept of personal library is introduced, which contains <p,t,c,f> entries, where p is metadata of the paper, t is a set of tags, c is comment of user and f gives a link to local copy of paper. Also a notion of explicit and implicit social networks is implied, which is used for information sharing and retrieval, here explicit network consists of references to friends or collaborators on OSNs and the implicit one consists of references to researches whose profiles are close to user's. Users' personal library and social network together are defined as users' federated library on which operations like querying a paper, tagging and commenting a paper, navigating from papers to people and navigating from keyword to people etc. are performed. For maintaining personalized social networks gossip based protocol is employed for periodic information exchange between nodes, where cosine similarity of two nodes is calculated to ascertain whether a particular node qualifies for being in user's implicit social network. PAPEER's paper recommendation to a target set of users was evaluated giving a recall of 70%, but a lower precision of 10%. No other considerations like privacy, security etc. Were taken into account in system design.

Privacy

As most people enjoying the benefits of social networks are also concerned with the way their service providers keep the rights to use their information in any way, letting the possibility of important data getting abused, privacy is the most basic issue to be catered for by decentralization of OSNs.

This section discusses some work relevant to the data privacy control as well as the privacy of behaviors and interactions of users.

Vafopoulos (2006) identifies Information Society as a two faced entity, the positive facet being the knowledge based development and other the personal data abuse. People in this society contribute towards it by interacting, learning and sharing valuable information but the paradigm also threatens the misuse of data by unauthorized accesses raising privacy issues.

The fact that OSNs can process fake data gave rise to the key idea of None of Your Business (NOYB) by Guha et al. (2008) work. A novel and interesting approach is suggested to keep users' data private while retaining most of the functionality. NOYB uses encryption to encode users' data atoms (parts of data) by indexing to a dictionary of valid data atoms build by observing OSNs profiles, thus OSNs can't tell that the data is not legitimate. Theses indexes can be coded using any encryption technique, authors used AES for demonstration and evaluation of the work. Existing key management system are also proposed to be used for key distribution purposes, though it was not part of the authors' implementation, which is in the form a Firefox extension, having button controls on profile pages for encryption and decryption. Manual verification affirmed the reasonability of encrypted profiles without leaking private information but only a small user-base was used.

A pioneering work by Buchegger et al. (2009) truly proposes and takes a step towards taking a move in the direction of a decentralized peer to peer approach coupled with encryption to address the privacy concern of centralized, where OSN functionalities like log in, friend search, addition, removal and updating of content etc. are implemented. For the early prototype a two tier architecture is developed with OpenDHT as look-up service and peers who can communicate and exchange data directly after first lookup. Privacy stems from the removal of any central entity from the picture and security is proposed (not implemented in this prototype) to be ensured by encryption and key management techniques.

Cutillo et al. (2009a) proposed a p2p social network architecture for ensuring privacy and co-operation among peers through trust relationships. The system has an underlying DHT architecture, providing p2p identifier based global access to the content and a trust identification service, which is responsible for preventing impersonation attacks by granting pseudonym, a unique identifier and authentication certificates to each node. An unusual view of system is also introduced in the proposed architecture called matryoshkas; where user is at the center of concentric rings of nodes with inner most ring being the most trusted ones, playing the role of replicas and granting privacy controlled access to the content by using public key cryptography (PKC). Fine grained access control is also made available as access policies can be defined both at individual and group levels. The implementation was in progress at the time of publication, thus no practical evaluation is done.

An extension to the work of Cutillo et al. (2009a) is done by the same authors (Cutillo et al. 2009b) with a particular focus on studying the feasibility of Safebook in terms of systems' responsiveness and availability of data. The simulations conducted in this paper shows that for a node with 3 to 4 shells (concentric rings around user) and up to 23 trusted nodes replicating its data, probability of data availability is up to 90%. And for this setup, for initial 90% look ups, overall look up delay can be estimated below 13.5 seconds.

Persona by Baden et al. (2009) provides users with fine grain privacy control by employing a combination of attribute based encryption (ABE) and public key cryptography (PKC). Granularity of privacy control allows users to define restrictions on individual and group level, these groups though anticipated to be classified by transparent relationships like co-leagues etc. can contain any diverse relationships. Each user in Persona network generates an asymmetric key-pair as PKC defines and distributes public key to users it wants to communicate with and ABE is employed for encryption to groups providing the flexibility to share with unions and intersections of groups.

Interaction among users of Persona is realized by applications which are used for every OSN function, may it be maintaining profile, sharing of collaborative data or resource management. The proposed solution is implemented as a Firefox extension and can be integrated with Facebook to allow users enjoy its privacy enabled application while continuing to be on familiar OSN. Median load time and median size of encrypted profile data was evaluated to be 2.3 seconds and 20.4KB respectively, which are reasonable enough.

PrPl by Seong et al. (2010) is a decentralized architecture providing fine grain privacy control and an API for allowing social applications to run on different administrative domains. Data in PrPl can be stored on personal servers or entrusted to a paid or free add-supported service, also it can be kept at various locations (possibly encrypted). A per user service called Personal Cloud Butler keeps track of storage distributions and shares the data with friends based on private preferences on access control employing trust certificates and communicating with other users' butler services. A decentralized identity management system OpenID is used for identity management in the system, it is responsible for authentication of users and butler services. An expressive query language SociaLite based on Datalog is implemented for development of social applications on top of DOSNs, which allows applications to request data from butler services running on different administrative domains. Applications for sharing personal information (PEOPS) and music streaming (Jinzora) were implemented for demonstration. One drawback of this otherwise good architecture is that no replication strategies were implemented owing to the assumption of data storage spaces being highly available, which is not a casual assumption to make.

A contact discovery scheme is introduced by De Cristofaro (2011) to achieve private discovery of mutual contacts in collaborative applications, where users maintain their contact lists themselves, without involving any third party like a central server. The need may arise when two unfamiliar/strange users want to discover their social proximity using the mutual friends' knowledge to build a relationship, ideally they wouldn't want their other contacts being revealed. Contact discovery scheme (CDS) consists of 4 protocols; Init() initializes the security parameters, AddContact(U↔V) adds V to U's contact list and issues a contact certificate which is used to ensure warranted claims on relationships, RevokeContact(U,V) revokes the contact certificate of U from V intersecting V with U's contact list, Discover(U↔V) is used to discover mutual contacts between U and V; it takes U and V's inputs as (role,CL,partner); role is either initializer or responder, CL is set of contact certificates and partner is the supposed partner, that is other user, and uses Okamoto's technique for RSA-based, identity- based key agreement is combined with padding (to hide size information) to output list of mutual contacts called shared contact list (SCL). For each transmission Index Hiding Message Encoding (IHME) is used so no useful information can be learned. Contact revocation is achieved by maintaining a list of revoked contacts which is taken in as an additional input by Discover(U↔V) allowing V to know U's revoked contacts. Nothing is done about hiding the size of contact lists and contact revocation list is public and while Discover(U↔V) doesn't allow privacy breach for un-common friends, revoked contacts are not private, which might be desired for many reasons. Also this approach is limited to individual contacts and does not take into account chain contacts and common communities etc., which is usually an indication of users' tastes and interests and can be a base for relationships.

An improvement of the work of De Cristofaro et al. (2011) by De Cristofaro et al. (2013) introduces another CDS which instead of IHME uses interleaved IHME, which divides the messages in smaller chunks, thus improving system's computational and communication complexities. Also more flexible contact discovery is now possible where a user need not include full contact list in the input to Discover(U↔V) protocol, but a subset can be used depending on nature of relation e.g. personal or business etc., meaning concept of common communities is realized. Yet this work still lacks in addressing chain relations and contact lists' size hiding.

In this work by Mega et al. (2011) authors concerned with privacy violation of centralized OSNs address the question whether it is possible to build a decentralized OSN over a social overlay, i.e., an overlay network whose links among nodes mirror the social network relationships among the nodes' owners? Main focus of the work is on the key OSN functionality of disseminating profile updates, gossip protocols are generally suitable for such purposes. But it was found that mainstream gossip protocols were inefficient because of characteristic properties of social networks, so a flooding protocol with each message piggybacking histories was proposed with inverse probability heuristic. The system was evaluated, using simulation over a crawled real world social network, depicting acceptable latency, foster load balancing across nodes, and churn tolerance. But the network was assumed to be immutable in terms of relationships, also simulation network workload was not realistic, which makes it hard to validate if the system would really perform well in real world scenarios.

Vis-à-vis by Shakimov et al. (2011) seeks to preserve users' location information privacy which is shared with a particular group and is not desirable to be disclosed to the world. It is a decentralized framework designed to interoperate with OSNs based on Virtual Individual Server (VIS: a personal virtual machine running on cloud; it self-organizes itself into overlay networks according to social groups). A Vis-a-Vis group descriptor is embedded in a centralized OSN's group, which when loaded by a user is interpreted and rewritten by a Vis-a-Vis browse extension to include the information downloaded from the appropriate VISs of individual users. The framework needs the users to trust acquired cloud service but stringent terms of business doesn't allow the service to abuse information as OSNs can as the payback for free service. The proposed framework was compared with a Vis-a-Vis implemented using centralized approach focusing on operation latencies, performance differences were found but justified by the authors as the fact that network latency dominates Vis-à-Vis' back end services latency, reduces the meaning of perceived performance differences.

DECENT by Jahid et al. (2012) is a modular and object-oriented DOSN architecture. It leverages a DHT to store user data and uses cryptography to realize confidentiality and integrity of user-owned content and the focus is a blog-like wall rather than chat messages. The architecture being modular has three separate components, the data objects, cryptography and DHT, interacting with each other via interface. This modularity causes freedom to use any kind of cryptography and any type of DHT.

Cachet is a decentralized OSN by Nilizadeh et al. (2012) that provides strong security and privacy and improves on DECENT. The main difference between them is that Cachet introduces social caches to improve the performance of the system by not incorporating the pull-based grasping of variety of single data items from many different sources. Due to this the nodes enforce social trust relation for maintaining secure (SSL) connection with rest of online contacts to get updates directly as quickly as possible. Cachet uses a DHT to store data and uses ABE (Attribute based Encryption) to ensure confidentiality. ABE is a public key encryption technique, where user's secret key and cypher text depend upon attributes such as kind subscription type, country he/she lives in, social groups etc. Decryption is only possible when user attribute match cypher text attributes. The authors observed this violation of privacy, but not addressed it completely, header was just hidden from storage system whereas the users could still find the headers and see plain text of access policies in ABE. For the sake of efficiency, information caching was involved and unencrypted information was stored on nodes that fulfills the ABE policy which are the ones able to decrypt. In this way user is able to know intended users for which the contents will be encrypted and can also trace the requests of people who can decrypt this information.

An approach to predict the propagation of social Data on DOSN is proposed in the work of Tandukar et al. (2012). Feedback of shared content is tracked to analyze interaction level and the priority of new social data is determined from previous history of recorded interactions between two users. The response value in feedback varies from .3 to .9. The relationship model is defined as:

$$S_A^B\left(I\right) = \alpha * S_A^B\left(I\right)_p + \left(1 - \alpha\right) * F$$

The new strength S is derived from the Previous Strength for the interest area I. The parameter a, is a linear function (a could be 0, 1) of number of data produced by user in a particular area. For propagation of the message a threshold value should be specified, if the strength of relationship is more than that threshold only then data will be propagated. The relationship model is defined in user's device as the system is based on decentralized architecture. Filtration process is done at sender side to reduce network traffic. As the relationship strength for interest I in user A for user B fades away, user B will not get social data related to interest I from user A. If user B want to get data from user A fro interest I, user B can send data to user A related to that interest area I, It will increase the strength of relationship as high as possible.

Bodriagov et al. (2013) discuss and compare different encryption schemes in context of their suitability to OSNs and identifies dynamic identity based broadcast encryption (DIBBE); a stateless, dynamic and cost efficient scheme, for data confidentiality and security. The approach uses four algorithms; Setup generates a secret master key (MK) and a group public key (GPK), MK is then taken as input by Extract algorithms which outputs a private key for each user. The Encrypt algorithm uses set of receivers (S) and GPK to produce (Header, K); K being a symmetric key for data encryption and Header, an encryption of this key for S. Encrypted data is in (Header, encrypted) form allowing only users in S to decrypt it with their private keys. For decryption, a symmetric key K is produced by Decrypt algorithm which takes GPK, Header, user's private key and ID as input. MK requirement by this approach restricts it in a way; it does not allow to encrypt for a group for whom membership doesn't exist, same goes for friends of friends.

Mahdian et al. (2013) proposed MyZone which employs a decentralized p2p architecture to realize OSN functionalities, while using a centralized server for initial user registration and finding other peers. The work focuses on small scale private communities while it is claimed that MyZone can be used for large-scale OSNs. Users' data is kept on their own nodes while availability is ensured by replicating it on a few trusted nodes. The centralized server called certification authority, is trusted to be non-malicious and resilient to malicious nodes, and it authenticates users, while communication protection is achieved by encryption methods. Authors conjectured that the benefits of absolute availability and consistency overweigh the added complexity, so a best effort is made to achieve an always available weakly consistent profiles' view. Users of MyZone have to decide for themselves the peer nodes where they should replicate their data, which may not be easy and efficient as this requires something more than trust like information about the resources and availability of the other node.

Decentralization gives user the control over his/her data and establish control access policies for who can access it or not. This is usually done by cryptography which is of two types generally the one which reveals the access policies and the one which don't. There is trade-off between these two of performance and privacy. Bodriagov et al. (2014) analyze the predicate encryption (PE) and adapt it to the context of DOSN. A univariate polynomial construction for the access control policies in PE is proposed, which significantly increases performance but at the same time it leaks some part of the access policy to users with access rights. Bloom filters were used for the sake of decreasing decryption time and identified objects which can be decrypted by any particular user. Evaluation is performed on the news feed. This work is limited to or gives best performance for group encryption or for small number of individual identities. Also the semantics of access control policies, useful to define access control criteria, policy validation process and dynamic policy allocation, are completely ignored.

Decentralization removes the control of a central service provider, enabling user to have more control over his data and preserve privacy. To prevent unauthorized access, Nasim et al. (2014) provide a light weighted privacy preserving and readily available component named as extensible Access Control Markup language (XACML) along with Security Assertion Markup Language (SAML) with secret key authentication. It allow user to share or keep personal information from other users and is robust against a range of attacks. Most of the languages are proprietary and also existing access control models are application dependent whereas in decentralized environment access control components should be interoperable, collaborative and agreeing on uniform policies. Due to the fact that there are diverse users with different requirements to control the access, rule base control access is used as it is more expressive and flexible. XACML is used because of its standardization and high expressiveness regarding constraints. The work introduced a new profile structure to protect user privacy and also their social connections, along with providing implementation and analysis of common access policy using XACML and SAML for privacy features. As XACML doesn't ensure authentication and authorization, so SAML, an XML based language for authentication and authorizing data was used. This work is somehow more suitable and user friendly for environment where every user hosts its own web server. Another issue with this work is that it oversees availability concerns, for which replicas of trusted servers and cloud services can be used for hosting. This work removed the need of OSN providers, its powerful enough that identity theft is not an easy task anymore and network leaks is reduced. Problem with this approach is, it's now more sensitive to Denial of services attack which makes the server or any network resource temporarily unavailable to user. Redundancy can resolve this problem only if the data owners don't have control over server otherwise it will give rise to further trust issues.

Usually everything comes with good and bad aspects, and so is the case with DOSNs. Greschbach et al. (2012) identify new privacy challenges in DOSNs specifically privacy breaches stemming from metadata (e.g. size etc.) and discusses general techniques to solve or mitigate them. The concern is as content storage, access right management, retrieval and other administrative tasks of the service become the obligation of the users, it is non-trivial to hide the metadata of objects (Harvesters, the nodes that request data from system) and information flows (network sniffers can observe traffic), even when the content itself is encrypted, as a result inferences from metadata might invade users' privacy. Also relay and storage nodes can possibly exploit the way data storage, encryption and communication is implemented in a DOSN and may turn into a powerful attacker. Moving towards the possible solutions, authors present padding as one way to hinder inferences based on size but also realize that it still allows inferences from the order of magnitude. Another better but complex approach is to split up the content in uniform sized blocks and hide the connection between them. To hide structure information, an encryption scheme concealing the indices and links along with data objects is a possible solution. Obfuscation of information flow can be achieved by routing through a mix of socially related nodes, caching also helps by minimizing message exchange and de-co-relating it from specific user actions. Noise (dummy traffic) which costs higher network load can be used where other measures are not applicable/effective.

Scalability

Scalability issues also arise in case of centralized service paradigm, due to huge number of people joining the OSNs. To take an apparent example Facebook had 10,000 servers in April 2008, and had to acquire a total of 30,000 till October 2009 (Miller, 2013), and this is only the number of servers, while their maintenance also costs a fortune to the service providers. Also network bandwidth needs to be scalable enough to accommodate the traffic generated by a huge number of users. This section explains some of the research ideas and their results pertaining to the scalability aspect.

A solution to the scalability problem of centralized OSNs is proposed in the form of a modular p2p framework by Graffi et al. (2008). The framework uses PAST, an extension to FreePastry, as the underlying structure and builds plugins for incorporating the OSN functionalities like maintaining friend lists, photo albums etc. An information cache is used to contain retrieved objects while a storage dispatcher module processes data so that it is in a storable form. Having a layer of plugins for providing all high level functionalities, the system is easily extendable thus new functionalities can be realized in the form of plugins and put to work easy and fast.

To address the issues of scalability and high costs of centralized OSNs a decentralized storage architecture called user assisted OSN (uaOSN) is proposed in the work of Kryczka et al. (2010) to distribute the storage load of users' published content (typical large sized contents e.g. photos, videos etc.) among the OSN's users with the purpose of letting the provider keep control while reducing service provision costs. uaOSN provider only keeps basic information like profiles and social graphs, queries for other content are addressed to the provider which replies with the storage place information so it acts like an indexer. This storage place can either be placed on desktop machines of users or set-top boxes/residential routers with a hard disk, a third possibility is to use a cloud service. Deployment of data is easy on desktop machines of users but they are not likely to be available 24/7, a crucial requirement for OSNs, replication techniques with focus on the locality principle can be employed to cater for this, and in case of data being stored on strangers' machines some encryption technique should be used for privacy purposes with the provider as a trusted third-party and key issuer. On the other hand routers and cloud service provide high availability but content deployment is costly on routers and using cloud service means users have to pay for storage space. uaOSN is claimed to bring reduction of costs and robustness to Denial of Service (DoS) attacks benefits to the providers along with higher availability and better access benefits to the users. However, the work has no implementation of the proposed architecture nor does it validates the claims made.

Cuckoo by Xu et al. (2010) is a peer to peer socio-aware (makes use of inherent relationships) microblogging service (a restricted version of OSN) compatible with Twitter architecture to improve scalability, reliability and availability requirements.

A structured p2p overlay network utilizing Pastry as the underlying overlay is created, where on joining, new nodes build their routing tables, leaf and neighborhood sets. For querying, a hybrid approach is used; DHT is employed for locating rare items while for popular items simple flooding is put to use. For content dissemination push method is deployed, which is replicating the micro-content among followers, who also acts as replicas if the original publisher is down. In case the publisher cannot push to all its followers' gossip based push between neighbors is used. Availability of content in case of an unpopular node not being online and none of its friends either is the responsibility of the service providers, in which exclusive case users will fetch the content from the service provider and a not peer node. Things may have worked fine if they were put to work but the system is not deployed thus no validation.

The issues of scalability and reliability are attempted to be dealt with by deploying a distributed browser consisting of multiple browser nodes for running collaborative applications by Shinjo et al. (2011). Each browser node is like a regular Web browser called Subspace. It is operated by a single user, able to communicate and collaborate with other nodes. An application on distributed browser can run across multiple nodes making use of any of the resources associated with those nodes, thus letting multiple users share a single application. The distributed browser was realized by implementing an extension of Google Chrome (Process Manager), which runs collaborative applications written in JavaScript performing process management and IPC. Authentication and secure inter-node communications were accomplished reusing the overlay network and social features of Skype (RPC Module). Co-browsing applications (sharing webpage, handing over control of a web session), Comment-sharing application with access control and an extension of Chrome's Screen Capture extension to capture and send screen image (along with annotations) to a remote user were developed for the testing purpose, all of which worked as anticipated, however no interactive and delay sensitive application was built and tested. A more concerning issue is the dependence on central servers of Skype, which leads us back to where we actually started the journey.

The work of Thilakarathna et al. (2012) addresses the high communication costs and battery usage issues of distributed social networks hosted on smartphones by using a replication strategy which is aware of connectivity among peers. The devices comprising the network are grouped into tribes for content replication on the basis of a combined criterion using bipartite b-matching and a greedy heuristic, which works in iterations building a solution and in each iteration it adds a node without violating capacity constraints. These tribes exploit time elasticity of content sharing for serving it through low-cost network connections. It was found via experiments that on average compared to the non-mobile approaches, this approach allows a content generator to reduce network bandwidth and battery usage up to 43% and 41% respectively.

Availability

The downtime of OSNs' servers raise the issue of data availability and motivates towards the decentralized paradigm. And once the systems get to decentralization, data availability may become an issue depending on the storage machines and the chance of their round the clock availability, for example ordinary users machines in peer to peer systems are not expected to be running all the time. So it is to be addressed how decentralized system would ensure data availability. This section takes the availability view of DOSNs research work.

In the work of Shakimov et al. (2009) three decentralized data storage schemes, where users' data is stored on a virtual individual server (VIS) are presented and privacy, cost and availability trade-offs are studied. The difference in three schemes involves the placement of VISs, which can either being on cloud, users' desktop machine with socially informed replicas or a hybrid of both. It was concluded that use of first scheme would incur a lot of cost, while providing high availability, also stringent terms of service between users' and service provider would tend to keep privacy. Using desktop machines on the other hand would raise availability issues even with replicas, nevertheless it is the most cost effective and privacy preserving approach. The hybrid scheme resort to use cloud based standby when neither desktop machines nor replicas are available, combining the benefits of both approaches and reducing their drawbacks simultaneously.

Remote storage of data leads to availability and resilience, the problem of maximization of data availability in distributed replicated system is studied in the paper by Rzadca et al. (2010). In decentralized systems each peer seeks to find a replication partner by maximizing his own availability.

Authors analyzed that even if a peer have complete knowledge of all other peers availabilities and peers are willing to replicate, achieving replication with minimal size is NP hard problem. Model introduced in this research is composed of n peers (representing users), for simplicity it is assumed that all peers are homogeneous. The ith peer is expressed as Pi and Peer availability av(I,t) is the proximity of peer p being online at time t, likewise unavailability auv(I,t).

Peers form replication groups {Gk} where each member replicates data of all other members and unavailability of a group is defined as uav{Gk, t}. This grouping have some advantages over pair based allocation i.e groups are automatically formed secondly it becomes easier to optimize some of the systems. Each peer want it data to replicated well, so I minimizes its dav(i) by forming a group with nav(I,t) as small as possible. Goal is to minimize the size of replication groups Min s= IGkI. It has been analyzed through simulations that locality aware policies are less efficient as compared to global randomized allocation, however the equitable heuristic works better then random allocation. It is proved that peers with high availability will only replicate each other. Many propositions are introduced but they require computational complexities and most of them are NP hard. More experimentation is required to test the proposed heuristic in real world scenarios.

Narendula et al. (2012a) focus on maximizing availability while keeping the privacy intact, a privacy friendly Decentralized OSN MY3 is proposed to this end. MY3 facilitates many properties which existing OSN already have such as access friends contents, finding their geographic locations, access time prediction, implicit trust on friends and many more. MY3 preserve user privacy by exercising controlled access over the contents, also replication strategies are presented by which system's performance and availability is maximized. This paper doesn't do any data encryption, rather it relies on trust relation between friends. Thus an approach to select a subset of friends which are included in a user's trusted proxy set for the sake for profile replication is provided with. The supporting argument put forward by authors is that the trust between friends can actually replace the need for content encryption hence removing the need of key management. The assumption makes the implementation easier but there exist a storage burden to persistently store stale contents of big user profiles, impose an overhead, due to which user profiles need to be small.

Supernova by Sharma, et al. (2012) is a super peer based self-organizing DOSN; which focuses on availability of data when a peer is down for the purpose of investigating whether such a system is sustainable or not given diverse participation behaviors and capacities. It was found that availability was 60% or less for 60% nodes. Replication of a user's encrypted data to a set of users after an agreement of terms is done, theses replica nodes called storekeepers handle updates while the user is down. Super peers are responsible for keeping track of availability patterns of users so they can be suggested to users as storekeepers, they may also do storekeeping for users with no or overloaded friends etc., also they keep track of a user's storekeepers/replicas. This costs super peers storage space, computational power and network bandwidth, so there should be enough incentives for users with enough resources to act as super peers (may be running on end user or a cloud service) which are not focused on other than saying this can simply be altruism, reputation or monetary gain.

Narendula et al. (2012b) analyzed the effect of different parameters such as total replicas, placement policy and user time, on the availability of content in Decentralized OSN, by performing simulations. Firstly the global availability was observed and then users' content; available only to their friends was considered. Three different strategies of replica placement has been studied on datasets of Facebook and Twitter; first strategy was based on greedy approach which will maximize the availability of contents, next was based on the users' friends which are most active and last was a simpler one which was to place replicas randomly. Of these three, the second strategy, which makes use of states related to users' friends who are most active with approximately 40% replication factor was found to give the highest availability of content to its friends. Problem may arise with this approach as the assumption of trust (users' trust on friends) can result in security breaches also not considering the consistency factor in replicas such as user activity updates are not communicated etc. can also prove to be problematic.

The motivation behind the work of Koll et al. (2013) is to find a systematic solution providing good availability with minimum cost and overhead. It is claimed to overcome the technical and economic issues of deployment, limited robustness and also difficulty of discriminating the users as they depend on other nodes related to it. To overcome these, a generic approach for placing the user data replicas is proposed, named SOUP (Self-Organized Universe of People). SOUP comprises of variety of mechanisms, based on interchanging the experiences among the nodes which are socially related, which results in efficient distribution of replicas to the mirror nodes to the whole OSN. SOUP induces benefit of robustness to OSN, also is adaptive and resilient to any malicious activities. It is also scalable as it can scale up to large number of users and quickly converges to a stable state. Measuring the storage and bandwidth consumption of SOUP by deploying its prototype to Amazon EC2 Virtual Machine revealed that during all the time of experiments, one workstation was fully available and attracted the profiles very quickly. Another observation is that SOUP perform slightly worse in the scenario when online time distribution is uniform due to which it is unable to exploit the heterogeneity of nodes characteristics which enable good selection of mirrors.

Sonet by Schwittmann et al. (2013) is a federated online social network architecture for providing privacy and high availability of data. User contents are both encrypted and decrypted on the end user devices, so they are not visible to OSN Provider. A novel aliasing approach along with secure algorithms for establishing mutual friendship is used for hiding the social graph from OSN Provider. Authentication does not require the user to reveal their identities which saves potential threat of attacker. This work focuses on improving data availability by using replication scheme (to mitigate server failures) which keeps the social graph hidden. This work differs from others as it obfuscates the social graph by single direction pseudonyms in combination with replication. In the proposed system, the application client interact with its own storage server which saves the overhead of a lot of smaller time span connections to third parties. Even though, extensive cryptographic operations are used, still performance evaluations suggested the application execute on mobile devices very efficiently.

The main goal of the work of Shahriar et al. (2013) is to increase availability with minimum cost and overhead. A DHT based replication scheme is presented where the main contribution is the concept of β-availability groups, where at any given time, at least β members of a replication group are supposed to be online. Users' uptime is tracked by the structured overlay which act as agent finding the match for the purpose of forming the replication group. Simulation-based experimentation indicated that groups based on 2-availability can probably provide much higher resilience to failures but at the same time require some overhead for the creation of groups.

Diaspora by Schulz et al. (2013) is aimed at building a reliable and usable decentralized online social network. The architecture is based on a client–server model where every user has his own server instance (Pod) which is used for storage, communication and access control. Since there is no data or service replication, Pods must always be online for reliable service provision. A Pod can be hosted either on own hardware or by a service provider (cloud service) Data is stored unencrypted on the pod, protected by an access control mechanism. As Diaspora offers access control based on the group and user concept which is not a fine grain one, it is unable to cover the cases which are based on dynamic rules or when a fine grain control like granting access to the whole group but a particular user is required.

Reliability and Security

People having their important, not to be lost data stored on the servers of OSNs, need to be sure their data would never be lost but regrettably that will exactly be the case if the service shuts down. So a solution in the form of decentralization also aims to provide reliability. Security aspect deals with things like authentication, authorization, non-repudiation etc. in DOSNs.

Layered identity based Kademelia like infrastructure (Likir) by Aiello et al. (2008) is a modification of Kademelia by Maymounkov et al. (2002), with the aim of avoiding a number of potential attacks like routing poisoning, eclipse attack, distributed denial of service, man in the middle etc. caused by malicious nodes. The architecture is based on a certification authority (CS) either centralized or decentralized responsible for associating node Ids with users' identities for identity management and non-repudiation using public key cryptography. Likir not only incurs an overhead with respect to number and size of messages exchange among nodes when compared to Kademlia but it also introduces cryptography operations' computational costs.

In their work Forsyth et al. (2013) focus on the problem of managing updates' consistency to ensure data reliability in an unstructured decentralized OSN. A cache structure capable of efficiently supporting updates is proposed; data cache is updated with data update information at a local level and then this information is used to push data updates to peers, also a path cache is maintained on a peer which stores metadata about data updates used to allow updates to propagate and facilitates random walks for item search. Random walk forwards query to neighbors until the target is found or search aborted using social graph as well as cache (data and path) on minimum distance successful search path. Future update can then be applied on same path due to the fact that path information is stored, this results in consistent replicas. Peers only look into subset of neighbors, who they know, have the data copy and don't contact peers for updates which are not part of search ensuring better performance. Simulated evaluations showed a trade-off between freshness of data and performance, also assumption of peers not being involved in malicious activity can cause issues in real world scenarios, and as the master manages and records all updates, it is required to be available at all times else delays will occur.

The work of Chilukaet al. (2015) is concerned with analysis of heavy churn impact on decentralized social network based on Sybil defense scheme (SNSD) robustness property. They found that heavy churn rate disintegrates the social overlay network into many disconnected components which results in poor network connectivity, also naïve approach can improve the performance in terms of network connectivity but its side effect result in poor network resilience. A new design approach was proposed which maintains trade-off between the network connectivity and network attack resilience by introducing a new heuristic; Minimum Expansion Contribution (MinEC). It was proposed that each node add links to only selective few "k" of its 2-hop neighbors based on MinEC, the idea behind MinEC is that 2-hop link is formed between nodes depending on the common neighbors between those nodes at the same time penalizing the degree of nodes. MinEC can be compared to 2- hop in terms of network connectivity and with 1-hop in terms of network attack resilience. Along with that it also preserves the fast mixing property. Architecture model is based on the dataset measurement of Yahoo Instant Messenger and Skype. Hypothesis of this paper is "Adding links from each node to all its 2-hop neighbors has significant unintended consequence of creating a large number of new 2-hop attack edges between honest and Sybil nodes" Since it will result in too many attack edge which will pose threat to robustness which require few and limited edges so for this hybrid of one-hop and 2-hop is proposed K 2-hop neighbors benefiting from advantages of both strategies, But finding optimal value of k is a non-trivial task. The hypothesis was validated by disconnection probability and escape probability and showed better performance. This work still lacks in guarantying to provide high network connectivity in heavy churn, which might require to go beyond typical 2-hop neighborhood for each node and not involving any malicious node. No better value of k is provided, it needs a lot of attention. Yet the work can be extended for social routing system in heavy churn behavior.

Vegas by Durr et al. (2012) is designed as a highly restrictive, secure and privacy preserving peer to peer OSN, which does not attempt to achieve the functionality of standard OSNs like Facebook etc. but instead allows for domain specific relaxations based on desired degree of privacy and security. Clients communicate through secure asynchronous communication channels called exchangers, which allow for delay-tolerant information exchange similar to a mail box. Privacy and security is preserved by the use of symmetric key encryption technique, where a pair of keys is used for each trusted node, this is an overhead but authors assume it negligible because their model restricts the relationships to a limited number (real trusted friends only). To ensure availability of data/profile information, concept of datastore was introduced, which represents the abstract concept of a user-writable and world-readable storage space. Each piece of data is stored as a single encrypted file and only the user or and his/her friends can access it by knowing datastore addresses and directory mapping information preserving privacy. Vegas attempts to provide a completely secure and privacy preserving OSN, so there is a compromise on functionality, also it is not possible to examine social graph structure and users' interaction behavior.

Aiello et al. (2012) proposed LotusNet, a p2p platform for development of social network services (SNSs) aimed to provide a good trade-off between privacy, security and service requirements. System architecture is based on a DHT modification called Likir by Aiello et al. (2008) which provides strong identity management at overlay level and a two way authentication between peers. Social network functionality is realized in widgets on top of DHT. For access control, signed grants issued by data owner containing identities of owner and granted user, an expiration time and a compressed list of allowed content types are used. Also published content is encrypted to avoid breach by index nodes and a single encryption key is shared with known contacts. Framework is implemented in the form of a java library, it can host several, and possibly inter-connected SNSs because no assumption was made about the structure of applications but large scale experimentation in real world setting is not conducted.

CONCLUSION

The centralized OSNs have their issues like privacy breach, scalability costs, availability concern etc., these raised the need for a more reliable architecture model, which will cater for these problems and still provide all the functionalities. Peer-to-Peer architecture is inherently suitable; scalability problem is addressable as users entering the network bring their own resources, privacy can be ensured using distributed storage concept of p2p model and availability concern can be dealt with by implementing replication strategies.

Move to the DOSN brings availability, data privacy and access control benefits for the users while if not completely removed from the picture, OSN providers enjoy a reduction in scalability costs. On the other hand, the fact is nothing can come as a one face all good entity, so does not DOSN; users do incur some cost as their resources are now being used and for better availability some paid storage service like a cloud service may need to be acquired. Moreover, if service providers get completely out of picture, they lose their business.

REFERENCES

Aiello, L. M., Milanesio, M., Ruffo, G., & Schifanella, R. (2008, September). Tempering Kademlia with a robust identity based system. In *Peer-to-Peer Computing, 2008. P2P'08. Eighth International Conference on* (pp. 30-39). IEEE. doi:10.1109/P2P.2008.40

Aiello, L. M., & Ruffo, G. (2012). LotusNet: Tunable privacy for distributed online social network services. *Computer Communications*, *35*(1), 75–88. doi:10.1016/j.comcom.2010.12.006

Baden, R., Bender, A., Spring, N., Bhattacharjee, B., & Starin, D. (2009, August). Persona: An online social network with user-defined privacy. [). ACM.]. *Computer Communication Review*, *39*(4), 135–146. doi:10.1145/1594977.1592585

Bodriagov, O., & Buchegger, S. (2013). *Encryption for peer-to-peer social networks* (pp. 47–65). Springer New York.

Bodriagov, O., Kreitz, G., & Buchegger, S. (2014, March). Access control in decentralized online social networks: Applying a policy-hiding cryptographic scheme and evaluating its performance. In *Pervasive Computing and Communications Workshops (PERCOM Workshops), 2014 IEEE International Conference on* (pp. 622-628). IEEE.

Buchegger, S., & Datta, A. (2009, February). A case for P2P infrastructure for social networks-opportunities & challenges. In *Wireless On-Demand Network Systems and Services, 2009. WONS 2009. Sixth International Conference on* (pp. 161-168). IEEE. doi:10.1109/WONS.2009.4801862

Buchegger, S., Schiöberg, D., Vu, L. H., & Datta, A. (2009, March). PeerSoN: P2P social networking: early experiences and insights. In *Proceedings of the Second ACM EuroSys Workshop on Social Network Systems* (pp. 46-52). ACM.

Chiluka, N., Andrade, N., Pouwelse, J., & Sips, H. (2015, April). Social Networks Meet Distributed Systems: Towards a Robust Sybil Defense under Churn. In *Proceedings of the 10th ACM Symposium on Information, Computer and Communications Security* (pp. 507-518). ACM. doi:10.1145/2714576.2714606

Cutillo, L. A., Molva, R., & Strufe, T. (2009, February). Privacy preserving social networking through decentralization. In *Wireless On-Demand Network Systems and Services, 2009. WONS 2009. Sixth International Conference on* (pp. 145-152). IEEE. doi:10.1109/WONS.2009.4801860

Cutillo, L. A., Molva, R., & Strufe, T. (2009). Safebook: A privacy-preserving online social network leveraging on real-life trust. *Communications Magazine, IEEE*, *47*(12), 94–101. doi:10.1109/MCOM.2009.5350374

De Cristofaro, E., Manulis, M., & Poettering, B. (2011, January). Private discovery of common social contacts. In *Applied Cryptography and Network Security* (pp. 147–165). Springer Berlin Heidelberg. doi:10.1007/978-3-642-21554-4_9

De Cristofaro, E., Manulis, M., & Poettering, B. (2013). Private discovery of common social contacts. *International Journal of Information Security*, *12*(1), 49–65. doi:10.1007/s10207-012-0183-4

Durr, M., Maier, M., & Dorfmeister, F. (2012, September). Vegas--A Secure and Privacy-Preserving Peer-to-Peer Online Social Network. In *Privacy, Security, Risk and Trust (PASSAT), 2012 International Conference on and 2012 International Confernece on Social Computing (SocialCom)* (pp. 868-874). IEEE.

Forsyth, S., & Daudjee, K. (2013, July). Update Management in Decentralized Social Networks. In *2013 IEEE 33rd International Conference on Distributed Computing Systems Workshops* (pp. 196-201). IEEE. doi:10.1109/ICDCSW.2013.54

Frey, D., Kermarrec, A. M., & Leroy, V. (2009). PAPEER: Bringing Social Networks into Research.

Graffi, K., Podrajanski, S., Mukherjee, P., Kovacevic, A., & Steinmetz, R. (2008, December). A distributed platform for multimedia communities. In*Multimedia, 2008. ISM 2008. Tenth IEEE International Symposium on* (pp. 208-213). IEEE. doi:10.1109/ISM.2008.11

Greschbach, B., Kreitz, G., & Buchegger, S. (2012, March). The devil is in the metadata—New privacy challenges in Decentralised Online Social Networks. In*Pervasive Computing and Communications Workshops (PERCOM Workshops), 2012 IEEE International Conference on* (pp. 333-339). IEEE.

Guha, S., Tang, K., & Francis, P. (2008, August). NOYB: privacy in online social networks. In *Proceedings of the first workshop on Online social networks*(pp. 49-54). ACM. doi:10.1145/1397735.1397747

Jahid, S., Nilizadeh, S., Mittal, P., Borisov, N., & Kapadia, A. (2012, March). DECENT: A decentralized architecture for enforcing privacy in online social networks. In *Pervasive Computing and Communications Workshops (PERCOM Workshops), 2012 IEEE International Conference on* (pp. 326-332). IEEE. doi:10.1109/PerComW.2012.6197504

Koll, D., Li, J., & Fu, X. (2013). *With a Little help from my friends: replica placement in decentralized online social networks*. Technical Report IFI-TB-2013-01, Institute of Computer Science, University of Goettingen, Germany.

Kryczka, M., Cuevas, R., Guerrero, C., Yoneki, E., & Azcorra, A. (2010, April). A first step towards user assisted online social networks. In *Proceedings of the 3rd workshop on social network systems* (p. 6). ACM. doi:10.1145/1852658.1852664

Mahdian, A., Han, R., Lv, Q., & Mishra, S. (2013). Results from a Practical Deployment of the MyZone Decentralized P2P Social Network. *arXiv preprint arXiv:1305.0606.*

Maymounkov, P., & Mazieres, D. (2002). Kademlia: A peer-to-peer information system based on the xor metric. In Peer-to-Peer Systems (pp. 53-65). Springer Berlin Heidelberg. doi:10.1007/3-540-45748-8_5

Mega, G., Montresor, A., & Picco, G. P. (2011, August). Efficient dissemination in decentralized social networks. In *Peer-to-Peer Computing (P2P), 2011 IEEE International Conference on* (pp. 338-347). IEEE. doi:10.1109/P2P.2011.6038753

Miller, R. (2013, October 13). Facebook Now Has 30,000 Servers [article]. Retrieved August 6, 2015 from http://www.datacenterknowledge.com/archives/2009/10/13/facebook-now-has-30000-servers/

Narendula, R., Papaioannou, T. G., & Aberer, K. "A decentralized online social network with efficient user-driven replication."*Privacy, Security, Risk and Trust (PASSAT), 2012 International Conference on and 2012 International Confernece on Social Computing (SocialCom)*. IEEE, 2012. doi:10.1109/SocialCom-PASSAT.2012.127

Narendula, R., Papaioannou, T. G., & Aberer, K. (2012, June). Towards the realization of decentralized online social networks: an empirical study. In*Distributed Computing Systems Workshops (ICDCSW), 2012 32nd International Conference on* (pp. 155-162). IEEE. doi:10.1109/ICDCSW.2012.62

Nasim, R., & Buchegger, S. (2014, December). XACML-Based Access Control for Decentralized Online Social Networks. In *Proceedings of the 2014 IEEE/ACM 7th International Conference on Utility and Cloud Computing* (pp. 671-676). IEEE Computer Society. doi:10.1109/UCC.2014.108

Nilizadeh, S., Jahid, S., Mittal, P., Borisov, N., & Kapadia, A. (2012, December). Cachet: a decentralized architecture for privacy preserving social networking with caching. In *Proceedings of the 8th international conference on Emerging networking experiments and technologies* (pp. 337-348). ACM. doi:10.1145/2413176.2413215

Paul, T., Famulari, A., & Strufe, T. (2014). A survey on decentralized Online Social Networks. *Computer Networks*, *75*, 437–452. doi:10.1016/j.comnet.2014.10.005

Rzadca, K., Datta, A., & Buchegger, S. (2010, June). Replica placement in p2p storage: Complexity and game theoretic analyses. In *Distributed Computing Systems (ICDCS), 2010 IEEE 30th International Conference on* (pp. 599-609). IEEE.

Schulz, S., & Strufe, T. (2013, June). d 2 Deleting Diaspora: Practical attacks for profile discovery and deletion. In *Communications (ICC), 2013 IEEE International Conference on* (pp. 2042-2046). IEEE.

Schwittmann, L., Boelmann, C., Wander, M., & Weis, T. (2013, July). SoNet--Privacy and Replication in Federated Online Social Networks. In *Distributed Computing Systems Workshops (ICDCSW), 2013 IEEE 33rd International Conference on* (pp. 51-57). IEEE.

Seong, S. W., Seo, J., Nasielski, M., Sengupta, D., Hangal, S., Teh, S. K., & Lam, M. S. et al. (2010, June). PrPl: a decentralized social networking infrastructure. In *Proceedings of the 1st ACM Workshop on Mobile Cloud Computing & Services: Social Networks and Beyond* (p. 8). ACM.

Shahriar, N., Chowdhury, S. R., Sharmin, M., Ahmed, R., Boutaba, R., & Mathieu, B. (2013, July). Ensuring Beta-Availability in P2P Social Networks. In*Distributed Computing Systems Workshops (ICDCSW), 2013 IEEE 33rd International Conference on* (pp. 150-155). IEEE. doi:10.1109/ICDCSW.2013.91

Shakimov, A., Lim, H., Ćaceres, R., Cox, L. P., Li, K., Liu, D., & Varshavsky, A. (2011, January). Vis-a-vis: Privacy-preserving online social networking via virtual individual servers. In *Communication Systems and Networks (COMSNETS), 2011 Third International Conference on* (pp. 1-10). IEEE.

Shakimov, A., Varshavsky, A., Cox, L. P., & Cáceres, R. (2009, August). Privacy, cost, and availability tradeoffs in decentralized OSNs. In *Proceedings of the 2nd ACM workshop on Online social networks* (pp. 13-18). ACM. doi:10.1145/1592665.1592669

Sharma, R., & Datta, A. (2012, January). Supernova: Super-peers based architecture for decentralized online social networks. In *Communication Systems and Networks (COMSNETS), 2012 Fourth International Conference on*(pp. 1-10). IEEE.

Shinjo, Y., Guo, F., Kaneko, N., Matsuyama, T., Taniuchi, T., & Sato, A. (2011, October). A distributed web browser as a platform for running collaborative applications. In *Collaborative Computing: Networking, Applications and Worksharing (CollaborateCom), 2011 7th International Conference on* (pp. 278-286). IEEE. doi:10.4108/icst.collaboratecom.2011.247088

Tandukar, U., & Vassileva, J. (2012). Selective propagation of social data in decentralized online social network. In *Advances in User Modeling* (pp. 213–224). Springer Berlin Heidelberg. doi:10.1007/978-3-642-28509-7_20

Thilakarathna, K., Petander, H., Mestre, J., & Seneviratne, A. (2012, October). Enabling mobile distributed social networking on smartphones. In *Proceedings of the 15th ACM international conference on Modeling, analysis and simulation of wireless and mobile systems* (pp. 357-366). ACM. doi:10.1145/2387238.2387299

Vafopoulos, M. (2006). Information Society: the two faces of Janus. In *Artificial Intelligence Applications and Innovations* (pp. 643-648). Springer US. doi:10.1007/0-387-34224-9_75

Xu, T., Chen, Y., Zhao, J., & Fu, X. (2010, June). Cuckoo: towards decentralized, socio-aware online microblogging services and data measurements. In *Proceedings of the 2nd ACM International Workshop on Hot Topics in Planet-scale Measurement* (p. 4). ACM. doi:10.1145/1834616.1834622

Chapter 4

Texture–Based Evolutionary Method for Cancer Classification in Histopathology

Kiran Fatima
National University of Computer and Emerging Sciences (NUCES), Pakistan

Hammad Majeed
National University of Computer and Emerging Sciences (NUCES), Pakistan

ABSTRACT

Real-world histology tissue textures owing to non-homogeneous nature and unorganized spatial intensity variations are complex to analyze and classify. The major challenge in solving pathological problems is inherent complexity due to high intra-class variability and low inter-class variation in texture of histology samples. The development of computational methods to assists pathologists in characterization of these tissue samples would have great diagnostic and prognostic value. In this chapter, an optimized texture-based evolutionary framework is proposed to provide assistance to pathologists for classification of benign and pre-malignant tumors. The proposed framework investigates the imperative role of RGB color channels for discrimination of cancer grades or subtypes, explores higher-order statistical features at image-level, and implements an evolution-based optimization scheme for feature selection and classification. The highest classification accuracy of 99.06% is achieved on meningioma dataset and 90% on breast cancer dataset through Quadratic SVM classifier.

INTRODUCTION

Real-world histology textures are much different from synthetic textures acquired in a controlled environment. The histology tissue textures have inherent non-stationary, heterogeneous and unorganized spatial intensity variations where different image regions can have different textural characteristics including scale, orientation, contrast or visual appearance. For this reason, adaptive approaches with quantitative methods for Computer-Aided Diagnosis (CAD) were employed in the past for the accurate diagnosis of cancers (Dundar et al., 2011), (Niwas, Palanisamy, Chibbar, & Zhang, 2012), (Irshad, Gouaillard, Roux,

DOI: 10.4018/978-1-4666-9767-6.ch004

Copyright © 2016, IGI Global. Copying or distributing in print or electronic forms without written permission of IGI Global is prohibited.

& Racoceanu, 2014). Major issues that need to be addressed regarding such challenging pathological problems include capturing the cellular architecture differences, removal of image artifacts and noise that arises in the tissue fixation, slide preparation and staining procedures. Diverse computer-aided techniques have been employed in the past with a varying degree of success for the solution of complex histopathological problems. Recent years have witnessed a significant growth of quantitative research studies on applications of digital pathology (Irshad et al., 2014), (Huang and Lai, 2010), (Al-Kadi, 2015) as a result of current progress in high-throughput whole-slide tissue scanning technology.

In almost all the types of cancer diagnosis, the classification system proposed for a specific type fails on other types. This is due to the variation in tissue architecture and structures. Therefore, unsupervised identification and analysis of these variations is essential for designing a generic classifier. Such a process can be designed by proposing tolerant methods for structure segmentation, feature extraction, feature selection and classification. This work is an attempt in this direction.

The morphometric analysis at the nuclei level has found wide application in histological image analysis (Dundar et al., 2011), (Irshad et al., 2014), (Huang et al., 2010). The morphometric characteristics of nuclei components are likely to present dominant role in the discrimination process of cancer grades and subtypes. However, the precise segmentation of the nuclei from biopsy images is found a complex and challenging task. Segmentation methods like thresholding, region growing, watershed, and active contours detect imprecise contours for the nuclei with heterogeneous texture, non-crisp boundaries, touching, and overlapping (Gurcan et al., 2009), (Irshad, Veillard, Roux, & Racoceanu, 2014). Segmentation may not suit the histological classification problems where the cancer types or subtypes have high intra-class and low inter-class variations in nuclei shapes, nuclei characterizing different tumor subtypes present in an image, and large number of overlapping and touching nuclei.

Histology texture classification problems are challenging to solve owing to inherent complexities of tissue textures including the non-homogeneous nature and the high intra-class variability and low inter-class differences in the texture of tumor samples. The textural analysis scans the image as a whole rather than its constituents and captures the variations among the texture patterns to classify images. Hence, the holistic approach of texture analysis may suit more for the classification of cancer types or subtypes which possess some distinguishing textural patterns. Histology texture classification primarily involves following main steps as: extraction of most representative features to maximally capture and portray the intrinsic tissue texture, selection of highly distinguishing and predictive features that are robust with respect to noise present in histology slides, and selection of an optimal classifier to recognize patterns even in the presence of large variations in the data and weak descriptors.

In this chapter, a texture-based optimized evolutionary abstract feature selection and classification framework is proposed and tested on the pathological classification of grade-I benign meningioma and intraductal proliferative breast lesions with significantly high accuracy. The proposed framework exploits higher-order textural statistics, classifier-based optimal selection of texture features, and classification through the best SVM kernel. This research work answers some very pertinent questions. They are:

- Is the texture analysis at image level more appropriate than morphometric analysis at nuclei level to discriminate cancer grades or subtypes?
- Is the combination of three color channels more informative than a single color channel?

The subsequent sections of this chapter are organized as follows: In the Section Related Work, a brief overview of the literature is presented. In the Section Proposed Framework, the proposed work is discussed in detail. The experiments and results are discussed in the Section Experiments and Results. Finally, the chapter is concluded with an outlook to the future research.

RELATED WORK

In past few years, automated prognosis and grading of cancers using pathological whole-slide images has been widely explored in various fields. The literature includes research studies on hepatocellular carcinoma (Huang et al., 2010), (Atupelage et al., 2013), prostate carcinoma (Kwak, Hewitt, Sinha, & Bhargava, 2011), (Ali, Veltri, Epstein, Christudass, & Madabhushi, 2011), renal cell carcinoma (H.-J. Choi and H.-K Choi, 2007), breast cancer (Dundar et al., 2011), (Niwas et al., 2012), (Irshad et al., 2014), (Dong et al., 2014), follicular lymphoma (Sertel, Lozanski, Shana'ah, & Gurcan, 2010), (Oztan, Kong, Gurcan, & Yener, 2012), brain tumor astocytomas (Glotsos et al., 2008), (Papageorgiou et al., 2008); and brain tumor meningiomas (Qureshi, Rajpoot, Nattkemper, & Hans, 2009), (Al-Kadi, 2010), (Fatima, Arooj, & Majeed, 2014), (Al-Kadi, 2015). The cancer grading and classification techniques are usually categorized on account of features computation methods as: first, which make morphometric analysis at nuclei level to perform region of interest and structure or nuclei segmentation. These techniques mainly relied on geometrical or statistical textural features for capturing histological nuclei characteristics considered by pathologists (Huang et al., 2010), (Dong et al., 2014), (Dundar et al., 2011), (Irshad et al., 2014), (Sertel et al., 2010). Second, the techniques which perform the texture analysis at image level and scan the overall textural patterns to capture the underlying characteristics and the spatial organization of the intensity variations (Qureshi, Sertel, Rajpoot, Wilson, & Gurcan, 2008), (Qureshi et al., 2009), (Al-Kadi, 2010), (Al-Kadi, 2015). In (Fatima et al., 2014), a novel hybrid classification framework based on image-level texture features and nuclei shape analysis is proposed for meningioma subtypes classification. The segmentation and classification results obtained through all these techniques primarily depend on the inherent complexity and nature of the problem.

In this work, the authors have explored multiple color channels and performed more sophisticated evolution-based optimized features selection for histopathological image classification. In the proposed work a generic technique is employed which is not dependent on the nature of problem and dataset. The framework is evaluated on two histology datasets of different problems and complexity. The major findings of the proposed work are:

- The texture analysis at image level is found more appropriate than morphometric analysis at nuclei level for the recognition and detection of histology patterns.
- The optimal feature sets attested the remarkable contribution of all the color channels for the discrimination of cancer grades or subtypes. In different scenarios, the significance of color channels can be ranked but their individual role cannot be ignored.

PROPOSED FRAMEWORK

The proposed framework works by first decomposing the input RGB image into its constituent color channels. Next, the grey-scale morphological operations are performed on each color channel to highlight the inherent textures. This is followed by extracting the higher-order statistical run-length matrix features from the morphologically processed images. Lastly, an optimized evolutionary search mechanism is adopted to find an optimal combination of extracted features. For the classification, a binary SVM is trained for each subtype and then tested on the unseen data. The architecture of the proposed framework is shown in Figure 1.

Pre-Processing

The digitized histological samples used in this research are true color RGB images. In order to investigate the role of each color channel in the process of cancer classification, the input images are decomposed into constituent R, G, B color channels and are utilized in further processing.

In the proposed work, the grey-scale morphology (Ternberg, 1986) is employed for the quantitative analysis of geometrical structures of all the input images. The basic aim of performing morphological processing on sample images is to eliminate possible noise, to emphasize the inherent texture and to segment the cell nuclei from the cytoplasmic background. The two basic operations of mathematical morphology are dilation and erosion. Dilation is basically employed for bridging gaps or filling holes. On the other hand, erosion is used to eliminate unwanted details. In order to preprocess histology images, Morphological gradient (*Mg*) – the difference between dilation and erosion of a sample image (Gonzalez and Woods, 2009) – is calculated by using the equation 1 for all the color channels of each image under consideration.

$$Mg = \left(I\left(x,y\right) \oplus s\left(x,y\right) \right) - \left(I\left(x,y\right) \ominus s\left(x,y\right) \right)$$

where *I(x,y)* is a grey-scale image and *s(x,y)* is a structuring element that is a sub-image or window utilized as a filter.

Figure 1. Architecture of the proposed framework

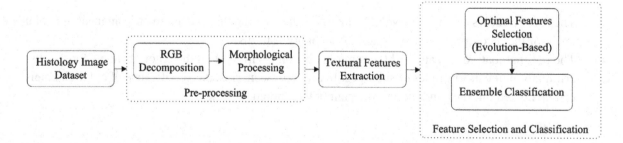

To find the optimal shape and size of the structuring element, the experiments are performed with the squares of 3x3, 5x5 and 7x7 pixels. A 5x5 pixels square of ones is found suitable according to the morphology of cell nuclei. As an example, the red color channel image for the meningioma subtype (Meningothelial) and corresponding morphological processed image are shown in Figure 2.

Feature Extraction

In the proposed work, statistical textural analysis of the histological images is performed to capture the overall intrinsic textural patterns and trends of cancer specimens. A string of consecutive pixels with the same grey-level value in a specific linear direction constitute a grey-level run. For a given image sample, a Run-Length Matrix (RLM) $P(i, j|\theta)$ is defined as the number of runs with pixels of grey-level i and run length j for a given orientation θ (Galloway, 1975).

In order to extract textural features on the basis of grey-level statistics, run-length matrices are generated for four orientations ($0°$, $45°$, $90°$ and $135°$) across all the three color channels. The eleven statistical features are computed from the generated run-length matrices (Tang, 1998). These features are: Short Run Emphasis (SRE), long run emphasis (LRE), Grey-Level Non-uniformity (GLN), Run-Length Non-uniformity (RLN), Run Percentage (RP), Low Grey-Level Run Emphasis (LGLRE), High Grey-Level Run Emphasis (HGLRE), Short Run Low Grey-Level Emphasis (SRLGLE), Short Run High Grey-Level Emphasis (SRHGLE), Long Run Low Grey-Level Emphasis (LRLGLE), Long Run High Grey-Level Emphasis (LRHGLE).

Feature Selection and Classification

In the proposed work, the process of feature selection is formulated as an optimization problem. The main goal is to formulate a reduced feature subset that achieves the highest possible value for the classification accuracy averaged over all the histological grades or subtypes. The RLM feature set extracted from all the color channels is used for identification of optimal combination of features. An evolution-based optimization technique Genetic Algorithm (GA) in combination with Support Vector Machine (SVM) is applied to perform a heuristic search to identify and select most relevant features that improves overall classification results. A binary SVM classifier with optimal feature subset is trained for each subtype and tested on unseen data.

Figure 2. Red color channel image of meningioma subtype (Meningothelial) and corresponding morphological processed image

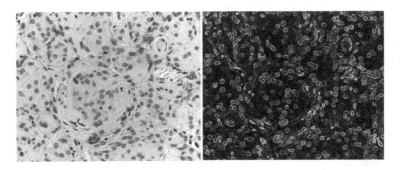

An evolutionary individual; that is, a chromosome is used to represent a feature subset selected from the space of all the possible feature subsets. Each chromosome is a binary string which presents a set of active or inactive genes. Active genes indexes characterize the features which will participate in the classification task. The length of the chromosome is 132, having 44 genes for RLM features from each red, green and blue colour channel respectively. The indexes used for the eleven RLM features calculated for different orientations for a colour channel are given in Table 1.

The structure of chromosome used in the optimized evolutionary feature selection scheme is given in Figure 3.

The initial genetic population consists of a set of randomly generated individuals in which each individual represents a chromosome, a binary string of active and inactive features. Next step is genotype to phenotype conversion where features are selected based on the gene value of each individual. SVM classifier is used to evaluate the fitness of each individual; that is, a candidate feature subset. The SVM classifier is trained on the selected feature subset from the training data while the feature subset from testing data is used to calculate the classification accuracy. The overall classification accuracy; that is, averaged over all subtypes is used as a fitness value for each individual. For genetic operations, the individuals are selected by performing the tournament selection. A set of seven individuals with highest fitness values is marked by the selection function to have a competition for the parents selection. Two-point crossover

Table 1. Proposed arrangement of a chromosome for the selection of the best features. Each feature encompasses four values corresponding to four orientations (0°, 45°, 90° and 135°).

Feature	Index Range
Short Run Emphasis (SRE)	1-4
Long Run Emphasis (LRE)	5-8
Grey-Level Non-uniformity (GLN)	9-12
Run-Length Non-uniformity (RLN)	13-16
Run Percentage (RP)	17-20
Low Grey-Level Run Emphasis (LGLRE)	21-24
High Grey-Level Run Emphasis (HGLRE)	25-28
Short Run Low Grey-Level Emphasis (SRLGLE)	29-32
Short Run High Grey-Level Emphasis (SRHGLE)	33-36
Long Run Low Grey-Level Emphasis (LRLGLE)	37-40
Long Run High Grey-Level Emphasis (LRHGLE)	41-44

Figure 3. Structure of chromosome used in the optimized evolutionary feature selection scheme. The length of chromosome represents set of 132 RLM features for three RGB color channels.

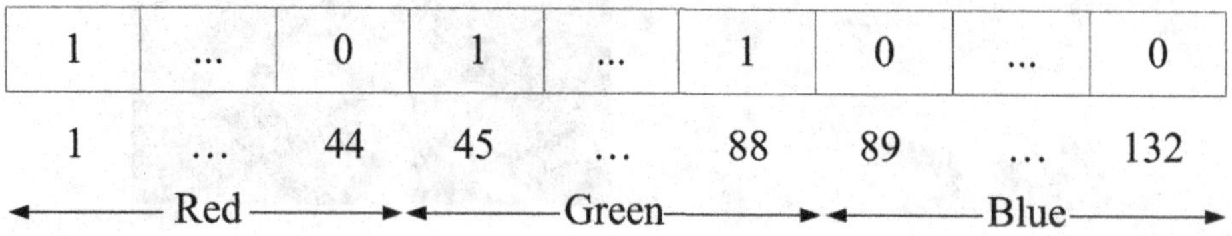

and uniform mutation operators are employed to create the remaining population of the next generation from the selected individuals. To have an expectation of fast convergence, a suitably higher crossover rate is maintained while using the already explored regions. The value of mutation probability is kept reasonably small to induce less genetic variety and to allow specification of the optimal solution. Two elite individuals are used in addition to most-fit individuals evolved as a result of genetic operations to create new population for the next generation.

A particular run or generation set is terminated when there was no improvement in the fitness value for a number of generations. To fine tune the best individual and to avoid premature convergence on a local optimal solution, suitably large number of runs are performed and the search space is explored efficiently. The architecture of the optimized evolutionary feature selection scheme is given in Figure 4.

The detailed set of evolutionary parameters with optimal values is given in Table 2.

One versus all decomposition strategy is adopted to solve the multi-class pathological classification problem employing SVM binary classifiers. One binary classifier is learned for each class (subtype or

Figure 4. Architecture of the optimized evolutionary feature selection scheme

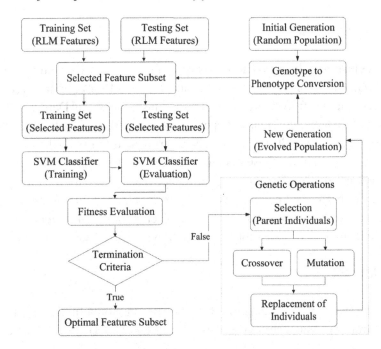

Table 2. Parameter values used for experimentation

Parameter	Value
Population Size	150
Chromosome Length	132
Selection Mechanism	Tournament (Size = 7)
Crossover Type	Two Point (Prob = 0.8)
Mutation Type	Uniform (Prob = 0.2, P_r=0.01)

grade) to distinguish it from the remaining classes. The classification label of a test image is specified by the ensemble decision of four base classifiers on account of decision function value f(*x*). Three kernel functions of SVM classifier (Linear, Gaussian RBF and Quadratic) are explored. For RBF SVM, the optimal value for γ; that is, width of Gaussian function is found through the grid-search method using cross validation in the range {2^{-5},..., 2^6} and the γ value with the highest cross validation accuracy is selected. For the estimation of separating hyper-plane, Least Squares (LS) (Suykens and Vandewalle, 1999) method is used.

EXPERIMENTS AND RESULTS

The evaluation of a framework is highly dependent on the selection of training and evaluation images. The efficacy, competency and the robustness of the proposed framework is ensured by employing the 5-folds cross validation scheme. The mean value of the classification accuracy for 5-folds is reported.

Datasets

Meningioma Tumor Dataset

This dataset comprises histology images of four subtypes of grade-I benign meningioma. These subtypes are: Meningothelial (*Mn*), Fibroblastic (*Fb*), Transitional (*Tr*) and Psammomatous (*Ps*). The diagnostic brain tumor samples are attained from neurosurgical resections at the Bethel Department of Neurosurgery, Bielefeld, Germany. For each meningioma subtype, data of five patients is collected and for each patient, four images having dimension of 1300x1030 pixels are truncated to obtain 16 images per patient and 80 images per subtype. The final database contains 320 images in total. The images of a meningioma patient with similar morphometric characteristics introduce bias in the classification process if the training and evaluation is not performed patient wise. Therefore, in each fold, all the images of one patient of each subtype are left-out for testing and the images of remaining four patients are used for training. The representative RGB images of four subtypes of benign meningioma are shown in Figure 5.

Breast Cancer Dataset

This dataset comprises breast biopsies diagnosed as Ductal Carcinoma In Situ (DCIS) or Usual Ductal Hyperplasia (UDH) from the Massachusetts General Hospital (MGH). 20 cases of UDH and 60 cases

Figure 5. RGB images of meningioma subtypes. From left to right (a-d) are images of Meningothelial, Fibroblastic, Transitional, and Psammomatous subtypes.

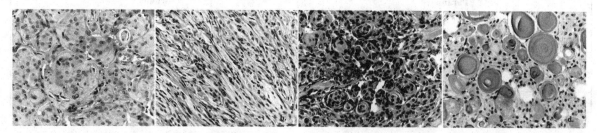

of DCIS (20 for each low, intermediate or high grade) are used in this study for experimentation. The representative RGB images of UDH and three grades of DCIS (low, intermediate or high) are shown in Figure 6.

Results of Optimized Evolutionary Feature Selection and Classification

A feature set having 132 features extracted from all the colour channels is used for histopathological classification. To analyze and compare impact of different feature sets on classification results, two different experiments are performed. In first experiment classification is performed with the complete set of RLM features through RBF, Linear, and Quadratic SVM classifiers for both datasets. For meningioma dataset the results are reported in Table 3 and for breast cancer dataset the results are reported in Table 4.

In second experiment evolution-based optimized feature selection is performed and three optimal feature subsets are attained through RBF, Linear, and Quadratic SVM. The Table 5 presents the classification results obtained for four meningioma subtypes.

Figure 6. RGB images of UDH and three grades of DCIS. (a) UDH, (b) DCIS Low, (c) DCIS Intermediate and (d) DCIS High.

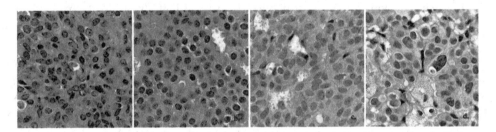

Table 3. Classification accuracy by using complete feature set (132 features) for Meningioma Tumor dataset. F_O is the count of the features used. Acc_{Mn}, Acc_{Fb}, Acc_{Tr} and Acc_{Ps} are % accuracy of Mn, Fb, Tr and Ps subtypes. $Acc_{Overall}$ is the mean accuracy of four meningioma subtypes.

Classifier	F_O	Acc_{Mn}	Acc_{Fb}	Acc_{Tr}	Acc_{Ps}	$Acc_{Overall}$
SVM_RBF	132	50	61.25	53.75	83.75	62.19
SVM_Linear	132	66.25	47.50	88.75	96.25	74.69
SVM_Quadratic	132	67.50	73.75	78.75	78.75	74.69

Table 4. Classification accuracy by using complete feature set (132 features) for Breast Cancer dataset. F_O is the count of the features used. Acc_{UDH}, Acc_{DCISL}, Acc_{DCISM} and Acc_{DCISH} are % accuracy of UDH, DCIS-Low, DCIS-Medium and DCIS-High. $Acc_{Overall}$ is the mean accuracy of UDH and three grades of DCIS.

Classifier	F_O	Acc_{UDH}	Acc_{DCISL}	Acc_{DCISM}	Acc_{DCISH}	$Acc_{Overall}$
SVM_RBF	132	60	50	50	50	52.50
SVM_Linear	132	65	20	30	55	42.5
SVM_Quadratic	132	50	20	30	65	41.25

Table 5. Classification accuracies for optimal feature sets selected through evolutionary technique using RBF, Linear and Quadratic SVM. F_O is number of optimal features. Acc_{Mn}, Acc_{Fb}, Acc_{Tr} and Acc_{Ps} are % accuracy of Mn, Fb, Tr and Ps subtypes. $Acc_{Overall}$ is the mean accuracy of four meningioma subtypes.

Classifier	F_O	Acc_{Mn}	Acc_{Fb}	Acc_{Tr}	Acc_{Ps}	$Acc_{Overall}$
SVM_{RBF}	17	80	83.75	93.75	96.25	88.44
SVM_{Linear}	17	88.75	92.5	100	100	95.31
$SVM_{Quadratic}$	20	97.5	100	98.75	100	99.06

For RBF SVM, 88.44% accuracy is achieved with 17 features. Similarly, accuracy of 95.31% with 17 features and 99.06% with 20 features is achieved with Linear SVM and Quadratic SVM, respectively. The best case of optimal feature selection resulted in 25% improvement in accuracy by using ~6 times reduced feature subset (see Table 3). The proposed work achieved the considerably high accuracy; that is, more than 97% for all the subtypes of meningioma.

Table 6 presents the classification results obtained for *UDH* and three grades of *DCIS* (low, medium and high) through the optimized evolutionary feature selection scheme.

For RBF SVM, 77.5% accuracy is achieved with 9 features. Similarly, the accuracy of 83.75% is achieved with 12 features and 90% with 14 features for Linear and Quadratic SVM, respectively. The proposed method has not only improved the accuracy of each subtype substantially but has improved the overall accuracy by ~40% by using ~10 times less features (see Table 4).

The percentage of features selected from R, G, B color channels through evolutionary feature selection scheme using RBF, Linear, and Quadratic SVM is shown in Figure 7 for meningioma dataset and in Figure 8 for breast cancer dataset. For meningioma subtypes classification, the Quadratic SVM with the highest accuracy selected more features from red and blue color channels. While, RBF SVM with the lowest accuracy selected more features from red color channel. For breast cancer classification, with Linear and Quadratic SVM more features are selected from red color channel. The RBF SVM with lowest accuracy selected more features from green color channel. Comparing the role of features from three color channels and three SVM kernels, the red and blue color channel features are highly ranked through the optimized evolutionary feature selection and classification scheme.

Table 6. Classification accuracies for optimal feature sets selected through evolutionary technique using RBF, Linear and Quadratic SVM. F_O is number of optimal features. Acc_{UDH}, Acc_{DCISL}, Acc_{DCISM} and Acc_{DCISH} are % accuracy of UDH, DCIS-Low, DCIS-Medium and DCIS-High. $Acc_{Overall}$ is the mean accuracy of UDH and three grades of DCIS.

Classifier	F_O	Acc_{UDH}	Acc_{DCISL}	Acc_{DCISM}	Acc_{DCISH}	$Acc_{Overall}$
SVM_{RBF}	9	95	45	90	80	77.5
SVM_{Linear}	12	95	70	85	85	83.75
$SVM_{Quadratic}$	14	90	85	90	95	90

Figure 7. Percentage of optimal features selected from R, G, B color channels through RBF, Linear and Quadratic SVM for Brain Tumor dataset

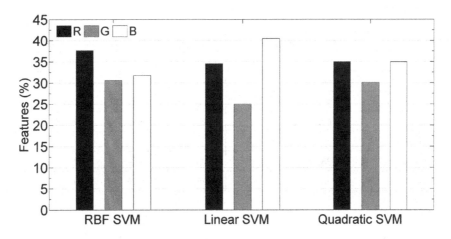

Figure 8. Percentage of optimal features selected from R, G, B color channels through RBF, Linear and Quadratic SVM for Breast Cancer dataset

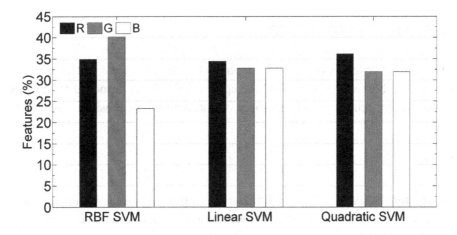

Performance Comparison with Different Classifiers

The performance of various classifiers is investigated by classifying the best feature subset obtained through Quadratic SVM for both datasets through a diverse group of classifiers widely used in medical imaging applications (Irshad et al., 2014), (Fatima et al., 2014), (Al-Kadi, 2015). These classifiers include functional classifiers like Gaussian RBF SVM, Linear SVM, and MultiLayer Perceptron (MLP); decision tree (Random Forest) (Breiman, 2001); probabilistic (Naive Bayes); and Instance-based Learners (kNN) (Aha, Kibler, & Albert, 1991).

The classification results for meningioma tumor dataset are presented in Table 7. MLP presented the highest value for overall accuracy and for two subtypes of meningioma *Fb* and *Ps* while, linear SVM classified the *Mn* and *Tr* subtype with comparatively high accuracy.

Table 7. Performance comparison using different classifiers for meningioma tumor classification. Acc$_{Mn}$, Acc$_{Fb}$, Acc$_{Tr}$ and Acc$_{Ps}$ are % accuracy of Mn, Fb, Tr and Ps subtypes. Acc$_{Overall}$ is the mean accuracy of four meningioma subtypes.

Classifier	Acc$_{Mn}$	Acc$_{Fb}$	Acc$_{Tr}$	Acc$_{Ps}$	Acc$_{Overall}$
SVM$_{RBF}$	58.75	56.25	67.5	87.5	67.50
SVM$_{Linear}$	66.25	48.75	83.75	91.25	72.5
SVM$_{Quadratic}$	**97.5**	**100**	**98.75**	**100**	**99.06**
MLP	62.5	61.25	73.75	96.25	73.44
Random Forest	51.25	60	51.25	83.75	61.56
Naive Bayes	38.75	51.25	55	72.5	54.38
kNN	46.25	53.75	48.75	91.25	60

The classification results for breast cancer dataset are presented in Table 8. RBF SVM presented the highest value for overall accuracy and also classified the UDH and three grades of DCIS with comparatively high accuracy.

FUTURE RESEARCH DIRECTIONS

In future, the behavior of other statistical and morphometric features across different color models will be investigated. The authors will also explore the applications of the proposed framework for grading and classification of other cancer types like kidney, breast, lymphoma, prostate, liver and lungs cancers.

CONCLUSION

In this chapter, a texture-based evolutionary framework is proposed for the histopathological classification of cancer specimens. The basic objective of the proposed work is to achieve promising classification

Table 8. Performance comparison using different classifiers for breast cancer classification. Acc$_{UDH}$, Acc$_{DCISL}$, Acc$_{DCISM}$ and Acc$_{DCISH}$ are % accuracy of UDH, DCIS-Low, DCIS-Medium and DCIS-High. Acc$_{Overall}$ is the mean accuracy of UDH and three grades of DCIS.

Classifier	Acc$_{UDH}$	Acc$_{DCISL}$	Acc$_{DCISM}$	Acc$_{DCISH}$	Acc$_{Overall}$
SVM$_{RBF}$	75	35	70	75	63.75
SVM$_{Linear}$	60	30	40	70	50
SVM$_{Quadratic}$	**90**	**85**	**90**	**95**	**90**
MLP	70	35	60	65	57.5
Random Forest	75	35	65	55	57.5
Naive Bayes	60	30	45	30	41.25
kNN	50	30	55	60	48.75

results by catering inherent complexity and prevailing the variations in the opinion of different pathologists given at different timings. The proposed framework explored grey-level run-length matrix features across different color channels and employed an evolution-based optimization technique to select an effective and prognostic set of features using three kernel functions of SVM classifier. The optimal feature set selected through Quadratic SVM performed classification with considerably high accuracy as compared to Linear and RBF SVMs. The classification results revealed that RLM features from red and blue color channels are more discriminative as compared to green color channel features in most of the scenarios but the importance of green channel RLM features is also evident from the experimental findings.

ACKNOWLEDGMENT

The authors would like to thank Dr. Nasir M. Rajpoot, Associate Professor, Department of Computer Science, University of Warwick, United Kingdom for the provision of Meningioma dataset of the Institute of Neuropathogy, Bielefeld, Germany. The authors would also like to thank Dr. Humayun Irshad and Dr. Andrew Beck, from Beck Lab, BIDMC & Harvard Medical School, USA for sharing histopathological Breast Cancer dataset.

REFERENCES

Aha, D. W., Kibler, D., & Albert, M. K. (1991). Instance-based learning algorithms. *Machine Learning*, *6*(1), 37–66. doi:10.1007/BF00153759

Al-Kadi, O. S. (2010). Texture measures combination for improved meningioma classification of histopathological images. *Pattern Recognition*, *43*(6), 2043–2053. doi:10.1016/j.patcog.2010.01.005

Al-Kadi, O. S. (2015). A multiresolution clinical decision support system based on fractal model design for classification of histological brain tumours. *Computerized Medical Imaging and Graphics*, *41*, 67–79. doi:10.1016/j.compmedimag.2014.05.013 PMID:24962336

Ali, S., Veltri, R., Epstein, J. I., Christudass, C., & Madabhushi, A. (2011). Adaptive energy selective active contour with shape priors for nuclear segmentation and gleason grading of prostate cancer. In *Proceedings of Medical Image Computing and Computer-Assisted Intervention–MICCAI 2011*. Toronto, Canada: Springer. doi:10.1007/978-3-642-23623-5_83

Atupelage, C., Nagahashi, H., Yamaguchi, M., Abe, T., Hashiguchi, A., & Sakamoto, M. (2013). Computational grading of hepatocellular carcinoma using multifractal feature description. *Computerized Medical Imaging and Graphics*, *37*(1), 61–71. doi:10.1016/j.compmedimag.2012.10.001 PMID:23141965

Breiman, L. (2001). Random forests. *Machine Learning*, *45*(1), 5–32. doi:10.1023/A:1010933404324

Choi, H.-J., & Choi, H.-K. (2007). Grading of renal cell carcinoma by 3d morphological analysis of cell nuclei. *Computers in Biology and Medicine*, *37*(9), 1334–1341. doi:10.1016/j.compbiomed.2006.12.008 PMID:17331492

Dong, F., Irshad, H., Oh, E.-Y., Lerwill, M. F., Brachtel, E. F., Jones, N. C., … Beck, A. H. (2014). Computational pathology to discriminate benign from malignant intraductal proliferations of the breast. *PLoS ONE, 9*(12).

Dundar, M. M., Badve, S., Bilgin, G., Raykar, V., Jain, R., Sertel, O., & Gurcan, M. N. (2011). Computerized classification of intraductal breast lesions using histopathological images. *IEEE Transactions on Bio-Medical Engineering, 58*(7), 1977–1984. doi:10.1109/TBME.2011.2110648 PMID:21296703

Fatima, K., Arooj, A., & Majeed, H. (2014). A new texture and shape based technique for improving meningioma classification. *Microscopy Research and Technique, 77*(11), 862–873. doi:10.1002/jemt.22409 PMID:25060536

Galloway, M. (1975). Texture analysis using gray level run lengths. *Computer Graphics and Image Processing, 4*(2), 172–179. doi:10.1016/S0146-664X(75)80008-6

Glotsos, D., Kalatzis, I., Spyridonos, P., Kostopoulos, S., Daskalakis, A., Athanasiadis, E., & Cavouras, D. et al. (2008). Improving accuracy in astrocytomas grading by integrating a robust least squares mapping driven support vector machine classifier into a two level grade classification scheme. *Computer Methods and Programs in Biomedicine, 90*(3), 251–261. doi:10.1016/j.cmpb.2008.01.006 PMID:18343526

Gonzalez, R. C., & Woods, R. E. (2009). *Digital Image Processing* (3rd ed.). India: Pearson Education Inc.

Gurcan, M., Boucheron, L., Can, A., Madabhushi, A., Rajpoot, N., & Yener, B. (2009). Histopathological image analysis: A review. *IEEE Reviews in Biomedical Engineering, 2*, 147–171. doi:10.1109/RBME.2009.2034865 PMID:20671804

Huang, P.-W., & Lai, Y.-H. (2010). Effective segmentation and classification for hcc biopsy images. *Pattern Recognition, 43*(4), 1550–1563. doi:10.1016/j.patcog.2009.10.014

Irshad, H., Gouaillard, A., Roux, L., & Racoceanu, D. (2014). Multispectral band selection and spatial characterization: Application to mitosis detection in breast cancer histopathology. *Computerized Medical Imaging and Graphics, 38*(5), 390–402. doi:10.1016/j.compmedimag.2014.04.003 PMID:24831181

Irshad, H., Veillard, A., Roux, L., & Racoceanu, D. (2014). Methods for nuclei detection, segmentation, and classification in digital histopathology: A review, current status and future potential. *IEEE Reviews in Biomedical Engineering, 7*, 97–114. doi:10.1109/RBME.2013.2295804 PMID:24802905

Kwak, J. T., Hewitt, S. M., Sinha, S., & Bhargava, R. (2011). Multimodal microscopy for automated histologic analysis of prostate cancer. *BMC Cancer, 11*(1), 62. doi:10.1186/1471-2407-11-62 PMID:21303560

Niwas, S. I., Palanisamy, P., Chibbar, R., & Zhang, W. (2012). An expert support system for breast cancer diagnosis using color wavelet features. *Journal of Medical Systems, 36*(5), 3091–3102. doi:10.1007/s10916-011-9788-9 PMID:22005900

Oztan, B., Kong, H., Gurcan, M. N., & Yener, B. (2012). Follicular lymphoma grading using cell-graphs and multi-scale feature analysis. In Proceedings of SPIE 8315, Medical Imaging 2012: Computer-Aided Diagnosis. doi:10.1117/12.911360

Papageorgiou, E., Spyridonos, P., Glotsos, D. T., Stylios, C. D., Ravazoula, P., Nikiforidis, G., & Groumpos, P. P. (2008). Brain tumor characterization using the soft computing technique of fuzzy cognitive maps. *Applied Soft Computing*, *8*(1), 820–828. doi:10.1016/j.asoc.2007.06.006

Qureshi, H., Rajpoot, N., Nattkemper, T., & Hans, V. (2009). A robust adaptive wavelet-based method for classification of meningioma histology images. In *Proceedings of MICCAI'2009 Workshop on Optical Tissue Image Analysis in Microscopy, Histology, and Endoscopy (OPTIMHisE)*. Academic Press.

Qureshi, H., Sertel, O., Rajpoot, N., Wilson, R., & Gurcan, M. (2008). Adaptive discriminant wavelet packet transform and local binary patterns for meningioma subtype classification. In *Proceedings of Medical Image Computing and Computer-Assisted Intervention–MICCAI 2008*. New York: Springer. doi:10.1007/978-3-540-85990-1_24

Sertel, O., Lozanski, G., Shana'ah, A., & Gurcan, M. N. (2010). Computer-aided detection of centroblasts for follicular lymphoma grading using adaptive likelihood-based cell segmentation. *IEEE Transactions on Bio-Medical Engineering*, *57*(10), 2613–2616. doi:10.1109/TBME.2010.2055058 PMID:20595077

Suykens, J., & Vandewalle, J. (1999). Least squares support vector machine classifiers. *Neural Processing Letters*, *9*(3), 293–300. doi:10.1023/A:1018628609742

Tang, X. (1998). Texture information in run-length matrices. *IEEE Transactions on Image Processing*, *7*(11), 1602–1609. doi:10.1109/83.725367 PMID:18276225

Ternberg, S. R. S. (1986). Grayscale morphology. *Computer Vision Graphics and Image Processing*, *35*(3), 333–355. doi:10.1016/0734-189X(86)90004-6

Chapter 5
Ceaseless Virtual Appliance Streaming:
Creation and Transmission of Virtual Packs over Network

Shahid Nawaz
National University of Sciences and Technology, Pakistan

Asad Waqar Malik
National University of Sciences and Technology, Pakistan

Raihan ur Rasool
National University of Sciences and Technology, Pakistan

ABSTRACT

Cloud computing is modus operandi of manipulating server clusters hosted at secluded sites on Internet for storage, processing, and retrieval of data. It tenders suppleness, disaster recovery, competitiveness, and cutback in capital and operational cost for ventures, principally small and medium ones, which hold meager resource base. Virtualization at plinth of cloud computing sanctions utilizing physical hardware stratum to frame and administer virtualized infrastructure, storage areas, and network interfaces. Virtual machines, administered on clouds to seize inherent advantages of virtualization, are fabricated on storage area networks (Armbrust et al., 2009). But whenever user endeavors to access them from remote location it resulted in hundreds of megabytes of data reads and ensuing congestion in network. Question is how to instigate virtual machines and load their applications in minimal time. The ingenious Ceaseless Virtual Appliance Streaming system assures virtual machine's streaming just like video on demand. It trims down burden over existing resources and offers improved network utilization.

DOI: 10.4018/978-1-4666-9767-6.ch005

Copyright © 2016, IGI Global. Copying or distributing in print or electronic forms without written permission of IGI Global is prohibited.

BACKGROUND

Arpanet

Internet came into being with the birth of Arpanet (Advanced Research Project Agency Network) project in 1969, a premium packet switching network relying upon Transmission Control Protocol / Internet Protocol (TCP/IP) protocol suit to transmit data packets between sender and receiver. Funding of Arpanet was supported by Advanced Research Projects Agency (ARPA) of US Department of Defense. Concept and design of packet switching was put forward by US comuputer scientists Leonaord Kleinrock and Paul Bran in collaboration with their British counterparts Donald Davis and Lawrence Roberts at MIT Lincoln Laboratory, Massachusetts. For Arpanet the genesis of TCP/IP transmission protocol suit was developed by US electrical engineer Robert Kahn in association with his countryman and Internet pioneer Vint Cerf.

Foremost message carried on Arpanet was send from University of California (UC) to Stanford Research Institute (SRI) on October 29, 1969. It was consisted of word "login" but only letters "l" and "o" were carried before the system crashed and communication stalled. Therefore first message ever delivered on Arpanet was "lo". System recovered about an hour later and full message "login" was finally delivered. The permanent Arpanet connection between UC and SRI was established in November 1969. By March 1970 it stretched out its arms to US eastern coastal regions and by 1973 it broadened its area beyond the Atlantic Ocean through satellite transatlantic communication link with Norwegian Seismic Array (NORSAR) of Norway.

Concurrently London was also connected with the laying of terrestrial circuits. By 1975 Arpanet became thoroughly operational under the control of US Defense Communication Agency presently known as US Defense Information Systems Agency (DISA). In 1983 military and civilian networks were bifurcated, sinking the volume of Arpanet from 113 to 68 nodes. Gateways were constructed to deliver electronic mails (emails) between these isolated entities. In 1991 Arpanet was finally ceased to exist and substitute by Internet.

Figure 1. Arpanet in 1969

Rise of Internet

Internet is a worldwide constellation of interconnected network of computers and servers which harnessed TCP/IP protocol suite to deliver data between millions of interconnected private, public, and research networks and installations. It is a mesh up of extensive range of copper, optical, wireless, and satellite communication systems and is a premium carrier of wide range of Internet traffic such as hypertext documents, multimedia, emails, and telephony. As no single body or country is entitled to manage and monitor the Internet, therefore a non-profit organization known as Internet Society was formulated in 1992 to create a framework of policies and transmission protocols for smooth functioning of Internet along diverse communication regimes worldwide. Its headquarters is at Virginia, United States and is consisted of 130 member organizations.

Now the fundamental question arises that how people could be connected with the Internet backbone. The answer is that individual users and organizations can connect to the Internet by exploiting Digital Subscriber Line or dial-up modem offered by local Internet Service Provider (ISP) on monitory basis. ISPs are in their turn are associated to some larger networks and so on. Bigger communication organizations possess their own proprietary network backbones to make bond with diverse communication priecents worldwide with the aid of Point of Presence (PoP). ISPs append their network to the focal network vertebrae at PoP. The PoP are tied together at Network Access Points (NAP). In this way Internet becomes proficient to function appropriately without the explicit aid of any centralized authority.

Internet witnesses fabulous growth since its inception in 1991. The number of Internet users burgeoned to 3 billion in 2015 as per Mobile Industry Review statistics. According to Internet World Stats the highest number of Internet users is in Asia which is nearly equivalent to half of the Internet user populace. But when the number of Internet users regarding to regional population has taken into account, European and American zones are in lead of Asia. The percentage of the Internet users as per continent is represented in following graph.

Figure 2. Shows working of Internet through PoP and NAP

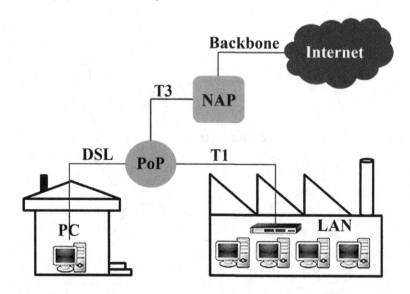

Figure 3. Internet Users per Continent 2014 (Source: Internet World Stats)

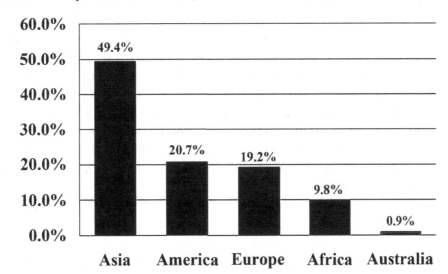

Cloud Computing

Cloud Computing incorporates both applications distributed as services over Internet and systems software and hardware in datacenters that offer those services (Armbrust et al., 2009). In contemporary high-tech world, organizations and business entities need servers, workstations, networking and communication devices, along with software licenses for their employees. But hardware and software are precious and in order to procure computing devices they ought to incur principal expenditures. Furthermore sparing of large sum of resources is mandatory to meet operational expenses for the maintenance and up-gradation of hardware. Along with hardware, the organizations have to expend hefty amount to procure software licenses to accommodate each of its employees. Whenever a new employee will be recruited, fresh licenses will be purchased for them. Accordingly organizations will have to set aside a principle share of its annual financial budget for hardware and software acquisition. But there is a substitute solution to the acquisition of hardware and software. Instead of procuring hardware and software license for each and every employee, a small application may be installed on workstations which will bind them with the web services offered by a remote cloud service provider. Local hosts then linked to web-based services of cloud to exploit necessary software from remote site which may range from simple word processing programmes to complex analytical models (Amanatullah, Lim, Ipung, & Juliandri, 2013). Organization will pay according to the usage of software as per agreement with the cloud service provider.

This mechanism incorporates innovative dimensions into IT industry. The workload has been shifted from on-premises workstations to the cluster of servers and computing devices mounted on cloud. Accordingly workstations do not need exclusive hardware to run and manage newest software to any further extent. The up-gradation and maintenance of costly computing infrastructures becomes the responsibility of cloud provider. Another benefit is that employees of client organization can access the cloud resources from anywhere at any time. They do not need to arrive at their offices to execute their local software applications. It offers greater mobility options to the organizations and its employees. Now organizations can move their office from one place to another and they do not need to shift their data centers with them.

Cloud computing is bifurcated into two sections, i.e., frontend and backend. Both sections are inter-connected through the Internet. Client only sees the frontend whereas backend is called the real cloud section. The frontend consists of a computer and application to establish connection with the cloud. Not all clouds need proprietary applications for the connection. Many services, like web-based email, utilize contemporary browsers to provide connection to their clients. At backend there are cluster of servers, networking devices, storage area networks, and applications. The applications include but not limited to data processing, simulations, video games, analytical programs, etc. A central server administers cloud resources and client requests. It runs protocols and a special type of software called 'middleware' to manage server farm. Intermittently server farm runs below its capacity. Therefore instead of putting more hardware in cloud infrastructure; virtualization of servers is valuable technique to extract maximum advantage from existing resources.

Streaming

Streaming is modus operandi of unremitting presentation and deliverance of data from source to receiver and is a separate entity from media itself. If a client first downloads a video file before execution, it cannot be labeled as a streaming. Delivery mechanisms are spontaneously fall into the category of either streaming or non streaming media. For example television and radio is inherently falls into the category of streaming media whereas books and CDs are non-streaming medium. During early days of streaming in 1990s it was not a fun to watch videos online. It was a stop-and-go process like a car stopping again and again on the red signal. Viewers spend more time on looking at the buffering status of media player instead of watching the video. But streaming has changes much since then. With the passage of time the hardware become cheaper and cheaper while processing power, memory, and storage capacity increases. The network bandwidth also increases tremendously and intelligent networking nodes take far less time to route packets as compared to 1991 when the Internet came into being. According to YouTube statistics in 2015 it has around 1 billion users who stream millions of videos per day.

The concept of streaming is as old as the people are. When a person talks to another person the sound waves carries information towards his ears. The brain then decodes the information to understand the meaning of the message. Similar is the case with television and radio. Information is travelled in the

Figure 4. Cloud computing resources access by end devices

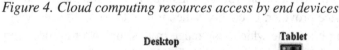
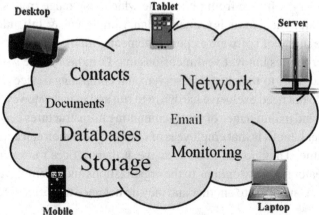

Figure 5. Streaming architecture from server to client

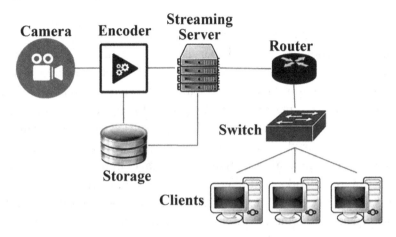

form of a satellite or cable signals from the source to receiver. The receiver decodes the electrical signals in the form of picture pixels and sound waves. The user than watch and listen the programmes over the television and radio. In case of video streaming, the streaming server streams the data over the network. The receiver may be a standalone media player or a plug-in attached with browser which decode the stream data to play the video. In this way a streaming server, transmission network, and decoder work together to allow people to watch videos and broadcasts (Cheng, Stein, Jin, & Zheng, 2008).

Video is a ribbon of still images which are displayed one after the other in sequence. Frame Per Second (FPS) is the number of frames which a media player can display one after the other in one second. If the frame rate is too slow then less data will be required to run the video, but in this case the video will flicker. The appropriate frame rate is the rate at which human brain can sense transition between the pictures. Movie projector uses 24 to 48 FPS to display picture at cinemas. Sometime video files are compressed using 'codec' software to reduces resolution and shuns unnecessary data to minimize the size of video files for their smooth streaming over network. Idea behind the codec is to create files that work well on lower bandwidth networks such as 56 kbps dial-up connections. Once file is encoded, it is uploaded on server from where user can access them. Some codec software can create files which run at different bit rates to support different connection types. Streaming media requires speedy transfer of data in correct order. Special kinds of protocols are used to divided files into small pieces and quickly deliver them in right order to the client. These protocols include Real-Time Streaming Protocol (RTSP), Real-Time Transfer Protocol (RTP), and Real-Time Transport Control Protocol (RTCP). They work jointly with TCP/IP which is active in background. TCP/IP further converts large data files into packets and before switching them among different routes. Massive Peer-to-peer (P2P) streaming structures have been effectively installed in Internet, distributing live multimedia content to large number of users at any particular time. A server's capacity has a vital role in P2P streaming over the Internet and any degradation in server capacity chiefly directed to moderate streaming qualities at peak times (Wu, Li, & Zhao, 2009). Live streaming needs some little modification in the architecture. It needs a camera that will capture the events, on-site encoder that encode that data into signals, and a satellite or terrestrial network that transfer the data simultaneously from place of event happening to the household viewers (Shi, Banikazemi, & Wang, 2008).

Virtual Machine

Virtual machine is software which permits diverse operating systems to run as guest over host operating system by means of virtualization layer called hypervisor. It is very helpful when a user wants to run an application not compatible with his host operating system. Virtual machine allows user to install guest operating system of his liking. For instance, a user can install Microsoft Windows as a guest operating system over Ubuntu through virtual machine software like 'virt-manager'. With installation of Windows, user can run Windows specific software such as Microsoft Office. Virtual machines construct virtualization layer between the host and guest operating systems to allocate virtual hardware resources to guest operating system. Guest operating system in unaware about the existence of host operating system between itself and hardware. It works in similar fashion as it is directly installed on hardware. Virtual hardware is mapped to real like hardware. For example virtual HDD is stored in a file at real HDD. Virtual machine can be accessed remotely through virtual network interface. User can install as much virtual machines on his computer as he likes depends he has enough storage capacity. All he required is a virtualization software to install and manage the virtual machines. Some virtual programs are available free of cost while others are proprietary and will have be purchased before their installation and management. Some popular virtualization programs include VMware, VSphere, Xen, Citrix, Windows Virtual PC, and Virt-Manager. In case of operating system level virtualization there is no need of hypervisor to manage virtualization layer. The host operating system possesses full hypervisor capabilities and the work of virtualization and allocation resources to different virtual servers is performed by itself without any third party help (Dawei & Rui, 2013).

Major limitation of virtual machine is that it shares hardware resources with host operating system. Therefore if computer has inadequate resources, it directly effects the working of virtual machine. For instance if a computer has 2 GB of memory available and in case of non-virtualization only 55% to 60% of it has been used by the operating system, but when the guest operation system will be installed over virtual machine, the memory usage will go up to 90% to 95%. Sometime memory swapping will be required to manage the memory between the two operating systems. It slows down things. For example Microsoft Windows was installed over and it consumes 50-60% of resources but when Ubuntu will be installed as guest operating system, it nearly doubles the usage of hardware resources. It shows that virtual machines can work well on high-tech devices.

Major advantage of virtual machine is its security and platform independence. It can run in a similar fashion on any system regardless of the difference in hardware architecture. Virtual machine also provide security, because, applications running over guest operating system have no direct connection with host operating system. Therefore they cannot damage the host operating system in case of any mall functioning.

Servers are powerful computers that host applications and files over network. Network administrators install applications at different servers to isolate them so that any damage to one application does not penetrate in server farm. It is also helpful to track errors in applications. It is a simple way to streamline server farm without much effort on part of the network administrator.

But there are limitations of this approach. In case of installation of one application per server, the server will be utilizing only the fraction of its resources. Servers are high-tech and expensive machines as compared to workstations and any underutilization of the server capacity increase capital and operational cost on part of the organization. Moreover with the expansion of computer network, the number of underutilized servers running single application increases. It requires more space to accommodate them. Another repercussion will be the increase in power consumption as more energy will be needed to run higher number of servers. An overcrowded data center requires expensive air conditioner units to cool down the server hardware so that they will provide optimal performance. Virtualization provides solution to all these problems. By using virtual machines, network administrator can install multiple guest operating systems and applications over a single server. He will transform one physical server into multiple virtual servers, each working independently of the other. In this way physical servers will be utilized at full capacity.

Companies can also take advantage of redundancy by installing same application on many virtual servers (Garfinkel & Rosenblum, 2003). In case if an application will become inconsistence, its workload will be simply shifted over similar application installed over different virtual server. It decreases the chances of interruption in the provision of services and increases the chances of disaster recovery in case of any physical system crash.

Virtual servers are also utilized by programmers to test applications in isolated environment. Instead of purchasing physical server for new application, network administrator can take advantage of concept of virtualization and use on-site servers to install and test new applications. They do not need to worry in case application malfunctions, because it is installed on guest operating system and have no direct connection to physical machine. In case of any problem in the application, it can be easily removed from the virtual server without damaging other applications and network.

With the passage of time, the server hardware becomes obsolete. New technologies replace the old ones. But some applications and operating systems require that outdated hardware or legacy system to function. Virtualization also comes forward to solve this issue. Network administrator simply creates hardware virtualization on modern and updated servers. The application does not see the difference. It performs as well as it was installed on legacy system. It gives time to company to shift to new application that can provide similar functionality and run on modern hardware. It is especially helpful when company who manufactured legacy system ceases to exist or no longer provides maintenance support for old systems.

Migration of virtual server from one physical server to another physical server is emerging concept. The migration of servers does not affect the functioning and working of applications. For migration the basic requirement is that both physical servers have similar hardware, processor and operating system (Maziku & Shetty, 2014). But with the emergence of new techniques, virtual server can be migrated from one physical server to another having different processor, but the limitation is that both processors are manufactured by same vendor.

Virtualization can be implemented in three different ways such as full virtualization, para virtualization, and operating system level virtualization. All three ways of virtualization have some common properties. The physical server is called host, whereas virtual server is called guest. Each system uses different approach to provide physical resources to virtual server.

Limitations of Virtualization

Some applications need high processing power to execute their task. Virtualization divides resources between physical server and virtual servers. Moreover hypervisor also need processing power to perform its functions. It slows down the system as a whole. The task which may take few seconds to complete in case of non virtualization, may be struck in the middle of execution and takes hours to complete. In extreme cases the system will crash if does not fulfill the processing requirements of the task. Therefore, a network administrator must take into consideration the expected usage of CPU before taking decision on virtualization about creating multiple virtual servers.

Migration is another limitation of virtualization. In order to migrate a virtual server from one physical server to the other, the processor on both physical servers must come from same vendor. Migration may be needed during maintenance work on physical server and porting reduces the downtime of application. It means that all company must purchase its physical servers from same vendor to support migration if it is anticipated to be required in future.

Virtual Appliance

Virtual appliance is defined as the image file of a virtual machine which contains pre-configured operating system and a single application. The basic idea behind the creation of a virtual appliance is that application will be delivered and operated in an easy and simplified manner (Kecskemeti, Terstyanszky, Kacsuk, & Nemeth, 2013). To achieve this purpose, only necessary components of operating system which are required in the execution an application are included. Virtual appliance can be installed as a virtual machine running on some virtualization programme. The deployment of virtual appliance also take care of the issues related to the installation and configuration of hardware drivers. A single file is delivered to the user, who can download it and run its intended application. In this way resources which are required for maintenance of virtual machine also reduced. The virtual appliances have proven record of excellence in the deployment and maintenance of network applications. The virtual appliances can be packaged and distributed as an Open Virtualization Format (OVF) which is an open standard format. It allows the virtual appliances to be run on virtual machines. The OVF is not vendor specific. Large variety of processors and hypervisors support this format.

Virtual appliance offers several benefits over traditionally installed applications on operating systems. They work in isolation of other virtual appliance and in case of security breach; other virtual appliances are not affected (Epstein, Lorenz, Silvera, & Shapira, 2010). Whereas in case of traditional application deployments approach if an application is affected by virus it can influence the whole system. Sometimes whole system crashes due to single application. Moreover virtual appliances encapsulate pre-configured application dependencies in a single unit. It is easy to get a file of virtual appliance and deploy it on virtual machine.

Figure 6. Difference between virtual machine and virtual appliance

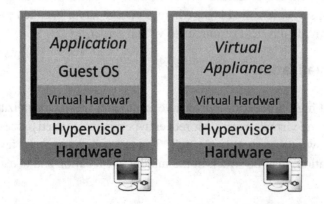

How to Make the Streaming of Virtual Appliance Possible?

Major hurdle in the usage of virtual appliances is that it cannot be streamed from server to client. It is therefore required to work out some mechanism which can treat bytes of virtual appliance file exactly like video frames. Then with the arrival of first few byte of virtual appliance at client end, the file may starts functioning. An intelligent streaming server can isolate the segment of application as required by user. It can judge this by looking at past usage history of a particular user or the current actions performed on virtual appliance.

For simple understanding of the concept, it is assumed that virtual appliance is consisted of a computer game consisted of many parallel stages. With the start of game a player can select one of those stages. When he completes that stage he will go to the next one. The next stage may also consist of parallel stages. The user will have to select one of them. This process of selection will continue till end of game. The Intelligent Streaming Server (ISS) can determine what next stage the user will play. ISS can determine it by using two methods:

1. Previous History Method,
2. Current Actions Method.

Previous History Method

In this method the ISS will look at the log files of the user which were created during his previous sessions. On the basis of previous history ISS will discover the stages previously played by user. It will create a package of those stages and transmit them one after the other. It is taken as assumption that user will play same stages of game. For instance a game consists of 8 stages. Some stages come after the other while some stages comes in parallel and users has to play any one of them.

According to above-mentioned history user played Stage 1 (Start), Stage 2 (A), Stage 3 (B), and Stage 4 (Finish). When user login and selects same game, the ISS will match his user ID with his previous session, create a package of those stages, and delivers it to user. ISS will withhold all other stages of the game.

Figure 7. Stages of the game as played by user in his previous session are shown by red circle

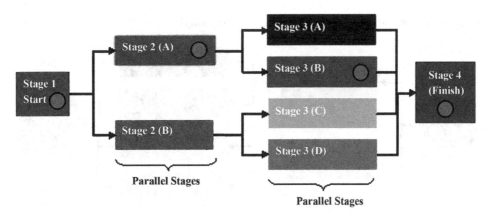

Advantages of Previous History Method

1. User will get a package of only 4 stages instead of all 9 stages of a game. It greatly reduces the size of virtual appliance file. Compression is also applied to further reduce the file's size.
2. The reduced size of file helps in smooth and swift transmission of packets from source to receiver over network. Smaller the size of file, quicker its transmission to user and vice versa.
3. Small file's size consumes less processing power of internal network nodes, which can be utilized to transmit packets of other files.

Limitations of Previous History Method

1. ISS maintains log file of previous sessions of current customers but in case of new customer who first time logged in to play the game, there will be no log file. Therefore there is no way to determine the stages of game which he is expected to play.
2. Current user may want to try another parallel stage next time. ISS using previous history method approach already matched the user ID and its previous session and packaged a file for that particular user. It then transmits that packaged file to the user. It means that user will have to play the stages of the games which he already played in his previous session.
3. If the user did not reach the end of game due to one reason or the other, the end stage will not be send to him by the ISS because it was not detected in his previous session. ISS only packaged those stages in file, which were already played.
4. With the increase in number of users, the volume of log files increase. It put burden on the processing power and storage capacity of ISS.

Current Action Method

Utilizing current action method, the ISS will determine which stages will be played by user in his current session.

ISS will not maintain the log file of previous sessions of the users. After login user will select a game among a list of games. ISS will send only first stage (start) of the game and all other stages are withheld.

Figure 8. Stages of the game and user action to guess next stage

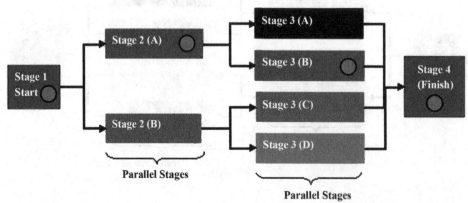

When user reached at the end of stage 1 (start), ISS will determine whether he want to play Stage 2 (A) or Stage 2 (B) based on user's action. When the ISS will determine the next stage on the basis of user's action it will send the packaged file of only that stage to the user. Various colours are used to match the user action and the next stage. This process will go on till the game has been finished.

Advantage of the Current Action Method

1. There will be no need to maintain the log files of users over the server which saves the storage capacity of the server.
2. ISS guesses the next stage on the basis of current user action, therefore user can select any parallel stage in his next session.
3. It reduces the size of file. ISS send stage 1 (start) to the user on every new session. After applying compression, the file consisting of only one stage is smaller than the file consisting of several stages. It needs lesser bandwidth to transmit smaller files.

Limitations of Current Action Method

1. It required complex algorithm to match the current user action and the next coming stage that he will probably play.
2. Before the user will finish playing current stage the package file of next stage must be received by him otherwise there will be a delay between the two stages. It affects the flow of the software execution.

Ceaseless Virtual Appliance Streaming (CVAS)

The major idea behind the concept of Ceaseless Virtual Appliance Streaming (CVAS) project is that virtual appliance can be executed by client just like streaming of videos. The streaming of virtual appliance is not possible in the same way as the streaming of video. The basic difference is that video consists of independent frames whereas virtual appliance file is packaged unit of application and necessary operating system. If a single bit is missed during its transmission from the ISS to the client side, the file cannot be executed. Therefore in order to execute file by the user, he must first download it from the server. The CVAS project makes the streaming of file possible by first dividing into virtual packs and then by sending appropriate virtual packs in the forms of wads to the client.

For ease of simplicity the above mentioned example of game has been taken to explain the concept of virtual packs and wads. The whole game consists of eight stages. But player cannot play all eight stages at a time. He must go in sequence from stage 1 (start) to stage 4 (Finish). There are parallel set of stages available at stage numbers 2 and 3. At stage 2 he can choose from 2 (A) and 2 (B). He cannot play both. Similarly at stage number 3 there are four parallel stages and user can play any one of them during his complete session from beginning till end. The CVAS project divides the game into 8 virtual packs each contain one stage. The virtual pack is a complete set of packaged file totally independent of other virtual pack files. It required change in basic programming of game to make the independent sets of virtual packs. Each virtual pack consists of a game portion and necessary operating system to execute it independently.

It is assumed that the size of each stage of the game is 20 MB. Therefore the size of the whole game is 160 MB. By using traditional method of playing online game, the user first download the whole game of 160 MB before start playing game. Depends upon network conditions it takes several minutes to few hours to download that game. But by using CVAS project the user don't need to download whole game of 160 MB at a time. He only needs only first stage of 20 MB to start his game. When a user logon to the system and selected the game from a list of game, the virtual pack consisting of the first stage has been delivered. Therefore he can start playing game by just receiving 20 MB out of 160 MB. When he reaches at the end of stage and before going to the next stage there comes a decision point at which ISS decided which next stage the user will want in future depends if the next stage is divided into many parallel stages or not. If coming stage is not consisted of many parallel stages then ISS delivers the virtual pack of the next stage. The matters becomes complicated when the next stage is consisted of parallel stages and user have to decide in previous stage that which parallel stage he will play in the next stage of game. The decision points shown with the same color as the color of the next stage of game. For ease of understanding it is assumed when user choose a color at the end of the stage, the ISS will detect this and send the virtual pack of that stage to the user. The CVAS method makes alteration in code to divide the game into virtual packs and to detect which virtual pack is needed next.

Once virtual pack has been selected all of its wads are sent to the user. In this way user don't need to download whole game and can play it stage by stage. As the game is sent in the form of virtual packs containing all necessary operating system support, there will be compatibility issues on the user end.

Future Research Directions

The CVAS is suitable where virtual appliance can be easily divided into independent virtual packs and the previous stages do not affect the outcome of coming stages. But this is not true for every type of

Figure 9. Working of CVAS to select and deliver virtual pack from server to client

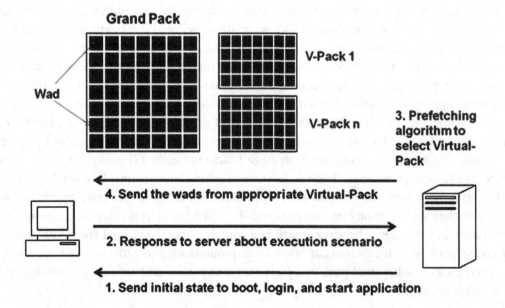

virtual appliance. For example a virtual appliance of software does not work well if it is broken into virtual packs which can work independently unless there is a mechanism that can bring forward the calculations of previous virtual pack into next virtual pack.

CONCLUSION

It is demonstrated that by dividing virtual appliance into virtual packs and sending only those packs to the user which are needed by him greatly reduce transmitting time, bandwidth consumption, and burden on processing power of internal nodes of the network. To achieve this objective some altercations are needed in the programming code of the software to convert it from one single unit to number of independent virtual packs. When ISS will detect which next virtual pack is required by the user, it will send all wads of that virtual pack to the user. The user can start using his virtual appliance with the receiving of the first virtual pack. The CVAS project thus work like streaming of video where media player can start playing video when it gets first 24 frames. The users do not need to wait for lengthy download times. It shows that CVAS method is superior to the traditional technique of downloading file before its use.

REFERENCES

Amanatullah, Y., Lim, C., Ipung, H. P., & Juliandri, A. (2013). *Toward Cloud Computing Reference Architecture: Cloud Service Management Perspective*. Paper presented at the International Conference on ICT for Smart Society (ICISS), Jakarta, Indonesia.

Armbrust, et al. (2009). Above the Clouds: A Berkeley View of Cloud Computing. Berkeley Technical Report. University of California.

Cheng, B., Stein, L., Jin, H., & Zheng, Z. (2008). Towards Cinematic Internet Video-On-Demand. In *Proceedings of the 3rd ACM SIGOPS/EuroSys European Conference on Computer Systems*. ACM.

Dawei, L., & Rui, W. (2013). *Large-Scale IP Network Testbed Based on OS-level Virtualization*. Paper presented at the International Conference on Cloud Computing and Big Data (CloudCom-Asia), Fuzhou, China.

Epstein, A., Lorenz, D. H., Silvera, E., & Shapira, I. (2010). *Virtual Appliance Content Distribution for a Global Infrastructure Cloud Service*. San Diego, CA: INFOCOM IEEE. doi:10.1109/INFCOM.2010.5462176

Garfinkel, T., & Rosenblum, M. (2003). A Virtual Machine Introspection Based Architecture For Intrusion Detection, San Diego, California. In *Proceedings of The Internet Society's 2003 Symposium on Network and Distributed Systems Security IEEE*. IEEE.

Kecskemeti, G., Terstyanszky, G., Kacsuk, P., & Nemeth, Z. (2013). Towards Efficient Virtual Appliance Delivery with Minimal Manageable Virtual Appliances. IEEE Transaction on Services Computing, 7(2), 279-292.

Maziku, H., & Shetty, S. (2014). *Towards a Network Aware Virtual Machine Migration: Evaluating the Cost of Virtual Machine Migration in Cloud Data Centers*. Paper presented at the 3rd International Conference on Cloud Networking (CloudNet), Luxembourg.

Shi, L., Banikazemi, M., & Wang, Q. B. (2008). *Iceberg: An Image Streamer For Space And Time Efficient Provisioning Of Virtual Machines*. Paper presented at the International Conference on Parallel Processing – Workshops, Portland, OR.

Wu, C., Li, B., & Zhao, S. (2009). Diagnosing Network-wide P2P Live Streaming Inefficiencies. In Proceedings of INFOCOM IEEE. IEEE.

KEY TERMS AND DEFINITIONS

Grand Pack: Grand Packs are independent units of software contain necessary functionality to complete task.

Streaming: Streaming means simultaneous downloading and execution of files by user.

Virtual Appliance: Virtual appliance is a preconfigured image of virtual machine having all necessary configuration such as just-enough operating system.

Virtual Machine: Virtual machine is defined as an emulation of physical computer system. It allows different operating systems to run as a guest operating system over host operating system using virtualization layer called hypervisor.

Virtualization: Virtualization is a process to create virtual software over host operating system.

Chapter 6
Performance Evaluation of Routing Metrics in Wireless Multi–Hop Networks

Usman Ashraf
King Faisal University, Saudi Arabia

Syed Salman Haider Rizvi
Air University, Pakistan

Mohammad Faisal Azeem
Air University, Pakistan

ABSTRACT

In the world of wireless communication technologies, the new standard IEEE 802.11n (MIMO) has revolutionized the available wireless bandwidth. Significant industrial and academic research has been initiated on this new technology around the world. Moreover, international as well as local manufacturers are highly interested in commercialization and performance improvement of this new technology. This is a research project in which we will perform comprehensive benchmarking of IEEE 802.11n in wireless multi-hop environments. In this project we evaluate the performance of routing metrics: Hop Count (HC) and Expected Transmission Count (ETX) on a test bed at A-Block Air University.

1. INTRODUCTION

Today, the Internet plays a vital role in providing connectivity-related services to people all around the world. Wireless Local Area Networks (WLANs) provide one of the fundamental blocks of the integration of the wireless devices to the wired Internet. Traditionally, WLANs provide us a centralized control and assume wired connectivity between the Access Points. However, with the new technologies, the concept of wireless multi-hop networks was introduced in order to have more flexible and practical deployments in remote and harsh environments. Wireless Multi-hop Networks (WMNs) are formed by

DOI: 10.4018/978-1-4666-9767-6.ch006

Copyright © 2016, IGI Global. Copying or distributing in print or electronic forms without written permission of IGI Global is prohibited.

using independent wireless or mobile nodes which interconnect wirelessly to create a wireless multihop backbone. However, more recently, Wireless Multihop Networks such as community mesh networks have become immensely popular all around the world and can play a significant role in providing high-speed last-mile wireless Internet broadband to users spread over large geographical regions (Broch, 1998). Therefore, wireless multihop networks will also have a major role in facilitating the proliferation of the cloud computing to end users in the coming years. As leaps and bounds are achieve in advancing the state of the art of cloud computing, the last-mile connectivity of end users will play an increasingly important role in the overall benefits reaped by the community.

Wireless technologies have also significantly improved during the last decade and wireless multihop networks such as wireless mesh networks have become significantly important. A wireless technology that has played an important role in pushing the bandwidth limits of wireless communication is the IEEE 802.11n commonly known an MIMO (Multiple-Input-Multiple-Output).

Routing protocols for wireless networks have been extensively researched during the recent years and significant research has been done in optimizing these protocols. Another important factor in the performance of these routing protocols is the routing metric which is being used. The routing metric is basically the performance metric which the routing protocols consider the most important and they select end-to-end routes between devices based on this metric. In this chapter, we will study the performance of contemporary routing metrics on a wireless test-bed and see their performance. The following are the objectives of this chapter:

- To study the performance of wireless multi hop network in a real test-bed environment.
- To study the performance of different metrics like Hop Count and Expected Transmission Time (ETX) on Dual Band Radio (2.4ghz, 5ghz).
- To analyze the performance of metrics and radio (throughput, packet loss and latency).

2. BACKGROUND

Although the optical fiber has large advantages in bandwidth and transmission loss, the cost of installation and maintenance, especially for rural areas, limit their application to access network services. Most 802.11 WLAN networks today are bridged by using wired technology i.e., Access Points are connected with each other through physical links (typically Ethernet). The dependency on wired network should be removed because of the following reasons:

- This dependency results in inflexibility as it becomes infeasible to extend the coverage of the WLAN beyond the deployment of the backbone wired network.
- Due to their design, centralized structures such as WLANs do not work efficiently for contemporary applications including wireless games which require a different type of connectivity such as peer-to-peer.
- A fixed topology disables the selection of more efficient paths across the network.

Next, the demand that comes from having the ability to communicate wherever and whenever has led to an inevitable trend in wireless access. Thus, the multi-hop wireless network (WMN) have been created with the additional WLAN access points are connected through Internet gateways wire wireless links to other access points using decentralized architectures. WMN hold the promise of overcoming emerging needs and promises to provide seamless last-mile wireless connectivity to users.

2.1 Wireless Multi-Hop Network

An ad hoc network is a collection of wireless devices which interconnect wirelessly to form a network without using any existing network infrastructure or centralized point. Since the range of each wireless device is eventually limited, typically multiple wireless hops are required to transmit data from one data to the other node. The name wireless multihop networking comes from this fact of multiple wireless hops. These types of networks are particularly useful in ad hoc deployment scenarios where traditional infrastructure is not available or has been destroyed. Every node in the network works autonomously, and collectively the entire network transmits packets on each nodes' behalf, achieving multihop networking. Every node basically runs a routing protocol that allows ad hoc nodes to discover "multi-hop" paths through the network. The idea of ad hoc networking sometimes also called infrastructure-less networking, since the mobile nodes in the network establish routing among themselves dynamically, and create their own network "on the fly".

2.2 Routing Protocols

A routing protocol is required every time that a packet must be transmitted to the destination across the multihop network. The routing protocol decides the end-to-end route for the packet. Routing protocols have been a popular interest area in wireless networks and a large number of routing protocols have been proposed for these types of networks. The main job of these protocols is to find a route across the network and deliver the packet to its destination. Routing protocols can be classified on a number of parameters, but in general, they are divided into three main categories: On-Demand (reactive), Table-Driven (Proactive) and Hybrid (Royer, 1999).

On-demand protocols work on the principle of establishing routes when required i.e. when a node needs to send data to a destination to which it does not have a route, it establishes the route. To achieve this, the node typically initiates a route discovery process which spreads a route request message across the network. Eventually, one of the route request packets arrives at the destination and a route is established across the network. The main advantage of reactive routing protocols is that they do not require periodic exchange of routing messages to establish routes and as such do not overburden the wireless network with useless routing packets. On the other hand, their biggest disadvantage is that they introduce some latency in the establishment of routes since the route must be established at the spot before actual data transfer can happen. Popular protocols in this category are AODV and DSR.

Table-drive or proactive protocols on the other hand, work on the principle of maintaining routes at all times by periodic exchange of routing messages. The routing information is periodically transmitted throughout the network in order to make sure that every node in the network has up-to-date information and has accurate routing tables. Existing routes are also periodically updates based on the new routing information received. Proactive protocols have the advantage that they do not introduce any latency and routing of data can immediately happen since the route is always available. However, they have the disadvantage of introducing significant routing overhead by periodic exchange of routing messages even though most routes are up to date. Popular protocols in this category are OLSR and DSDV.

There are some hybrid routing protocols which combine elements from both the proactive and reactive families of routing protocols. These protocols are relatively rare and sometimes offer combined advantages of both the families of protocols.

3. ROUTING METRICS

Routing protocols select end-to-end routes through the network based on some metric which enables it to select "better" routes through the network. Commonly used metrics include bandwidth, interference, delay etc. A good routing metric should address issues related to key features such as interference, and performance. While a number of routing metrics have been proposed in the literature, we focus on the more popular ones and discuss their working.

3.1 Hop Count

Number of hops is the key metric routing and more common in conventional networks, including WMNs and allows us to determine how many hops away the target is from the source. Many routing protocols such as DSR, AODV, OLSR and Destination Sequence Distance Vector (DSDV) use hop count as its base count metric. Hop count ranks routes based purely on the path length. It is simple and offers a high level of efficiency since its calculation is relatively straightforward. The base versions of all ad hoc protocols necessarily implement this metric. However, it was shown in research that selecting the shortest route is not the best solution in all circumstances and there are other more important considerations such as link-quality and bandwidth, which must be given more preference to achieve better end-to-end results. For example, it was shown the sometimes selecting the shortest route selects links which have poor quality (in terms of packet losses) lead to suboptimal results. Nevertheless, the hop count metric remains the most widely implemented metric.

3.2 Expected Transmission Count (ETX)

The Expected Transmission Count (ETX) metric is the most popular routing metric that was proposed to replace the hop count metric. The main motivation was that the number of hops was not the optimal choice for route selection in wireless networks and therefore the ETX was introduced. The ETX metric basically counts the expected number of transmissions (including retransmissions) required to successfully send a packet over a wireless link. This metric basically captures the link-quality in the sense that it gives weight to the total number of transmissions that were required for successful delivery. This metric helps select routes with minimal packet losses on the intermediate links. ETX is one of the most popular routing metric and most contemporary routing metrics are based on the ETX metric. In ETX, neighboring nodes exchange small HELLO (or probe) packets periodically (roughly once a second). Using a sliding window of time, every node calculates the number of probes received both in the forward and reverse directions on the link. Nodes calculate the Expected Transmission Count (ETX) as the product of forward delivery ratio d_f i.e. the ratio of probes that the neighbor successfully received during the last t seconds and d_r the ratio of probes that the node successfully received from the corresponding neighbor in the reverse direction. The ETX link metric for a link becomes

$$ETX = \frac{1}{d_f \times d_r}$$

The authors proposing the ETX metric also proposed using a time window of 10 seconds to calculate the metric. A window this long is sufficient enough to dampen the effects of frequent fluctuations in the link qualities. Since the value of the ETX metric is based on the probe loss ratio, which directly affects performance, therefore, this implies that a path with low ETX value has low congestion, low packet loss ratio, and thus a high yield.

4. IEEE 802.11n (MIMO)

The designers of wireless systems face many challenges in meeting the demand for wireless communication for higher data rates, better service, fewer dropped calls, and higher network capacity, including the limited availability of the problems of radio frequency spectrum and transmission caused by several factors such as fading and multipath distortion. These needs require new techniques to improve spectral efficiency and reliability. The technology of Multiple Input Multiple Output (MIMO) promises a cost-effective way to provide these capabilities. MIMO uses multiple antennas at both transmitter and receiver to improve communication performance. It is one of several forms of smart antenna technology. The MIMO technology has attracted significant attention, offering a substantial increase in the achievable throughput and the wireless range without additional bandwidth or transmission power increase. This is achieved by a higher spectral efficiency (more bits per second per hertz of bandwidth) and diversity (reduced fading).

Because of these appealing properties, MIMO is a hot topic of wireless research. The increasing demand for capacity in wireless systems has motivated researchers to explore ways to achieve higher performance in a given bandwidth. Recent research has shown that in a multipath environment, the use of space-time coding with multiple antennas at both ends of the link can increase the capacity of the wireless channel. MIMO is actually an underlying technique for transporting data. It operates at the physical layer and enables its use with virtually any wireless transmission protocol. For example, MIMO can be used with the popular IEEE 802.11 (Wi-Fi) technology. For these reasons, MIMO eventually become the standard for carry almost all wireless traffic. MIMO is one of the most economical ways of increasing bandwidth, range and will become a key technology in wireless systems. To properly evaluate the performance of these algorithms requires a comprehensive understanding of MIMO and models that capture this sophisticated spatial behavior as done by Gesbert (1999).

For MIMO, there are four different types of communication models or multiple antenna systems, namely Single-Input-Single-Output (SISO), Single-Input-Multiple-Output (SIMO), Multiple-Input-Single-Output (MISO) and Multiple-Input-Multiple-Output (MIMO). Single Input Single Output (SISO), as shown in Figure 1, is the most basic version and is based on a single antenna at both the sender and the receiver. This one is the simplest one in the communication model. It has been used in TV, radio and Wi-Fi systems. The other is model is Single Input Multiple Output (SIMO) in which we have multiple antennas at the receiver where both antennas are used at the receiving side or the one which gives the best result. Another one is Multiple Input Single Output (MISO) in which we have multiple antennas at the sender (transmitter) side while single antenna at the receiver side. Finally we have MIMO (Multiple

Figure 1.

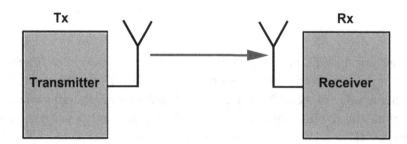

Input Multiple Output) shown in Figure 2, in which we had multiple antennas at both the sender and receiver side. For example if we had 2x2 at both the sender and receiver the throughput will be doubled. This is the most common model.

MIMO has other features as well like Precoding, spatial multiplexing, coding diversity and frame aggregations which are given below:

4.1 Precoding

Precoding refers to multi-stream beam forming. Generally, it is considered that all spatial processing that occurs in the transmitter. In single-stream beam forming, all of the transmit antennas send the same signal with appropriate phase weighting such that the gain of signal power is maximized at the receiver input. The benefits of beam forming include increasing the gain of the received signal by constructively adding the signals emitted from different antennas as well as reducing the effect of multipath fading.

4.2 Spatial Multiplexing

Spatial multiplexing can only be achieved by MIMO antenna configuration. In spatial multiplexing, a high-speed signal is split into several low-rate streams and subsequently, each stream is transmitted from different antennas, but on the same frequency channel. The successful reception of these signals at the receiver depends on whether these signals have sufficiently different spatial signatures. Spatial multiplexing is a powerful technique for increasing the channel capacity in a higher signal to noise ratio (SNR). The maximum number of spatial streams is limited by the lesser of the number of antennas at the sender or receiver.

Figure 2.

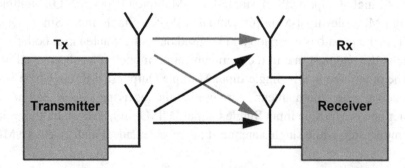

4.3 Coding Diversity

Coding diversity techniques are typically employed when the transmitter does not have channel knowledge. In this technique, the signal is encoded using a technique called space-time coding. The signal is transmitted from the transmitting antennas using full (or near orthogonal coding). Diversity coding breaks the independent fading in the multiple antenna links to enhance signal diversity. However, since there is no channel information available, therefore the benefits of beam-forming or array-gain cannot be achieved.

4.4 Frame Aggregation

It is the feature of 802.11n and MIMO in which two frames will be transmitted at the same time from one antenna. Transmitting every frame involves some overhead such as radio-level head, Media access control (MAC) header, and the header of acknowledgment which will eventually consume more bandwidth than a normal transmission. By transmitting multiple frames together, some optimizations can be realized.

5. MAIN FOCUS OF THE CHAPTER

5.1 Introduction

For the project we will use TP-Link Wi-Fi routers as the nodes on which we will install OpenWRT OS. Below are the details of the hardware used and the software installed. Also we will discuss the performance evaluation tool used and the functions that can be used on IPERF.

5.2 Hardware: TP-Link TL-WDR4300 (ver. 1.7)

For the performance evaluation we are using TP Link model TL-WDR 4300 Version 1.7.It is a dual band (two radio) of frequency 2.4Ghz and 5Ghz with gigabit Ethernet. Its theoretical speed is 750 Mbps. It is dual stream (2x2) on 2.4 GHz and triple stream (3x3) on 5Gh. The details of the interfaces are given below:

- CPU: Atheros AR9344@560MHz
- Flash: 8 MB
- RAM: 128MB
- Network: 4 ports
- WAN: 1 port
- Bandwidth: 300 Mbps (radio0)
- 450 Mbps (radio1)

Figure 3 shows the web based interface of the router.

Figure 3. Web based interface of the router

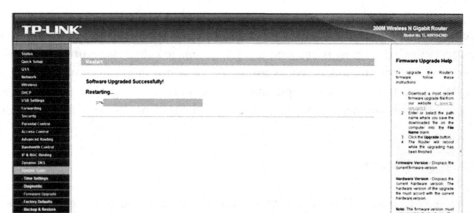

5.3 Operating System: OpenWRT (OS for Wi-Fi)

OpenWRT is an operating system / embedded operating system based on the Linux kernel, and is mainly used to route network traffic. It is a free and Open source OS (Openwrt). OpenWRT framework allows you to modify your embedded operating system according to your particular needs. Some of the main components are the Linux kernel, util-linux, uClibc and BusyBox. Components are optimized for size to be small enough to fit into the limited storage and memory available on home routers.

It can be used both as a Command-line interface also as a web interface using package LuCi. There are more than 3500 packages (software) available on OpenWRT. The OS can be run on many devices like smart phones, laptops and PC based on x86 architecture.OpenWRT many versions came into the market but all OS will not work on the same device due to the compatibility problem. For our device Attitude Adjustment (12.09) was supported. Figure 4 shows the command line interface of OpenWRT.

5.4 Components of OpenWRT

Some of the main components that this OS used are given below:

- **Uclibc:** It is a C library used for embedded Linux systems. It is smaller than glibc but all the functionalities are available in this library but in the compressed size. For porting any application from glibc to uclibc recompilation is needed.
- **Opkg:** Opkg is just like installer for installing any software. It is light weight package management system.It is also used in many embedded linux system.
- **BusyBox:** OpenWRT support most of the commands that are supported by a Unix OS. All the libraries support these command are condensed into single busybox. Commands like Vi editor are symbolic linked into this busybox.

Figure 4.

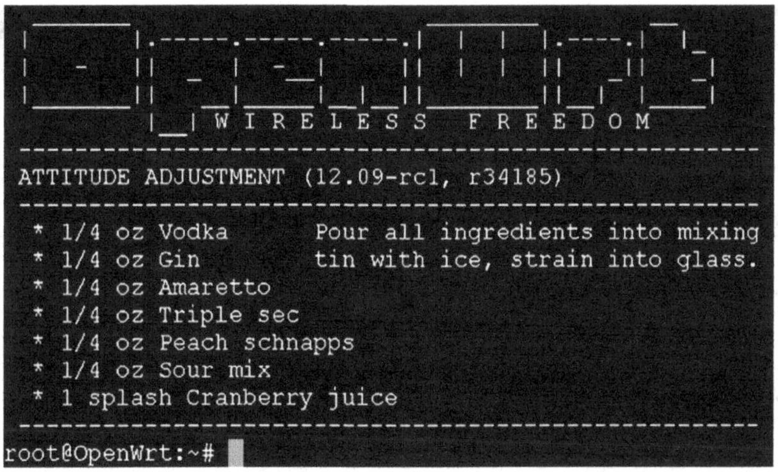

```
 |     |.------.------.   |  |   |.-----.|  |
 |  -  ||  _  |  _  |   ||  |   ||  |  ||  _   -|
 |  |  ||  _  |  _|   ||  |   ||  |  ||   _|
 |__|  | |  |  | |  | |_||  |   ||  |  |  |_|
       |__| W I R E L E S S   F R E E D O M
----------------------------------------------------
ATTITUDE ADJUSTMENT (12.09-rc1, r34185)
----------------------------------------------------
  * 1/4 oz Vodka       Pour all ingredients into mixing
  * 1/4 oz Gin         tin with ice, strain into glass.
  * 1/4 oz Amaretto
  * 1/4 oz Triple sec
  * 1/4 oz Peach schnapps
  * 1/4 oz Sour mix
  * 1 splash Cranberry juice
----------------------------------------------------
root@OpenWrt:~#
```

- **LuCi:** OpenWRT was introduced as a command line interface shell. Later on after the development in the OS LuCi was introduced so users can easily access the wireless router by using the web page. All the basic operations are available on this web page package but some commands need to run on command line shell.

Figure 5 shows the Luci interface.

5.5 OpenWRT Buildroot

For installing any package firstly we will have to compile the source code and make its executable. OpenWRT buildroot provides you to compile your code and makes it executable. Here we can specify the architecture of our hardware according to which our code will be compiled and its executable will be created. This buildroot automatically check for the dependency packages and download the dependency source code and compile it along with the code we are compiling.

In the buildroot shown in Figure 6, where in target system we specify which type of architecture our hardware is using and in the target profile we are specifying the model using this architecture. So according to these conditions our code will be compiled.

5.6 Network and Wireless Files

The two files that are most important for OpenWRT and the routing protocol are wireless and network files. In the network file we define each interface and for each interface we will set the IP. Also the switch inside the router will be configured in this file. The network and the wireless files are located at the location '/etc/config/network' and '/etc/config/wireless'.

Figure 5.

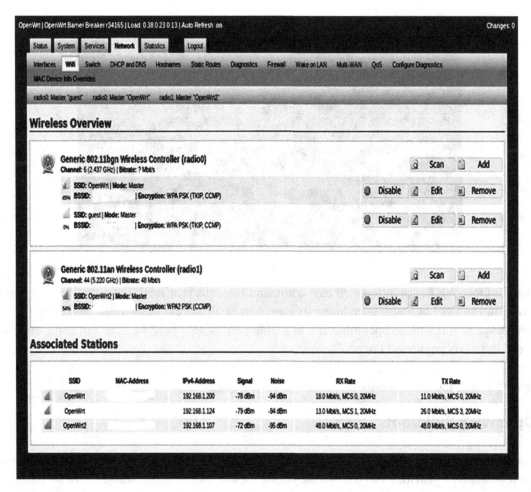

Network File

```
config interface 'loopback'
            option ifname 'lo'
            option proto 'static'
            option ipaddr '127.0.0.1'
            option netmask '255.0.0.0'
config interface 'lan1'
            option ifname 'eth0.1'
            option proto 'static'
            option ipaddr '192.168.2.8'
            option netmask '255.255.255.0'
```

Figure 6. Openwrt BuildRoot

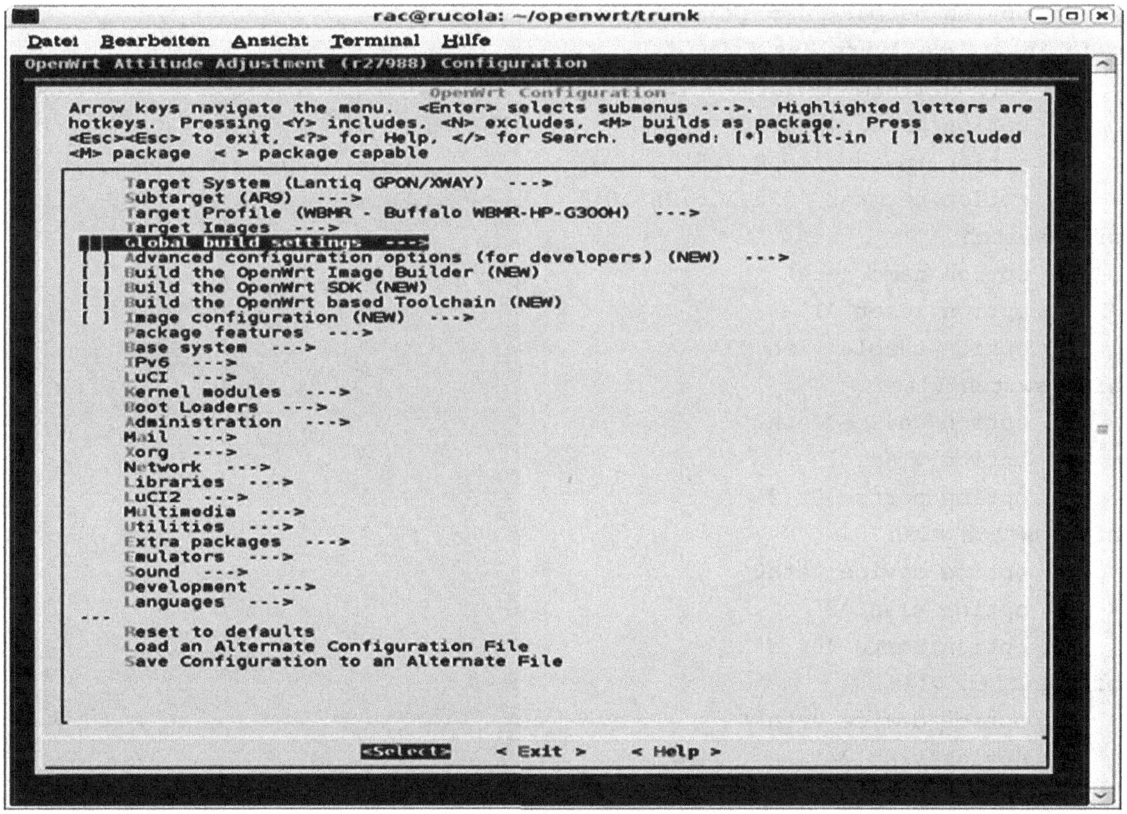

```
config interface 'lan2'
                option ifname 'eth0.2'
                option proto 'static'
                option ipaddr '10.2.0.1'
                option netmask '255.255.255.0'
config interface 'lan3'
                option ifname 'eth0.3'
                option proto 'static'
                option ipaddr '10.3.0.1'
                option netmask '255.255.255.0'
config interface 'lan4'
                option ifname 'eth0.4'
                option proto 'static'
                option ipaddr '192.168.10.3'
                option netmask '255.255.255.0'
                option gateway '192.168.10.9'
config interface 'wireless'
        option ifname 'wlan0'
        option proto 'static'
```

```
        option ipaddr '10.0.1.8'
        option netmask '255.255.255.0'
config interface 'wireless2'
        option ifname 'wlan1'
        option proto 'static'
        option ipaddr '10.0.1.8'
        option netmask '255.255.255.0'
config switch
        option name 'eth0'
        option reset '1'
        option enable_vlan '1'
config switch_vlan
        option device 'eth0'
        option vlan '1'
        option ports '0t 2'
config switch_vlan
        option device 'eth0'
        option vlan '2'
        option ports '0t 3'
config switch_vlan
        option device 'eth0'
        option vlan '4'
        option ports '0t 5'
config switch_vlan
        option device 'eth0'
        option vlan '3'
        option ports '0t 4'
```

In the network file we will define the IP for each interface. Switch and vlan will also be created in this file. In the portion i.e 'config interface lan' we are defining the IP of the interface. In the line config interface lan1 we are giving the user defined name for the device which can be anything. In the line option ifname we are giving the physical hardware ID i.e eth0.1 is the physical name of our hardware.In the rest of the lines ipaddr subnet ang gateway we are defining normal IP address.In the same way we will define the rest of interfaces like lan2, lan3, lan4, wan, radio0 and radio1. In the next phase we are defining and creating the switch. For the switch we will define vlans in which we will define the ports of the switch where in the device we will define the switch ID. In the vlan we will give user oriented name like 'option vlan 3' number could be anything like here we are giving the number 3 and the number could be anything define by the user.

Wireless File

```
config wifi-device 'radio0'
        option type 'mac80211'
        option channel '11'
```

```
        option macaddr 'c0:4a:00:40:87:1b'
        option hwmode '11ng'
        option htmode 'HT20'
        list ht_capab 'LDPC'
        list ht_capab 'SHORT-GI-20'
        list ht_capab 'SHORT-GI-40'
        list ht_capab 'TX-STBC'
        list ht_capab 'RX-STBC1'
        list ht_capab 'DSSS_CCK-40'
        option txpower '15'
        option country 'US'
config wifi-iface
        option device 'radio0'
        option network 'wireless'
        option mode 'adhoc'
        option ssid 'OpenWrt'
        option encryption 'none'
config wifi-device 'radio1'
        option type 'mac80211'
        option channel '36'
        option macaddr 'c0:4a:00:40:87:1c'
        option hwmode '11na'
        option htmode 'HT20'
        list ht_capab 'LDPC'
        list ht_capab 'SHORT-GI-20'
        list ht_capab 'SHORT-GI-40'
        list ht_capab 'TX-STBC'
        list ht_capab 'RX-STBC1'
        list ht_capab 'DSSS_CCK-40'
        option txpower '10'
        option country 'US'
config wifi-iface
        option device 'radio1'
        option network 'wireless2'
        option mode 'adhoc'
        option ssid 'OpenWrt'
        option encryption 'none'
```

In the wireless file we are using two radios in the same router. In the first phase (config wifi-iface) we tell the physical hardware and its mode and the network associated with it. The second part is about the attributes of the radio in which we tell the hardware mode like a/b/g/n, transmit power in the decibels, the country and the channel associated with the. Likewise, we will the define the second radio in the same style like we done with the first radio.

5.7 OLSRd (Optimized Link State Routing Daemon)

The routing protocol used for the multi hop network was OLSRd.OLSRd is a proactive routing protocol so the routing table is known in advance. Some parameters need to be defined so the daemon should know how to the protocol should run. The parameters are defined in a conf file known as olsrd.conf. The file is located in '/etc/olsrd.conf '. The configuration of this file is given below. This is the least configuration that any olsrd should contain.

```
DebugLevel          1
ClearScreen         yes
LinkQualityLevel    2
UseHysteresis       no
Interface "wlan1" "wlan0"
{
  HelloInterval     2.0
  HelloValidityTime 20.0
}
```

Some of the above words explanation is given below

- DebugLevel [0-9]: It sends the debug output to the terminal. Setting the value will not send output to the terminal or stdout and the protocol will be run in background
- LinkQualityLevel [0-2]: Setting the value to 0 will turn off the link quality (ETX) and Hop Count will be activated. For the value 1 only MPR will
- Interface: This field requires which interface should be used for OLSR, here we are using both interfaces of radio Ethernet (LAN) ports can also be included here.

5.8 IPERF

IPERF is a network benchmarking tool used in our project. It can calculate throughput, jitter and packet loss. Both TCP and UDP packets can be measured using this tool.IPERF can be easily install on the OpenWrt using the package managing tool OPKG.

The server side IPERF can be run by the command 'iperf -s' while the client side can be run as 'iperf –c 10.0.1.1' the IP should match the server IP and it should be included in the olsrd.conf file. Running with command will run the iperf in the TCP mode.

The upd can be run by using the argument –u i.e 'iperf -s -u' and the client side should also contain the '-u' argument.The result will contain the datagram loss and bandwith. The default bandwith speed is 5 Mb/sec but it can be changed by using the argument –b 'iperf –c 10.0.1.1 –u –b 10m'. Time can also be defined by using the argument '–t' i.e 'iperf –c 10.0.1.1 –t 10'. Time argument will be in seconds. The interval for the result can be set by using '-i' argument and the result will be displayed for that interval otherwise default interval will be for one second. Figure 7 shows the Iperf interface.

Figure 7.

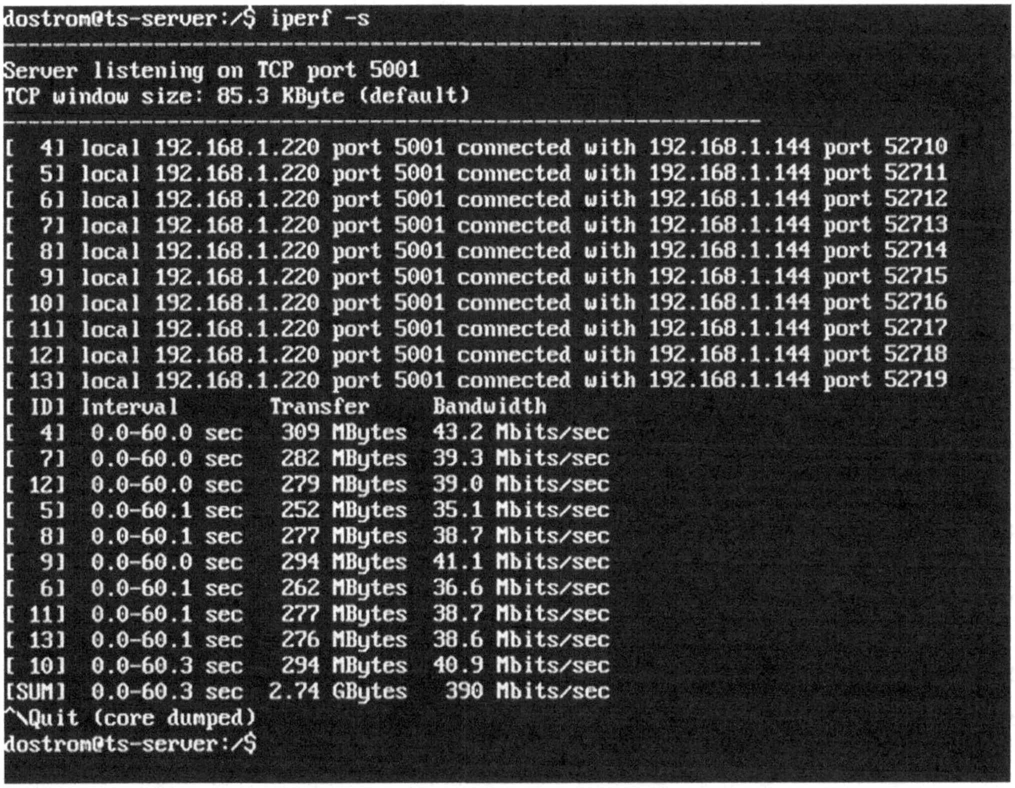

```
dostrom@ts-server:/$ iperf -s
---------------------------------------------------------------------
Server listening on TCP port 5001
TCP window size: 85.3 KByte (default)
---------------------------------------------------------------------
[  4] local 192.168.1.220 port 5001 connected with 192.168.1.144 port 52710
[  5] local 192.168.1.220 port 5001 connected with 192.168.1.144 port 52711
[  6] local 192.168.1.220 port 5001 connected with 192.168.1.144 port 52712
[  7] local 192.168.1.220 port 5001 connected with 192.168.1.144 port 52713
[  8] local 192.168.1.220 port 5001 connected with 192.168.1.144 port 52714
[  9] local 192.168.1.220 port 5001 connected with 192.168.1.144 port 52715
[ 10] local 192.168.1.220 port 5001 connected with 192.168.1.144 port 52716
[ 11] local 192.168.1.220 port 5001 connected with 192.168.1.144 port 52717
[ 12] local 192.168.1.220 port 5001 connected with 192.168.1.144 port 52718
[ 13] local 192.168.1.220 port 5001 connected with 192.168.1.144 port 52719
[ ID] Interval        Transfer     Bandwidth
[  4]  0.0-60.0 sec   309 MBytes   43.2 Mbits/sec
[  7]  0.0-60.0 sec   282 MBytes   39.3 Mbits/sec
[ 12]  0.0-60.0 sec   279 MBytes   39.0 Mbits/sec
[  5]  0.0-60.1 sec   252 MBytes   35.1 Mbits/sec
[  8]  0.0-60.1 sec   277 MBytes   38.7 Mbits/sec
[  9]  0.0-60.0 sec   294 MBytes   41.1 Mbits/sec
[  6]  0.0-60.1 sec   262 MBytes   36.6 Mbits/sec
[ 11]  0.0-60.1 sec   277 MBytes   38.7 Mbits/sec
[ 13]  0.0-60.1 sec   276 MBytes   38.6 Mbits/sec
[ 10]  0.0-60.3 sec   294 MBytes   40.9 Mbits/sec
[SUM]  0.0-60.3 sec  2.74 GBytes   390 Mbits/sec
^\Quit (core dumped)
dostrom@ts-server:/$
```

6. PERFORMANCE EVALUATION

The performance evaluation of different routing metrics on different radios is the major theme of this project. The result contains the performance difference between the radios used such as radio0 2.4 Ghz, radio1 5.0 Ghz and for the both radios simultaneously. The result for the radios is done on two metrics known as Hop Count (HC) and Expected Transmission Time (ETX). The result contains the three major network benchmarking tools like Throughput, Latency and datagram loss.

6.1 Testbed

The multi hop test bed contains 14 nodes which are placed in the 'A Block, Air University, Islamabad'. Figure 8 shows the testbed used. The circles are showing the node number, in the performance evaluation we will calculate the results from node 1 to node 14.

6.2 Results

The results here shown for the two routing metrics and for the two radios. Each test ran for 30 minutes. In the each graph we are comparing results for the two radios and for both radio simultaneously. As the

Figure 8.

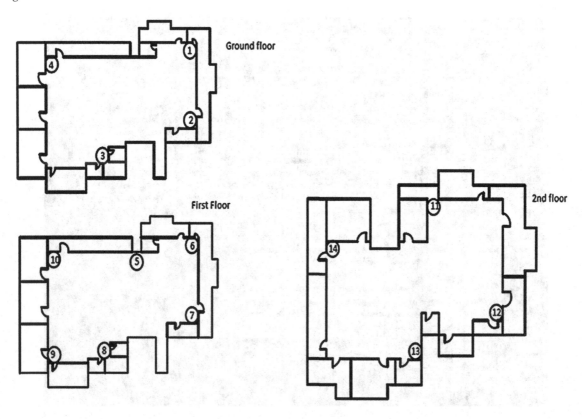

results were taken in a limited area so we had to reduce the transmission power in order to have real time testbed. The radio0 power was reduced to 15db (decibels) and radio1 power to 10db. The radio0 was using the channel 11 and the radio1 was using the channel 36. The distance from each node to other is approximately 10 meters minimum.

6.2.1 Hop Count (HC) Results

In the HC metric our OLSRd radio0 following the route from node 1 - 5 - 14, while the radio1 following the path (route) 1- 6 - 14, and by using both radio simultaneously route becomes $1 - 2 - 14$. Note that the whole route is followed by radio0 which

Figure 9 shows the result for throughput of Hop Count on different radios. The above result shows that using both radio simultaneously giving us better throughput while the radio1 is almost near to that. Packet Loss also known as datagram loss in the term of UDP results are given below in Figure 10. We are sending packets at 5 Mb/sec.

In the above results of packet loss the better performance is again by both radio simultaneously. While the radio0 performance is worst with the loss of 33% packet in a second. Figure 11 shows the result of latency also known as round trip time. The result was taken using the command ping an (ICMP) packet.

Figure 9. Throughput – hop count (Mbits/sec)

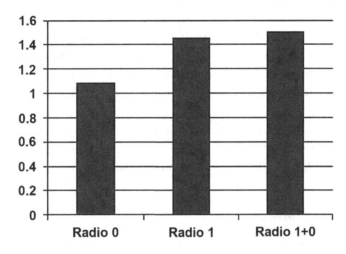

Figure 10. Packet loss – hop count (%)

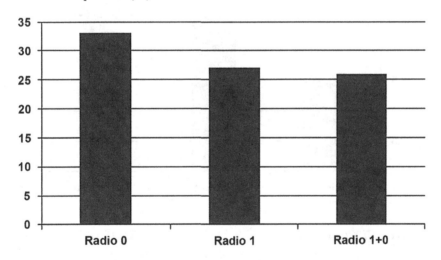

Figure 11. Latency – hop count (ms)

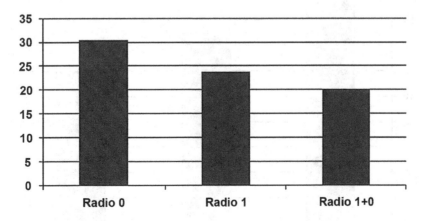

6.2.2 Expected Transmission Time (ETX) Results

In the ETX metric our OLSRd radio0 following the route from node 1 – 6 - 10 - 14, while the radio1 following the path (route) 1- 2 - 4 - 14, and by using both radio simultaneously route becomes 1 - 7 - 8 - 14. Note that the route from 1 - 7 and 8 - 14 followed by radio1, while from the node 7 - 8 is followed by radio0. Figure 12 shows the result for throughput of Expected Transmission Time (ETX) on different radios.

In the above results the throughput for both radio simultaneously is having more fine results than the other while radio0 had a worst result. Almost double difference can be seen from the result. Figure 13 shows the results for packet loss in which we will send our packets at the rate of 5 Mb/sec.

Figure 12. Throughput – ETX (Mbits/sec)

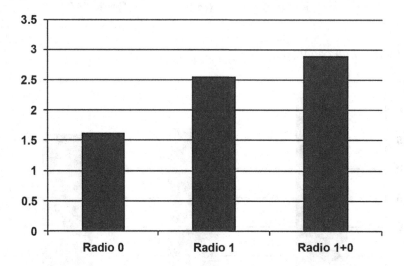

Figure 13. Packet loss – ETX (%)

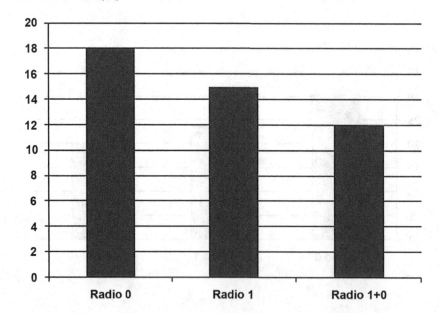

Here, in terms of packet loss, both radio simultaneously achieved the better as compared to the both radios but the results are not as worst as was the case of Hop Count. Below is the result of latency for ETX (shown in Figure 14) on the different radios

Latency for both radios simultaneously is better than other so again the results are in favor of dual band radio. In general the results are very clear which shows using dual band radio having multiple channels can seriously increase in the performance. We will have a look in conclusion with details why we are having good results with this dual band radio.

7. CONCLUSION

Wireless multi hop networks have attracted the attention of many researchers due to its widespread applications and there are a number of hardware available. During the recent years many new routing metrics are being proposed but not all of them are implemented and evaluated. However, the routing metrics evaluation in this project is already evaluated but not for the dual-band of 802.11n. In this report we are comparing the routing metrics over the dual band radio of 802.11n. We had tested the performance on the both radios separately and also simultaneously. The overall performance was much impressive during both radio was activated in the daemon. However the performance of Radio1 which was running at the band of 5.0 GHz was much better than the Radio0 running on band 2.4 GHz.Note that the IP of both radio band was the same and the role of daemon was that to choose which band. The performance was depends on some of the factors which are given below.

Hardware

The Radio0 at 2.4 GHz was using dual stream 2x2 while Radio1 was using triple stream 3x3 so the bandwidth will be more of 5GHz than 2.4 GHz.But the range will be more of radio0 than radio1 because attenuation increase with the increase of frequency.

Figure 14. Latency – ETX (ms)

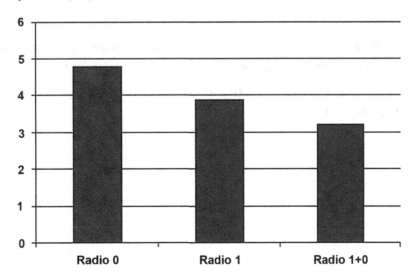

Channels

In radio0 2.4 GHz only 3 non-overlapping channels (1, 6, 11) are available while radio1 5 GHz had 23 non-overlapping channels which are higher than the 2.4 GHz. Most of our devices like microwave, cord less phones etc. using the frequency 2.4 GHz due to which a lot of interference is experienced. The 5 GHz using the channel which is unique by the time also a lot of channels are available in this frequency mode. So the 5 GHz will be going to have less interference

Metric

Routing metrics have a significant impact on the performance of multi hop network. The ETX routing metric calculates the link quality based on probe loss ratio and when more than one routes are available, it chooses the route with minimum link-loss, resulting in stable performance. The Hop Count metric on the other hand, just counts the number of hops and chooses the path with minimum number of hops. In our case we had the best result when using the ETX metric and dual band radio simultaneously. Also the channels used on that band matters due to the interference. Therefore, after considering several factors based on the channels, the metric and the bands used (dual-band), we conclude that using dual band with ETX metric outperforms ETX with single-band. Link-rate aware metric like ETT (Expected Transmissions Time) will give better result in multi-rate multi-radio situations.

REFERENCES

Broch, J. (1998). A performance comparison of multi-hop wireless ad hoc network routing protocols. In *Proceedings of the 4th annual ACM/IEEE international conference on Mobile computing and networking*. ACM. doi:10.1145/288235.288256

Gesbert, D., Bölcskei, H., Gore, D., & Paulraj, A. J. (2002). Outdoor MIMO wireless channels: Models and performance prediction. *Communications. IEEE Transactions on*, *50*(12), 1926–1934. doi:10.1109/TCOMM.2002.806555

OpenWRT website: http://openwrt.org/

Royer, E. M., & Toh, C. K. (1999). A review of current routing protocols for ad hoc mobile wireless networks. *Personal Communications, IEEE*, *6*(2), 46–55. doi:10.1109/98.760423

Tirumala, A., Dunigan, T., & Cottrell, L. (2003). Measuring end-to-end bandwidth with Iperf using Web100. No. SLAC-PUB-9733.

Chapter 7
Mobile Cloud Computing Future Trends and Opportunities

Sajid Umair
National University of Sciences and Technology, Pakistan

Muhammad Nauman Zahoor
National University of Sciences and Technology, Pakistan

Umair Muneer
National University of Sciences and Technology, Pakistan

Asad W. Malik
National University of Sciences and Technology, Pakistan

ABSTRACT

Due to wide variety of smart phones and capability of supporting heavy applications their demand is increasing day by day. Increase of computation capability and processing power Mobile cloud computing (MCC) becomes an emerging field. After cloud computing mobile cloud provide significant advantage and usage with reliability and portability. Challenges involved in mobile cloud computing are energy consumption, computation power and processing ability. Mobile cloud provides a way to use cloud resources on mobile but traditional models of smart phones does not support cloud so researchers introduce new models for the development of MCC. There are certain phases that still need improvement and this field attracts many researchers. Purpose of this chapter is to analyze and summarize the challenges involved in this field and work done so far.

INTRODUCTION

Over the past years, computing in cloud is becoming as advanced as it endorsed software for the devices operated on internet. It provides a lot of utility ways for the user to access any application as they want. Now people are using more reliable ways to use software's being a service on a cloud instead the install all the infrastructure on their own machines. As we know that Cloud structure consists of many datacenters and they are also maintained by providers. The providers such as Google, Amazon, and Microsoft provide their services to consumers on demand and they have maintained it on the cloud at different locations (S. Prerez, 2009). All in all severe crashes and failures are avoided and high reliability is due to computation technology.

DOI: 10.4018/978-1-4666-9767-6.ch007

Copyright © 2016, IGI Global. Copying or distributing in print or electronic forms without written permission of IGI Global is prohibited.

This chapter covers the main contents like the current trend, challenges and future practices of cloud computing. By the increasing usage of handheld devices is directly proportional to its power consumption which leads to many other factors such as memory management and less computational power. As by the time internet and technology is increasing every person would prefer to do his work by using fewer resources. Cloud computing meet their needs as they required because everything is on cloud distributed and virtualized. According to some research base mobile applications are estimated to rise 88% per annum from 2009 to 2014 (J. G. Ruay-Shiung Chang et al. 2013).

MCC has made our life easier in an effective way. Handheld devices along with internet connections made life more comfortable. With this technology we can move our more intensive tasks on cloud. To comprehend the main challenges in Mobile Cloud Computing one should get the domain knowledge and deep understandings of cloud computing.

This section displays the distributed computing, base in cloud flow examination patterns and issues identified with Mobile Cloud Computing. The Mobile Cloud Computing comprises of cloud, portable, processing gadget and remote channels, and asset suppliers. Point of MCC is to give clients straightforwardness so they can get everything on their cell phones with unwavering quality. It gives administrations like programming on the cloud, handling force, financially savvy arrangements and dependability and accessibility. In its most straightforward structure, MCC is a structure where capacity and handling of registering happens outside cell phone; though, assets can be investigated on the portable. There are numerous distributed computing applications. A standout amongst the most unmistakable employments of Mobile Cloud Computing is in e-business where one can offer or purchase things through their cell phones. These errands incorporate online installment, ticketing and bank exchanges and so on. There are a few confinements with this methodology like security issue, system idleness and so forth. E-learning or virtual learning is an essential commitment to training by this innovation. Cloud make it less demanding so that addresses features, presentations everything is accessible on the cloud. Cloud versatile figuring has sway on medicinal area too, one can without much of a stretch take assistance from specialists siting a large number of miles away; this is conceivable because of cloud adjustment in diverse parts.

Distributed computing has sway on portable keeping money and versatile recreations and so on (A. B. E. Cuervo et al.2010). With the approach of PDAs and their backing for expansive applications like computer games, picture preparing and e-keeping money and so on. Their many-sided quality and interest of computational assets is expanded. There is still sure application that requests a major computational power and telephones react moderate (P. B. M. Satyanarayanan et al.2009). To take care of this issue industry need to consider and change programming or equipment to satisfy it prerequisites (C. Mascolo, 2010). Equipment assets can't be improved because of configuration issues however programming should be possible. Calculation change is a strategy where we can move our reckoning undertaking on the cloud. Change of the processing on the cloud improves the execution of the application and tackles the issue of battery utilization and permits us to run application that is not able to keep running on cell phones. (Amazon, 2011) Numerous utilizations of distinctive area have moved their backing on cloud, for example, (T. P. X.Yang and and J. Shen, 2010), healthcare (T. P. a. I. M. C. Doukas, 2010) and business.

Many distributions point out the centrality of MCC. Creator examines two models and presents a method to proficiently get to the assets (R. F. a. I. Khalife, 2011). Creators exhibited the difficulties in the field of versatile cloud. This section shows the late improvement in MCC and stress on difficulties and future patterns. This section likewise (C. L. H. T. Dinh et al.2011) and (X. K. L. Guan et al.2011) exhibits the contrasts in the middle of cloud and portable cloud structural planning and components influencing the Mobile Cloud Computing on the cloud. In the future we discuss different topics like building design, writing survey, portable distributed computing models, correlation of versatile cloud models are exhibited, advantages and disadvantages. Toward the end, chapter is finished up with discriminating audit and future territories and changes.

MCC ARCHITECTURE

Cost effective services is basic and necessary required for cloud users to be provided by service providers. These services play an important role for small customers to grow their business and increase their productivity. Main resource consuming tasks are sent to cloud and computation takes place there. The results are then sent back to mobile user. This practice helps in increasing battery life by bypassing CPU intensive tasks to cloud rather than mobile devices instead. There are some threats as well which are being faced by these technologies and need to be catered. There are some serious concerns that need to be addressed while we are dealing with Mobile Cloud Computing. Some of these concerns are bandwidth latency and mobile devices, battery power, latency in network, communication service threats etc. Services are provided in the form of infrastructure as a service (IAAS), platform as a service (PAAS) and software as a service (SAAS). Figure 1 shows MCC architecture. Services can be obtained using two techniques. 1). by directly accessing their mobile network. 2). by accessing through access points. Satellite and base station connections are used to connect mobile devices to cloud service providers. Telecom networks provide internet connectivity which is used by mobile users to get connected to cloud servers.

Main components of this design are mobile users, telecom industry, internet services providers and cloud services providers. Wi-Fi or mobile data connections are used by users to get connected through satellite or with the help of base stations. Using mobile devices requests are sent through network to get processed. Final processing take place on cloud and results are compiled there. Network provider works as a middleware and provide services to mobile users from the cloud providers. There are several Mobile Cloud Computing applications that are using the cloud with the help of internet directly. Figure 2 shows

Figure 1. Mobile cloud computing architecture

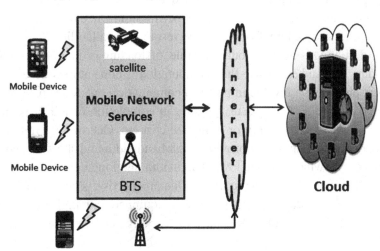

Figure 2. Detail view of architecture

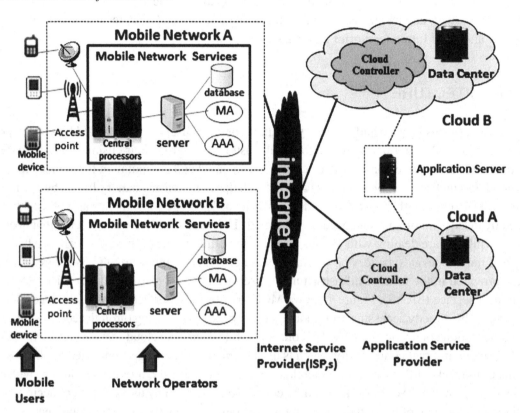

a more detailed view of the architecture. Using internet services requests of clients are sent cloud for processing. There are two networks that are involved in the mentioned picture. For processing purposes multiple servers are used by cloud service providers to accommodate multiple requests from clients

Another main and important feature of Mobile Cloud Computing is use of Computation Offloading. There is a systematic process which is used for making decision in offloading. The process is explained in Figure 3. Main requirement to get connected is user permission. Once user grants the permission the network availability is checked and confirmed. Cloud resources availability is checked in next phase. After that feasibility of moving is done. If found feasible, offloading is done. Required data and details are moved. If offloading is found expensive then computation is done at local level.

There are different prospective involve in perform computation on cloud. A user may take consideration cost of network, cloud cost and security issues in completion of job. It is an important point what user desire is whether to save energy or minimize cost etc. One of the limits is communication channel; if it is wireless connection then it provides high bandwidth and shorter delays as compared to third generation connections which provide lower bandwidth and long delays. So for both choices user may select one connection that is according to needs. One prospective is how much hardware resources available in smart phone. Now today's mobile phones are equipped with high memory some have more processing power other may have energy efficiency. So it is user's choice to select the most appropriate phone for computations.

Figure 3. Offloading of mobile cloud computing

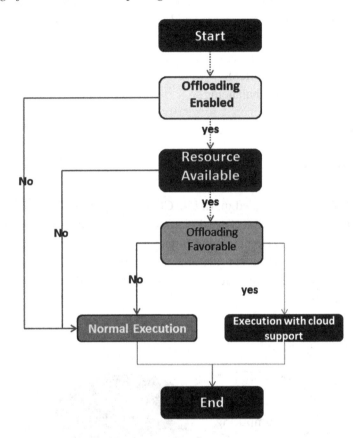

BACKGROUND

With increasing use of mobile devices this technology has emerged a lot. Along with mobile technology wireless technology is also becoming increasingly popular. Demand of both technologies is increasing on each passing day. According to a survey there is an 18.1% increase in mobile and Mobile Cloud Computing market (J. G. Ruay-Shiung Chang et al.2013). Space is provided by Mobile Cloud Computing. As use of MCC is increasing it is resulting in energy efficiency. Main reason of obtaining energy efficiency is transfer of resource consuming applications to operate on cloud servers rather than mobile devices. Mobile Cloud Computing is a very worthy and modern field. There are many authors, whom published their research papers in this field. L. Zhon and B. Wang in (B. W. L. Zhong and H. Wei, 2012) discuss the role of internet in MCC. Abdullah Gani and Han Qi (A. G. Han Qi, 2012) explained the infrastructure and architecture of the mobile cloud computing. Both the authors have discussed different challenges in this field. Authors have also pointed out main reasons why MCC is important and needs to evolve even more. According to a survey (S.A.Z. Sanaei and A. Gani, 2012) MCC usage is increasing very rapidly and this increase is resulting in getting more revenue generated. According to the current "Visiongain" report, Mobile Cloud Computing market will produce $45 billion in profit up to the year 2016 (J. G. Ruay-Shiung Chang et al.2013). There are many fields in which Mobile Cloud Computing

MCC can be used. Some of those fields are sensor data applications, natural language processing, social networking, image processing, multimedia search and so many others. Some of other features of MCC are described as under.

1. Avoiding limitations of hardware field.
2. Easy access of the data and load balancing.
3. Removal of regional restrictions.
4. Efficient Task Processing.

Mobile Cloud Computing

Processing and storage of data is combined in Mobile Cloud Computing processing to for one structure. Three services are combined i.e. Mobile Cloud Computing, cloud computing and wireless network computing. Main concept of MCC is explained in Figure 4.

Mobile Cloud Computing gives different facilities, like virtualization, scalability, flexibility, mobile cloud service connectivity, mobility, multi-tenancy, mobile utility billing etc. Figure 5 shows a much detail version of these facilities.

Figure 4. Combine architecture model

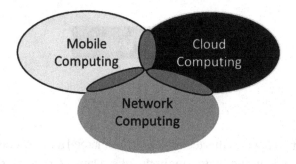

Figure 5. Facilities or features of mobile cloud

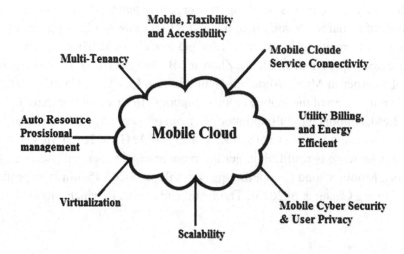

Mobile Cloud Computing is a Buzz Word

Demand of this technology i.e. Mobile Cloud Computing is increasing. According to Gartner Group; globally, mobile application storage and downloading have reached to 17.7 billion in the year 2011 (Gartner, 2014). That was 117 percent increased, which were greater than downloads in 2010. According to a survey, this increase will reach to the 185 billion at the end of 2014 (Gartner, 2014).

Now we will discuss some of motivations behind Mobile Cloud Computing. Initially, increasing battery life, processing power and also a time of mobile devices is important. Next motivation is to remove the limitations from the current mobile devices. Another important one is to increase the resource sharing and using computational resources in cloud Infrastructures. Different benefits are provided by Mobile Cloud Computing such as sharing of applications and mobile information. Another benefit is increasing sharing of resources and utilization the resources in the networks. Expansion of the enterprise mobile connectivity to the cloud community from mobile users which includes social media cloud users and social networks is also an important benefit. Customers also provide benefit from Mobile Cloud Computing such as converting the mobile devices into personal desktops, virtual and portable that provides unlimited storage.

Mobile cloud provides services and resources to the users. The services include cloud computing or mobile application. Resources include mobile data storage or wireless internet. Different deployed models are

1. **Ad-Hoc Mobile Cloud:** In this model the services contribute to the mobile users, to form an ad-hoc mobile network.
2. **Private Mobile Cloud:** In this model with the help of wireless internet the service provider allots the resources of mobile cloud to the group of users.
3. **Mobile Community Cloud:** This model is also related to the Mobile Cloud Computing that renders the resources to its clients, to form many mobile social networking communities through the wireless internet.

Research in MCC

Some of the subjects and research fields in the MCC are describe below

1. Mobile Cloud Infrastructure: This field tells us that how we construct the cost and energy effective mobile cloud model. In this field the mobile cloud provide the storage to the mobile client and provide the resources to the mobile user.
2. **Engineering for MCC:** This Research field tells us that how we use the well-structured and cost effective model for the development of the Mobile Cloud Computing and applications. This field also define the techniques and methodologies to improve the mobile cloud computing.
3. **Mobile Networking for MCC:** This field tells us the intelligent connection and energy efficient communication between the devices, network, and computer. Mobile networking in the mobile cloud is to take the place of the widely varied wireless networks and internet.

MCC Generations

First Generation

On personal mobile cloud First generation is based on. The main features of first generation are basically the services that are deployed and maintained in the data center of Mobile Cloud Computing. As the other important point is that the mobile communication is heterogeneous network and mainly operated by the current network. Other big feature of this system is scalability. This feature is also related to synchronization as the contents of mobile and application data are synchronized. Other important feature includes mobility. Figure 6 is related to the concept of showing the infrastructure that supports the wireless and internet. At the same time Figure 6 shows the first generation of the personal mobile cloud.

Second Generation

On Cloud based mobile cloud infrastructure the second generation is based on. It has different no of benefits and features. In the datacenter all the services are maintained. Second generation contains some new features e.g. On-demand service. It means that the services, data and contents are provided on demand to the mobile cloud. It also provides scalability. Figure 7 shows the complete architecture of second generation.

Third Generation

According to the survey of the Virgin Media Business CEO, Mark Heraghty, the mobile data usage growth causes to increase shifts that how in enterprise mobiles are used (L. Cocking, 2012). Figure 8 shows the picture of third generation that consists of four layers.

The first layer is Computing cloud layer. The second layer is Network layer. The third layer is Mobile cloud layer and the fourth layer is Mobile Layer.

Figure 6. Personal Cloud infrastructures (First Generation Model)

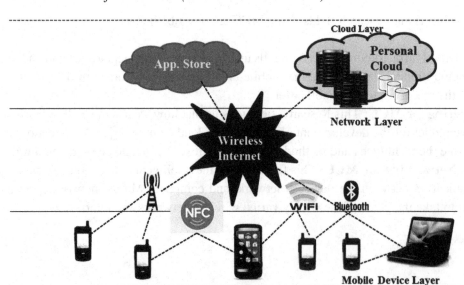

Figure 7. Second Generation: Mobile Cloud infrastructures

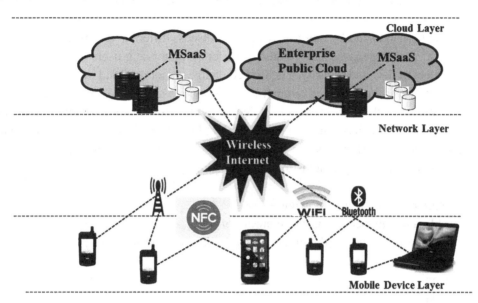

Figure 8. Third Generation: Mobile Cloud Service infrastructures

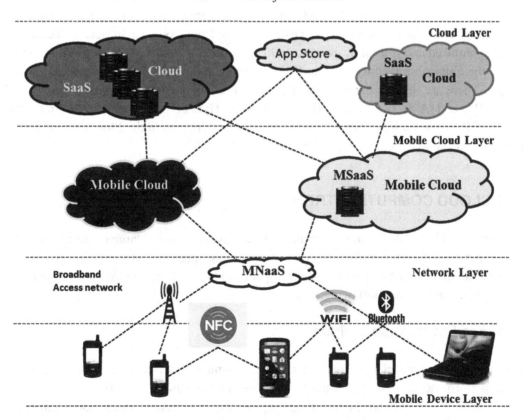

RESEARCH CHALLENGES AND ISSUES OF MOBILE CLOUD COMPUTING

S. W. L. Niroshinie Fernando and Wenny Rahayu (2013) discuss different sort of challenges and issues in the field of MCC and these issues are related to different factors e.g users operations, application services, management of data and security. The first challenge is mobile cloud infrastructure. Privacy is second one. Mobility is third one. Green computing is fourth one and mobile SaaS is last one.

Personal information of the mobile users is collected by the providers and in turn is like equivalent to gold mining. As a result it can be said that cloud is silver line. As when the data is stored in hard disk or USB, when the USB or hard disk is lost data is also lost. But when we move towards cloud, these problems remain no more. Some problems in cloud computing are following.

1. Physical location of data is not known to users.
2. If some problem in data occurs, user is unaware of that.
3. When the user want to change the cloud provider, data migration also becomes one other main problem.
4. In case when the cloud provider is damaged, then there is a high risk that how we will be able to recover our data.

Mobile Cloud Computing also has the same major problems which are known as mobility problem. The other main challenge that Mobile Cloud Computing community faced is the physical threats in case of mobile device being lost. Other big challenge occurs when from mobile; a Subscriber Identity module (SIM) card is removed and is used by everyone. One other major challenge in Mobile Cloud Computing is when the Subscriber Identity Module (SIM) cards is removed from the mobile and is accessed by everyone. There are some research papers related to the thin clients are Think Air (A. A. S. Kosta and P. Hui 2011) and (A. B. E. Cuervo et al.2010) and also Hyrax (E. Marinelli, 2009). In the research paper (Y. C. a. R. K. Dejan Kovachev, 2009) the other important area in the Mobile Cloud Computing infrastructures related to the computation offloading is discussed.

MOBILE CLOUD COMPUTING TRENDS

Some different models are designed so that main objectives like running large computation within the cloud and to achieve efficiency at the same time. So adopting specific model depends on objectives of the user. Specific models fulfill specific users prospective and they are considered as more useful. We have four basic models that are following.

Performance Enhancement Model

The main purpose of the model by using cloud resources to improve performance. Apps take a little time where high performance is offloaded to the cloud. Here are some useful models.

Cloud Cloning: Cloud of application cloning is a procedure which is sent to the cloud. It mainly works on harmonization plan. Consistency and unprocessed parts of the application by pointing to existing clone is maintained. Execution is complete (S. I. B.-G.Chun et al. 2010). The application of this model for the processing of the application is sent to the smart phone back in the division is dynamic and depends on cloud resources and processing power. Cloud cloning planning a mobile user tries to use whenever, it automatically blocks and the appropriate size distribution for this application. Migration takes place at certain intervals and on completion. The application is processed on back-loaded. Cloning detailed view of mobile cloud data shown in Figure 9.

Energy Enhancement Model

This type of model is mainly focused on cloud resources efficiently by using smart phones to minimize energy consumption. It's time to reduce overhead cloud applications are using.

μ Cloud: This model reliability, portability, supporting role in the application takes from different sources and that this configuration. At one time, a component loaded on the mobile phone and something called hybrid cloud implementation process (M. A. K. M. Satyanarayanan et al. 2005). Different as they can implement a middleware they need. The input parameter, local memory and configuration information is stored to identify a component (Y. G. V. March et al .2011). Dependency graph and the edges of their order execution as well as represent the components are represented. When a component implemented in full, resulting in the production of the component being input. This process continues until the ingredients are at the end.

Hybrid Application Models

Hybrid models such as energy efficiency and to achieve multiple objectives are devised. Using a model of multiple objectives are achieved because these types of models, are more suitable.

Think Air: This model in the cloud (A. A. S. Kosta et al.2011) smart phone supports the method level changes on this clone smartphone running parallel themes from the quality of service. A programmer

Figure 9. Cloud cloning model

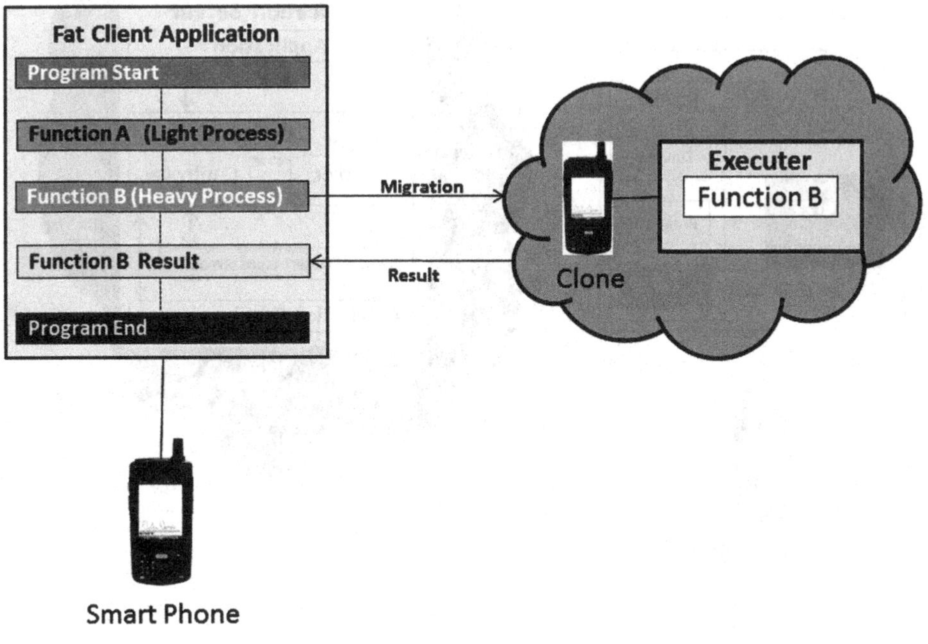

can offload to the cloud for the implementation, so that resource-intensive methods to explain. When a method is called, was called to the way of the future to track the movement Think PROFILER. Method of execution controller takes the decision about the location and thus improves the performance and energy consumption saves time

Cuckoo: It is more versatile models and programming for the community provides an easy to use and that they are familiar with the existing tools can be integrated (N. P. R. Kemp et al. 2012). Due to the increasing demand of the Android platform is built. Cuckoo in the application to develop, create and name a project developer must write. In the next phase of counting of the parts are separated and run on the cloud, Android, is to use the existing model. This approach is also useful for improving the performance and energy is shrinking.

COMPARISON OF DIFFERENT MOBILE CLOUD MODELS

From the above discussion, it is apparent that most of the models are not considered all the concerns of the cloud computing. The advantages and disadvantages are there for every model but the security and privacy of any cloud application is not always given the importance needed, is the biggest disadvantage. Below, in Table 1, model comparisons are shown. As discussed above, we have different models for different requirements. For performance based model, clone cloud which enhances the mobile perfor-

Figure 10. Think Air model

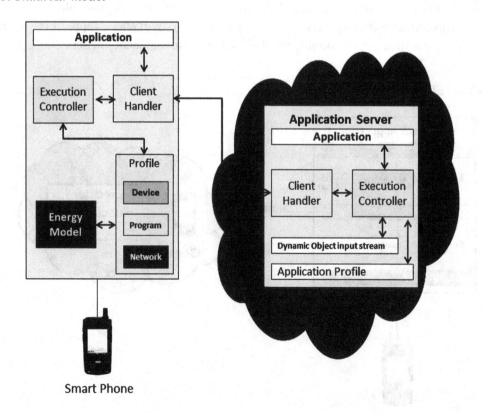

Smart Phone

Table 1. Model comparison

Model	Ba	S	Latency	Platform	Pr	MC
μ Cloud	Low	Low	Low	Android	Low	Energy
Cuckoo	Low	Low	Medium	Android	Low	High
Clone Cloud	High	Low	Low	Dalvik VM	Low	Performance
Think Air	Low	Low	Low	NDK (Java)	Low	High

Ba- Bandwidth; **Mc**- Model Category; **Pr**- Privacy; **S**- Security

mance and μ for increasing energy efficiency; hybrid approach which caters both of the requirements but there are still certain concerns which are not handled yet. Below table mention some requirements which are necessary to handle.

PROS AND CONS OF MOBILE CLOUD COMPUTING

There are a lot of reasons like communication, portability, scalability there for cloud computing give solution to mobile cloud. Mobile Cloud Computing has a lot of uses and solves different problems and challenges. Few advantages are given below

1. **Battery Consumption:** Due to increasing processing power in smart phones, lots off feature and application consume battery very fast. So this is the major issue in present situation. There are many solutions for increasing battery life but by doing computation on the cloud save cost, battery life and time.
2. **Privacy:** Privacy is a serious issue for the sake of hiding information of the user or company. Trusting the cloud is a problem and how to handle in case of discrepancy. So use communication channel or use decryption and encryption technique is used in the cloud. For the secure communication we use Virtual private network.
3. **Memory Requirement:** Memory requirement is a major concern due to large memory requirements of applications. To overcome this problem, mobile user can use cloud resources to store and save applications and necessary material using wireless networks. It also saves time and energy for the smart phones.
4. **Scalability:** It is the most desirable feature with the advent of cloud computing. Scalability support is necessary for the development of models in Mobile Cloud Computing. Every application can be enhanced if it is able to be scalable along with the ability to incorporate more attributes and modules in its development. So cloud applications must be scalable to adapt to any configuration. The dependency of scalability is on Mobile Cloud Computing model and domain of the application. For instance Amazon services are fully automated and user can change the components upon its needs. This important feature helps to configure this application on different platform and addition of any new module causes no effect on the whole system. Similarly Google engine (Google app engine, 2011) designed for stateless web applications and storage capability which make it scalable on different prospective.

There are many advantages of mobile cloud computing for business community as well, such as the fact that Mobile cloud computing helps to save money for businesses. By allowing organizations and users to share resources and applications with least amount of investment on hardware and software, mobile cloud computing apparatus helps a lot to shrink investment expenses. For enterprise or individual user, mobile cloud computing offers less technical setup and operations which lower price structure.

CONCLUSION

A survey related to MCC has been presented in this chapter and provides different trends and challenges. Evolution is happening as mobile usage is increasing on each passing day. Up to 35% revenues are coming from mobile devices and mobile applications (US Mobile Data Market Updates, 2010). Role of cloud computing is evident from the fact that large computation, time efficiency and many other factors are achieved through this technology. People want to use mobile for as many applications as possible. Some applications can only be executed using combination of mobile and cloud. This is the reason why this has become a hot topic in this area. This field has potential to do business and services mobility with the help of cloud. More focus is to overcome limitations of mobile by using cloud servers for computation. As discussed above, different Mobile Cloud Computing models have been presented; one thing common in all is that they are lacking privacy of the application. Security needs to be ensured to make data protected from attack that comes outside from cloud. Mobile Cloud Computing privacy framework is used to take care of this issue. A virtual private network is created that handle activates and authentication framework. To make it more secure and reliable a standard framework is required to be created to handle data management as well. This chapter gives us ideas about new areas of research related to this field that are required to work upon.

REFERENCES

Amazon simple storage service (2011). Available: www.aws.amazon.com/s3/

Chun, S. I. B.-G., Maniatis, P., & Naik, M. (2010). Clonecloud: boosting mobile device applications through cloud clone execution. *arXiv preprint arXiv: 1009.3088,*

Cocking, L. (2012). *The Future of Mobile Cloud Infrastructure.* Available: http://www.guardtime. com/2012/08/13/the-future-of mobile cloud- infrastructure/

Cuervo, A. B. E., Cho, D.-k., Wolman, A., Saroiu, S., Chandra, R., & Bahl, P. (2010). Maui: making smartphones last longer with code offload. *8th international conference on Mobile systems, applications, and services,* pp. 49–62. doi:10.1145/1814433.1814441

Cuervo, A. B. E., Cho, D.-k., Wolman, A., Saroiu, S., Chandra, R., & Bahl, P. (2010).Making smartphones last longer with code offload. In *8th international conference on Mobile systems, applications, and services,* pp. 49–62.

Dejan Kovachev, Y. C. R. K. (2009). *Mobile Cloud Computing: A Comparison of Application Models.* Middleware Springer.

Dinh, C. L. H. T., Niyato, D., & Wang, P. (2011). *A survey of mobile cloud computing: architecture, applications, and approaches.* Wireless Communications and Mobile Computing.

Doukas, T. P. I. M. C. (2010). Mobile healthcare information management utilizing cloud computing and Android OS. In *Engineering in Medicine and Biology Society (EMBC), Annual International Conference of the IEEE.,* pp. 1037–1040, Aug. 31-Sept. 4 2010.

Gartner. Available: http://www.gartner.com/newsroom/id/1529214

Guan, X. K. L., Song, M., & Song, J. (2011), A survey of research on mobile cloud computing. In *Computer and Information Science (ICIS) IEEE/ACIS 10th International Conference on. IEEE,* pp. 387– 392. doi:10.1109/ICIS.2011.67

Han Qi, A. G. (2012). Research on Mobile Cloud Computing: Review, Trend and Perspectives. In *Proceedings of the Second International Conference on Digital Information and Communication Technology and its Applications (DICTAP), IEEE,* pp. 195-202.

Kemp, N. P. R., Kielmann, T., & Bal, H. (2012). Cuckoo: a computation offloading framework for smartphones. Mobile Computing, Applications, and Services (Vol. 76, pp. 59–79). Springer. doi:10.1007/978-3-642-29336-8_4

Khalife, R. F. I. (2011). Mobile cloud computing educational tool for image/video processing algorithms. In Digital Signal Processing Workshop and IEEE Signal Processing Education Workshop (DSP/SPE), pp. 529–533, 4-7 Jan 2011.

Kosta, A. A. S., Hui P., Mortier, R., & Zhang, X. (2011). Unleashing the Power of Mobile Cloud Computing using ThinkAir. *Computing Research Repository.*

March, Y. G. V., Leonardi, E., Goh, G., Kirchberg, M., & Lee, B. S. (2011). μcloud: Towards a new paradigm of rich mobile applications. *Procedia Computer Science, 5,* 618–624. doi:10.1016/j.procs.2011.07.080

Marinelli, E. (2009). *Cloud Computing on Mobile Devices using MapReduce* (Master Thesis Draft). Computer Science Dept., Carnegie Mellon University (CMU).

Mascolo, C. (2010). The power of mobile computing in a social era. *IEEE Internet Computing, 14*(6), 76–79. doi:10.1109/MIC.2010.150

Niroshinie Fernando, S. W. L., & Rahayu, W. (2013). Mobile cloud computing: A survey. *Future Generation Computer Systems, 29,* 84–106.

Prerez, S. (2009). *Why cloud computing is the future of mobile.* Available: http://www.readwriteweb.com

Ruay-Shiung Chang, J. G., & Gao, V. Jingsha He; Roussos, G.; Wei-Tek Tsai, "Mobile Cloud Computing Research - Issues, Challenges and Needs," *Service Oriented System Engineering (SOSE), 2013 IEEE 7th International Symposium on* pp. 442, 453, 25-28 March 2013.

Sanaei, S. A. Z., Gani, A., & Khokhar, R. H. (2012) "Tripod of requirements in horizontal heterogeneous mobile cloud computing," *Proceedings of the 1st International Conference on Computing, Information Systems, and Communications.*

Satyanarayanan, M. A. K. M., Helfrich, C. J., & Hallaron, D. R. O. (2005). Towards seamless mobility on pervasive hardware. Pervasive and Mobile Computing, 1, 157–189.

Satyanarayanan, P. B. M., Caceres, R., & Davies, N. (2009). The case for VM-based cloudlets in mobile computing. *IEEE Pervasive Computing / IEEE Computer Society [and] IEEE Communications Society*, *8*(4), 14–23. doi:10.1109/MPRV.2009.82

US Mobile Data Market Updates. (2010). Chetan Sharma Consulting. Retrieved from http://www.chetansharma.com/usmarketupdateq32010.html

Yang, T. P. X., & Shen, J. (2010). On 3g mobile e- commerce platform based on cloud computing. In *Ubimedia Computing (U-Media), 3rd IEEE International Conference on. IEEE,* pp. 198–201, 5-6 July 2010.

Zhong, B. W. L., & Wei, H. (2012). Cloud Computing Applied in the Mobile Internet. In *7th International Conference on Computer Science & Education (ICCSE),* pp. 218-221. doi:10.1109/ICCSE.2012.6295061

Chapter 8
A Survey of Cloud–Based Services Leveraged by Big Data Applications

S. ZerAfshan Goher
National University of Sciences and Technology, Pakistan

Barkha Javed
National University of Sciences and Technology, Pakistan

Peter Bloodsworth
National University of Sciences and Technology, Pakistan

ABSTRACT

Due to the growing interest in harnessing the hidden significance of data, more and more enterprises are moving to data analytics. Data analytics require the analysis and management of large-scale data to find the hidden patterns among various data components to gain useful insight. The derived information is then used to predict the future trends that can be advantageous for a business to flourish such as customers' likes/dislikes, reasons behind customers' churn and more. In this paper, several techniques for the big data analysis have been investigated along with their advantages and disadvantages. The significance of cloud computing for big data storage has also been discussed. Finally, the techniques to make the robust and efficient usage of big data have also been discussed.

INTRODUCTION

The rapid advancement of the technology has proliferated the numbers of devices connected to the internet such as laptops, mobile devices, cameras, thermostats, wifi routers, electronic appliances, wireless sensors and more. According to a survey conducted by the Gartner, there are nearly fourteen billion devices connected to the internet so far and the number is expected to increase about twenty to hundred billion by the year 2020 (*Gartner Says 4.9 Billion Connected "Things" Will Be in Use in 2015*, 2014). The ever growing number of electronic devices using internet produces tremendous data streams and

DOI: 10.4018/978-1-4666-9767-6.ch008

Copyright © 2016, IGI Global. Copying or distributing in print or electronic forms without written permission of IGI Global is prohibited.

aids to the concept of internet of things (IoT) where every day physical machines can be connected to the internet using wireless, RFID & sensor technologies (Gubbi, Buyya, Marusic, & Palaniswami, 2013). This extracted information from the raw data is exploited to draw smart decisions automatically such as the temperature and moisture sensor present in a wrist watch can help to adjust room temperature accordingly. Beside advantages, this growing interest in harnessing the internet has produced a massive amount of heterogeneous data that is difficult to handle by the conventional enterprise systems (Bandyo-padhyay & Sen, 2011). This voluminous data is generated frequently at a high speed and is commonly referred to as big data. Big data is sheer volume of data that is so diverse and complex to be processed by a conventional database management system (DBMS) (Fan & Bifet, 2012). In order to handle this massive scale of data, data storage techniques need to be redefined. In this work, a survey of some of the important data storage techniques from the perspective of big data has been conducted.

The big data is originated from multiple sources and is therefore lacks a common standard pattern. Big data format can be categorized into three main classes which are: structured, semi-structured and unstructured data (Wu, Zhu, Wu, & Ding, 2014). The data in a structural approach is stored in the form of tables, where each table is composed of several rows and columns. The data stored in this format can be easily stored, analyzed and queried, whereas, the unstructured data lacks any fixed pattern and is found on a large scale such as website contents, blog entries, PDF files, radar data, satellites images, videos, social media data, business documents and more. The semi structured data lies in between; it is a type of structured data that does not own a rigid format. In semi-structured data, markers and tags are used to identify certain content of the data such as xml. Email is one of the examples of semi-structured data that has some fixed field (i.e. sender, receiver, date and time) along with some unstructured data (i.e. attachment and email body). The unstructured data is however generated more quickly than the other types of data and represents 80 percent of all the informatics data, whereas, structured and semi-structured schemes only captures five to ten percent of data (*Structured, semi-structured and unstructured data*, 2014). The management of this massive amount of data is beyond the capabilities of conventional DBMS and requires a scalable infrastructure that could mine data to gain useful insights. For instance, the text based sentiment analysis of the customer-centric data from social media helps to understand and to predict the customer behavior towards a particular product or campaign.

Data analytics is the core part of big data, sophisticated quantitative methods i.e. computational mathematics, data mining, machine learning, and artificial intelligence are used to perform analysis and to discover hidden patterns for enhancing business productivity (Fisher, DeLine, Czerwinski, & Drucker, 2012). Big data requires a scalable architecture and high processing power to operate large volume of distributed data. However, the high adoption cost associated with the hardware procurement makes it difficult for enterprises to leverage the up-to-date tools and technologies to process volumetric data. Cloud computing is a viable option in such scenarios as it reduced the resource acquisition cost by implementing pay-as-you-go model (Vaquero, Merino, Caceres, & Lindner, 2009). The elasticity of cloud technology makes it a good candidate to manage the big data applications. Cloud facilitates on the fly expansion of underlying infrastructure i.e. when the resource demands increases beyond the capacity of an enterprise then the cloud resources can be reserved with minimum effort. This relief user from the burden of over-provisioning where an enterprise invests heavily to build up its infrastructure, however, in case of low resource demands the added capacity goes underutilized which reduced revenue streams. Cloud-oriented big data analytics provides pre-built setup to support data-driven decision making (Buyya, Yeo, Venugopal, Broberg, & Brandic, 2009).

In order to better manage the massive amount of data, cloud provides three different service models known as platform as a service (PAAS), software as a service (SAAS) and infrastructure as a service (IAAS) to businesses and thus enables them to select the most appropriate service model according to their requirements. Software as a service lies at the top of the cloud service stack. It provides various functionalities such as automatic updates, patch management, global accessibility, easy software administration and software compatibility across a wide range of businesses. SAAS helps big-data clients to perform data analysis by subscribing to a public cloud provider. The PAAS, on the other hand, provides pretested technologies and platform to lower the risks of new system development. Businesses having low capital can use PAAS to build, run and test their application. In addition, PAAS also provides advanced applications that offer cost-effective solutions to analyze volumetric data effectively. The infrastructure as a service presents the lowest level of abstraction (Armbrust et al., 2009). The IAAS's users can access the underlying hardware of a virtual datacenter by using virtual machines. In case of high workload, IAAS assists users to add capacity by deploying more virtual machines. The cloud service model enables enterprises to better assess big data value before using any significant company resources.

Keeping the aforementioned factors in mind, this paper discusses some of the key factors related to big data realm such as the literature regarding data stores used for big data storage and processing. Moreover, the selection and adoption of the most suitable cloud provider to run big data applications has also been discussed.

LITERATURE REVIEW

Data Stores for BigData Processing

Initially, relational database management system (RDBMS) was used to store data as it provides a convenient relational-structure to save and access data with enforced relationship between the tables. Beside many advantages, the RDBMS failed to cope with the rapid growth of data and is subjected to several problems. Among the several issues raised by the RDMS, the lower performance is the most critical one. As the number of tables in the relational database increases its performance becomes a bottleneck, therefore, it is not considered as a scalable solution to handle big data. Further, RDBMS supports a rigid-schema that restricts it from operating disparate data (Pavlo et al., 2009). To enhance performance, traditional RDBMS is complemented by new database technologies i.e. NewSQL, NoSQL and parallel databases to manage the peta bytes of data. The first step in this regard was the evolution of parallel databases which strives to resolve the low performance issues of RDBMS. It was introduced to improve query execution time by utilizing multiple hard disks and CPUs simultaneously (Hashem et al., 2015). Parallel databases assist in executing several operations in parallel such as data loading, indexing and data querying. The Gamma, one of the popular parallel databases, speeds up the query execution time by splitting a given query and assigns it to multiple DBMS nodes for processing. In this scheme, the data analysis is executed concurrently at each node. The parallelization feature is largely used in business intelligence for data analysis such as discovering data interrelationships. However, one of the shortcomings of the parallel databases is that they are solely used to handle structured data.

NewSQL is another form of modern relational database management system that provides efficient execution time for online transaction processing (OLTP) while guaranteeing ACID properties of traditional database system (Kumar, Bhushan, Gupta, Sharma, & Gupta, 2014). It provides a user-friendly structure for large-scale data storing and management. However, similar to parallel database NewSQL also promotes schema-oriented data management. The strict relational schema can be a limitation to certain applications such as blogs over the web, which contains different set of attributes that are difficult to capture in a relational format. Moreover, there is always an excessive amount of time and money required to load unstructured data in traditional databases, therefore, new technologies have emerged to manage data without relying heavily on data schema. In order to deal with unstructured data effectively, high-profile cloud providers i.e. Amazon, IBM, Google, Microsoft and Rackspace provide cloud-based database platforms (i.e. Hadoop and NoSQL) to store the data generated by big data applications.

NoSql databases present a completely different infrastructure to handle heavy workload of data. It provides a mechanism to store and retrieve data in other than the tabular form and is primarily used for analytical processing of extensive datasets (Moniruzzaman & Hossain, 2013). It is distributed in nature and enables parallel execution of large-scale data across a set of commodity servers. The data in this scheme is not composed of tables and SQL is not used as a query language. Some of the popular examples of NoSql are Bigtable, HBase, Redis, Cassandra and Voldemort. NoSQL databases are open source and so have a price advantage over other commercial databases. The advanced functionalities of NoSql such as online transaction processing (OLTP), predictive analysis, business intelligence and social networking make it suitable for big data paradigm. NoSQL databases are further categorized into four classes which are: key-value stores, wide-column stores, document stores and graph databases.

The key-value stores, commonly known as key-value database save data in the form of text based values in a hash table. In order to locate records, alpha-numeric identifier known as key is used to search for an exact match. Due to its simplicity and fast data retrieval, this scheme is used by Amazon and linkedin to manage their user profiles and product details. Dynamo, Redis, Riak are the examples of key-value stores . On the other hand, a document database as the name implies is used to manage and store documents in a standard data exchange format i.e. Xml, Json and Bson. This type of database has efficient query processing and indexing features and is generally used to store semi-structured data such as email messages and xml documents. Lotus notes, Clusterpoint, Apache CouchDB, MongoDB, and OrientDB are some of its popular examples. Similarly, the wide-column database is another form of a distributed database which replicates Google file system and BigTable data storage structure. This type of database is used for large-scale batch-oriented data processing and is explicitly use for predictive analysis. Wide-column data store correlates the data and finds the hidden patterns to make decision making more intelligent. Some of the widely used column databases are Accumulo, Druid, HBase, Vertica.

Moreover, in some situations the relationship among the various data components is crucial to consider for accurate data processing i.e. representing the data of social networks. The graph databases were evolved to emphasize data relationships graphically. The graph database is similar to an object oriented database where the nodes in the graph represent an object and the edges represent data relationship. This type of database is required when the relationship between the data nodes is more important than the data itself, for instance, pattern detection, network analysis, bio-informatics, and recommendations engines. Graph databases are commonly used by the yahoo, facebook and Amazon to analyze and model their customer's behavior and to forecast future demands. Allegro, Neo4J, InfiniteGraph, OrientDB, Virtuoso and Stardog are some of the examples of graph databases. The Apache Hadoop is another well-known industry initiative to develop cost-efficient software for scalable, reliable, distributed storage and computing (Chen, Alspaugh, Katz, 2012). The leading big data practitioners such as Google, Apple, Facebook are currently running Hadoop as their analytical engine. Hadoop has in fact become a defacto standard to manage intensive and heterogeneous data in a dynamic environment like cloud. It is coded in java and has two main parts known as Hadoop distributed file system (HDFS) and MapReduce. Hadoop distributed file system runs on the top of a local file system and is used to save extremely large amount of datasets i.e. petabyte, and zettabyte. HDFS is highly fault tolerant and can scale to thousands of machines as necessary. Nodes in this scheme are divided in to two types known as master and slave. The master node receives the incoming data, divides it into manageable units and after partitioning assigned it to one or more slaves for further processing. Moreover, it is also the responsibility of master node to maintain file system namespace and to control access to files by users.

The MapReduce, a staple of Hadoop, is widely preferred by the cloud providers. It is a computational platform that takes input of large-scale data and distributes it to several servers known as Hadoop cluster for parallel processing. MapReduce contains two functions known as mapper and reducer. The reducer function splits a given problem into manageable chunks and speeds up the processing whereas the mapper performs the data filtering tasks. Several reducers can run in parallel as they are independent of each other. A task that would take twenty hours to execute on RDBMS will only take less than three minutes when distributed across Hadoop clusters. In order to make MapReduce fault tolerant, after performing every operation the data is stored on a disk to reduce data loss which incurs significant overhead (Jian, Ooi, Shi, & Wu, 2010). In addition, another problem with MapReduce is that it only performs the one-pass batch processing of the data. This increases the execution time of complex multi-pass analysis functions (i.e. graph processing and data exploration) which are the core part of big data analytics. Moreover, it provides a procedural programming interface and the execution of interactive applications over such a platform requires the data sharing across various MapReduce steps. One of the possible solutions to allow data sharing in MapReduce is to write data into distributed file system which causes data duplication. Further, experiments revealed that while running complex machine learning algorithms on MapReduce this overhead consumed more than ninety percent of the execution time which is undesirable. In order to resolve this problem, an innovative open source structure known as spark was evolved that is much faster than Hadoop to perform real time stream processing.

To reduce the data duplication overhead and to speedup execution, the spark it keeps the data in memory rather than to replicate it over disks. Spark utilizes resilient distributed datasets (RDDs) to keep data in memory. RDDs can be defined as the group of objects that are distributed across a set of cluster nodes to work concurrently (*Cluster Computing Comparisons: MapReduce vs. Apache Spark*, 2014). In this scheme, after capturing the data it is immediately forwarded to the analytical engines for further refinement and the results are dispatched to the dashboard. This type of processing is being used by all types of big data applications i.e. recommendation engines provided by the various domains. To implement security spark creates a *Linage Graph* by mapping the data transformation at the every step of processing in the form of a graph. In case of any failure, the sequence of nodes found in the linage graph is used to rebuild the lost information. Besides advantages, one of the limitations of spark is the absence of distributed database storage. Therefore, big data projects usually require installing spark on the top of the Hadoop to perform complex operations. By incorporating both technologies, the data analytics applications running on the spark can make use of the data stored in the Hadoop distributed file system (HDFS). However, the selection among Hadoop and Spark depends on the nature of the application i.e. if an organization only produces and manages limited amount of data then in this case spark would be a good solution and there will be no need to combine it with Hadoop. The following table shows the major differences between the aforementioned big data storage techniques.

Table 1. Comparison of data stores used for BigData

Datastore	Distributed Computing	ACID Compliance	Schema rigidity	Language	Examples
RDBMS	×	√	√	SQL	Oracle, postgresql,sql server, MySql SQLite
NewSQL	√	√	√	API program	MySQL Cluster, Google Spanner, Clustrix, VoltDB, MemSQL, Pivotal's SQLFire
NoSQL	√	×	×	SQL	DynamoDB,Hbase,MangoDB, BigTable, SimpleDB, Redis
Hadoop	√	√	×	API program	Hive, Pig, Zoo keeper, Cassandra, spark

Cloud Solutions for BigData Processing and Storage

The emergence of IoT has brought many innovations in the society. The widespread of the internet technologies have converted conventional cities in to smart ones and thus contributed to the exponential data growth. A smart city utilizes the information and communication technologies to raise the quality of life of its citizens. It contains tools and technologies to discover the hidden information from the large scale datasets daily generated by a society. The discovered knowledge can be then used to provide better transport services, energy efficient mechanisms, improved public security, waste management and better health solutions for the public. The goal of smart cities is to provide better urban governance and planning using smart hardware and software such as RFID, smart phones, smart house hold appliances without compromising data security. The management of smart cities is quite a challenging task due to several reasons: i) Heterogonous data format i.e. structured, unstructured and semi-structured ii) data reliability iii) requirements of cross-thematic applications such as energy, transport, water etc. In order to handle the massive amount of data produced by the smart cities, cloud-based big data analytics architecture was proposed by (Naphade, Banavar, Harrison, Paraszczak, & Morris, 2011). The model was implemented by integrating the Hadoop and Spark technologies.

To provide a unified view of data, the architecture was divided into three tiers. In the model, the lower layer was responsible to collect the diverse data from multidisciplinary sources. After data gathering, the data was classified into different categories on the basis of its characteristic. The lower layer was also equipped with certain repositories to provide data storage for the processed data. The middle layer was the resource and data mapping layer which links the data stored in the repositories. The major challenge in implementing the data linkage was the heterogeneity of the data. During processing the data mapping layer worked to explore the common data-patterns to inter-relate data components. The top layer of the system contained analytical engine that process data for application specific purposes. This layer utilized the linked data from the middle layer to perform queries and to generate results.

Data warehouse is another strategy used to analyze the hidden data patterns of an organization (Lyon, 2014). A data warehouse represents central repositories that are used to store current and historical data from disparate locations. It refers to any technology that is used to store data for later analysis it could be a relational database or Hadoop. The data in a data warehouse is organized in a subject-oriented manner i.e. sales, inventory etc. A data warehouse captured and stored data in an unmodified way. However, if the changes are required then separate copies of the modified data is created and stored. It used on line analytical processing tools (OLAP) to perform data analysis and to generate reports. The main objective of a data warehouse is to draw smart decisions based on the reliable data available in a corporation.

There are various types of data warehouse such as data mart, online analytical processing (OLAP), online transaction processing (OLTP) and predictive analytics. The data mart is primarily used to collect and save records of a single department. It manages subject-wise records to improve the internal functions of an organization. However, due to single-subject focus it is used to get data from limited sources. OLAP on the other hand, use data mining techniques to maintain data in multi-dimensional schemas. While the OLAP is used to analyze data, the OLTP is used to control every day transactions. It contains detailed data to support data integrity and fast query processing. Contrary to the OLAP, OLTP arranges data in a highly normalized relational structure. In order to deal with failure, it performs data backup on regular basis. The last type of the data warehouse is known as predictive analysis which used sophisticated mathematical models to uncover the hidden data meaning to predict future trends. Predictive analysis operates on historical data to improve customer relationship management. Beside advantages, one of the limitations of a data warehouse is its inability to manage unstructured and semi-structured data. However, new analytical data warehouse techniques have been introduced to manage heterogeneous set of data. It contains automated business intelligence tools to convert data in to structured format and then to store it.

The big data and data warehouse can be used collectively to facilitate advanced operations for instance, a company can utilize the data gathered from its social networking platform with the data present in the data warehouse to update the friend circle of a user (Kambatla, Kollias, Kumar, Grama, 2014). The extracted knowledge is helpful to find out the social influence of a user. The data is then pushed back to the data warehouse so that a campaign manager can manage it accordingly. Moreover, brokerage system can incorporate data warehouse and big data analytics techniques to keep records of the raw click stream on a website. In this method, the data from the web is gathered by utilizing the Hadoop and is then forwarded to the data warehouse which maps it with the organization marketing campaigns. After successful mapping, customer preferences are analyzed and relevant investment suggestions can be forwarded to the customer. The Hadoop and MapReduce solutions are increasingly being coupled by the data warehouse to leverage the capabilities of both technologies. By technological coupling, Hadoop jobs can use data warehouse as a data source and can forward the queries to the data warehouse for further processing.

In order to utilize big data applications conveniently the selection of a suitable big data public cloud platform is a challenging task as it entails consideration of right big data technologies, suitable platform selection, economical cloud resources, performance of cloud resources, location, capacity, quality of services etc. At present number of IAAS and PAAS providers are leveraging their services for big data analytics; selection of most suitable and economical resources of which is a time consuming task as customers are required to compare each and every provider for their applications. The diverse models of cloud providers further exacerbate this challenge. Further, customers often rely on well-known cloud providers for big data services (*How to choose the best cloud big data platform*, 2015). However, emerging cloud providers such as JoyentCloud and Qubole also provide strong big data credentials. Similarly, there are also other emerging cloud providers who are working to improve their services. The customers are often unaware or reluctant to consider new and emerging providers which limit the business of emerging providers.

The selection of a suitable public cloud provider requires comparison among providers which is a challenging task. Therefore, a platform is required which assist in automatic selection of a suitable cloud provider. A platform similar to (Javed, Bloodsworth, Rasool, Munir, & Rana, 2015) is required for the selection of big data cloud services. This system provides automated selection based on customers' requirements. However for big data cloud services, the system must accommodate features such as choice of big data technologies for respective application, locality of data center as big data mostly require large data transfer etc. Furthermore, for selection of suitable resources/ providers resource monitoring tools such as Otus (Ren, Lopez, & Gibson, 2011) can be integrated with a cloud-based system. Such integration will assist customers to automatically monitor resources during selection and comparison of cloud providers and will simplify big data management.

FUTURE RESEARCH DIRECTIONS

The massive amount of big data makes it difficult to be managed by the conventional data storage systems. Therefore, many organizations and IT industry are moving towards the cloud due to its promising solutions for large-scale data management. Cloud computing provides virtual data centers with large-scale capabilities to handle the dynamic workload. Enterprises can get the required services by selecting a suitable cloud provider. However, despite great advancement, cloud is still in its infancy due to the security and privacy concerns. Cloud based data management can be made more robust by incorporating security mechanisms. This will provide more confidence to users and motivates them to leverage cloud services for big data analytics without any security concerns.

CONCLUSION

Due to the growing interest in harnessing the hidden significance of data, more and more enterprises are moving to data analytics. Data analytics require the analysis and management of large-scale data to find the hidden patterns among various data components and to gain useful insight. The derived information is then used to predict the future trends that can be advantageous for a business to flourish such as the knowledge about customers' likes/dislikes, reasons behind customers' churn and more. In this work, several techniques for the big data analysis have been investigated along with their advantages and disadvantages. The significance of cloud computing service model for big data storage has also been discussed. The literature shows the significance of cloud computing in acting as a facilitator to manage big data. Form the above discussion, it can be concluded that the cloud computing appears as a potential solution for the risks faced by the big data applications such as the unanticipated data bursting, immense storage and computing power needs.

The cloud not only provides on-demand IT infrastructure to handle the spikes in the demands but also provides efficient database management tools and technologies to handle the massive data growth. The cloud-based analytics services help the low-funded enterprises to improve their internal operations and to forecast their future demands by leveraging cloud resources. Moreover, the cloud pricing model assists enterprises to increase their capital by reducing customer's churn to a minimum level. The only problem faced by the cloud adoption is of security and privacy which can be overcome by introducing robust security mechanisms. Furthermore, the availability of large number of public cloud providers makes the selection and comparison of cloud providers quite challenging. An automated system is therefore required that could select the most suitable and economical platform for cloud-based big data processing and storage. Such a system will also benefit providers other than well-known providers who provide strong big data credentials.

REFERENCES

Armbrust, M., Fox, A., Griffith, R., Anthony, D. J., Randy, H. K., Konwinski, A., . . . Zaharia, M. (2009). *Above the Clouds: A Berkeley View of Cloud Computing*. University of California at Berkley, USA. Technical Rep UCB/EECS-2009-28.

Bandyopadhyay, D., & Sen, J. (2011). Internet of things: Applications and challenges in technology and standardization. *Wireless Personal Communications, 58*(1), 49–69. doi:10.1007/s11277-011-0288-5

Buyya, R., Yeo, C., Venugopal, S., Broberg, J., & Brandic, I. (2009). Cloud Computing and Emerging IT Platforms: Vision, Hype, and Reality for Delivering Computing as the 5th Utility. *Future Generation Computer Systems, 25*(6), 599–616. doi:10.1016/j.future.2008.12.001

Chen, Y., Alspaugh, S., & Katz, R. H. (2012). Interactive analytical processing in big data systems: A cross-industry study of mapreduce workloads. *Proceedings of VLDB Endowment, 5*(12), 1802–1813. doi:10.14778/2367502.2367519

Fan, W., & Bifet, A. (2012). Mining Big Data: Current Status and Forecast to the Future. *SIGKDD Explorations Newsletter, 14*.

Fisher, D., DeLine, R., Czerwinski, M., & Drucker, S. (2012). Interactions with big data analytics. *Interaction, 19*(3), 50–59. doi:10.1145/2168931.2168943

Gartner. (2014). *Gartner Says 4.9 Billion Connected "Things" Will Be in Use in 2015*. Retrieved July 5, 2015, from http://www.gartner.com/newsroom/id/2905717

Gubbi, J., Buyya, R., Marusic, S., & Palaniswami, M. (2013). Internet of things (iot): A vision, architectural elements, and future directions. *Future Generation Computer Systems, 29*(7), 1645–1660. doi:10.1016/j.future.2013.01.010

Hashem, I., Yaqoob, I., Anuar, N. B., Mokhtar, S., Gani, A., & Khan, S. U. (2015). The rise of "big data" on cloud computing: Review and open research issues. *Information Systems, 47*, 98–115. doi:10.1016/j.is.2014.07.006

Javed, B., Bloodsworth, P., Rasool, R., Munir, K., & Rana, O. (2015). *Cloud Market Maker: An automated dynamic pricing marketplace for cloud users, 2015*. .10.1016/j.future.2015.06.004

Jian, D., Ooi, B. C., Shi, L., & Wu, S. (2010). The performance of mapreduce: An in-depth study. *Proceedings of VLDB Endowment, 3*(1-2), 472–483. doi:10.14778/1920841.1920903

Kambatla, K., Kollias, G., Kumar, V., & Grama, A. (2014). Trends in big data analytics. *Journal of Parallel and Distributed Computing, 74*(7), 2561–2573. doi:10.1016/j.jpdc.2014.01.003

Kumar, R., Bhushan, B., Gupta, S., Sharma, Y., & Gupta, N. (2014). Apache Hadoop, NoSQL and NewSQL Solutions of Big Data. *International Journal of Modern Computer Science, 3*.

Lyon, L. (2014). *Integrating Big Data into the Enterprise Data Warehouse*. Retrieved July 2, 2015, from http://www.databasejournal.com/features/db2/integrating-big-data-into-the-enterprise-data-warehouse/

Moniruzzaman, A., & Hossain, S. (2013). Nosql database: New era of databases for big data analytics-classification, characteristics and comparison. *International Journal of Database Theory & Application*, *6*(4), 1–14.

Naphade, M., Banavar, G., Harrison, C., Paraszczak, J., & Morris, R. (2011). Smarter cities and their innovation challenges. Computer, 44, 32–39.

Nolle, T. (n.d.). *How to choose the best cloud big data platform. A vendor cloud platform comparison guide.* Retrieved July 4, 2015, from http://searchcloudapplications.techtarget.com/tip/How-to-choose-the-best-cloud-big-data-platform

Pavlo, A., Paulson, E., Rasin, A., Abadi, D. J., DeWitt, D. J., Madden, S., & Stonebraker, M. (2009). A comparison of approaches to large-scale data analysis. In *Proc. ACM International Conference on Management of Data (SIGMOD'09)*. New York: ACM.

Philip, N. (2014). *Cluster Computing Comparisons: MapReduce vs. Apache Spark*. Retrieved July 5, 2015, from http://www.qubole.com/blog/big-data/spark-vs-mapreduce/

Ren, K., López, J., & Gibson, G. (2011). Otus: Resource Attribution in Data-intensive Clusters. In *Proceedings of the second international workshop on MapReduce and its applications*. doi:10.1145/1996092.1996094

Ronk, J. (2014). *Structured, Semi-Structured and Unstructured Data*. Retrieved July 2, 2015, from https://jeremyronk.wordpress.com/2014/09/01/structured-semi-structured-and-unstructured-data/

Vaquero, L. M., Merino, L. R., Caceres, J., & Lindner, M. (2009). A break in the clouds: Towards a cloud definition, *ACM Computer Communication. RE:view*, *39*, 50–55.

Wu, X., Zhu, X., Wu, G. Q., & Ding, W. (2014). Data mining with big data. *Transactions on Knowledge and Data Engineering: IEEE*, *26*(1), 97–107. doi:10.1109/TKDE.2013.109

KEY TERMS AND DEFINITIONS

Big Data: A large volume of data that is gathered form heterogeneous sources and is difficult to manage by traditional database systems.

Cloud Computing: An innovative model of delivering various IT applications and services over the internet. User can access cloud services anywhere in the world by using a web browser. Virtualization is considered as the core part of the cloud that enables access to the underlying infrastructure of data-centers in the form of virtual machines.

Data Analytics: Techniques that are used to find the hidden meaning of data such as data mining, artificial intelligence etc. Data analytics is used to take smart decisions that cause innovation in the internal processes of an enterprise.

Parallel Database: Parallel databases are used for the efficient processing of volumetric data. This type of database is used for the parallel execution of several operations such as data loading, processing and evaluating queries.

Relational Database System: Tools and techniques that are used to store data in relational format. The relational databases provide a convenient mechanism to store and manage data in a schema-oriented manner.

Chapter 9
Need of Hadoop and Map Reduce for Processing and Managing Big Data

Manjunath Thimmasandra Narayanapppa
BMS Institute of Technology, India

A. Channabasamma
Acharya Institute of Technology, India

Ravindra S. Hegadi
Solapur University, India

ABSTRACT

The amount of data around us in three sixty degrees getting increased second on second and the world is exploding as a result the size of the database used in today's enterprises, which is growing at an exponential rate day by day. At the same time, the need to process and analyze the bulky data for business decision making has also increased. Several business and scientific applications generate terabytes of data which have to be processed in efficient manner on daily bases. Data gets collected and stored at unprecedented rates. Moreover the challenge here is not only to store and manage the huge amount of data, but even to analyze and extract meaningful values from it. This has contributed to the problem of big data faced by the industry due to the inability of usual software tools and database systems to manage and process the big data sets within reasonable time limits. The main focus of the chapter is on unstructured data analysis.

INTRODUCTION

Big data is the collection of datasets that are huge in size and difficult to handle by commonly used data processing tools and its applications. These datasets are unstructured and usually originated from various sources such as social media, scientific applications, social sensors, surveillance cameras, electronic health records, web documents, archives, web logs and business applications. They are larger in the size

DOI: 10.4018/978-1-4666-9767-6.ch009

Copyright © 2016, IGI Global. Copying or distributing in print or electronic forms without written permission of IGI Global is prohibited.

with fast data in/out. Organizations would be interested in capturing and analyzing these datasets because they can add considerable value to the decision making process. However, such processing may involve complex workloads, which move the boundaries of what are possible using traditional data management and data warehousing techniques and technologies. Further, big data must have high value and ensure trust for decision making process. These data come from diverse sources and heterogeneity is one more important property besides volume, variety, velocity, value and veracity. Data gets collected and stored at unprecedented rates. Moreover the challenge is not only to store and manage the large amount of data, but even to analyze and extract meaningful values from it. This has contributed to the problem of big data faced by the industry due to the inability of usual database systems and software tools to manage and process the big data sets within reasonable time limits. Processing of Big data can consist of various operations depending on usage like culling, classification, indexing, highlighting, searching, faceting, etc.

Two significant data management trends for processing the big data are relational DBMS products meant for analytical workloads (also called analytic RDBMSs, or ADBMSs) and the non-relational systems (sometimes called NoSQL systems) meant for processing multi-structured data. A non-relational system can be used to generate analytics from big data or to pre-process big data before consolidated into a data warehouse.

Analytic RDBMS - ADBMS

An analytic RDBMS is an integrated solution for managing the data and generating analytics that offers better price/performance, simplified management and administration. The performance improvements are achieved by making use of massively parallel processing architectures, data compression, enhanced data structures and the capability to push analytical processing into DBMS.

Non-Relational Systems

Non-relational systems are useful for processing the big data where most of data is multi-structured. These are particularly popular with the developers who prefer to use procedural programming language, rather than a structured language such as SQL, to process the data. These systems support different types of data structures including document data, key-value pairs and graphical information.

One of the most important non-relational systems is the Hadoop distributed processing system introduced by open source Apache Software Foundation. Apache defines the Hadoop as, a framework for running applications on large hardware cluster built of commodity hardware. It includes a distributed file system (HDFS) which can distribute and manage bulky data across the nodes of a hardware cluster to offer high throughput. Hadoop makes use of the MapReduce programming model to divide the application processing into small fragments that can be executed on multiple nodes of same cluster to provide massively parallel processing. The Hadoop also includes Pig and Hive languages for generating and developing MapReduce programs. Hive includes Hive-QL, which provides subset of SQL.

The main focus of the chapter is on unstructured data analysis. The unstructured data is the information that either does not fit well into relational tables or does not have pre-defined data model. As compared to others the fastest growing type of data is the unstructured data. Some of examples are imagery, sensors, telemetry, video, log files, documents and email data files. Big data is a collection of techniques and technologies that involve new forms of integration to uncover hidden values from large datasets that are complex, diverse and of a massive scale. There are several techniques for gathering, storing, processing, and analyzing big data. This chapter covers the systematic approach for big data problem and the optimal solution using Hadoop cluster, Hadoop Distributed File System (HDFS) for data storage, use of parallel processing to process large data sets and use of Map Reduce programming framework. The techniques share common characteristics of high availability, scale-out and elasticity. Map Reduce, in conjunction with Hadoop Distributed File System (HDFS) and HBase, is a modern approach to analyze unstructured data. The Hadoop clusters are effective means of processing massive data, and this can be optimized with the right architectural approach. Big data analytics is the process of examining big data to uncover hidden patterns, unidentified correlations and other valuable information which may be used to make better business decisions. More data may lead to more accurate analyses. More accurate analyses may lead to better confident decision making. Further, better decisions can lead to greater operational efficiencies, cost reductions and reduced risk.

LITERATURE SURVEY

The term Big Data has been devised to describe the exponential increase, obtain ability and use of information in both structured and unstructured forms. The increase in big data has been driven by escalating volumes of detailed information originating from organizations, mass media and multimedia, social networking platforms and the 'Internet of Things'. Data analytics, the analysis of large data sets has become a fundamental element for both private sector and public sector organizations who wish to compete through ever-evolving technology, productivity advancement, and innovation in research and development. It is also imperative to note the value of what can be termed 'small data'. For small businesses in more traditional sectors the types of business data becoming available will be of smaller volume, slower velocity and narrower variety. Nonetheless, enhanced use of this data in a smart way, and application of analytical techniques can realize business value.

For the purposes of this chapter, data analytics is understood as the mining, analysis, interpretation and purposeful utilization of Data, including Big Data. This process of extracting and analyzing data to generate economic value has been noted as a key future requirement for enterprises and organizations across all sectors. The term big data has become ubiquitous. Due to a shared origin between industry, academia and the media there is no single integrated definition, and various stakeholders present diverse and often contradictory definitions. Jonathan Stuart Ward and Adam Barker attempts to gather the various definitions which have gained some extent of traction and to furnish a clear and concise definition.

As suggested by Google Trends, there are number of technologies which are commonly suggested as being involved in the big data. NoSQL provisions including Amazon Dynamo, CouchDB, MongoDB, Cassandra et al play a critical role in storing large amount of unstructured and vastly variable data. Related to the exploit of NoSQL data stores there is a series of analysis tools and methods including text mining, MapReduce, NLP, machine learning, statistical programming and information visualization. To merit the use of the term big data the application of one of these technologies alone is not sufficient. Rather, trends recommend that it is the combination of a number of technologies and the use of significant data sets that merit the term. The definitions surveyed here all encompass the following: Bigdata is a term that describes the storage and analysis of large and complex data sets using a series of techniques including, but not restricted to: NoSQL, MapReduce and machinelearning.

Apache hadoop is a major innovation in the IT market place last decade. From humble beginnings Apache Hadoop has become a world-wide adoption in data centers. It brings parallel processing in hands of average programmer. As more data centers supports hadoop platform, it becomes imperative to migrate existing data mining algorithms onto hadoop platform for increased parallel processing efficiency. With the introduction of big data analytics, this trend of movement of the existing data mining algorithms to hadoop platform has become rampant. A. N. Nandakumar and Nandita Yambem(2014) explored the current migration activities and challenges in migration.

As data clustering has attracted a significant amount of research attention, so many clustering algorithms have been proposed in the past decades. However, the enlarging data in applications makes clustering of very large scale of data a challenging task. Zhao (2009) proposed a fast parallel k-means clustering algorithm based on MapReduce, which has been widely embraced by both industry and academia. They used speedup, scale up and size up to evaluate the performances of their proposed work. The results show that the proposed algorithm can process large datasets on commodity hardware effectively. One of the problems noticed when testing the Parallel K-means is that, the speed up is not linear. The main reason is that communication overhead increases as we increase the dataset size.

Jimmy Lin and Chris Dyer (2010) gave a very detailed explanation of applying EM algorithms to text processing and fitting those algorithms into the MapReduce programming model. The EM fits naturally into the MapReduce programming model by making each iteration of EM one MapReduce job: mappers map over independent instances and compute the summary statistics, while the reducers sum together the required training statistics and solve the M-step optimization problems. In this work, it was observed that when global data is needed for synchronization of hadoop tasks, it was difficult with current support from hadoop platform.

Zhenhua(2010) applied K-Means algorithm for remote sensing images in Hadoop. One of important lessons learnt while doing this experiment is that hadoop operates only on text and when image has to be represented as text and processed, the overhead in representation and processing is huge even for smaller images. Kang and Christos Faloutsos applied hadoop for graph mining in social networking data. One of the main observations here is that some of the graph mining algorithms cannot be parallelized, so estimated solutions are needed. Anjan Kumar (2012) have implemented Apriori algorithm on Apache Hadoop platform. Contrary to the believe that parallel processing will take less time to get Frequent item sets, they experimental observation proved that multi node Hadoop with differential system configuration (FHDSC) was taking more time. The reason was in way the data has been portioned to the nodes. Gong-Qing Wu (2009) implemented C4.5 decision tree classification algorithm on apache hadoop. In this work, while constructing the bagging ensemble based reduction to construct the final classifier many duplicates were found. These duplicates could not have avoided if proper data partitioning method have been applied.

Support vector machines have been used successfully in many classification tasks. Their computation and storage requirements increase rapidly with the number of training vectors. Zganquan (2012) sun explored the applicability of SVM on Map Reduce platform. Through his experiments he concluded that the Map reduce is able to reduce the training time and the computation time for SVM, the portioning method was very unclear. No relationship between the portioning technique and the performance could be derived. If the portioning heuristics are part of hadoop platform, it would have given fewer burdens to the programmers.

EM algorithm estimates the parameters for hidden variables by maximizing the likelihood. EM is an iterative approach that alternates between performing a expectation step (E-Step) and Maximization step (M-Step). Jiangtao Yin (2012) proposed an EM with frequent updates to convert EM as a parallel algorithm. The cost of frequent updates is very high in Hadoop clusters. To alleviate this problem mechanism based on updates to closest node must be devised. Also heuristics methods must be formed to reduce the frequent updates to block updates. Naïve Bayes is a probabilistic classifier which fits properly to Map reduce architecture. Apache Mahout Implementation of Naïve Bayes has very good performance and reduced the training time. But still improvements can be made it platform is able to support block key value updating mechanism.

The buzz-word big-data refers to the large-scale distributed applications which work on unprecedentedly big data sets. Apache's Hadoop and Google's MapReduce framework are the defacto software systems for big data applications. The surveillance regarding these applications is that they produce a huge amount of intermediate data, and this plentiful information is thrown away once the processing completes. Motivated by this surveillance, a data-aware cache framework for the big-data applications, which is termed as Dache which is explored by Yaxiong Zhao and Jie Wu (2013). In this Dache, tasks present their intermediate results to the cache manager. Before initiating its execution, a task queries the cache manager for likely matched processing outcome, which could accelerate its execution. A fresh cache description method and a cache request and reply protocols are designed. Dache is implemented by extending the related components of the Hadoop. Testbed experiment results show that Dache significantly optimizes the completion time of MapReduce jobs and it also saves a significant chunk of the CPU execution time.

UNSTRUCTURED ANALYTICS

As unstructured data is collected in unprecedented levels, the analysis, rather than the storage of this data becomes a challenge. To address this problem set, new techniques and paradigms are being developed and implemented. This chapter explores one such implementation of unstructured data analytics. The way data storage is viewed has been varying constantly. The current trend for data storage is Hadoop which provides a flexible data storage mechanism for storing extremely huge amount of data and to handle the data intensive scientific applications. It uses the MapReduce programming model and stores the data in HDFS (Hadoop Distributed File System).Hadoop is an Apache open source distributed computing framework, and have been applied in many sites such as Amazon, Face book and Yahoo, and so on. It is a distributed system infrastructure, take advantage of the power of clusters, with high-speed computing and storage ability. It assumes that computing elements and storage will fail, so keep multiple working copies of data to ensure the re-distribution process of the failure of the node. It works in parallel and speed up processing speed through parallel processing. The most central part of the Hadoop framework is: MapReduce and HDFS.

MapReduce as a Data Processing Model

MapReduce, introduced by Dean and Ghemawat in 2004, is a framework for large scale data processing using commodity clusters. Its greatest advantage is the easy scaling of data processing over multiple computing nodes. In the MapReduce model, the data processing primitives are called mappers and reducers. In the mapping phase, the MapReduce takes the input data and feeds each data element to the mapper. In the reducing phase, reducer processes all the outputs from the mapper and arrives at a final result. In general, the mapper is meant to filter and transform the input into something that the reducer can aggregate over. Before developing the MapReduce programming model, Google used hundreds of separate implementations to process and compute large datasets. Most of the computations were quite simple, but the input data was very large. Hence the computations needed to be distributed across hundreds of computers in order to finish calculations in a reasonable time. The MapReduce framework is highly efficient and scalable, and thus can be used to process large datasets. When the MapReduce framework was introduced, Google rewrote its web search indexing system to use the new framework. The indexing system produces the data structures used by Google web search. More than 20 Terabytes of input data was used for this operation. For the first time the indexing system ran as a sequence of eight MapReduce operations, later new phases have been added. Overall, an average of hundred thousand MapReduce jobs is run daily on Google's clusters, more than twenty Petabytes of data processed every day.

The idea of MapReduce is to hide the complex details of data distribution, fault tolerance, parallelization, and load balancing. Like Google's MapReduce, Hadoop uses many machines in a cluster to distribute data. The parallelization doesn't necessarily have to be performed over many machines in a network. There are different implementations of MapReduce for parallelizing computing in various environments. Hadoop is a distributed file system that can run on clusters ranging from a single computer up to many thousands of computers. Hadoop framework was inspired by two systems from Google File System and MapReduce. The framework transparently distributes data, allocates tasks, and parallelizes computations across cluster nodes in a shared-nothing architecture. It is widely used in large scale data centers such as those operated by Google, Amazon and Facebook.

MapReduce is a simple programming model which used for data processing. The same program, Hadoop can run the MapReduce programs write in various languages. Most importantly, MapReduce program is parallel essentially, so we can give the large-scale data analysis to any operators with enough machines. MapReduce has the advantage of handling large data sets, so it is so suitable for cloud computing platform. MapReduce's core task is to divide the data into different logic blocks, programs written with the distributed properties model, can process on distributed clusters in parallel. Its input data is the set of key / value pairs, the output is also the set of key / value pairs. Users will need to divide work into two blocks: Map and Reduce. First Map process each block separately in parallel, the results of these logic blocks are reassembled into a different sort collections, they are processed by the Reduce at last. MapReduce data process model is shown in Figure 1.

Figure 1. MapReduce process architecture

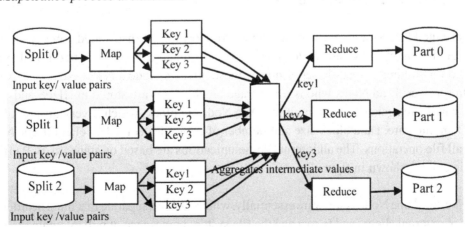

A user-defined Map function takes an input pair, and then generates an intermediate key/value pairs set. MapReduce library put all values with the same intermediate key together, then pass them to the Reduce function. The function is expressed as:

map (in_key, in_value) → (out_key, intermediate_value) list

User-defined Reduce function accepts an intermediate key and related value, it combined the value to form a set of comparatively small value set, and usually this collection is smaller than the input. The function is expressed as:

reduce (out_key, intermediate_value list) → out_value list

A MapReduce execution passes through three phases; Map, Shuffle, and Reduce. In the Map phase, every map task applies the *map* function on its input split. There are no ordering requirements for the input of the Map phase, i.e., a map task can process any part of the input. In the Shuffle phase, the reduce tasks copy and sort their respective parts of the intermediate outputs produced by all map tasks. In the Reduce phase, the reduce tasks apply the *reduce* function on their inputs to produce the output of the MapReduce job. In contrast to the Map phase, the Reduce phase has ordering requirements, i.e., a reduce task cannot apply the *reduce* function on its input unless the respective parts of all the map tasks' outputs are ready and sorted.

MapReduce programs can be run in three modes:

1. **Standalone Mode:** Only run a Java virtual machine, no distributed components. This mode does not use HDFS file system, but use native Linux file system.
2. **Pseudo-Distributed Mode:** Start several JVM process on the same machine, each hadoop daemon runs in a separate JVM process, do "pseudo distributed" operation.
3. **Fully-Distributed Mode:** The real run on multiple machines distributed mode. Which, Standalone mode using the local file system as well as local MapReducer job runner, distributed mode using HDFS and MapReduce daemons?

HDFS - Hadoop Distributed File System

Hadoop Distributed File System, provide underlying support for the distributed computing storage. To client users, HDFS architecture can create, delete, move, or rename the file like traditional architecture, but it is based on building a specific set of nodes, these nodes include a Name Node, who provide the original data services; Data Node, who is file storage blocks. Files are stored in HDFS and are divided into blocks, which are again copied to multiple Data Nodes in block, which is very different from traditional RAID architecture. Data block size and number of copies is decided by client users. Name Node can control all file operations. The all internal communications are based on standard TCP / IP protocol. HDFS architecture is shown in figure 2.

1. **NameNode:** Name Node is software essentially, which run on a separate machine, in order to control access of external clients and to manage the file system namespace, it will maintain the file system tree and the tree index of all files and directories. Name Node will store file system Meta-data in

Figure 2. HDFS Architecture

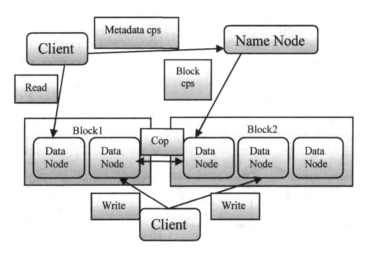

memory, and every file block information is stored in Data Node. This information saves on local disk permanently in two forms: namespace image and edit the log. The user does not need to know the specific location of the node When programming, servers provide storage and location-block services.

2. **DataNode:** Data Node is the basic unit of file storage which is a software running on a separate machine; the Block is stored in the local file system, save the Meta-data of Blocks, and sent all messages of existing Blocks often to Name Node. The Hadoop cluster contains only one Name Node and various DataNodes. Data Node usually connects all systems by a switch in the form of tissue rack. Data Node reacts read and write request from the client. Name Node dependent the message from each Data Node heartbeat. Each message contains a report of the block, according to the report, Name Node verify the block map, and other file system metadata. If Data Node cannot send heartbeat messages, Name Node will take remedial measures and re-copied Block that missing on this node.

3. **Client:** Client is the applications which need for a distributed file system. Their relationship is as follows:
   a. Client send file written request to the NameNode
   b. According to file block configuration and file size, NameNode returned file information of its management section to the Client.
   c. Client divides file into multiple Blocks, according to DataNode address information, write to each DataNode Block orderly.

Files in HDFS are split into smaller blocks, usually of size 64MB, and each block is stored separately in a Data Node and replicated according to specified replication factor to provide data durability. The HDFS client contacts the Name Node to get the location of each of the block, and then interacts with the DataNodes responsible for the data. The Hadoop MapReduce Framework shown in figure3 consists of two components that control the job execution process: the central component called JobTracker and

Figure 3. Hadoop MapReduce Framework

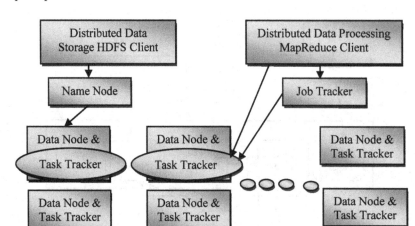

a number of distributed components are called TaskTrackers. Based on the location of job's input, the JobTracker schedules tasks to run on several TaskTrackers and coordinates their execution. The Task-Trackers run tasks allocated to them and send progress reports to the job tracker.

MapReduce's execution model consists of two phases, map and reduce. Map tasks can be run parallel and which are distributed across different nodes. The input data which is stored in HDFS prior to initiating the job, is divided into splits, and for each of the split a map task is assigned to Task Tracker on a node that is close to the split. The map computation starts when its input split is fetched by Task-Tasker, which processes the input split according to the map function presented by the programmer, produces intermediate data in the form of <key, value> pairs, and partitions them for the reduce tasks. In the second phase, the TaskTrackers assigned to do reduce task fetch the intermediate data from the map. The TaskTrackers combine the different partitions, perform the reduce computation, and results are stored back into HDFS (Figure 4).

Figure 4. Data Processing in Hadoop

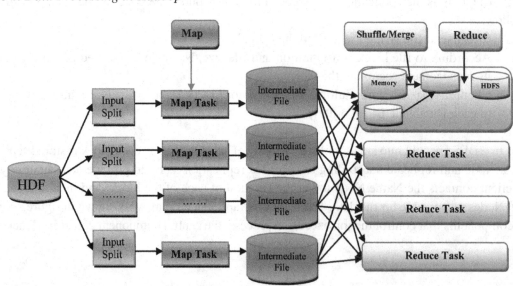

DISCUSSION AND CHALLENGES

Challenges with Big Data

So far, researchers are not able to unify around the essential features of big data. Big data put forward new challenges for data management and analysis, and even for the whole it industry. There are three important aspects which encounter with problems in processing big data, and are presented in detail as follows.

1. **Big Data Storage and Management:** Current technologies of data management systems are not able to satisfy the needs of big data, and the increasing speed of storage capacity is much less than that of data, thus a revolution re-construction of information framework is desperately needed. There is a need to design hierarchical storage architecture. Besides, prior computer algorithms are not able to effectively storage data that is directly acquired from the actual world, due to the heterogeneity of the big data. However, they do excellent in processing homogeneous data. Therefore, how to re-organize data is one big problem in big data management. Virtual server technology can exacerbate the difficulty, raising the prospect of overcommitted resources, especially if communication is poor between the application, server and storage administrators. We also need to solve the bottleneck problems of the high concurrent I/O and single-named node in the present Master-Slave system model.

2. **Big Data Computation and Analysis:** While processing a query in big data, speed is a significant demand. However, the process may take time because mostly it cannot traverse all the related data in the whole database in a short time. In this case, index will be an optimal choice. At present, indices are only aiming at simple data, while big data is becoming more complicated. The combination of appropriate index for big data and up-to-date preprocessing technology will be a desirable solution when we encountered this kind of problems. Application parallelization and divide-and-conquer is natural computational paradigms for approaching big data problems. But obtaining additional computational resources is not as simple as just upgrading to a bigger and more powerful machine on the fly. The traditional serial algorithm is inefficient for the big data. If there is enough data parallelism in the application, users can take benefit of the cloud's reduced cost model to use hundreds of computers for a short time costs.

3. **Big Data Security:** By using online big data application, a lot of companies can greatly reduce their IT cost. However, security and privacy affect the entire big data storage and processing, since there is a massive use of third-party services and infrastructures that are used to host important data or to perform critical operations. The scale of data and applications grow exponentially, and bring huge challenges of dynamic data monitoring and security protection. Unlike traditional security method, security in the big data is mainly in the form of how to process data mining without exposing sensitive information of users. Besides, current technologies of privacy protection are mainly based on static data set, while data is always dynamically changed, including data pattern, deviation of attribute and addition of new data. Thus, it is a challenge to implement effective privacy protection in this complex situation. In addition, legal and regulatory issues also need attention.

Hadoop vs. Traditional

While Hadoop has lived up to much of the hype, there are some circumstances where running work-loads on a traditional database systems may be the better solution. For companies questioning which functionality will better serve their big data business requirements, here are some key questions to be asked when choosing between Hadoop and a traditional database.

- **Data being analyzed is structured or unstructured?**
  - **Structured Data:** The data that resides within the fixed confines of a file or record is known as structured data. Due to the fact that structured data – even in large volumes – can be entered, stored, queried, and examined in a simple and straightforward way, this type of data is best functioned by a traditional database systems.
  - **Unstructured Data**: Data that comes from a various of sources, such as text documents, emails, photos, audio files, social media posts and videos, is referred to as unstructured data. Being the both complex and huge, unstructured data cannot be managed or efficiently queried by a traditional database. Hadoop's ability to aggregate, join, and analyze multi-source data without having to structure it first allows the organizations to gain deeper insights very quickly. Thus Hadoop is the perfect fit for companies looking to store, analyze and manage large volumes of unstructured data.
- **Scalable analytics infrastructure is needed?**

Companies whose data workloads are static and predictable will be better served by the traditional database systems. Companies challenged by growing data demands will want to get advantage of Hadoop's scalable infrastructure. Scalability allows adding the servers on demand to accommodate increasing workloads. As the cloud-based Hadoop service, Qubole provides more flexible scalability by spinning the virtual servers up or down within minutes in order to accommodate fluctuating workloads.

- **Hadoop implementation will be cost-effective?**

The Cost-effectiveness is always a concern for many companies looking to adopt the new technologies. In order to consider a Hadoop implementation, companies need to make sure that realized benefits of a Hadoop deployment compensate the costs. Otherwise it would be better to stick with the traditional databases to meet data storage and analytics needs. Hadoop has a several things going for it that make the implementation more cost-effective than the companies may realize. Hadoop saves the money by combining open source softwares with the commodity hardware. Cloud-based Hadoop platforms such as the Qubole reduce costs further by removing the expense of physical servers and the warehouse space.

Hybrid systems, which integrate traditional relational databases with Hadoop platforms, are gaining the popularity as cost-effective ways for the companies to leverage the benefits of both platforms.

- **Is fast data analysis critical?**

Hadoop was designed for large distributed data processing that addresses every file in the database, and this type of processing takes time. For some tasks where fast performance isn't critical, such as scanning historical data, running end-of-day reports to reviews daily transactions, and performing analytics where a slower time-to-insight is acceptable, the Hadoop is ideal.

On the other hand, in cases where organizations rely on time-sensitive data analytics, a traditional database is the better fit. That's because shorter time-to -insight isn't about analyzing large unstructured datasets, which Hadoop does so well. It's all about analyzing smaller data sets in real or near-real time; this is what traditional databases are well equipped to do.

Hybrid systems are also a best fit to consider, as they allow companies to use traditional databases to run small, highly interactive workloads while using Hadoop to process huge, complex data sets.

- **Which approach is best?**

While the benefits of big data analytics in providing deeper insights that lead to competitive benefit are real, those benefits can only be realized by companies that exercise due diligence in making sure that Hadoop is the analytics tool that best serves their needs.

CONCLUSION

This Chapter explores the need of Hadoop data cluster, Map Reduce programming framework and HDFS for processing and managing big data, so it mainly concentrated on the unstructured data analysis. Big Data is not a new concept but it is very challenging. It includes scalable storage index and a distributed approach for retrieving the required results. It is a basic fact that data is too large to process conventionally. We also discussed the key issues, involving cloud storage and computing architecture. It also explores which functionality will better serve big data business by comparing Haddop with that of traditional data bases. In general, the analytics systems aim for the following: Scale-out: To support huge datasets (multiple terabytes or petabytes) and very high request rates, designed so that the request can be done via a horizontal set of commodity servers. Elasticity: While scale out provides the ability to have large systems, elasticity allows to add more capacity to a running system, and shifting load to them. High availability: The use of commodity hardware means that failures are relatively common, so automated recovery is critical and part of the design.

REFERENCES

M. G. Jaatun, G. Zhao, & C. Rong (Eds.). (2009). Parallel K-Means Clustering Based on MapReduce. In *Proceedings of CloudCom 2009* (LNCS), (vol. 5931, pp. 674–679). Springer-Verlag.

Kang & Faloutsos. (n.d.). Big Graph Mining: Algorithms and Discoveries. *SIGKDD Explorations, 14*(2).

Koundinya, Srinath, Sharma, Kumar, Madhu, & Shanbag. (2012). Map Reduce Design and Implementation of apriori Algorithm for Handling Voluminous Data. *Advanced Computing: An International Journal, 3*(6).

Lin, J., & Dyer, C. (2010). *Data-Intensive Text Processing with MapReduce*. Academic Press.

Nandakumar & Yambem. (2014). A Survey on Data Mining Algorithms on Apache Hadoop Platform. *International Journal of Emerging Technology and Advanced Engineering*, 4(1).

Sun, Z. (2012). Study on Parallel SVM Based on MapReduce. Paper presented at Conference on Worldcomp.

Wang et al. (Eds.). (2010). Parallel K-Means Clustering of Remote Sensing Images Based on MapReduce. In *Proceedings of WISM 2010* (LNCS), (vol. 6318, pp. 162–170). Springer-Verlag.

Ward, J. S., & Barker, A. (2013). *Undefined By Data: A Survey of Big Data Definitions.* arXiv:1309.5821v1 (cs.DB)

Wu. (2009). MReC4.5: C4.5 Ensemble Classification with MapReduce. *chinagrid*.

Yin. (2012). Accelerating Expectation-Maximization Algorithms with Frequent Updates. In *Proceedings of 2012 IEEE International Conference on Cluster Computing*. IEEE.

Zhao, Y., & Wu, J. (2013). Dache: A Data Aware Caching for Big-Data Applications Using the MapReduce Framework. In *Proc. 32nd IEEE Conference on Computer Communications, INFOCOM 2013*. IEEE Press. doi:10.1109/INFCOM.2013.6566730

Chapter 10
Big Data Virtualization and Visualization on Cloud

Farid Ahmad
Adama Science and Technology University, Ethiopia

ABSTRACT

Data virtualization is the procedure of combining data from different sources of information to develop a solo, logical and virtual view of facts so that it can be accessed by front-end resolutions such as applications, dashboards and portals without having to know the data's exact storingsite. Several organizations ride multiple types of database management systems, such as Oracle and SQL servers, which do not work fine with one another. Therefore, enterprises face new challenges in data integration and storage of huge amounts of data. With data virtualization, commercial handlers are able to get real time and consistent information speedily, which supports them to take foremost corporate decisions. The process of data virtualization involves abstracting, transforming, federating and delivering data from unequal sources. The key objective of data virtualization technology is to deliver a single point of access to the data by aggregating it from a wide range of data sources.

INTRODUCTION

The mainstream of big data solution is now provided in three forms; software-only, as an application or cloud-based. Decisions linking which way to obtain will depend, amongst other belongings, on issues of data neighborhood, solitude and guideline, human resources and project requirements. Numerous organizations choose on behalf of a hybrid way out. via on command cloud assets to enhancement in-house deployments. It is a elementary truth that data that is too big to process predictably is also too big to transportation everyplace. IT is undergoing an inversion of priority; it is the lineup that wishes to be in motion, not the data. If you would like to examine data from the Ethiopia Census. It's a lot easier to execute your code on Amazon's web services setup, which hosts such data locally, and won't cost you time or money to transport it.

Virtualization is a foundational innovation material to the execution of both distributed computing and enormous information. It gives the premise to a significant number of the stage ascribes needed to

DOI: 10.4018/978-1-4666-9767-6.ch010

Copyright © 2016, IGI Global. Copying or distributing in print or electronic forms without written permission of IGI Global is prohibited.

get to, store, investigate, and deal with the appropriated processing segments in enormous information situations. Virtualization, the procedure of utilizing PC assets to impersonate different assets; is esteemed for its ability to expand IT asset usage, proficiency, and adaptability. One essential use of virtualization is server solidification, which helps associations expand the usage of physical servers and conceivably save money on framework costs. Be that as it may, you discover numerous advantages to virtualization. Organizations that at first engaged exclusively on server virtualization are presently perceiving that it can be connected over the whole IT framework, including programming, storage, and networks.

BACKGROUND

whereas we are at an near the beginning phase in the advancement of big data, it is not at all too near the beginning to dig up ongoing with good practices so that you can pull what you are learning and the understanding you are gaining. As with every vital rising technology, it is significant to recognize why you need to leverage the technology and have a actual sketch in place. Several organizations begin their big data journey by experiment with a sole project that might offer some material benefit. By selecting a project, you have the autonomy of testing with no risk capital expenditures

There are some of the best, most comprehensive, sophisticated-yet-flexible visualization tools available and all are capable of handling big data. Many of these tools are Open-Source, free applications that can be used in conjunction with one another or with your existing design applications, using JavaScript, JSON, SVG, Python, HTML5 or drag-and-drop functionality with no programming required at all. Others are comprehensive business intelligence platforms capable of sophisticated data analysis and reporting, complete with a multitude of ways to visualize your data. Cloud computing normally begins with virtualization. Virtualization is acute to cloud computing because it shortens the transfer of services by providing a platform for optimizing multifaceted IT resources in a mountable way, which is what makes cloud computing so cost effective. Virtualization can be applied very broadly to objective about everything you can visualize including hardware, operating systems, memory, networks, storage and applications.

Basics of Virtualization

Virtualization disunites resources and accommodations from the underlying physical distribution environment, enabling you to engender many virtual systems within a single physical system. One of the primary reasons that companies have implemented virtualization is to amend the performance and efficiency of processing of a diverse commix of workloads. Rather than assigning a dedicated set of physical resources to each set of tasks, a pooled set of virtual resources can be expeditiously allocated as needed across all workloads. Reliance on the pool of virtual resources sanctions companies to amend latency. This incrementation in accommodation distribution speed and efficiency is a function of the distributed nature of virtualized environments and avails to amend overall time-to-value. Utilizing a distributed set of physical resources, such as servers, in a more flexible and efficient way distributes paramount benefits in terms of cost savings and ameliorations in productivity.

Virtualization put into practice several advantages, including the following:

- Virtualization of physical assets (e.g. servers, storage, and networks) enables extensive enhancement in the exploitation of these assets.
- Virtualization enables improved control over the usage and performance of your IT resources.
- Virtualization can provide a level of automation and standardization to Optimize your computing environment.
- Virtualization provides a foundation for cloud computing.

Although being able to virtualize resources adds a huge amount of efficiency, it doesn't come without a cost.

The Importance of Virtualization to Big Data

Understanding big data challenges ordinarily requires the administration of extensive volumes of profoundly disseminated information stores alongside the utilization of register and information escalated applications. In this manner, you require an exceptionally proficient IT environment to bolster big data. Virtualization gives the added level of proficiency to make big data stages a reality. In spite of the fact that virtualization is actually not a prerequisite for big data examination, programming systems, for example, MapReduce, which are utilized as a part of big data situations, are more effective in a virtualized situation. Virtualization has three attributes that backing the adaptability and working proficiency needed for enormous information situations:

- **Encapsulation:** A virtual machine can be represented (and even stored) as a single file, so you can identify it facilely predicated on the accommodations it provides. For example, the file containing the encapsulated process could be a consummate business accommodation. This encapsulated virtual machine could be presented to an application as a consummate entity. Thus, encapsulation could forfend each application so that it does not interfere with another application. One of the most consequential requisites for prosperity with big data is having the right level of performance to fortify the analysis of astronomically immense volumes and varied types of data. As you commence to leverage environments such as Hadoop and MapReduce, it is critical that you have a fortifying infrastructure that can scale. Virtualization integrates efficiency at every layer of the IT infrastructure. Applying virtualization across your environment will avail to achieve the scalability required for big data analysis. As a result, your entire IT environment needs to be optimized at every layer, from the network to the databases, storage, and servers. If you only virtualize your servers, you may experience bottlenecks from other infrastructure elements such as storage and networks. If you only fixate on virtualizing one element of your infrastructure, you are less liable to achieve the latency and efficiency you require. The following describes how virtualization of each element across the IT environment — servers, storage, applications, data, networks, processors, recollection, and accommodations can have a positive impact on immensely big data analysis.
- **Partitioning:** In virtualization, many applications and operating systems are fortified in a single physical system by partitioning (disuniting) the available resources.

- **Isolation:** Each virtual machine is isolated from its host physical system and other virtualized machines. Because of this isolation, if one virtual instance crashes, the other virtual machines and the host system are not affected. In integration, data is not shared between one virtual instance and another.

Server Virtualization

In server virtualization, one physical server is partitioned into multiple virtual servers. The hardware and resources of a machine including the desultory-access-recollection (RAM), CPU, hard drive, and network controller can be virtualized (logically split) into a series of virtual machines that each runs its own applications and operating system. A virtual-machine (VM) is a software representation of a physical machine that can execute or perform the same functions as the physical machine. A thin layer of software is genuinely inserted into the hardware that contains a virtual machine monitor, or hypervisor. The hypervisor can be thought of as the technology that manages traffic between the VMs and the physical machine.

Server virtualization utilizes the hypervisor to provide efficiency in the utilization of physical resources. Of course, installation, configuration, and administrative tasks are associated with establishing these virtual machines. This includes license management, network management, and workload administration, as well as capacity orchestrating. Server virtualization avails to ascertain that your platform can scale as needed to handle the immensely colossal volumes and varied types of data included in your sizably voluminous data analysis. You may not ken the extent of the volume or variety of structured and unstructured data needed afore you commence your analysis. This dubiousness makes the desideratum for server virtualization even more preponderant, providing your environment with the capability to meet the unanticipated demand for processing profoundly and immensely large data sets.

Network Virtualization

Network virtualization, software-defined networking provides an efficient way to utilize networking as a pool of connection resources. Networks are virtualized in a kindred fashion to other physical echnologies. In lieu of relying on the physical network for managing traffic between connections, you can engender multiple virtual networks all utilizing the same physical implementation. This can be subsidiary if you require to define a network for data accumulating with a certain set of performance characteristics and capacity and another network for applications with different performance and capacity. Inhibitions in the network layer can lead to bottlenecks that lead to unacceptable latencies in immensely colossal data environments. Virtualizing the network avails reduce these bottlenecks and amend the capability to manage the immensely colossal distributed data required for big data analysis.

Processor and Memory Virtualization

Processor virtualization avails to optimize the processor and maximize performance. Recollection virtualization decouples recollection from the servers. In astronomically immense data analysis, you may have reiterated queries of immensely colossal data sets and the engenderment of advanced analytic algorithms, all designed to probe for patterns and trends that are not yet understood. These advanced analytics can require lots of processing power (CPU) and memory (RAM). For some of these computations, it can take a long time without sufficient CPU and recollection resources. Processor and recollection virtualization can avail speed the processing and get your analysis results sooner.

Application Virtualization

Application foundation virtualization gives a proficient approach to oversee applications in connection with client request. The application is epitomized in a manner that expels its conditions from the fundamental physical PC framework. This serves to enhance the general reasonability and convenience of the application. Furthermore, the application base virtualization programming normally takes into consideration systematizing business and specialized use strategies to verify that each of your applications influences virtual and physical assets in an anticipated manner. Efficiencies are picked up in light of the fact that you can all the more effortlessly appropriate IT assets as indicated by the relative business estimation of your applications. As such, your most discriminating applications can get top need to draw from pools of accessible processing and stockpiling limit presently. Application foundation virtualization utilized as a part of mix with server virtualization can help to guarantee that business administration level assentions (SLAs) are met. Server virtualization screens CPU and memory use, yet does not represent varieties in business need when assigning assets. For instance, you may oblige that all applications are treated with the same business-level need. By executing application foundation virtualization notwithstanding server virtualization, you can guarantee that the most high priority applications have top-need access to assets. Your enormous information applications may have critical IT asset prerequisites, because of the vast volumes of information or the rate at which that information is produced. Your big data surroundings need to have the right level of consistency and repeatability to verify that the applications have entry to the obliged assets. Application framework virtualization can guarantee that every application conveyed for a big data investigation has admittance to the process power.

Data and Storage Virtualization

Data virtualization can be habituated to engender a platform for dynamic linked data accommodations. This sanctions data to be facilely probed and linked through a cumulated reference source. As a result, data virtualization provides an abstract accommodation that distributes data in a consistent form regardless of the underlying physical database. In additament, data virtualization exposes cached data to all applications to ameliorate performance. Storage virtualization coalesces physical storage resources so that they are more efficaciously shared. This reduces the cost of storage and makes it more facile to manage data stores required for immensely colossal data analysis.

Data and storage virtualization play a consequential role in making it more facile and less costly to store, retrieve, and analyze the astronomically immense volumes of expeditious and varying types of data. Recollect that some sizably voluminous data may be unstructured and not facilely stored utilizing traditional methods. Storage virtualization makes it more facile to store astronomically immense and unstructured data types. In a big data environment, it is propitious to have access to a variety of operational data stores on demand. For example, you may only need access to a columnar database infrequently. With virtualization, the database can be stored as a virtual image and invoked whenever it is needed without consuming valuable data center resources or capacity.

Implementing Virtualization to Work with Big Data

Virtualization avails makes your IT environment astute enough to handle big data analysis. By optimizing all elements of your infrastructure, including hardware, software, and storage, you gain the efficiency needed to process and manage sizably voluminous volumes of structured and unstructured data. With astronomically immense data, you require to access, manage, and analyze structured and unstructured data in a distributed environment. Big data surmises distribution. In practice, any kind of MapReduce will work better in a virtualized environment. You require the capability to move workloads around predicated on requisites for compute power and storage. Virtualization will enable you to tackle more sizably voluminous quandaries that have not yet been scoped. You may not ken in advance how expeditiously you will require to scale. Virtualization will enable you to fortify a variety of operational big data stores. For example, a graph database can be spun up as an image.

Virtualized environment require be adequately managing and governing to comprehend cost savings and effectiveness benefits. If you rely on big data services to explain your analytics challenges, you need to be secure that the virtual environment is as well managed and secure as the physical environment. Some of the benefits of virtualization, including ease of provisioning, can easily lead to management and security problems without proper oversight. Virtualization makes it easy for developers to create a virtual image, or a copy, of a resource. As a result, many companies have implemented virtualization only to find that the number of virtual images spirals out of control.

Defining the Cloud in the Context of Big Data

Cloud computing is a method of providing a set of shared computing resources that include applications, computing, storage, networking, development, and deployment platforms, as well as business processes. Cloud computing turns traditional soloed computing assets into shared pools of resources predicated on an underlying Internet substructure. In cloud computing, everything from compute power to computing infrastructure and from to you as an accommodation to be operational in the authentic world, the cloud must be implemented with prevalent standardized processes and automation. Many businesses leverage cloud accommodations for everything from backup to Software as a Accommodation (SaaS) options such as customer relationship management (CRM) accommodations. With the magnification of mobile computing, more consumers, professionals, and corporations are engendering and accessing data with cloud-predicated accommodations. The average consumer may be sent an online coupon for a favorite store; a quality control manager in a manufacturing plant might amass sensor data from a variety of machines to determine whether a quality quandary subsists. These scenarios are predicated on the cloud-predicated data accommodations infrastructure. A popular example of the benefits of cloud fortifying big data can be noted at both Google and Amazon.com. Both companies depend on the capability to manage massive amounts of data to move their businesses forward. These providers needed to come up with infrastructures and technologies that could fortify applications at a massive scale. Consider Gmail and the millions upon millions of messages that Google processes per day as a component of this accommodation. Google has been able to optimize the Linux operating system and its software environment to fortify e-mail in the most efficient manner; therefore, it can facilely support hundreds of millions of users. Even more importantly, Google is able to capture and leverage the massive amount of data about both its mail users and its search engine users to drive the business. Likewise, Amazon.com, with its IaaS data centers, is optimized to fortify these workloads so that Amazon can perpetuate to offer incipient accommodations and support a growing number of customers without breaking the bank. To grow its retail business, Amazon must be able to manage data about its merchandise, its buyers, and its channel of partner merchants.

Cloud Deployment Models

The two types of deployment models for cloud computing are public and private. These are offered for general purport computing needs as opposed to concrete types of cloud distribution models. We examine the distribution models later in the chapter. In the meantime, take a visual examination of the distinctions between public and private cloud models and how you might utilize them.

The Private Cloud

A private cloud is a set of hardware, networking, storage, accommodations, application, and interfaces owned and operated by an organization for the utilization of its employees, partners, and customers. A private cloud can be engendered and managed by a third party for the exclusive utilization of one enterprise. The private cloud is a highly controlled environment not open for public consumption. Thus, the private cloud sits abaft a firewall. The private cloud is highly automated with a fixate on governance, security, and compliance.

Automation supersedes more manual processes of managing IT accommodation to fortify customers. In this way, business rules and processes can be implemented inside software so that the environment becomes more prognosticable and manageable. If organizations are managing a big data project that demands processing massive amounts of data, the private cloud might be the best cull in terms of latency and security.

The Public Cloud

The public cloud is a set of hardware, networking, storage, accommodations, applications, and interfaces owned and operated by a third party for use by other companies and individuals. These commercial providers engender a highly scalable data center that obnubilates the details of the underlying infrastructure from the consumer. Public s are viable because they typically manage relatively perpetual or straightforward workloads. For example, electronic mail is a very simple application. Therefore, a cloud provider can optimize the environment so that it is best suited to fortify a sizably voluminous number of customers, even if it preserves many messages. Likewise, public cloud providers offering storage or computing accommodations optimize their computing hardware and software to fortify these categorical types of workloads. In contrast, the typical data center fortifies so many different applications and workloads that it cannot be facilely optimized. A public cloud can be very efficacious when an organization is executing an involute data analysis project and needs extra computing cycles to handle the task. In additament, companies may opt to store data in a public cloud where the cost per gigabyte is relatively inexpensive when compared to purchased storage. The overriding issues with public clouds for big data are the security requisites and the amount of latency that is acceptable.

All public clouds are not identically tantamount. Some public clouds are scalable managed accommodations with a high caliber of security and a high caliber of accommodation management.

Understanding Cloud Deployment and Delivery Models

Two key cloud models are consequential in the discussion of big data; public clouds and private clouds. For those organizations that adopt cloud deployment and distribution models, most will utilize a cumulating of private computing by an external company for the shared utilization of a variety of customers who pay a per-utilization fee). How these companies balance public and private providers depends on a number of issues, including privacy, latency, and purport. It is paramount to understand these environments and what they betoken for a potential big data deployment. In that way, you can determine whether you might want to utilize a public cloud IaaS, for example, for your big data projects or if you optate to perpetuate to keep all your data on premises. Or, you might want to utilize an amalgamation of both. So, we outline these deployment and distribution models first and then verbalize more about what they denote to big data.

The most popular cloud delivery models are described in the following.

Infrastructure as a Service

Infrastructure as a Service (IaaS) is single of the mainly clear-cut of the cloud computing services. IaaS is the deliverance of computing services including hardware, storage, networking, and data center space based on a charter model. The end user of the service acquires a resource and be charged for that resource based lying on amount used and the period of that usage. You find both public and private versions of IaaS.

Platform as a Service

Platform as a Service (PaaS) is a mechanism for combining IaaS with an distracted set of middleware services, software development, and deployment tools that allow the organization to have a consistent way to create and deploy applications on a cloud or on premises. A PaaS offers a consistent set of programming or middleware services that ensure that developers have a well-tested and well-integrated way to create applications in a cloud environment. A PaaS environment brings development and deployment together to create a more manageable way to build, deploy, and scale applications. A PaaS requires an IaaS.

Software as a Service

Software as a Service (SaaS) is a business application created and hosted by a provider in a multitenant model. Multitenancy refers to the situation where a single instance of an application runs in a cloud environment, but serves multiple client organizations (tenants), keeping all their data separate. Customers pay for the service per user either on a monthly or yearly contract model. The SaaS model sits on top of both the PaaS and the foundational IaaS.

Data as a Service

Because this is a book about big data, we also want you to know about another delivery model called Data as a Service (DaaS). DaaS is closely related to SaaS. DaaS is a platform-independent service that would let you connect to the cloud to store and retrieve your data. In addition, you find a number of specialized data services that are of great benefit in a big data environment. For example, Google offers a service that can process a query with 5 terabytes of data in only 15 seconds. This type of query would typically take ten times as long with a typical data center. Hundreds of specialized analytic services have been developed by companies like IBM and others. In fact, a number of cloud characteristics make it an important part of the big data ecosystem:

- **Scalability:** Scalability with regard to hardware refers to the capability to go from small to large amounts of processing power with the same architecture. With regard to software, it refers to the consistency of performance per unit of power as hardware resources increase. The cloud can scale to large data volumes. Distributed computing, an integral part of the cloud model, really works on a "divide and conquer" plan. So if you have huge volumes of data, they can be partitioned across cloud servers. An important characteristic of IaaS is that it can dynamically scale. This means that if you wind up needing more resources than expected, you can get them.
- **Often low up-front costs:** If you use a cloud provider, up-front costs can often be reduced because you are not buying huge amounts of hardware or leasing out new space for dealing with your big data. By taking advantage of the economies of scale associated with cloud environments, the cloud can look attractive. Of course, you will need to do your own calculation to evaluate whether you are interested in a public cloud, private cloud, hybrid cloud, or no cloud.
- **Pay as you go:** A typical billing option for a cloud provider is Pay as You Go (PAYG), which means that you are billed for resources used based on instance pricing. This can be useful if you're not sure what resources you need for your big data project.
- **Fault tolerance:** Cloud service providers should have fault tolerance built into their architecture, providing uninterrupted services despite the failure of one or more of the system's components.
- **Elasticity:** Elasticity refers to the capability to expand or shrink computing resource demand in real time, based on need. One of the benefits of the cloud is that customers have the potential to access as much of a service as they need when they need it. This can be helpful for big data projects where you might need to expand the amount of computing resources you need to deal with the volume and velocity of the data. Of course, this very feature of the cloud that makes it attractive to end users means that the service provider needs to design a platform architecture that is optimized for this kind of service.
- **Resource pooling:** Cloud architectures enable the efficient creation of groups of shared resources that make the cloud economically viable.
- **Self-service:** With self-service, the user of a cloud resource is able to use a browser or a portal interface to acquire the resources needed, say, to run a huge predictive model. This is dramatically different than how you might gain resources from a data center, where you would have to request the resources from IT operations.

Making Use of the Cloud for Big Data

Limpidly, the very nature of the cloud makes it an ideal computing environment for big data. So how might you utilize big data together with the cloud?

Here are some examples:

- **PaaS in a private cloud:** PaaS is an entire infrastructure packaged so that it can be acclimated to design, implement, and deploy applications and accommodations in a public or private cloud environment. PaaS enables an organization to leverage key middleware accommodations without having to deal with the intricacies of managing individual hardware and software elements. PaaS vendors are commencing to incorporate big data technologies such as Hadoop and MapReduce into their PaaS offerings. For example, you might want to build a specialized application to analyze prodigious amounts of medical data. The application would make utilization of authentic-time as well as non-authentic-time data. It's going to require Hadoop and MapReduce for storage and processing. What's great about PaaS in this scenario is how expeditiously the application can be deployed. You won't have to wait for internal IT teams to get up to speed on the incipient technologies and you can experiment more liberally. Once you have identified a solid solution, you can bring it in house when IT is yare to fortify it.

- **SaaS in a hybrid cloud:** Here you might want to analyze "voice of the customer" data from multiple channels. Many companies have come to realize that one of the most consequential data sources is what the customer cerebrates and verbalizes about their company, their products, and their accommodations. Getting access to voice of the customer data can provide Providers in the big data Cloud Market Cloud players come in all shapes and sizes and offer many different products. Some are household names while others are recently emerging. Some of the cloud providers that offer IaaS accommodations that can be utilized for big data include Amazon.com, AT&T, GoGrid, Joyent, Rackspace, IBM, and Verizon/Terremark.

- **IaaS in a public cloud:** In this scenario, you would be utilizing a public cloud provider's infrastructure for your big data accommodations because you don't want to utilize your own physical infrastructure. IaaS can provide the engenderment of virtual machines with virtually illimitable storage and compute potency. You can pick the operating system that you optate, and you have the flexibility to dynamically scale the environment to meet your desiderata.

An example might be utilizing the Amazon Elastic Compute Cloud (Amazon EC2) accommodation, detailed later in the chapter, to run an authentic-time predictive model that requires data to be processed utilizing massively parallel processing. It might be an accommodation that processes astronomically immense-box retail data. You might want to process billions of pieces of click-stream data for targeting customers with the right ad in authentic time.

However, cloud companies and cloud service providers are withal offering software targeted concretely for big data. Where to be meticulous when utilizing cloud services Cloud-predicated accommodations can provide an economical solution to your big data needs, but the cloud has its issues. It's consequential to do your homework afore moving your big data there. Here are some issues to consider:

- **Performance:** Because you are fascinated with getting performance from your accommodation provider, ascertain that explicit definitions of accommodation-level accedences subsist for availability, support, and performance. For example, your provider may tell you that you will be able to access your data 99.99 percent of the time; however, read the contract. Does this uptime include scheduled maintenance?

- **Data access:** What controls are in place to ascertain that you and only you can access your data? In other words, what forms of secure access control are in place? This might include identity management, where the primary goal is forfending personal identity information so that access to computer resources, applications, data, and accommodations is controlled congruously.
- **Location:** Where will your data be located? In some companies and countries, regulatory issues avert data from being stored or processed on machines in a different country.
- **Data integrity:** You require to ascertain that your provider has the right controls in place to ascertain that the integrity of your data is maintained.
- **Compliance:** Ascertain that your provider can comply with any compliance issues particular to your company or industry.
- **Costs:** Little costs can integrate up. Be meticulous to read the fine print of any contract, and ascertain that you ken what you operate to do in the cloud.
- **Data transport:** Be sure to decipher how you get your data into the cloud in the first place. For example, some providers will let you mail it to them on media. Others insist on uploading it over the network. This can get expensive, so be conscientious.

CONCLUSION

The potency of the cloud is that users can access needed computing and storage resources with little or no IT support or the desideratum to purchase more hardware or software. One of the key characteristics of the cloud is elastic scalability: Users can integrate or subtract resources in virtually authentic time predicated on transmuting requisites. The cloud plays a consequential role within the big data world. Dramatic changes transpire when these infrastructure components are cumulated with the advances in data management. Horizontally expandable and optimized infrastructure fortifies the practical implementation of big data. The organizations that decide to be leaders will uncover new business opportunities and implement new business processes before the followers realize what has happened. It is rare to have a chance to be among the first to enter an entirely new realm of data and analysis. Don't let your organization miss the chance that is sitting in front of you today. Begin to uncover the ways that the analysis of big data can change how your organization does business. Now it is clear that big data virtualization and visualization on cloud plays the significance role for IT peoples.

REFERENCE

Hurwitz, J., Nugent, A., Halper, & Kaufman. (2013). Big Data For Dummies. John Wiley & Sons.

Chapter 11
Essentiality of Machine Learning Algorithms for Big Data Computation

Manjunath Thimmasandra Narayanapppa
BMS Institute of Technology, India

T. P. Puneeth Kumar
Acharya Institute of Technology, India

Ravindra S. Hegadi
Solapur University, India

ABSTRACT

Recent technological advancements have led to generation of huge volume of data from distinctive domains (scientific sensors, health care, user-generated data, finical companies and internet and supply chain systems) over the past decade. To capture the meaning of this emerging trend the term big data was coined. In addition to its huge volume, big data also exhibits several unique characteristics as compared with traditional data. For instance, big data is generally unstructured and require more real-time analysis. This development calls for new system platforms for data acquisition, storage, transmission and large-scale data processing mechanisms. In recent years analytics industries interest expanding towards the big data analytics to uncover potentials concealed in big data, such as hidden patterns or unknown correlations. The main goal of this chapter is to explore the importance of machine learning algorithms and computational environment including hardware and software that is required to perform analytics on big data.

INTRODUCTION

Every day, 2.5 quintillion bytes of data are created and 90 percent of the data in the world today were produced within the past two years (IBM, 2012). Our capability for data generation has never been so powerful and enormous ever since the invention of the information technology. As another example, in 2012, the first presidential debate between President Barack Obama and Governor Mitt Romney generated

DOI: 10.4018/978-1-4666-9767-6.ch011

Copyright © 2016, IGI Global. Copying or distributing in print or electronic forms without written permission of IGI Global is prohibited.

more than 10 million tweets in 2 hours (Twitter, 2012). Among all these tweets, the specific moments that generated the most discussions revealed the public interests, such as the discussions about vouchers and Medicare. Such online discussions provide a new means to sense the public interests and generate feedback in real- time, and are mostly appealing compared to standard media, such as TV broadcasting, newspapers or radio. Another example is Flickr, a picture sharing site, which receives on an average 1.83 million photos (Michel, 2015). Assuming the size of each photo is 2 megabytes (MB), this requires 3.6 terabytes (TB) of storage disk every single day. In fact, as an old saying states: "a picture is speaks a thousand words," the billions of pictures collected by Flicker are a treasure tank for us to explore the human society, public affairs, social events, disasters, and so on, only if we have the powerful technology to harness the enormous amount of data. The above examples show the rise of Big Data applications where data collection has grown tremendously and is beyond the ability of commonly used software tools to acquire, manage, and process within an "acceptable elapsed time." An essential challenge facing by applications of Big Data is to explore the large volumes of data and extract useful information or knowledge for future actions (Rajaraman & Ullman, 2011).

Machine learning is a branch of artificial intelligence that allows us to make our application intelligent without being explicitly programmed. Machine learning concepts are used to enable applications to take a decision from the available datasets. A combination of machine learning and data mining can be used to develop various applications such as spam mail detectors, self-driven cars, face recognition, speech recognition, and online transactional fraud-activity detection. There are many popular organizations that are using machine-learning algorithms to make their service or product understand the need of their users and provide services as per their behavior. Google has its intelligent web search engine, which provides a number one search, spam classification in Google Mail, news labeling in Google News, and Amazon for recommender systems. There are many open source frameworks available for developing these types of applications/frameworks, such as R, Python, Apache Mahout, and Weka (Han Hu, Wen, Chua, Xuelong Li, n.d).

In the basic computational model of CPU and memory, the algorithms runs on the CPU and access the data that is in the memory, its need to bring in the data from disk into memory, but once the data is in memory, and the algorithm runs in the data that is on memory. This is the familiar model considered to implement all kinds of algorithms such as machine learning, statistics etc. wherever the data is so big, that it cannot fit into memory at the same time. That's where data mining comes in. In traditional data mining algorithms, since the data is a big, only portion of the data bring into memory at a time and process the data in batches, finally writes the results back to disk. But sometimes even this is not sufficient. Now if you take ten billion webpages, each of 20 KB, you have, total dataset size of 200 TB. Now, when you have 200 TB, let us assume that by using the traditional computational model, traditional data mining model. And all this data is stored on a single disk, and we have read tend to be processed inside a CPU. Now the fundamental limitation here is the data bandwidth between the disk and the CPU. The data has to be read from the disk into the CPU, and read bandwidth for most modern SATA disk is around 50MB a second, so we can read data at 50MB a second, it means its takes 4 million seconds that is 46 days. To do something useful with the data, it's going to take even longer time. Such a long time is unacceptable, we need a better solution to read and process the Big Data. One of the solutions for this kind of problem is to split the data into chunks on multiple disks and CPUs. Now read the chunks of the data from the multiple disks and process it in parallel in multiple CPUs. That will cut down read and process time by a lot. For example, if you had a 1,000 disks and CPUs, 4 million seconds come down to 4,000 seconds. This is the fundamental idea behind the idea of cluster computing.

The architecture that has emerged for cluster computing is something is show in the Figure 1.in the figure the racks consisting of number of commodity Linux nodes. Commodity Linux nodes will be used because they are very cheap. Each rack has 16 to 64 of these commodity Linux nodes and these nodes are connected by a gigabit switch. So there is 1 Gbps bandwidth between any pair of nodes in rack. Of course 16 to 64 nodes is not sufficient. Multiple racks are lined up and connected by backbone switches. Each backbones is a higher bandwidth switch can transfer two to ten gigabits between racks, these goup og racks form a datacenter. This is the classical traditional architecture that has emerged over the last few years for storing and mining massive datasets.

The traditional machine learning algorithm which are designed for traditional computing environment consisting of singe memory and single disk are not capable of mining big data on a distributed environment like hadoop, however a scalable machine learning algorithms provided by mahout library can run on distributed environment like hadoop HDFS.

LITERATURE SURVEY

Because of the massive, heterogeneous, multisource and dynamic characteristics of application data involved in a distributed environment, one of the most important challenges of Big Data is to carry out computing on the petabyte or even the Exabyte level data with a complex computing process involving scalable machine learning algorithms and complex computing platform. Therefore, utilizing a parallel Computing infrastructure like hadoop cluster, its corresponding programming language support to analyze and mining the distributed data are the critical goals for Big Data analytics.

Designing and developing large scale machine learning algorithm has attracted a significant amount of research attention, many such algorithms have been proposed in the past decades. However, designing the machine learning algorithms to work on massive datasets present on distributed platforms really a challenging task.

Figure 1. Architecture of a cluster

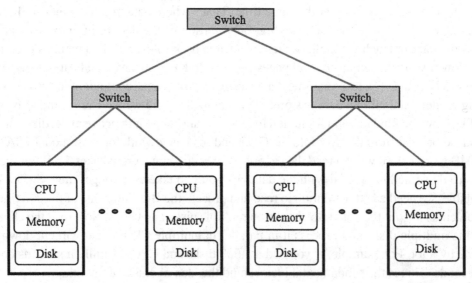

Xindong Wu, Xingquan Zhu, Gong-Qing Wu, and Wei Ding (2014) presented a HACE theorem that suggests key characteristics of big data and proposes a Big Data processing model for data mining, that model involves demand-driven aggregation of information sources, mining and analysis, user interest modeling, and security and privacy considerations. It also discusses issues in the data-driven model and also in the Big Data revolution

Jainendra Singh (2014) have analysed the challenging issues in the data-driven model and discussed the Machine Learning (ML) approach to the security problems encountered in big data applications, technologies and theories.

A. N. Nandakumar and Nandita Yambem (2014) explored the current activities and challenges in migration of existing data mining algorithms onto hadoop platform for increased parallel processing efficiency. Even identified the current gaps and open research areas in migration process.

Jiby Joseph, Omar Sharif and Ajit Kumar (2014) proposed a solution for Predictive Maintenance in Automotive Industry using machine learning on big data platform and demonstrates how Machine Learning can enable accurate prediction of failure events in the production line of automotive industries. Discussed the Applications of Machine Learning in Different Industries.

Jimmy Lin and Chris Dyer (2010) give a very detailed explanation of applying EM algorithms to text processing and fitting those algorithms into the MapReduce programming model. The EM fits naturally into the MapReduce programming model by making each iteration of EM one MapReduce job: mappers map over independent instances and compute the summary statistics, while the reducers sum together the required training statistics and solve the M-step optimization problems. In this work, it was observed that when global data is needed for synchronization of hadoop tasks, it was difficult with current support from hadoop platform.

Kang and Christos Faloutsos (n.d) applied hadoop for graph mining in social networking data. One of the main observations here is that some of the graph mining algorithms cannot be parallelized, so estimated solutions are needed.

Anjan K Koundinya (2012) have implemented Apriori algorithm on Apache Hadoop platform. Contrary to the believe that parallel processing will take less time to get Frequent item sets, they experimental observation proved that multi node Hadoop with differential system configuration (FHDSC) was taking more time. The reason was in way the data has been portioned to the nodes.

Gong-Qing Wu (2009) implemented C4.5 decision tree classification algorithm on apache hadoop. In this work, while constructing the bagging ensemble based reduction to construct the final classifier many duplicates were found. These duplicates could not have avoided if proper data partitioning method have been applied.

BIG DATA ANALYTICS

Big data analytics (Han Hu, Yonggang Wen, Tat-Seng Chua, Xuelong Li, n.d) is the process of using analysis algorithms running on powerful supporting platforms to uncover potentials hidden in big data, such as hidden patterns or unknown relationships. According to the processing time requirement, big data analytics can be categorized into two different paradigms:

Streaming Processing

The start point for the streaming processing model is the assumption that the potential value of data depends on freshness of the data. Thus, the streaming processing paradigm analyzes data as soon as possible it arrives. In this paradigm, data arrives in a stream. In its continuous arrival, because the stream is fast and carries enormous volume, only a small share of the stream is stored in limited memory. One or few passes over the stream are made to find approximation results. Streaming processing technology have been studied for decades. Open source systems such as Storm, S4 and Kafka supports stream processing. The streaming processing paradigm is mainly used in online applications.

Batch Processing

In the batch-processing paradigm, data are stored first and then analyzed. MapReduce become the leading batch-processing model. The basic idea of MapReduce is that data are divided into small chunks. Then, these chunks are processed in parallel on a distributed platform to generate intermediate results. Finally the result is derived by aggregating all the intermediate results. This model schedules computation resources very close to data location, which avoids the communication overhead of data transmission. The MapReduce model is simple and widely applied in several fields such as bioinformatics, web mining, and machine learning.

In general the streaming processing paradigm is appropriate for applications in which data are generated in the form of a stream and speedy processing is required to obtain approximation results. Therefore, the streaming processing application domains are relatively narrow. Recently, most applications have adopted the batch-processing paradigm; even some real-time processing applications use the batch-processing paradigm to realize a faster response. Because the batch-processing paradigm is widely adopted, in this chapter we consider batch processing based big data platforms.

Previously the focus was on building the technologies to overcome various challenges of Big Data, todays focus is on enabling advanced Analytics on Big Data. Apache's open-source section carrying out many development activities in this regard and also there are number of start-ups booming with products for performing Advanced Analytics like supervised, un-supervised learning, predictive modelling, regression etc. on Big Data in Hadoop.

The following open source projects support big data analytics.

Hadoop

Apache Hadoop the Hadoop open source project from apache supports intensive processing of large datasets across distributed systems. It is designed to feature high performance and scalability on data-intensive applications, whereby data systems can scale up from a single sever to hundreds or thousands of computing nodes, each offering parallel computation and distributed storage. For further information

HBase

The HBase open source distributed database system is part of the apache Hadoop project. It is a noSQL, versioned, column-oriented data storage system that provides random real-time read/write access to big data tables and runs on top of the Hadoop Distributed File system

Hive

The Hive open source data warehouse system is also part of the apache Hadoop project. It provides data summarization, queries, and analysis of large datasets. Likewise, it incorporates a mechanism to feature ad-hoc queries via a general purpose SQL-like language, called HiveQL, while maintaining traditional map/reduce operations in those situations where complex logic can't adequately be expressed using HiveQL.

COMPUTATIONAL FRAMEWORK

Hadoop is specially designed for two core concepts: HDFS and MapReduce (Vignesh Prajapati, 2013). Both are related to distributed computation. MapReduce is believed as the heart of Hadoop that performs parallel processing over distributed data. Hadoop have its several distributions and tools that are compatible with its distributed file system, such as Hive, pig scripts and HBase.

Hadoop Distributed File System (HDFS)

HDFS is rack-aware filesystem of Hadoop, which is a UNIX-based data storage layer of Hadoop. HDFS is resulting from concepts of Google filesystem. Hadoop partition the data and computation across several (thousands of) nodes of the hadoop clusters, and executes the application computations in parallel, close to their data. On HDFS, data files are replicated as sequences of blocks in the cluster. A Hadoop cluster capable of scaling storage capacity, computation capacity and I/O bandwidth by simply adding commodity servers. HDFS can be accessed from applications in various different ways. Natively, HDFS provides a Java API for applications to use.

The Hadoop clusters at Yahoo! span around 40,000 servers and store 40 petabytes of data. Also, worldwide around one hundred other organizations are known to use Hadoop.

Characteristics of HDFS:

- Fault tolerant
- Able to handle large datasets
- Master slave paradigm
- Runs with commodity hardware
- Write once file access only

MapReduce

MapReduce is a programming model for processing huge datasets scattered on a large cluster. MapReduce is the core of Hadoop. Mapreduce programming model allows performing massive data processing across thousands of nodes configured with Hadoop clusters. Mapreduce paradigm is derived from Google MapReduce.

Hadoop MapReduce is a software framework for writing applications easily, which process huge amounts of datasets in parallel on large clusters (thousands of nodes) of commodity hardware in a fault-tolerant and reliable manner.

This MapReduce paradigm is separated into two phases, Map and Reduce that mainly deal with key and value pairs of data. The Map and Reduce task run sequentially in hadoop cluster to compute the final result; the output of the Map phase becomes the input for the Reduce phase

Large Scale Machine Learning

The most commonly accepted definition of "data mining" (A. Rajaraman and J. Ullman, 2011) is the discovery of "models" for data. Discovery of model can follow one of the several approaches such as statistical modeling, machine learning, computational and summarization.

Algorithms called "machine learning" not only summarize the data and also learn a model or classifier from the data, and thus discover something about data that will be seen in the future.

Data mining is going through a significant shift with the volume, variety, value and velocity of data increasing significantly each year. In the past, traditional data mining software was implemented by loading data into memory and running a single thread of execution over the data. The process was constrained by the amount of memory available and the speed of a processor. If the process could not fit it entirely into memory, the process would fail. The single thread of execution also failed to take advantage of multicore servers unless multiple users were on the system at the same time. The solution is to increase the machine configuration or parallelize with commodity hardware.

There are three different types of machine-learning algorithms for intelligent system development:

- Supervised machine-learning algorithms
- Unsupervised machine-learning algorithms
- Recommender systems

Supervised Machine-Learning Algorithms

In this section, we will be learning about supervised machine-learning algorithms.
The algorithms are as follows:

- Linear regression
- Logistic regression

Linear Regression

Linear regression is mainly used for predicting and forecasting values based on historical information. Regression is a supervised machine-learning technique to identify the linear relationship between target variables and explanatory variables. We can say it is used for predicting the target variable values in numeric form.

Logistic Regression

In statistics, logistic regression or logit regression is a type of probabilistic classification model. Logistic regression is used extensively in numerous disciplines, including the medical and social science fields.

It can be binomial or multinomial. Binary logistic regression deals with situations in which the outcome for a dependent variable can have two possible types. Multinomial logistic regression deals with situations where the outcome can have three or more possible types.

Unsupervised Machine Learning Algorithm

In machine learning, unsupervised learning is used for finding the hidden structure from the unlabeled dataset. Since the datasets are not labeled, there will be no error while evaluating for potential solutions.

Unsupervised machine learning includes several algorithms, some of which are as follows:

- Clustering
- Artificial neural networks
- Vector quantization

Clustering

Clustering is the task of grouping a set of object in such a way that similar objects with similar characteristics are grouped in the same category, but other objects are grouped in other categories. In clustering, the input datasets are not labeled; they need to be labeled based on the similarity of their data structure.

In unsupervised machine learning, the classification technique performs the same procedure to map the data to a category with the help of the provided set of input training datasets. The corresponding procedure is known as clustering (or cluster analysis), and involves grouping data into categories based on some measure of inherent similarity; for example, the distance between data points. Clustering used in the applications like Market segmentation, Social network analysis, Organizing computer network, Astronomical data analysis

Recommendation Algorithms

Recommendation is a machine-learning technique to predict what new items a user would like based on associations with the user's previous items. Recommendations are widely used in the field of e-commerce applications. Through this flexible data and behavior-driven algorithms, businesses can increase conversions by helping to ensure that relevant choices are automatically suggested to the right customers at the right time with cross-selling or up-selling.

For example, when a customer is looking for a Samsung Galaxy S IV/S4 mobile phone on Amazon, the store will also suggest other mobile phones similar to this one, presented in the Customers Who Bought This Item Also Bought windows

APPLICATIONS OF MACHINE LEARNING IN DIFFERENT INDUSTRIES

Machine Learning can be applied to high volumes of data in order to gain deeper insights and to improve decision making. Table 1 depicts some emerging applications of Machine Learning

Table 1. Machine learning applications across industries

Industries	Applications of Machine learning
Manufacturing	• Predictive maintenance or condition monitoring • Warranty reserve estimation • Propensity to buy • Demand forecasting • Process optimization • Telematics
Retail	• Predictive inventory planning • Recommendation engines • Upsell and cross-channel marketing • Market segmentation and targeting
Healthcare and Life Sciences	• Alerts and diagnostics from real-time patient data • Disease identification and risk stratification • Patient triage optimization • Proactive health management • Healthcare provider sentiment analysis
Travel and Hospitality	• Aircraft scheduling • Dynamic pricing • Social media – consumer feedback and interaction analysis • Customer complaint resolution • Traffic patterns and congestion management
Financial Services	• Risk analytics and regulation • Customer Segmentation • Cross-selling and up-selling • Sales and marketing campaign management • Credit worthiness evaluation

MACHINE LEARNING IN HADOOP

Some of the softwares that makes the machine learning possible on Hadoop are discussed below.

Mahout

Apache software came up with Apache Mahout to facilitate machine learning on Big Data, Mahout provides machine learning libraries that enables running various scalable machine learning algorithms on Hadoop in a distributed manner using the MapReduce paradigm. Currently, Mahout supports only Clustering, Classification and Recommendation Mining.

R

R is a Statistical tool consist of the packages designed specifically for executing machine learning algorithms on structured, semi-structured and un-structured data, but R alone not possible to support design of large scalable machine learning algorithms, that is where the RHadoop comes in, RHadoop is a collection of five R packages developed by Revolution Analytics that allow users to manage and analyze data with Hadoop using map-reduce programming model. The packages are compatible with open source Hadoop and other Hadoop distributions such as Cloudera, Hortonworks, mapR's. RHadoop provides a way to an analyst applying machine learning algorithm on large datasets using MapReduce paradigm. Similarly other softwares such as RHIPE, ORCH, Hadoop Streaming also makes R and Hadoop integration possible.

A BIG DATA FRAMEWORK FOR CATEGORIZING TECHNICAL SUPPORT REQUESTS USING LARGE SCALE MACHINE LEARNING

According to Arantxa Duque Barrachina and Aisling O'Driscoll (2014), technical support call centers regularly receive several thousand customer queries on a daily basis. Usually, the organisations discard the data related to customer enquiries within a relatively short period of time due to limited storage capacity. However, the use of big data platform and machine learning for big data analytics enables the call centers to store, manage, analyse and identify customer patterns, improve first call resolution and maximise daily closure rates. This chapter provides an overview on proof of concept (POC) end to end solution that make use of the Hadoop programming model, HABSE, HIVEQL and the mahout big data analytics library for categorizing similar support calls for large technical support data sets.

The PoC provides an end to end solution for conducting large scale analysis of technical support datasets using the open source Hadoop platform, Hadoop sub projects such as HBase, Hive and distributed clustering algorithms from the Mahout library. Figure 2 illustrates the architecture of the PoC end to end solution.

To process the technical support data by the Mahout, first it must be uploaded to HDFS, then run the Hadoop map-reduce job to convert the technical support data exported in CSV file format into Sequence File format of the Hadoop. A Hadoop Sequence File is a flat file consisting of binary key/value pairs.

Figure 2. PoC end to end Solution for analyzing large technical support data sets

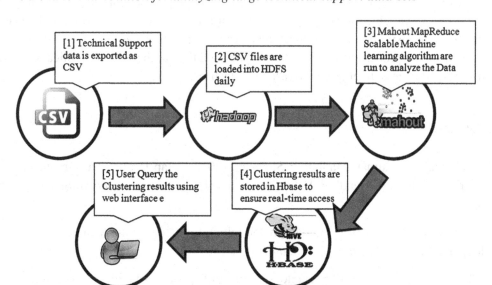

The goal of identifying related customer support calls based on their problem description is resolved by using distributed clustering machine learning algorithms provided by mahout library to analyse the data set, thereby finding support calls with a similar problem description and grouped into separate clusters.

Most importantly, Hadoop alone does not provide real-time data access capability since it is designed for batch processing. Thus, once the data analysis phase is completed using mahout's distributed machine learning algorithms, a Hadoop Mapreduce job stores the clustering results into a non-relational database such as Hbase, it is one of the Hadoop subproject by apache, so that technical support engineers can query the information in real-time from Hbase using SQL like language called hive query. The information stored includes the support call number, the cluster identifier and the probability of that support call belongs to a given cluster. When an engineer queries the support calls related to a particular case, the cluster to which such a case should belong is identified in Hbase, along with all support calls within that cluster sorted based on their cluster membership probability. An ordered list returned to the technical support contains support call identifier and its associated cluster membership probability. The support calls displayed at the top of the ordered list are more likely to contain similar problems to the specified technical support case and as a result are more likely to have the same solution. The end to end framework presented above integrates Hadoop platform and mahout scalable machine learning library to provide a well-designed end to end solution that addresses a real world problem, the same framework can be used for solving most of the real word big data problems of different industries.

CONCLUSION

This Chapter explores the need of Hadoop data cluster, Hadoop file system, Map Reduce programming framework Hadoop sub projects like Hive, Hbase for storing, managing and real time analysis of big data and also explores the importance of large scale machine leaning in big data analytics with a PoC. So it mainly concentrated on the big data analysis using large scale machine learning algorithms. This chapter also covers big data platform compering with traditional platform of data processing. Software tools which currently available for applying machine learning on hadoop platform have been explored. The various efforts in designing scalable machine learning algorithms have been surveyed. It also covers the batch and stream processing of big data analytics and list out the various application of machine learning in solving the big data problem of various industries.

REFERENCES

Anjan, Srinath, Sharma, Kumar, Madhu, & Shanbag. (2012). Map Reduce Design and Implementation of a Priori Algorithm for Handling Voluminous data-sets. *Advanced Computing: An International Journal, 3*(6).

Barrachina & O'Driscoll. (2014). A big data methodology for categorizing technical support requests using Hadoop and Mahout. *Journal of Big Data.*

Hu, Wen, Chua, & Li. (n.d.). Toward Scalable Systems for Big Data Analytics: A Technology Tutorial. *IEEE Access.*

IBM. (2012). *IBM What Is Big Data: Bring Big Data to the Enterprise*. Retrieved from http:// www-01. ibm.com/software/data/bigdata/

Joseph, J., Sharif, O., & Kumar, A. (2014). *Using Big Data for Machine Learning Analytics in Manufacturing*. Tata Consultancy Services Limited White Paper.

Kang & Faloutsos. (n.d.). Big Graph Mining: Algorithms and Discoveries. *SIGKDD Explorations, 14*(2).

Lin & Dyer. (2010). *Data-Intensive Text Processing with MapReduce*. Academic Press.

Michel, F. (2015). *How Many Photos Are Uploaded to Flickr Every Day and Month?* Retrieved from https://www.flickr.com/photos/franckmichel/6855169886/

Nandakumar, & Yambem. (2014). A Survey on Data Mining Algorithms on Apache Hadoop Platform. *International Journal of Emerging Technology and Advanced Engineering, 4*(1).

Prajapati, V. (2013). *Big Data Analytics with R and Hadoop*. Packet Publishing.

Rajaraman, A., & Ullman, J. (2011). *Mining of Massive Data Sets*. Cambridge Univ. Press. doi:10.1017/CBO9781139058452

Singh. (2014). Big Data Analytic and Mining with Machine Learning Algorithm. *International Journal of Information and Computation Technology, 4*.

Twitter. (2012). *Twitter Blog, Dispatch from the Denver Debate*. Retrieved from http://blog.twitter.com/2012/10/dispatch-from-denver-debate.html

Wu. (2009). *MReC4.5: C4.5 Ensemble Classification with MapReduce*. China Grid.

Wu, X., Zhu, X., Wu, G.-Q., & Ding, W. (2014). Data Mining with Big Data. *IEEE Transactions on Knowledge and Data Engineering, 26*(1).

Chapter 12
Big Data Virtualization and Visualization:
On the Cloud

Muhammad Adeel
International Islamic University, Pakistan

ABSTRACT

With the recent explosion of internet usage as well as more and more devices are being hooked up with the cloud, big data is becoming a phenomena to tackle with. Big data management was initially a question of concern for only the big commercial players such as Google, Yahoo, Microsoft and others. But it has now become a concern for others, too. According to recent estimates, big data will continue to grow from terabytes into exabytes and beyond. This data needs to be made available for an organization's own use as well can be made available for scientific and commercial needs to the interested entities. This can include different user segments such as academia, industry etc. Academic use of big data is for further research and enablement of big data over cloud, working with it in containers, usage in virtualized environments etc. This generates a need for a sustainable infrastructure which can hold and maintain big data with opportunities for extended processing.

INTRODUCTION

Big data is an all-encompassing term for any collection of data sets which has become too large and complex to be processed by any conventional means. This implies that such huge data will not be able to be stored in simple conventional storage. Such huge data has to be first of all collected and stored ready to be provided in accessible formats. Such Big Data may be logs, mobile, banking transactions, online user generated content such as blog posts and tweets, online searches and satellite images. The data through its processing and its visualization can result in precious hidden information to be found out from that data.

Moreover, big data refers to a collection of datasets that are huge in size and complex to handle by commonly used data processing tools and applications. These datasets can be structured as well as

DOI: 10.4018/978-1-4666-9767-6.ch012

Copyright © 2016, IGI Global. Copying or distributing in print or electronic forms without written permission of IGI Global is prohibited.

unstructured and often come from various sources such as social media, social sensors, scientific applications, surveillance cameras, archives, web documents, electronic health records, business applications and web logs. They are mammoth in size with sometimes even more data arriving at a very fast rate a.k.a streaming data. Further, big data should have high value and ensure trust for decision making. Also, these data come from heterogeneous sources and heterogeneity is another important property for this big data besides its variety, volume, velocity, value and veracity.

There are many technologies that support handling big data including parallel processing, distributed computing, cloud computing platforms, large storage systems and MapReduce. There is an urgent need to investigate the challenges of big data computing by leveraging the potential of cloud computing. The chapter will try to bring into focus the concepts related to big data virtualization and its visualization on top of cloud computing.

SIGNIFICANCE OF BIG DATA AND APPLICATIONS

Big data management was initially a question of concern for only the big commercial entities such as Google, Yahoo, Microsoft, big research organizations (such as Nasa which may have to deal with trillions of bytes of satellite imagery, massive capturing of space signals etc), governments and so on. With the recent explosion of internet usage we can see, that more and more devices are being hooked up with the cloud (internet), and there are multiple government, commerical and defence orgranizations which are collecting and/or interested in analysing this big data. According to recent estimates, this data will continue to grow from terabytes into exabytes and possibly even beyond. This data needs to be made available for scientific and commerical needs to the interested parties in addition to its normal use. This can include different user segments such as academia, industry etc. Academic use of big data can result in further research and enablement of big data over cloud, experiments on big data in cloud computing, cloud based big data research, application containers, big data in virtual environments etc. Commercial use of this data can be quite wide ranging such as sentiment analysis, customer behaviour, future trend analysis, pattern mining in big data and the like. This generates a need for a sustainable infrastructure which can hold and maintain big data with opportunities for extended processing, visualization and transformations. Big data has some distinguishing characteristics which makes it unique than traditional data and which are described below in some detail:

- **Volume:** Big data is typically in the order of terabytes, peta bytes and even more. It become obvious that such data cannot be stored in any traditional means easily.
- **Value:** Big data brings value. It may be holding precious gems of information ready to be mined. This information will remain hidden if it cannot be fully processed and analyzed.
- **Velocity:** Big data such as sensors data collected through traffic sensors, home devices sensors, public places sensors, space signals analysis data, flight data of a Boeing 737. It is obvious that such data will be arriving, in fact streaming at a very fast pace. This generates the need to filter the noise out and store the remaining interesting big data quickly.
- **Veracity:** The data validity or truthfulness is important nonetheless. The ultimate value to be derived from big data depends solely on the level of veracity in the big data. The big data has to be truly authentic and should contain only minor defects and errors.

Advances in digital sensors, communications, computation, and storage have created huge collections of data, capturing information of value to business, science, government, and society. For example, search engine companies such as Google, Yahoo!, and Microsoft have become quite successful in analyzing the huge World Wide Web and providing search, targeted ads and other related services from this big data. These companies typically process terabytes of data every day and keep on looking at new ways of providing and enhancing services over this data. This delivery of services over the world wide web has transformed people way of finding and making use of information on a daily basis. Just as search engines have transformed how we access information, other forms of big- data computing will transform the activities of research organizations, more big data companies, scientific researchers, medical practitioners.

According to (Bryant, Katz, & Lazowska, 2008), Wal-Mart recently contracted with Hewlett Packard to construct a data warehouse capable of storing 4 petabytes (4000 trillion bytes) of data, representing every single purchase recorded by their point-of-sale terminals (around 267 million transactions per day) at their 6000 stores worldwide. By applying machine learning to this data, they can detect patterns indicating the effectiveness of their pricing strategies and advertising campaigns, and better manage their inventory and supply chains.

Furthermore, it is stated by (Bryant, Katz, & Lazowska, 2008) that many scientific disciplines have become data-driven. For example, a modern telescope is really just a very large digital camera. The proposed Large Synoptic Survey Telescope (LSST) is said to scan the sky from a mountaintop in Chile, recording 30 trillion bytes of image data every day – a data volume equal to two entire Sloan Digital Sky Surveys daily! Astronomers will apply massive computing power to this data to probe the origins of our universe which will definitely be provided by the cloud. According to (Bryant, Katz, & Lazowska, 2008), The Large Hadron Collider (LHC), a particle accelerator that will revolutionize our understanding of the workings of the Universe, will generate 60 terabytes of data per day – 15 petabytes (15 million gigabytes) annually. Similar eScience projects are proposed or underway in a wide variety of other disciplines, from biology to environmental science to oceanography. These projects generate such enormous data sets that automated analysis is required. Additionally, it becomes impractical to replicate copies at the sites of individual research groups, so need arises for even combining the computational resources to run big data analysis programs for all of the affiliated scientists.

The authors, (Bryant, Katz, & Lazowska, 2008) further develop the argument for big data in modern medicine. According to them, Modern medicine collects huge amounts of information about patients through imaging technology (CAT scans, MRI), genetic analysis (DNA microarrays), and other forms of diagnostic equipment. Human genome code can take massive amount of storage for its subsequent analysis. By applying data mining to data sets for large numbers of patients, medical researchers are gaining fundamental insights into the genetic and environmental causes of diseases, and creating more effective means of diagnosis. These measurements can then be used to guide simulations of climate and groundwater models to create reliable methods to predict the effects of long-term trends, such as increased $CO2$ emissions and the use of chemical fertilizers.

Moreover, according to (Bryant, Katz, & Lazowska, 2008) the collection of all documents on the World Wide Web (several hundred trillion bytes of text) is proving to be a corpus that can be mined and processed in many different ways. For example, language translation programs can be guided by statistical language models generated by analyzing billions of documents in the source and target languages, as well as multilingual documents, such as the minutes of the United Nations. Specialized web crawlers scan for documents at different reading levels to aid English-language education for first graders to adults. Cross language information retrieval frameworks can automatically provide translation and document retrieval from multiple languages into the result set. A conceptual network of noun- verb associations, (Bryant, Katz, & Lazowska, 2008), has been constructed based on word combinations found in web documents to guide a research project at Carnegie Mellon University in which MRI (magnetic resonace imaging) images are used to detect how human brains store information. The above discussion provides enough background on the significance of big data and its applications in different domain areas through its virtualization and visualization.

With big data virtualization it can be provided as a unified service for the data requesting entities. Big data would leverage the support provided by cloud for the performance aspect of efficiency, scalability and reliability. In addition, experiments/processing on big data using Map Reduce etc are quite easy to setup and process if the data is first made available through virtualization. New big data processing techniques will be easy to just "plug in" to the system ("cloud") and analyze the results.

BIG DATA VIRTUALIZATION AND VISUALIZATION

Managing Big Data Virtualization and Visualization

Data virtualization, a hot research area relates to how heterogeneous big data may be accessed, administered, and optimize on cloud based infrastructure as if it were a single, logically unified resource. This enables the abstraction of the external interface of big data from its internal implementation. Such infrastructure will help the big data services to continue with the addition and deletion of new data continuously in the system. A global file system or some other naming convention which can uniquely identify data items (such as files).

According to Talia (2013) in Toward Cloud-Based Big Data Analytics.Although few cloud-based analytics platforms are available today, current research work anticipates that they will become common within a few years. Some current solutions are based on open source systems such as Apache Hadoop and SciDB, while others are proprietary solutions provided by companies such as Google, IBM, EMC, BigML, Splunk Storm, Kognitio, and InsightsOne. As more such platforms emerge, big data storage and services will become even more ubiquitous.

The starting point in big data virtualization is that of first making that data available in the first place. (Zhang et al., 2013) have addressed this problem by providing two online algorithms (OLM and RHFC). Their solution discussed how dynamically generated geo disperesed data can be efficiently moved into cloud for processing further by a MapReduce type framework. Both solutions by these authors successfully tackle the problem and report close-to-offline optimum performance for both algorithms.

Shekhar, Gunturi, Evans, and Yang (2012) have addressed the problem of fast increasing, location-aware datasets with characteristics that exceeds the capability of spatial computing technologies. Their paper addresses the emerging challenges posed by special Spatial Big Data (SBD). SBD examples include trajectories of cell- phones and GPS devices, vehicle engine measurements, tem- porally detailed road maps, etc. According to them, SBD has the potential to transform society via next-generation routing services such as eco-routing. This data has very domain specific applications and is usable by mobile companies, car manufacturers, internet search providers etc. Incidently this area also holds great promises as part of autonomous spatical computing.

One example of big data management is one adopted by wikipedia. At multiple terabytes in size, the text and images of Wikipedia are an example of big data, see Figure 1. It allows the readers to edit the encyclopedia as well. With terabytes of data and continous editing of content from user, wikipedia provides one major use case of big data management.

According to Ji, Li, Qiu, Awada, and Li (2012), an approach to handle the demands for managing big data is to have a hierarchichal storage architecture. The architecture will lend it towards speedy processing of big data in the cloud. The hierarchichal storage architecture would effectively virtualize and provide access to data as/from a single entity at the same time. Later on we will see, how Hadoop Distributed file system (HDFS) as well as Open Stack storage tries to address this big data virtualzation problem. The contribution by (Pääkkönen & Pakkala, 2015) is the introduction of a technology independent reference architecture for big data systems, which is based on analysis of published implementation architectures of big data use cases.

Industry is one of the biggest generators of big data. The research published by Tan, Zhan, Ji, Ye, and Chang (2015) aims to use industry generated big data for enhancing supply chain innovation capabilities. The technique is based on the deduction graph technique. The approach provides an analytic

Figure 1. Visualization of daily Wikipedia edits created by IBM (© 2015, Wikipedia, Used Under Open Source License)

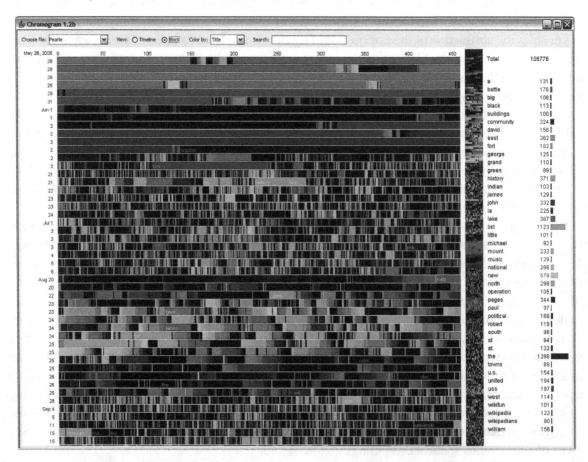

infrastructure for firms to incorporate their own competence sets with other firms. The results indicate that the proposed data analytic approach enable firms to utilize big data to gain competitive advantage by enhancing their supply chain innovation capabilities.

In the work by Ortiz, De Almeida, and Balazinska (2013), the authors provide a vision for personalized service level agreements in the cloud. In contrast to Amazon Elastic MapReduce and Google BigQuery services for big data virtualization and visualization which have specific pricing model and service level agreement (SLA) described at the level of compute resources (instance-hours or gigabytes processed). The authors propose a new abstraction, called a Personalized Service Level Agreement, where users are presented with what they can do with their data in terms of query capabilities, guaranteed query performance and fixed hourly prices.

HiTune (Dai, Huang, Huang, Huang, & Liu, 2011) is a system for analyzing cloud based big data. The system provides performance metrics for Hadoop. Although Big Data Cloud based technologies (e.g., MapReduce, Hadoop and Dryad) makes it easy to develop and run highly scalable applications, efficient provisioning and fine-tuning of these massively distributed systems remain a major challenge. In this paper, the authors describe a general approach to help address this challenge, based on distributed instrumentations and dataflow-driven performance analysis. Based on this approach, they have implemented HiTune, a scalable, lightweight and extensible performance analyzer for Hadoop. We report our experience on how HiTune helps users to efficiently conduct Hadoop performance analysis and tuning, demonstrating the benefits of dataflow-based analysis and the limitations of existing approaches (e.g., system statistics, Hadoop logs and metrics, and traditional profiling).

Starfish (Herodotou, Lim, Luo, Borisov, Dong, Cetin, & Babu, 2011) is a self tuning system for big data analytics. According to them, timely and cost-effective analytics over "Big Data" is now a key ingredient for success in many businesses, scientific and engineering disciplines, and government endeavors. The Hadoop software stack—which consists of an extensible MapReduce execution en-gine, pluggable distributed storage engines, and a range of procedural to declarative interfaces—is a popular choice for big data ana- lytics. Most practitioners of big data analytics—like computational scientists, systems researchers, and business analysts—lack the ex- pertise to tune the system to get good performance. Unfortunately, Hadoop's performance out of the box leaves much to be desired, leading to suboptimal use of resources, time, and money (in pay- as-you-go clouds). We introduce Starfish, a self-tuning system for big data analytics. Starfish builds on Hadoop while adapting to user needs and system workloads to provide good performance automat- ically, without any need for users to understand and manipulate the many tuning knobs in Hadoop. While Starfish's system architecture is guided by work on self-tuning database systems, we discuss how new analysis practices over big data pose new challenges; leading us to different design choices in Starfish.

According to Dai, Huang, Huang, Huang, and Liu (2011), there are dramatic differences between delivering software as a service in the cloud for millions to use, versus distributing software as bits for millions to run on their PCs. First and foremost, services must be highly scalable, storing and processing an enormous amount of data. For instance, in June 2010, Facebook reported 21PB raw storage capacity in their internal data warehouse, with 12TB compressed new data added every day and 800TB compressed data scanned daily. This type of "Big Data" phenomenon has led to the emergence of several new cloud infrastructures (e.g., MapReduce, Hadoop, Dryad, Pig and Hive), characterized by the ability to scale to thousands of nodes, fault tolerance and relaxed consistency. In these systems, the users can develop their applications according to a dataflow graph (either implicitly dictated by the programming/query model or explicitly specified by the users). Once an application is cast into the system, the cloud runtime is responsible for dynamically mapping the logical dataflow graph to the underlying cluster for distributed executions. With these Big Data cloud infrastructures, the users are required to exploit the inherent data parallelism exposed by the dataflow graph when developing the applications;on the other hand, they are abstracted away from the messy details of data partitioning, task distribution, load balancing, fault tolerance and node communications. Unfortunately, this abstraction makes it very difficult, if not impossible, for the users to understand the cloud runtime behaviors. Consequently, although Big Data Cloud makes it easy to develop and run highly scalable applications, efficient provisioning and fine-tuning of these massively distributed systems remain a major challenge. To help address this challenge, the authors attempt to design tools that allow users to understand the runtime behaviors of Big Data Cloud, so that they can make educated decisions regarding how to Improve the efficiency of these massively distributed systems – just as what traditional performance analyzers do for a single execution of a single program.

On performance aspect during big data virtualization and visualization, Dai, Huang, Huang, Huang, and Liu (2011) note: "Unfortunately, performance analysis for Big Data Cloud is particularly challenging, because these applications can potentially comprise several thousands of programs running on thousands of machines, and the low level performance details are hidden from the users by using a high level dataflow model." In this paper, the authors describe a specific solution to this problem based on distributed instrumentations and dataflow-driven performance analysis, which correlates concurrent performance activities across different programs and machines, reconstructs the dataflow-based, distributed execution process of the Big Data application, and relates the low level performance activities to the high level dataflow model.

In the internet of things (IOT) model, where almost everything we have will be "online", the amount of data generated qualifies as big data. Ninjablocks (ninjablocks.com) is one such service which can generate so big data through its sensor devices connected to the ninja cloud. Technologies supporting big data storage in the cloud are IBM DB2, Microsoft SQL Server, Postgresql open source server and also NoSQL databases.

Data virtualization allows the data-as-a-service model. Data accessible as uniform, single entity provides benefits to the interested clients. For commercial entities, big data in cloud can hold master data as well as helping in customer data integration (CDI) for the corporate clients. According to (Demirkan & Delen, 2013), Daas platforms use nosql which would really enable the storage / retrieval of semi structured data / records easily. Amazon offers simpleDB for this purpose. Although a distributed setup of relational databases is also possible to setup. Typically, the commerical data warehouse vendors provide visualization support for their data analytics offerings.

PNUTS (Cooper et al., 2008) is a system by yahoo for big data management over the cloud. PNUTS uses traditional computing systems to provide a geographically distributed, centrally managed service with automated load balancing and fail over.

Hadoop MapReduce provides an excellent open source framework for processing very large data sets over commodity hardware in parallel and fault tolerant manner. Hadoop processes input data in to very large distributed keys through map processes. It provides output with its reduce framework for towards the computer systems back.

Hadoop MapReduce

```
1.    package org.myorg;
2.
3.    import java.io.IOException;
4.    import java.util.*;
5.
6.    import org.apache.hadoop.fs.Path;
7.    import org.apache.hadoop.conf.*;
8.    import org.apache.hadoop.io.*;
9.    import org.apache.hadoop.mapred.*;
10.   import org.apache.hadoop.util.*;
11.
12.   public class WordCount {
13.
14.   public static class Map extends MapReduceBase implements Mapper<LongWritable, Text, Text,
      IntWritable> {
15.   private final static IntWritable one = new IntWritable(1);
16.   private Text word = new Text();
17.
18.   public void map(LongWritable key, Text value, OutputCollector<Text, IntWritable> output,
      Reporter reporter) throws IOException {
19.   String line = value.toString();
20.   StringTokenizer tokenizer = new StringTokenizer(line);
21.   while (tokenizer.hasMoreTokens()) {
22.   word.set(tokenizer.nextToken());
23.   output.collect(word, one);
24.   }
25.   }
26.   }
27.
28.   public static class Reduce extends MapReduceBase implements Reducer<Text, IntWritable, Text,
      IntWritable> {
29.   public void reduce(Text key, Iterator<IntWritable> values, OutputCollector<Text, IntWritable>
      output, Reporter reporter) throws IOException {
30.   int sum = 0;
31.   while (values.hasNext()) {
32.   sum += values.next().get();
33.   }
34.   output.collect(key, new IntWritable(sum));
35.   }
36.   }
37.
38.   public static void main(String[] args) throws Exception {
```

```
39.    JobConf conf = new JobConf(WordCount.class);
40.    conf.setJobName("wordcount");
41.
42.    conf.setOutputKeyClass(Text.class);
43.    conf.setOutputValueClass(IntWritable.class);
44.
45.    conf.setMapperClass(Map.class);
46.    conf.setCombinerClass(Reduce.class);
47.    conf.setReducerClass(Reduce.class);
48.
49.    conf.setInputFormat(TextInputFormat.class);
50.    conf.setOutputFormat(TextOutputFormat.class);
51.
52.    FileInputFormat.setInputPaths(conf, new Path(args[0]));
53.    FileOutputFormat.setOutputPath(conf, new Path(args[1]));
54.
55.    JobClient.runJob(conf);
57.    }
58.    }
59.
```

Map Reduce code (© 2015, https://hadoop.apache.org/docs/r1.2.1/mapred_tutorial.html)

SOLUTIONS AND RECOMMENDATIONS

As indicated in the above code, the mapper class is implemented in 18-25 lines, which has the task of splitting the input into key - value pairs. The combiner and in this case the reducer too is joining the output and then printing it.

The example elaborates the process of data crunching which in this case is just a locally running word cound program. Hadoop MapReduce (hadoop distributed file system, 2015) is provided with a highly scalable, fault tolerant and distributed file system which is designed to run on commodity scale hardware. The file system even supports streaming data access to facilitate batch type processing. Setting a farm of thousands of commodity hardware machines is cheap but it is not reliable compared to its costly counterparts.

Big data is getting bigger as part of an information explosion. Hadoop along with its processing tools provide a way to store big data in a fully virtualized manner (on HDFS). The tools provided as part of Hadooop and in addition to them by mostly the open source community enable powerful, time saving and efficient processing of that data.

One of the goals of Hadoop Distributed file system (HDFS) is to keep running while nodes keep on adding removing from the system. Moreover it runs on very large data sets (multi tera bytes of data sets i.e., big data). Hive is a datawarehouse infrastructure formed on top of Hadoop to provide further support for ad-hoc data summarization, query and analysis (visualization). Hive was created with Hadoop for analyzing massive amount of data pro vided by Hadoop for insight. As demonstrated earlier, even a simple MapReduce job can take some time to develop. Hive provides a language called HiveQL to transform SQL-like queries into MapReduce jobs which are then executeed on Hadoop. As SQL is part of almost all major relational database systems, it is easy to continue with in on Hadoop. Hive makes possible to readily use big data in Hadoop for computational problem solving. Hive is best used for summarizing, querying, and analyzing large sets of structured data where time is not of the essence (three open source hadoop, n.d.).

While Hive on MapReduce is very effective for summarizing, querying, and analyzing large sets of structured data, the computations Hadoop enables on MapReduce are slow and limited, which is where Spark (three open source hadoop, 2015) comes in.. Open sourced by Apache, Spark is a powerful Hadoop data processing engine which is touted to run 100x times faster than Hadoop MapReduce in memory and about 10x faster on disk.

The advantage for users is that Spark not only supports operations such as SQL queries, streaming data, and complex analytics such as machine learning and graph algorithms, it also allows these multiple capabilities to be combined seamlessly into a single workflow. In addition, Spark provides compatibility with Hadoop's Distributed File System (HDFS), HBase, and anyHadoop storage system, which means that all of an organization's existing data is immediately usable in Spark. And Spark's ability to unify big data analytics (e.g., virtualization and visualation) reduces the need for organizations to build separate processing systems to take care of their various computational needs.

Faced with the task of performing fast interactive analysis on a massive data warehouse of over 250 petabytes and counting, engineers at Facebook developed their own query machine called Presto. Unlike Spark, which runs programs both in memory and on disk, Presto runs in memory only. This functionality allows Presto to run simple queries on Hadoop in just a few hundred milliseconds, with more complex queries taking only a few minutes. In contrast, scanning over an entire dataset using Hive, which relies on MapReduce, can take anywhere from several minutes to several hours. Presto has also been shown to be up to seven times more efficient on the CPU than Hive. Plus Presto can combine data from multiple sources into a single query, allowing for analytics across an entire organization.

Today Presto is available as an open source distributed SQL query solution that organizations can use to run interactive analytic queries on data sources ranging from gigabytes to petabytes. With the ability to scale to the size of organizations as big as Facebook, Presto is a powerful query engine that has transformed the Hadoop ecosystem and could be transformative for organizations and entire industries as well.

MapR(mapr.com) is a complete distribution for Apache Hadoop that packages more than a dozen projects from the Hadoop ecosystem to provide you with both big data virtualization and graphic visualizatin. The MapR platform not only provides enterprise-grade features such as high availability, disaster recovery, security, and full data protection but also allows Hadoop to be easily accessed as traditional network attached storage (NAS) with read-write capabilities.

MapR delivers business-critical production success because of the advanced architecture of the MapR Data Platform, which is 100% binary compatible with the Apache Hadoop distributed file system (HDFS) to ensure plug-and-play compatibility and no vendor lock-in. The MapR Data Platform is a modern, true read-write capable, NFS-mountable distributed file-system written in C++ that directly accesses storage hardware – dramatically improving performance and ease of administration. Unlike other Hadoop distributions that require separate clusters for multiple applications, the data platform is built to process both distributed files and database tables in one unified layer – an engineering feat in its own right. This enables organizations to support both operational (e.g., HBase) and analytic apps (e.g., Apache Drill, Hive, or Impala) on one cluster, significantly reducing costs as you grow your Hadoop deployment.

Sap AG (the world top enterprise resource planning solutions provider) provides unprecedented insight with Hadoop and the SAP HANA platform for Big Data. This allows to extract maximum value from Big Data by combining the in-memory processing power of SAP HANA with Hadoop's storage and processing. Sap allows tapping into every valuable source of data in the organization and find valuable patterns which that lead to future growth. So Sap big data tools (Sap analytics, 2015) such as Sap IQ can be readily used for big data visualization in this case.

Analysts can further analyze streaming data in real time with SAP Event Stream Processor (SAP ESP) – and take immediate action.

Microsoft combines the power of open source Hadoop with its own cloud offering Microsoft Azure for big data virtualization as well as its visualization (Microsoft Excel is an option for it). Microsoft presents its approach to reveal new insights and drive better decision making with Azure HDInsight, a Microsoft Big Data solution powered by Apache Hadoop. The resulting insights are sharable to business users through Microsoft Excel. Azure is based on three major services which are HDInsight, SQL Database as relational database as a service and Storage. The storage is scalable to

- Geo-redundant storage across hundreds of miles
- With petabytes of storage
- Fastest performance in the industry
- Industry standard SMB file sharing across VMs
- Pay for what you use with competitive pricing
- REST, .NET, Java, C++, node.js, PowerShell and more

Microsoft Storage Points (http://azure.microsoft.com/en-us/services/storage/)

Ambari (Ambari, 2015) is a web-based tool for provisioning, managing, and monitoring Apache Hadoop clusters which includes support for Hadoop HDFS, Hadoop MapReduce, Hive, HCatalog, HBase, ZooKeeper, Oozie, Pig and Sqoop. Ambari also provides a dashboard for viewing cluster health such as heatmaps and ability to view MapReduce, Pig and Hive applications visually along with features to diagnose their performance characteristics in a user-friendly manner.

Much like Hadoop MapReduce along with the HDFS, the OpenStack is a fully cloud based offering for virtualizing and managing big data. In fact, open stack is a fully cloud based operating sytem that allows the managing of resources such as computing, storage and network all through central command and control. OpenStack big data virtualization capabilities scale to the size of petabytes of data for storage. Openstack writes data in multiple servers throughout the systems to ensure data integrity through replication. The storage options are is integrated and accessible through openStack compute and through the DashBoard. It is a fully open source distributed object based file system for big data ranging from terabytes to exabytes. OpenStack dashboard provides a graphical interface to manage cloud based resources but still falling short of providing full fledge big data visualization capabilities.

OpenStack Block Storage (Cinder) provides persistent block-level storage devices for use with OpenStack compute instances. The block storage system manages the creation, attaching and detaching of the block devices to servers. Block storage volumes are fully integrated into OpenStack Compute and the Dashboard allowing for cloud users to manage their own storage needs. In addition to local Linux server storage, it can use storage platforms including Ceph, CloudByte, Coraid, EMC (ScaleIO, VMAX and VNX), GlusterFS, Hitachi Data Systems, IBM Storage (Storwize family, SAN Volume Controller, XIV Storage System, and GPFS), Linux LIO, NetApp, Nexenta, Scality, Solid-Fire, HP (StoreVirtual and 3PAR StoreServ families) and Pure Storage.

Block storage is appropriate for performance sensitive scenarios such as database storage, expandable file systems, or providing a server with access to raw block level storage. Snapshot management provides powerful functionality for backing up data stored on block storage volumes. Snapshots can be restored or used to create a new block storage volume.(Open Stack, 2015)

As discussed earlier, big data can be deployed and used as part of a DaaS (Database as a service) framework. Trove is such a framework for openstack which allows full deployment of a cloud with encompassing features. Trove is basically data base as a service for openstack. It can utilize features of a relational or non relational database (MySQL or MongoDB, for example) to provide services. Trove as an implementor of big data enabling services provides a RESTFul api that supports JSON and XML to mange Trove instances.

Another cloud data virtualization technique is glusterFS (Gluster FS, 2015). GlusterFS is a scale-out network-attached storage file system. It has found applications including cloud computing, streaming media services, and content delivery networks. GlusterFS was developed originally by Gluster, Inc., then by Red Hat, Inc., after their purchase of Gluster in 2011. GlusterFS aggregates various storage servers over Ethernet or Infiniband RDMA interconnect into one large parallel network file system. It is free software, with some parts licensed under the GNU General Public License (GPL) v3 while others are dual licensed under either GPL v2 or the Lesser General Public License (LGPL) v3. GlusterFS is based on a stackable user space design.

Comparing open source as well as commercial big data offerings the open source offering seem to gain ground. For instance, OpenStack, Hadoop, Apache tools over Hadoop are all open source. In commercial technologies, Red Hat Storage Server was announced as a commercially-supported integration of GlusterFS with Red Hat Enterprise Linux. Moreover Google is using its BigTable deployed internally although it is part of the commercially offered Google cloud platform. PNUTS (Cooper et al., 2008) was offered by Yahoo as their data management platform for big data. Microsoft is offering its Azure platform for Big Data. The recent efforts are all toward being a part of the Open Stack software and enhancing from there. OpenStack Sahara project allows the interesting integration of Hadoop with OpenStack. This means OpenStack now allows a quite comprehensive big data virtualization through its supporting technologies along with its visualization.

Looking at commercial offering for big data management, the Google Bigtable (Chen, 2010) is a storage system by Google for virtualizing its big data and to use it for its computational needs. It is unlike relational data bases, is distributed and designed to scale to large data sets. Multiple google apps have been reported using big data as its backend storage provider i.e., Google Earth using Bigtable with around 70 terabytes of data (Chen, 2010). Bigtable is designed to store structured as well as semi structured data in distributed nodes across the network. Apache HBase provides big table like capabilities for Hadoop HDFS file system.

Much of big data is streaming data telling holding information about customer preferences, people sentiments, and even health care. The streaming data has to be passed through real time processing for which Hadoop is one very popular tool. Big data can provide big value to the enterprises and anyone who deploys but there is big effort involved. An underlying architecture is required which is suitable to be extended to accept further big data. The existing big data technologies (i.e., OpenStack, Hadoop) are in better position to extend themselves for processing further. This may not be completely possible for even very large traditional data base solutions of today.

Big data virtualization opens door for information enablement, analytics over the data such as data mining, knowledge discovery and so on. The tools do not need to go over heterogeneous sources to collect data. It would be present in one place, ready to be analyzed and results gathered from it for information consumers. Using big data analytics to fuel business growth is one of the top priorities for the enterprises. As discussed, both Hadoop and OpenStack are solid offerings in this area. Senior executives want to drive business decisions based on data analytics.

For intriguing big data business requirements, big data virtualization may be handled by the use of exclusive cloud based data storage services based on a traditional db provider which is then processed by an enterprise warehouse for analytics, decision making, data mining as well as visualization. Sap with Hana is a premium example, IBM analytics, Microsoft Analytics, Oracle ERPs services also fall in this area. Although as discussed earlier, open source technologies in conjunction with open source relational as well as non relational (nosql) databases can readily be deployed in the enterprise for the same purpose. This would require more efforts, but the end result can be almost always more flexible and rewarding. The initial setup cost of an open source setup can be significant, but later on there are very few if any licensing fees are involved which need to be paid to commercial big data visualization and analytics providers. Even more, the open source setup is very easy to accommodate to future changing requirements and needs.

Over the cloud, data security can have serious consequences. Data in the cloud has to be protected through security authorizations for intended users. If somehow the big data is compromised, this can be a significant loss. Big data can even be dependent on some country national laws and regulations where the data is actually stored. Large cloud providers may spread their data in different geographical locations around the globe for security purposes. A single interface to all data will allow the creation of information and its enablement in one place. New recovery processes are also required where big data gets in some catastrophe.

Big data visualization would emphasize upon the visualization of data. There are a lots of opportunities in this case. Statistics about the raw data can give valuable insight about the nature and form of original data. Almost always, this requires use of graphical libraries and toolkits to visualize trends in data. Clusters, graphs, trees and other visualizing tools can be used to capture and display the insight big data relationships thus helping decision making in the respective fields. For custom visualization, a high level programming language would be needed.

R is such a programming language for big data. The general consensus is that R compares well with other popular statistical packages, such as SAS, SPSS and Stata. In January 2009, the *New York Times* ran an article about R gaining acceptance among data analysts and presenting a potential threat for the market share occupied by commercial statistical packages, such as SAS. (Wikipedia_R, 2015)

The open source R language has also received Commercial backing. In 2007, Revolution Analytics was founded to provide commercial support for Revolution R, its distribution of R, which also includes components developed by the company (Wikipedia_R, 2015). Major additional components include: ParallelR, the R Productivity Environment IDE, RevoScaleR (for big data analysis), RevoDeployR, web services framework, and the ability for reading and writing data in the SAS file format.

In October 2011, Oracle announced the *Big Data Appliance*, which integrates R, Apache Hadoop, Oracle Linux, and a NoSQL database with the Exadata hardware. (Wikipedia_R), where Oracle R Enterprise is now one of two components of the "Oracle Advanced Analytics Option" (the other component is Oracle Data Mining). IBM offers support for in-Hadoop execution of R, and provides a programming model for massively parallel in-database analytics in R. There are numeous other major commercial software systems supporting connections to or integration with R.

Tibco offers a runtime version R as a part of Spotfire (Wikipedia_SpotFire). The following code illustrates the use of R programming language for very simple processing.

Example 1:

```
Hello World! Save the following code in a file called "demo.r"
### Initial MPI
library(pbdMPI, quiet = TRUE)
init()


comm.cat("Hello World!\n")

### Finish
finalize()
and use the command
mpiexec -np 2 Rscript demo.r
to execute the code where Rscript is one of command line executable program.
```

BIG DATA CHALLENGES IN DIVERSE DOMAINS

Big data is even a problem to handle in other scientific research fields as they progress i.e., Physics, Biology etc. According to (Marx, 2013), Biologists are joining the big-data club. With the advent of high-throughput genomics, life scientists are starting to grapple with massive data sets, encountering challenges with handling, processing and moving information that were once the domain of astronomers and high-energy physicists.

Furthermore, according to Marx, V. (2013), with every passing year, biologists turn more often to big data to probe everything from the regulation of genes and the evolution of genomes to why coastal algae bloom, what microbes dwell where in human body cavities and how the genetic make-up of different cancers influences how cancer patients fare. The European Bioinformatics Institute (EBI) in Hinxton, UK, part of the European Molecular Biology Laboratory and one of the world's largest biology-data repositories, currently stores 20 petabytes (1 petabyte is 10^{15} bytes) of data and back-ups about genes, proteins and small molecules. Genomic data account for 2 petabytes of that, a number that more than doubles every year.

Marx, V. (2013) puts the above presented data pile to be just one-tenth the size of the data store at CERN, Europe's particle-physics laboratory near Geneva, Switzerland. Every year, particle-collision events in CERN's Large Hadron Collider generate around 15 petabytes of data — the equivalent of about 4 million high-definition feature-length films. But the EBI and institutes like it face similar data-wrangling challenges to those at CERN, says Ewan Birney, associate director of the EBI.

In the work by (O'Driscoll, Daugelaite, & Sleator, 2013), the authors present and note:

- Ever improving next generation sequencing technologies has led to an unprecedented proliferation of sequence data.
- Biology is now one of the fastest growing fields of big data science.
- Cloud computing and big data technologies can be used to deal with biology's big data sets.
- The Apache Hadoop project, which provides distributed and parallelised data processing are presented.
- Challenges associated with cloud computing and big data technologies in biology

According to (O'Driscoll, Daugelaite, & Sleator, 2013), since the completion of the Human Genome project at the turn of the Century, there has been an unprecedented proliferation of genomic sequence data. A consequence of this is that the medical discoveries of the future will largely depend on our ability to process and analyse large genomic data sets, which continue to expand as the cost of sequencing decreases. The authors, (O'Driscoll, Daugelaite, & Sleator, 2013) provide an overview of cloud computing and big data technologies, and discuss how such expertise can be used to deal with biology's big data sets. In particular, big data technologies such as the Apache Hadoop project, which provides distributed and parallelised data processing and analysis of petabyte (PB) scale data sets will be discussed, together with an overview of the current usage of Hadoop within the bioinformatics community. Advances in next generation sequencing technologies has resulted in the generation of unprecedented levels of sequence data. Therefore, modern biology now presents new challenges in terms of data management, query and analysis. Human DNA is comprised of approximately 3 billion base pairs with a personal genome representing approximately 100 gigabytes (GB) of data, the equivalent of 102,400 photos.

FUTURE RESEARCH DIRECTIONS

The future holds great potential for big data. As big data will become more prevalent, technologies supporting it will also improve further. The emerging trend seems to be everyone shifting to the cloud such as a hybrid cloud, public cloud and a private cloud. As cloud cannot function without having some data to act on, the cloud technologies are focusing on big data component as well. OpenStack set of technologies seems to be the future area in which most research will take place and where cloud will be integrated with big data along with the technologies to process it.

CONCLUSION

The chapter has discussed big data virtualization and it visualization on the cloud. As cloud is the emerging new trend in computing, it is important to see how the big data fits into it. The discussion has tried to cover both academic research as well as commercial advancements and offering on big data. As discussed there are many existing technologies which are in different stages of development which can leverage and support big data accordingly.

REFERENCES

Bryant, R., Katz, R. H., & Lazowska, E. D. (2008). *Big-data computing: creating revolutionary breakthroughs in commerce, science and society.* Academic Press.

Cooper, B. F., Ramakrishnan, R., Srivastava, U., Silberstein, A., Bohannon, P., Jacobsen, H.-A., & Yerneni, R. et al. (2008). PNUTS:Yahoo!'s hosted data serving platform. *Proceedings of the VLDB Endowment, 1*(2), 1277–1288. doi:10.14778/1454159.1454167

Dai, J., Huang, J., Huang, S., Huang, B., & Liu, Y. (2011). HiTune: dataflow-based performance analysis for big data cloud. In Proc. of the 2011 USENIX ATC, (pp. 87-100). USENIX.

Demirkan, H., & Delen, D. (2013). Leveraging the capabilities of service-oriented decision support systems: Putting analytics and big data in cloud. *Decision Support Systems, 55*(1), 412–421. doi:10.1016/j.dss.2012.05.048

Design, H. D. F. S. (2015). Retrieved from http://hadoop.apache.org/docs/r1.2.1/hdfs design.html

Gluster, F. S. (2015). Retrieved from http://en.wikipedia.org/wiki/GlusterFS

Hadoop Ambari. (2015). Retrieved from http://hadoop.apache.org/

Hadoop Transform. (2015). Retrieved from http://opensource.com/business/15/3/three-open-source-projects-transform-hado

Herodotou, H., Lim, H., Luo, G., Borisov, N., Dong, L., Cetin, F. B., & Babu, S. (2011, January). Starfish: A Self-tuning System for Big Data Analytics. In CIDR (Vol. 11, pp. 261-272). Academic Press.

Ji, C., Li, Y., Qiu, W., Awada, U., & Li, K. (2012). Big data processing in cloud computing environments. In Proceedings of the International Symposium on Parallel Architectures, Algorithms and Networks, I-SPAN. doi:10.1109/I-SPAN.2012.9

MapReduce Tutorial. (2015). Retrieved from http://hadoop.apache.org/docs/r1.2.1/mapred tutorial.html

Marx, V. (2013). Biology: The big challenges of big data. [PubMed]. *Nature, 498*(7453), 255–260. doi:10.1038/498255a PMID:23765498

O'Driscoll, A., Daugelaite, J., & Sleator, R. D. (2013). 'Big data', Hadoop and cloud computing in genomics. [PubMed]. *Journal of Biomedical Informatics, 46*(5), 774–781. doi:10.1016/j.jbi.2013.07.001 PMID:23872175

OpenStack. (2015). Retrieved from http://en.wikipedia.org/wiki/OpenStack

Ortiz, J., De Almeida, V. T., & Balazinska, M. (2013, June). A vision for personalized service level agreements in the cloud. In *Proceedings of the Second Workshop on Data Analytics in the Cloud* (pp. 21-25). ACM. doi:10.1145/2486767.2486772

Pääkkönen, P., & Pakkala, D. (2015). *Reference Architecture and Classification of Technologies, Products and Services for Big Data Systems.* Academic Press.

Sap_Analytics. (2015). Big Data Research. Retrieved from www.sap.com/solution/big-data/software/hadoop/index.html

Shekhar, S., Gunturi, V., Evans, M. R., & Yang, K. (2012, May). Spatial big-data challenges intersecting mobility and cloud computing. In *Proceedings of the Eleventh ACM International Workshop on Data Engineering for Wireless and Mobile Access* (pp. 1-6). ACM. doi:10.1145/2258056.2258058

Talia, D. (2013). Toward cloud-based big data analytics. Retrieved from http://xa.yimg.com/kq/groups/16253916/1476905727/name/06515548.pdf

Tan, K. H., Zhan, Y., Ji, G., Ye, F., & Chang, C. (2015). Harvesting Big Data to Enhance Supply Chain Innovation Capabilities: An Analytic Infrastructure Based on Deduction Graph. *International Journal of Production Economics, 165*, 223–233. doi:10.1016/j.ijpe.2014.12.034

Wikipedia. _BigData. (2015). Visualization of daily Wikipedia edits created by IBM. Retrieved from http://en.wikipedia.org/wiki/Big_data

Wikipedia. _R. (2015). Retrieved from http://en.wikipedia.org/wiki/R_(programming_language

Wikipedia. _SpotFire. (2015). Retrieved from http://en.wikipedia.org/wiki/Spotfire

Zhang, L., Wu, C., Li, Z., Guo, C., Chen, M., & Lau, F. C. M. (2013). Moving big data to the cloud. In INFOCOM (pp. 405–409). IEEE. Retrieved from doi:10.1109/INFCOM.2013.6566804

Chapter 13
Resource Scheduling for Big Data on Cloud:
Scheduling Resources

K. Indira Suthakar
Thiagarajar College of Engineering, India

M. K. Kavitha Devi
Thiagarajar College of Engineering, India

ABSTRACT

Cloud computing is based on the concepts of distributed computing, grid computing, utility computing and virtualization. It is a virtual pool of resources which are provided to users via Internet. It gives users virtually unlimited pay-per-use computing resources without the burden of managing the underlying infrastructure. Cloud computing service providers' one of the goals is to use the resources efficiently and gain maximum profit. This leads to task scheduling as a core and challenging issue in cloud computing. This paper gives different scheduling strategies and algorithms in cloud computing.

INTRODUCTION

Cloud computing dates back to the 1960's when John McCarthy opined that "computation may someday be organized as a public utility". Amazon played a key role in cloud computing development by launching Amazon web service on utility basis in 2006. Before scheduling tasks on cloud computing, the characteristics of the cloud should be taken into account. Some of the characteristics of cloud include:

1. On-demand self service
2. Ubiquitous network access
3. Location independent resource pooling
4. Rapid elasticity
5. Pay per use

DOI: 10.4018/978-1-4666-9767-6.ch013

Copyright © 2016, IGI Global. Copying or distributing in print or electronic forms without written permission of IGI Global is prohibited.

Millions of user share cloud resources by submitting their computing task to the cloud system. Scheduling these millions of task is a challenge to cloud computing environment. Different scheduling strategies are proposed in the cloud resource scheduling environment. These strategies considers different factors like cost matrix generated by using credit of tasks to be assigned to a particular resource, quality of Service (QoS) based meta-scheduler and Backfill strategy based light weight virtual machine scheduler for dispatching jobs, QoS requirement heterogeneity of the cloud environment and workloads. Optimal resource allocation or task scheduling in the cloud should decide optimal number of systems required in the cloud so that the total cost is minimized and the SLA is upheld. Cloud computing is highly dynamic, and hence, resource allocation problems have to be continuously addressed, as servers become available/non-available while at the same time the customer demand fluctuates. Thus this study focuses on scheduling algorithms in cloud environment considering above mentioned characteristics, challenges and strategies.

TASK SCHEDULING TYPES

Cloud Service Scheduling

Cloud service scheduling is categorized at user level and system level. At user level scheduling deals with problems raised by service provision between providers and customers. The system level scheduling handles resource management within datacenter. Datacenter consists of many physical machines. Millions of tasks from users are received; assignment of these tasks to physical machine is done at datacenter. This assignment or scheduling significantly impacts the performance of datacenter. In addition to system utilization, other requirements like QoS, SLA, resource sharing, fault tolerance, reliability, real time satisfaction, etc. should be taken into consideration.

User Level Scheduling

Market-based and auction-based schedulers are suitable for regulating the supply and demand of cloud resources. Market based resource allocation is effective in cloud computing environment where resources are virtualized and delivered to user as a service. Development of a pricing model using processor-sharing for clouds, the application of this pricing model to composite services with dependency consideration and the development of two sets of profit-driven scheduling algorithms are proposed in. Service provisioning in Clouds is based on Service Level Agreements (SLA). SLA represents a contract signed between the customer and the service provider stating the terms of the agreement including non-functional requirements of the service specified as Quality of Service (QoS), obligations, and penalties in case of agreement violations. Thus there is a need of scheduling strategies considering multiple SLA parameters and efficient allocation of resources. A novel scheduling heuristic considering multiple SLA parameters for deploying applications in cloud. The scheduler algorithm that allows re-provisioning of resources on the cloud in the event of failures. The focus of model is to provide fair deal to the users and consumers, enhanced quality of service as well as generation of optimal revenue. A novel cloud scheduling scheme uses SLA along with trust monitor to provide a faster scheduling of the over flooding user request with secure processing of the request. A novel approach of heuristic-based request scheduling at each server, in each of the geographically distributed data centers, to globally minimize the penalty charged to the cloud computing system is proposed in. This approach considers two variants of heuristics, one based on the simulated annealing method of neighborhood searches and another based on FIFO scheduling. Based on the queuing model and system cost function, considering the goals of both the cloud computing service users and providers, proposes an algorithm to get the approximate optimistic value of service for each job in the corresponding no-preemptive priority M/G/1 queuing model. This approach guarantees the QoS requirements of the users' as well as the maximum profits for the cloud computing service providers. To deal with dynamically fluctuating resource demands, market driven resource allocation has been proposed and implemented by public Infrastructure-as-a-Service (IaaS) providers like Amazon EC2. In this environment, cloud resources are offered in distinct types of virtual machines (VMs) and the cloud provider runs an auction-based market for each VM type with the goal of achieving maximum revenue over time. A case study of single cloud provider and how to best match customer demand in terms of both supply and price in order to maximize the providers revenue and customer satisfactions while minimizing energy cost is proposed. Another auction-based mechanism for dynamic VM provisioning and allocation that takes into account the user demand for VMs when making VM provisioning decisions.

Static and Dynamic Scheduling

Static scheduling allows for pre-fetching required data and pipelining different stages of task execution. Static scheduling imposes less runtime overhead.

In case of dynamic scheduling information of the job components/task is not known before hand. Thus execution time of the task may not be known and the allocation of tasks is done on fly as the application executes. A job execution environment Flextic that exploits scalable static scheduling techniques to provide the user with a flexible pricing model and at the same time, reduce scheduling overhead for the cloud provider has been presented. The service request scheduling strategies in three -tier cloud structure, which consists of resource providers, service providers and consumers, should satisfy the objectives of the service providers and consumers. A dynamic priority scheduling algorithm (DPSA) is used to achieve above objectives. A new fault tolerant scheduling algorithm MaxRe is proposed in the cloud domain. This algorithm incorporates the reliability analysis into the active replication schema, and exploits a dynamic number of replicas for different tasks. A trust mechanism -`based task scheduling model is proposed in the cloud domain. Trust relationship is built among computing nodes, and the trustworthiness of nodes is evaluated by utilizing the Bayesian cognitive method. A feedback dynamic algorithm for preemptable job scheduling mechanism is proposed. A preemptable scheduling improves the utilization of resources in clouds and feedback procedure in above algorithms works well in the situation where resource contentions are fierce. In cloud computing, traditional way for task scheduling cannot measure the cost of cloud resources accurately by reason that each of the tasks on cloud systems is totally different between each other and introduces an optimized algorithm for task scheduling based on ABC (activity based costing) in cloud computing and its implementation. Also an experiment on different optimization strategies for cost -optimal dynamic scheduling in hybrid cloud environments is performed. To achieve QOS in cloud environment an improved backfill algorithm using balanced spiral (BS) method. It is used to analyze the various parallel job scheduling algorithms like EASY, conservative and CBA. In scheduling algorithm is proposed that measures both resource cost and computation performance and also improves the computation/communication ratio by grouping the user tasks according to a particular cloud resource's processing capability and sends the grouped jobs to the resource. Due to job grouping, communication of coarse-grained jobs and resources optimizes computation/communication ratio. A large number of cloud computing servers waste a tremendous amount of energy and emit a considerable amount of carbon dioxide. Green task scheduling is necessary to significantly reduce pollution and substantially lower energy usage.Green task scheduling approaches are proposed in the cloud domain. A fully decentralized scheduler aggregates information about the availability of the execution nodes throughout the network and uses it to allocate tasks to those nodes those are able to finish them in time.

As study considering the realistic network topology and communication model, proposes the Deadline, Reliability, Resources-aware (DRR) scheduling algorithm. Considering the failure and recovery scenario in the Cloud computing entities, proposes a Reinforcement Learning (RL) based algorithm to make job scheduling fault-tolerable while maximizing utilities attained in the long term. A new framework of task scheduling strategy for tree network.

Components of Task Scheduling in a Cloud

A hybrid cloud is a combination of both a private and a public cloud. The Figure 1 describes various the components of scheduling tasks in a hybrid cloud computing environment. The advantage of a hybrid cloud is the scalability of the resources. In a hybrid cloud computing environment the resources already available, is pooled up as a private cloud and extra resources required can be got from the public cloud on demand. To schedule the tasks in a hybrid cloud environment, the user submits the tasks to the scheduler in the private cloud and requests the Virtual Machine (VM) required for completing the task (Figure 1). The private cloud scheduler schedules the tasks on to the available virtual machines in the private cloud based on the scheduling strategy defined. If the task could not be completed using the resources in the private cloud then additional resources required are acquired from the public cloud service provider. A redirection strategy is used to redirect the tasks to the public cloud scheduler and the tasks are scheduled onto virtual machines in the public cloud.

TAXONOMY OF SCHEDULING ALGORITHMS

The Taxonomy of scheduling algorithms in the cloud environment based on task dependency for both the independent and dependent tasks is given in Figure 2. Based on the task dependency, the tasks can

Figure 1. Components of task scheduling

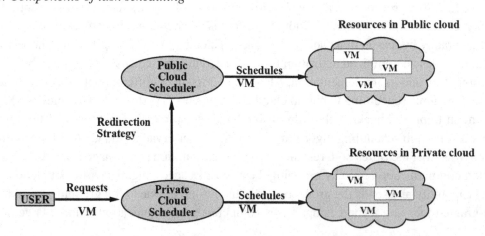

Figure 2. Task dependency classification

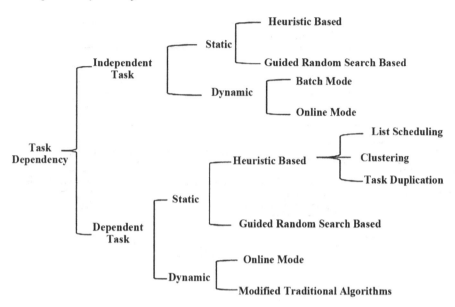

be classified as independent and dependent tasks. The tasks which do not require any communication between the tasks are called independent tasks. The dependent tasks differ from the independent tasks as the former have precedence order to be followed during the scheduling process. The main objective in scheduling the dependent tasks is to minimize the make span which is the total length of the schedule, by decreasing the time taken to execute each node called the Computation cost and the communication cost which is, the time taken to transfer data between the two nodes. Thus, the tasks dependency plays a vital role in deciding the appropriate scheduling strategy.

Static vs. Dynamic Scheduling Algorithms

As given in Figure 3, the algorithms for task scheduling can be broadly classified as static or dynamic based on the time at which the scheduling or assignment decisions are made. In the case of static scheduling, information regarding all the resources in the cloud and the complete set of tasks as well as all the independent sub tasks involved in a job is assumed to be available by the time the task is scheduled on the cloud. But in dynamic scheduling, a prior knowledge of the resources needed by the task and the environment in which it would be executed is unavailable as the jobs arrive in a real-time mode.

The static scheduling algorithms are further classified as heuristics based and guided random search based algorithms. The heuristics based class of algorithms makes the most realistic assumptions about a priori knowledge concerning process and system loading characteristics. It can be used in the scheduling problem which cannot give optimal answers but only require the most reasonable amount of cost and other system resources to perform their function. The guided random search based algorithms make random choices and guide them through the problem space. These algorithms are also called as "nature's heuristics" as they have a close resemblance to the phenomenon existing in nature. Genetic algorithm is an example of this type, which searches for a near-optimal solution in large solution spaces.

Figure 3. Dependent task-scheduling classification

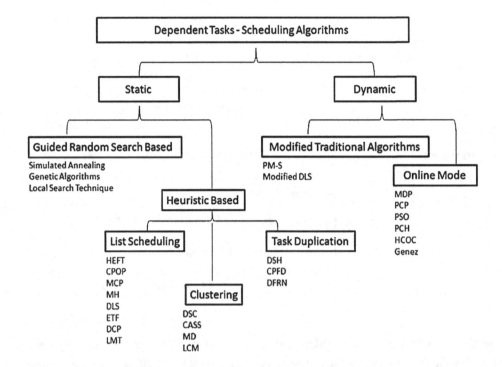

The dynamic scheduling algorithms can be used in two fashions namely on-line mode and batch mode. In the online mode, a task is scheduled onto a machine as soon as it arrives. Each task is scheduled only once and the scheduling result cannot be changed. Hence, on-line mode of dynamic scheduling can be applied, if the arrival rate of the tasks in the real-time is low. However, in the batch mode the tasks are collected into a set that is examined for scheduling at prescheduled times. While online mode heuristics consider a task for scheduling only once, batch mode heuristics consider a task for scheduling at each scheduling event until the task begins execution.

SCHEDULING INDEPENDENT TASKS

The various static and dynamic algorithms commonly used in scheduling the independent tasks are given in the Figure 4 and are discussed explains independent tasks may be further classified as coarsely grained and fine grained tasks based on the granularity. Granularity is the ratio of computation to the amount of communication. The Coarse-grained tasks communicate data infrequently and only after larger amounts of computations. The fine-grained tasks are small individual tasks in terms of code size and execution time. They have greater potential for parallelism but also greater overheads of processing and communication time.

Figure 4. Independent task-scheduling classification

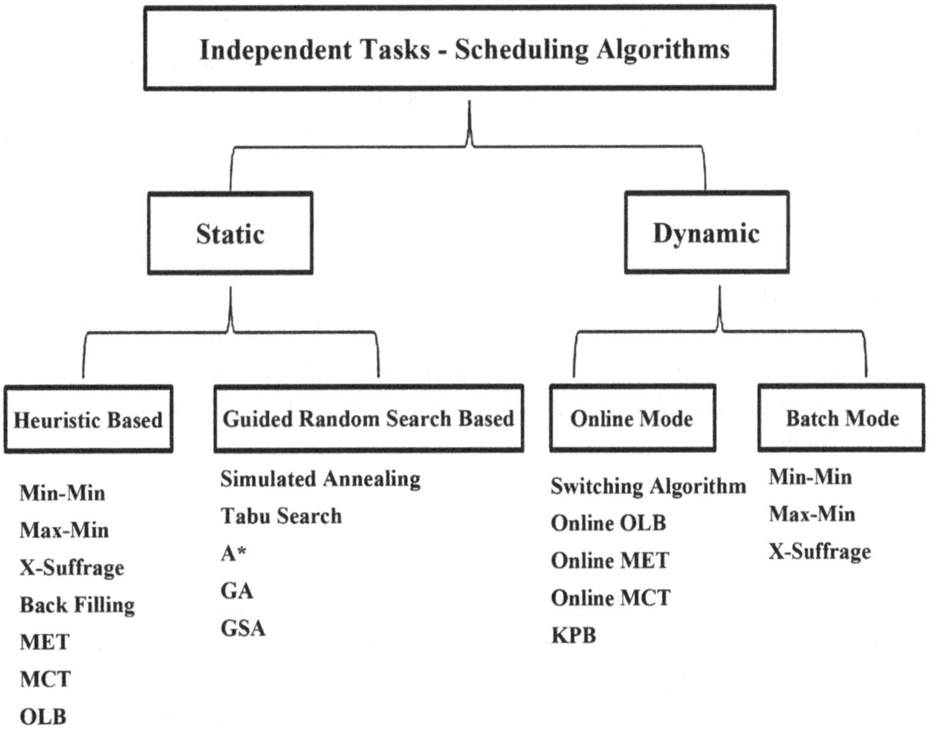

```
┌─────────────────────────────────────────────┐
│   Independent Tasks - Scheduling Algorithms   │
└─────────────────────────────────────────────┘
              │
      ┌───────┴────────┐
  ┌────────┐      ┌──────────┐
  │ Static │      │ Dynamic  │
  └────────┘      └──────────┘
```

Heuristic Based	Guided Random Search Based	Online Mode	Batch Mode
Min-Min	Simulated Annealing	Switching Algorithm	Min-Min
Max-Min	Tabu Search	Online OLB	Max-Min
X-Suffrage	A*	Online MET	X-Suffrage
Back Filling	GA	Online MCT	
MET	GSA	KPB	
MCT			
OLB			

Static Algorithms for Independent Tasks

The static algorithms used for scheduling the independent tasks can be broadly classified as Heuristic based and Random search based algorithms. The various heuristic based algorithms are discussed briefly in the following section.

Static - Heuristic Based Algorithms

Braun et al have done a detailed comparative study of various static scheduling algorithms for scheduling independent tasks. Some of the popular algorithms are OLB, MET, MCT, Max-Min etc.

Opportunistic Load Balancing (OLB)

The OLB scheduling algorithm tries to keep all the machines or resources available as busy as possible. Thus it assigns each task to the next immediately available machine in a random order. The tasks are assigned randomly irrespective of the expected execution time on that machine.

The advantage of OLB that it is simple and easy to implement as it does not require any extra calcula-tion. The disadvantage in OLB is that the mappings it finds can result in very poor make span as OLB does not consider expected task execution times, when assigning the tasks to the resources.

Minimum Execution Time (MET)

In contrast to OLB, the main objective of the Minimum Execution Time (MET) is to give each task to its best machine. Thus MET assigns each task, in arbitrary order, to the machine with the best expected execution time for that task, regardless of that machine's availability. Though MET is also very simple to implement, it can cause a severe load imbalance across machines as it ignores the availability of machines during the scheduling process.

Minimum Completion Time (MCT)

The motivation behind MCT is to combine the benefits of both OLB and MET and to avoid the circumstances in which OLB and MET perform poorly. The Minimum Completion Time algorithm schedules each task, in arbitrary order to the machine with the minimum completion time for that task. But the limitation of this approach is that all the tasks cannot be assigned to the machines that have the minimum execution time for them.

The Min-Min Heuristic

In the Min-min heuristic, the minimum completion time C for each task to be scheduled is calculated and the task with the overall minimum completion time is selected and assigned to the corresponding machine. Hence the algorithm is given the name Min-min. The scheduled task is removed from the set of tasks to be scheduled, and the process is repeated until all tasks are scheduled.

Similar to MCT the Min-min algorithm is based on the minimum completion time. However, MCT considers only one task at a time but the Min-min considers all the unscheduled tasks for each decision making step. The advantage of Min-min is that it assigns the tasks in the order that changes the machine availability status by the least amount that any assignment could. Thus more tasks can be assigned to the machines that complete them the earliest and also execute them the fastest.

The Max-Min Heuristic

In Max-min, the task with the longer execution time is assigned to the best machine available first and is executed concurrently with the remaining tasks with shorter execution times. This helps to minimize the penalties incurred from performing tasks with longer execution times at last.

The Max-min heuristic approach gives a more balanced load across machines and a better make span than the Min-min. Because in Min-min all of the shorter tasks would execute first, and then the longer running task would be executed while several machines sit idle. Thus the Max-min performs better than the Min-min heuristic if the number of shorter tasks is larger than that of longer tasks.

Min-min and Max-min algorithms are simple and can be easily amended to adapt to different scenarios. QoS Guided Min-min heuristic, Segmented Min-min algorithm are modifications of the existing min-min algorithm.

Xsuffrage

The idea behind Suffrage approach is, the task that would suffer the most, if it is not assigned to a machine should be given the first priority than the other tasks. The suffrage value of each task is defined as the difference between its best MCT and its second-best MCT. Conventional suffrage algorithms may have problems when the resources are clustered. An improved approach called XSuffrage by Casanova et al, gives a cluster level suffrage value to each task and experiments show it outperforms the conventional Suffrage approach.

Backfilling Algorithms

Backfilling is a policy of strategically allowing tasks to run out of order to reduce fragmentation or idle holes. The most popular backfilling strategies are the Conservative, Aggressive and Selective backfilling strategies. In conservative backfilling, jobs are given reservation as and when they arrive. Hence, if the jobs are longer, it is very difficult for other jobs to get a reservation ahead of previously arrived jobs. With Aggressive Backfilling, only the request at the head of the waiting queue called the pivot is granted a reservation and other requests are allowed to move ahead in the queue if they do not delay the pivot. Under selective backfilling a request is granted a reservation if its expected slowdown exceeds a threshold.

Static - Random Search Based Algorithms for Independent Task

Genetic Algorithm

GA is an evolutionary technique to perform search in a large solution space. In GA the various steps like population selection, seeding, crossover, and mutation are carried out for mapping the tasks on to the machines. While the advantages of the GAs are the generation of the good quality of output schedules, the disadvantages are: The scheduling times are usually much higher than the heuristic- based techniques. Also, the optimal set of control parameters obtained for one set of task scheduling may not be optimal for another set of tasks.

Simulate Annealing (SA)

SA is a search technique based on the physical process of annealing, which is the thermal process of obtaining low-energy crystalline states of a solid. SA theory states that if temperature is lowered sufficiently slowly, the solid will reach thermal equilibrium, which is an optimal state. By analogy, the thermal equilibrium is an optimal task-machine mapping (optimization goal), the temperature is the total completion time of a mapping (cost function), and the change of temperature is the process of mapping change. If the next temperature is higher, which means a worse mapping, the next state is accepted with certain probability.

Tabu Search (TS)

Tabu Search is a meta-strategy for guiding known heuristics to overcome local optimality. It is an iterative technique which explores a set of problem solutions, denoted by X, by repeatedly making moves from one solution to another solution *s'* located in the neighborhood *N(s)* of *s*. These moves are performed with the aim of efficiently reaching an optimal solution by minimizing some objective functions.

GSA

The Genetic Simulated Annealing (GSA) heuristic is a combination of the GA and SA techniques. In general, GSA follows procedures similar to the GA. However, for the selection process, GSA uses the SA cooling schedule and system temperature and a simplified SA decision process for accepting or rejecting a new chromosome.

A*

A* is a tree based search heuristic beginning at a root node that is a null solution. As the tree grows, nodes represent partial scheduling (a subset of tasks is assigned to machines), and leaves represent final scheduling (all tasks are assigned to machines). The partial solution of a child node has one more task scheduled than the parent node. Each parent node can be replaced by its children. To keep execution time of the heuristic tractable, there is a pruning process to limit the maximum number of active nodes in the tree at any one time. If the tree is not pruned, this method is equivalent to an exhaustive search. This process continues until a leaf (complete scheduling) is reached.

Dynamic Algorithms for Independent Tasks

Online Mode

The OLB, MET, MCT algorithms discussed in the previous section can also be used to schedule independent tasks dynamically in the online mode. The other algorithms include Switching Algorithm and the k-percent best (KPB).

SA (Switching Algorithm)

SA (Switching Algorithm) uses the MCT and MET heuristics in a cyclic fashion depending on the load distribution across the machines. MET can choose the best machine for tasks but might assign too many tasks to same machines, while MCT can balance the load, but might not assign tasks machines that have their minimum executing time. If the tasks are arriving in a random mix, it is possible to use the MET at the expense of load balance up to a given threshold and then use the MCT to smooth the load across the machines.

K-Percent Best (KPB)

KPB (K-Percent Best) heuristic considers only a subset of machines while scheduling a task. The subset is formed by picking the k best machines based on the execution times for the task. A good value of k schedules a task to a machine only within a subset formed from computationally superior machines. The purpose is to avoid putting the current task.

HEURISTIC MODEL FOR TASK EXECUTION SCHEDULING

Introduction

A cloud is a type of distributed system, it consist of, collection of interconnected and virtualized computers. It offers pool of resources like data, software and infrastructure etc, to the user. So the efficient utilization of cloud resources has become a major challenge in cloud computing. Scheduling in cloud is responsible for selection of best suitable resources for executing a task, by considering some static and dynamic parameters like makespan, cost, resource utilization; speed etc. Cloud service providers provide services to large scale cloud environment with cost benefits. Also, there are some popular large scaled applications like social networking and internet commerce. These applications can provide benefit in terms of minimizing the costs using cloud computing. Cloud computing is considered as internet based computing service provided by various infrastructure providers based on their need, so that cloud is subject to Quality of Service(QoS), Load Balance (LB) and other factors which have direct effect on user consumption of resources controlled by cloud infrastructure. In cloud scheduling process need to achieve several factors. So it needs to use effective algorithm for allocating proper task to the proper resources. Various task scheduling algorithms has been proposed by researchers, most important task scheduling algorithms are Min-Min, Max-Min etc.

Scheduling Process in Cloud

The main advantage of job scheduling algorithm is to achieve a high performance computing and the best system throughput. The available resources should be utilized efficiently without affecting the service parameters of cloud. Scheduling process in cloud can be categorized into three stages they are Resource discovering and filtering, Resource selection, and Task submission. In resource discovery datacenter broker discovers the resources present in the network system and collects status information related to them. During resource selection process target resource is selected based on certain parameters of task and resource. Then during task submission task is submitted to selected resources.

Scheduling

Scheduling theory for cloud computing is gaining consideration with day by day hike in cloud popularity. In general, scheduling is the process of mapping tasks to available resources on the basis of tasks' characteristics and requirements. It is an essential aspect in efficacious working of cloud as many task parameters need to be considered for proper scheduling. The available resources should be utilized efficiently without affecting the service parameters of cloud. Scheduling process in cloud can be generalized into three stages namely:

1. **Resource Discovering and Filtering:** Datacenter Broker discovers the resources present in the network system and collects status information related to them.
2. **Resource Selection:** Target resource is selected based on certain parameters of task and resource. This is deciding stage.
3. **Task Submissions:** Task is submitted to resource selected.

Response Based Scheduling

Task Grouping

Grouping means collection of components on the basis of certain behavior or attribute. By task grouping in cloud it is meant that tasks of similar type can be grouped together and then scheduled collectively. We can say that it is a behavior that supports the creation of 'sets of tasks' by some form of commonality. In the proposed framework tasks are grouped on the basis of constraint which can be deadline or minimum cost. Once the tasks are grouped, they can be judged for their priority and scheduled accordingly. Grouping, if employed to combine several tasks, reduces the cost-communication ration.

Prioritization

Priority determines the importance of the element with which it is associated. In terms of task scheduling, it determines the order of task scheduling based on the parameters undertaken for its computation. In the present framework, the deadline based tasks are prioritized on the basis of task deadline. The tasks with shorter deadline need to be executed first. So they are given more priority in scheduling sequence. The task list is rearranged with tasks arranged in ascending order of deadline in order to execute the task with minimum time constraint first. The cost based tasks are prioritized on the basis of task profit in descending order. This is appreciable as tasks with higher profit can be executed on minimum cost based machine to give maximum profit.

Greedy Allocation

Greedy algorithm is suitable for dynamic heterogeneous resource environment connected to the scheduler through homogeneous communication environment. Greedy approach is one of the approach used to solve the job scheduling problem. According to the greedy approach.

Deadline Constrained Based

To improve the completion time of tasks greedy algorithm is used with aim of minimizing the turnaround task of individual tasks, resulting in an overall improvement of completion time.

Turnaround Time = Resource Waiting Time + Task Length / Proc. Power of Resource

After calculating the turnaround time for each resource, the resource with minimum turnaround time is selected and task is executed there. The scheduler locates the best suited resource that minimizes the turnaround time. The turnaround time is calculated on the basis of expected completion time of a job. Once the scheduler submits a task to a machine, the resource will remain for some time in processing of that job. The resource status is updated to find out when the resource will be available to process a new job.

Minimum Cost Based

The resource with minimum cost is selected and tasks are scheduled on it until its capacity is supported. After scheduling each task the resource status is updated accordingly. Thus the selection of task and target resource is sequential once they are prioritized according to user needs.

*Cost of Task = (Task length / Proc Power of Resource) * Resource Cost*

Request Based Schedule

Scheduling Process

The process of scheduling can be viewed as service request scheduling (service provider and the Consumer) and resource scheduling (service provider and resource provider).

The process of service request scheduling occurs as:

1. Users submit their request to the service provider.
2. Service provider executes the request.
3. Process the request in the service request architecture.
4. Dynamic VM generation and dispatch at the resource provider site.

System Architecture

The major components in the service request scheduling are:

1. **Classifier:** Receives user request, process and classifies into smaller task units. These task units can be scheduled directly onto the scheduler but before that it needs to get assigned with random priorities. Priority can either be based on system state or the task characteristics. Once each task gets its unique priority these task units can be sent to the scheduler component to be scheduled.
2. **Scheduler:** Each scheduler contains several schedule units, each having its own priority based on the system design and the real situation. Scheduler pushes up the task units into appropriate schedule units based on the idleness and the saturation of each and every schedule unit. Scheduler units execute the task units based on the algorithm. The task unit with the lower deadline will be scheduled first to optimize the result.
3. **Compactor:** Summarizes the completed task units during each cycle and sends it to the resource provider.

Task Scheduling in Cloud Computing

Job Scheduling of cloud computing refers to dispatch the computing tasks to resource pooling between different resource users according to certain rules of resource use under a given cloud circumstances. At present there is not a uniform standard for job scheduling in cloud computing. Resource management and job scheduling are the key technologies of cloud computing that plays a vital role in an efficient cloud resource management.

Scheduling Policy

The following task scheduling algorithms are presently established in the cloud environments.

Ant Colony Optimization (ACO)-Inspired

A new Cloud scheduler based on Ant Colony Optimization is the one presented by Cristian Mateos and et.al. The goal of our scheduler is to minimize the weighted flowtime of a set of PSE jobs, while also minimizing Makespan when using a Cloud. In the ACO algorithm, the load is calculated on each host taking into account the CPU utilization made by all the VMs that are executing on each host. This metric is useful for an ant to choose the least loaded host to allocate its VM. Parameter Sweep Experiments (PSE) is a type of numerical simulation that involves running a large number of independent jobs and typically requires a lot of computing power. These jobs must be efficiently processed in the different computing resources of a distributed environment such as the ones provided by Cloud. Consequently, job scheduling in this context indeed plays a fundamental role. In this algorithm, Makespan and flow-time are evaluated. Evaluation results of this metrics show that ACO performance better than two other (Random and Best effort) algorithm.

Berger Model

Baomin Xu and et.al proposed for the first time an algorithm of job scheduling based on Berger model in cloud environment. The Berger model of distributive justice is based on expectation states. It is a series of distribution theories of social wealth. Expectation states formed by a series of theories are used to study actors and evaluate the impact of their behavior. Brief speaking, expectation states theories are to study the follow two issues. First, actor how to generate expectations of itself and other individual's according to the information (such as status, reward, and performance differences) around the world; Secondly, these expectations how to affect the behavior (such as participatory, and decision-making influence) of actors and others. Expectation states theories have been expanded and applied widely. State value theory of distribution justice is an important theoretical basis of the paper. It described that allocator how to use referential comparisons to establish the expectation for reward allocation. The expectations are used to evaluate the justice or injustice of distribution in a variety of circumstances. Through the expansion of CloudSim platform, job scheduling algorithm based on Berger model is implemented. The validity of the algorithm is verified on the extended simulation platform. By comparing of simulation results with the optimal completion time algorithm, the proposed algorithm in this paper is effective implementation of user tasks, and with better fairness.

Dynamic Level Scheduling (DLS) Algorithm

Wei Wang and et.al extend the traditional DLS algorithm by considering trustworthiness of resource nodes. This algorithm meets the requirement of user jobs in trust, and makes jobs scheduling based on directed acyclic graph (DAG) more reasonable. The main contribution of this study to scheduling systems is that it extends the t traditional formulation of the scheduling problem so that both execution time and reliability of applications are simultaneously accounted for. Evaluation the trustworthiness of machines in Cloud environment by proposed algorithm shows decrease the failure probability of the task assignments, and assurance of the execution of tasks in a security environment.

Min-Min Algorithm

The main idea of the Min-Min algorithm is as quickly as possible to dispatch each task to virtual machines as resources which can complete the task in the shortest possible time. Min-Min algorithm will execute short jobs in parallel and the long jobs will follow the short jobs. The shortcoming of this algorithm is the short jobs scheduled first, until the machines are leisure to schedule and execute long jobs. Min-min can cause both the whole batch jobs executed time get longer and unbalanced load. Even long jobs cannot be executed. Compared with the traditional Minmin algorithm, improved algorithm adds the three constraints (quality of service, the dynamic priority model and the cost of service) strategy which can change this condition. The experimental results of improved Min-Min algorithm show it can increase resource utilization rate, long tasks can execute at reasonable time and meet users' requirements.

Particle Swarm Optimization (PSO) Algorithm

Particle Swarm Optimization (PSO) as a meta-heuristics method is a self-adaptive global search based optimization technique introduced by Kennedy and Eberhart. The PSO algorithm is alike to other population-based algorithms like Genetic algorithms (GA) but, there is no direct recombination of individuals of the population.

The PSO algorithm focuses on minimizing the total cost of computation of an application workflow. As a measure of performance, Authors used cost for complete execution of application as a metric. The objective is to minimize the total cost of execution of application workflows on Cloud computing environments. Results show that PSO based task-resource mapping can achieve at least three times cost savings as compared to Best Resource Selection (BRS) based mapping for our application workflow. In addition, PSO balances the load on compute resources by distributing tasks to available resources.

Priority Based Job Scheduling (PJSC) Algorithm

Priority of jobs is an important issue in scheduling because some jobs should be serviced earlier than other those jobs can't stay for a long time in a system.

In cloud computing, the main objective of this algorithm is to propose a new priority based job scheduling algorithm called PJSC. The proposed algorithm is based on the theory of Analytical Hierarchy Process (AHP). The Analytical Hierarchy Process is a multi-criteria decision making (MCDM) and multi-attribute decision-making (MCDM) model. The PJSC algorithm is based on multiple criteria decision making model. The PJSC algorithm provided a discussion about some issues such as complexity, consistency and finish time. Evaluation result of this algorithm has reasonable complexity, also it decrease finish time (Makespan).

Round Robin Algorithm

The Round Robin algorithm mainly focuses on distributing the load equally to all the resources. Using this algorithm, the broker allocates one VM to a node in a cyclic manner. The round robin scheduling in the cloud computing is very similar to the round robin scheduling used in the process scheduling. The scheduler starts with a node and moves on to the next node, after a VM is assigned to that node.

Although round robin algorithms are based on simple rule, more load is conceived on servers and thus unbalancing the traffic. Result of Round Robin algorithm shows better response time and load balancing as compared to the other Algorithm.

HEURISTIC MODELS FOR TASK SCHEDULING

Heuristics are applied to find an optimal solution to the scheduling. Heuristic can be both static and dynamic. Static heuristic is applied when the numbers of tasks to be completed are known in prior. Dynamic heuristic can be used when the task arrival is dynamic in nature. This paper focus on heuristic algorithms such as Min-Min, Max-Min and Improved Min-Min. The dynamic heuristic is used in two ways. They are Online mode and batch mode. In online mode heuristic algorithms tasks are scheduled when they arrive in the system. In batch mode heuristic algorithm tasks are queued and collected into a set when they arrive the system.

Min-Min Algorithm

Min-Min algorithm is a type of batch mode scheduling algorithm, so all the arriving tasks are grouped in a queue then it is scheduled; group of tasks is called meta task. Min-Min algorithm first executes minimum sized tasks with resource which gives the minimum execution time so it is called as Min-Min algorithm. Min-Min scheduling is based on Minimum Completion Time (MCT); that is used to assign tasks to the resources having minimum expected completion time (Su, Li, Huang, Huang, Shuang, & Wang, 2013).

Initially a scheduler takes a set of unmapped/ unscheduled tasks and a set of available resources starting by task with minimum MCT to be mapped to next resources; this process is repeated until the unmapped set becomes empty. Briefly, expectation time produces a smaller makespan, which is a measure of throughput of heterogeneous computing systems like computational grids and If more tasks can be obtained, they can be mapped to resources to complete them earliest and executing them faster.

1. for all tasks Ti in meta-task Mv
2. for all resources Rj
3. Cij = Eij + rj
4. do until all tasks in Mv are mapped
5. for each task in Mv find the earliest completion time and the resource that obtains it.
6. find the task Tk with the minimum earliest completion time.
7. assign task Tk to resource that gives the earliest completion time.
8. delete task Tk from Mv.
9. update rj
10. update Cij for all i.
11. end do.

In Figure 2 rj represents the ready time of the resource Rj to execute a task, Cij and Eij represent the expected completion time and execution time of the tasks.

Max-Min Algorithm

It is also a type of batch mode scheduling algorithm it overcomes the limitations of Min-Min algorithm. Similar to Min-Min, a scheduler schedules tasks by expecting the Execution Time of the tasks and allocation of resources. Instead of selecting the minimum MCT, the maximum MCT is selected, that is why it is named Max-Min. It focuses on giving priority to large tasks over others small. The Max-Min algorithm is typical to the Min-Min algorithm, except for being different in; the word "minimum" would be replaced by "maximum". Officially Max-Min algorithm does better than Min-Min algorithm in cases when the number of short tasks is more than the longer ones. For example, if there is only one long task, the Max-Min algorithm executes many short tasks concurrently with the long one.

1. for all tasks Ti in meta-task Mv
2. for all resources Rj
3. Cij = Eij + rj
4. do until all tasks in Mv are mapped
5. for each task in Mv find the earliest completion time and the resource that obtains it.
6. find the task Tk with the maximum earliest completion time.
7. assign task Tk to resource that gives the earliest completion time.
8. delete task Tk from Mv.
9. update rj
10. update Cij for all i.
11. end do.

Max-Min Algorithm

In algorithm 2, the expected time of resource Rj is the time to become ready to execute a task after finishing the execution of all tasks assigned to it which is denoted by rj. Also Eij is the estimated execution time of task Ti on resource Rj whereas Cij is the Expected Completion Time that is the estimated execution time and ready time together.

Drawbacks

1. Min-Min algorithm attempts to assign the short tasks before the long one.
2. The Min-Min algorithm seems worse in the cases when the number of short tasks is much more than the long ones.
3. Max- Min algorithm can executes short tasks concurrent with the long task.

PROPOSED HEURISTIC ALGORITHM FOR TASK SCHEDULING

A typical data centre which consists of commodity machines connected through various high speed links in cloud computing. This environment is used to compute dissimilar and large group of tasks. Basically it is not possible to distinguish the tasks of one user from the other. Hence scheduling problem over here is going to be matching multiple tasks to multi machines as in Figure 5. The optimal matching is an optimization problem which possesses NP-complete complexity. In general the heuristic model is applied as a suboptimal algorithm in order to obtain good solution. In dynamic batch mode heuristic scheduling tasks are queued and collected into a set when they arrive in the system. The scheduling algorithm will start after a fixed period of time and according to some priority factor. This paper focused on most popular existing heuristic approach named Min-Min, in order to overcome the limitations of Min-Min algorithm the improved version of the Min-Min algorithm has been developed.

Improved Min-Min Algorithm

The Min-Min algorithm does not provide better performance when the number of short tasks is high. So the Max-Min Algorithm is used, it can execute short tasks concurrently with the long task on different resources, so it can achieve better Performance in terms of load balancing it will automatically decrease the makespan. So in order to avoid the drawbacks of Min-Min algorithm improved Min-Min algorithm is used. In this scheduling algorithm all the tasks should be sorted ascending. It means that tasks with minimum completion time are in front of the queue and tasks with maximum completion time are in rear of the queue. Then this algorithm like the Min- Min algorithm, computes minimum completion time of all tasks on available resources. After that, the resource according to the appropriate condition should be chosen. For selecting a task for Scheduling, it first computes the average of completion time and standard deviation of existing tasks.

EXPERIMENTAL RESULT

The performance of scheduling algorithms are calculated based on the following parameter.

Figure 5. Scheduling

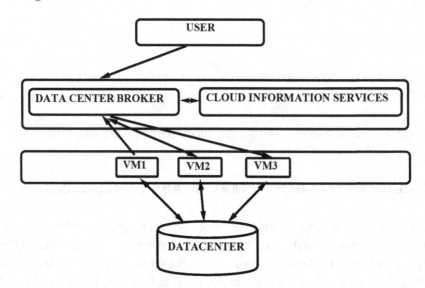

Figure 6. Heuristic models

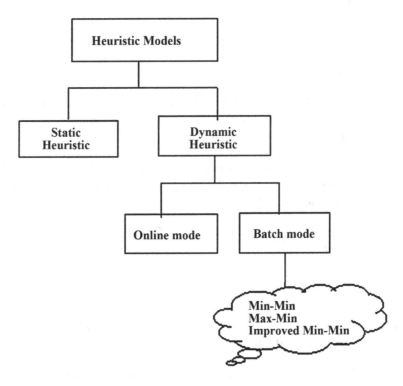

Make Span or Completion Time

Load Balancing

Make span or completion time represent the total time needed to execute the task by the available resource. Load balancing is the factor which is used to perform effective resource utilization. Min-Min algorithm works better if the number of smaller tasks is less and Max-Min algorithm works better if the number of larger tasks is less. To compare and evaluate the proposed algorithm with other algorithms such as Min-Min and Max-Min, a simulation environment known as cloudsim toolkit has been used. Here the number of tasks is given by considering various load conditions like light, medium and heavy. Then the corresponding make span produced by all the three algorithms are given. Performances of the algorithms are compared based on the values given in table1. The graphical representation for make span comparison is given in Figure 6.

REFERENCE

Su, S., Li, J., Huang, Q., Huang, X., Shuang, K., & Wang, J. (2013). Cost-efficient task scheduling for executing large programs in the cloud. *Parallel Computing Elsevier Publications*, *39*(4-5), 177–188. doi:10.1016/j.parco.2013.03.002

ADDITIONAL READING

Abrishami, S., & Naghibzadeh, M. (2012). Deadline-constrained workflow scheduling in software as a service Cloud. *Computer Science & Engineering and Electrical Engineering. Scientia Iranica, 19*(3), 680–689. doi:10.1016/j.scient.2011.11.047

Agarwal, A., & Jain, S. (2014). Efficient Optimal Algorithm of Task Scheduling in Cloud Computing Environment. [IJCTT]. *International Journal of Computer Trends and Technology, 9*(7), 344–349. doi:10.14445/22312803/IJCTT-V9P163

Arabi, E. K., El-Sisi, A., Tawfeek, M. A., & Torkey, F. A. (2013). Intelligent Strategy of Task Scheduling in Cloud Computing for Load Balancing. [IJETTCS]. *International Journal of Emerging Trends & Technology in Computer Science, 2*(6), 12–22.

Azar, Y., Ben Aroya, N., Devanur, N. R., & Jain, N. (2013). Cloud Scheduling with Setup Cost. *Preceedings of the 25th ACM symposium on parallelism in algorithms and architecture, 298-304.*

Brian Bouterse & Harry Perros. (2012). Scheduling Cloud Capacity for Time - Varying Customer Demand. *1st International Conference on Cloud Networking, IEEE Publications, 137-142*

Buyya, R., Vecchiola, C., & Thamarai Selvi, S. (2013). *Mastering Cloud Computing Foundations and Applications Programming*. Elsevier Publications.

Buyya, R., Yeo, C. S., & Venugopal, S. (2008), Market oriented cloud computing: vision, hype, and reality for delivering IT services as computing utilities. *Proceedings of the tenth conference on high performance computing and communications (HPCC 2008, IEEE Press, Los Alamitos, CA). Dalian, China, 5-13.* doi:10.1109/HPCC.2008.172

Ioannis, A., Moschakis, Helen D. Karatza. (2010). Evaluation of gang scheduling performance and cost in a cloud computing system. *Springer Publications, 59*(2), 975–992.

Israr, H. (2013). Architecture level mapping of cloud computing with Grid computing. *International Journal of Engineering Sciences & Emerging Technologies, 5*(1), 7–11.

Jiao, X. Z., You, C. H., & Yang, Y. (2007). An Optimization Method of Workflow Dynamic Scheduling Based on Heuristic GA. *Computer Science, 34*(2).

Mateos, C., Pacini, E., & Garino, C. (2013) An ACO-inspired algorithm for minimizing weighted flowtime in cloud-based parameter sweep experiments.

Judeans & Ghemawat, S. (2004) MapReduce: simplified data processing on large clusters. *Sixth Symposium on Operating System Design and Implementation (OSDI'04),1-13.*

Lin, W., Liang, C., Wang, J. Z., & Buyya, R. (2012). Bandwidth-aware divisible task scheduling for cloud computing. *Software-practice and experience. John Wiley & Sons Library, 44*(2), 163–174.

Mell, P. & Grance, T. (2011), The NIST Definition of Cloud Computing. *NIST Special Publication 800-145.*

Supreeth, S., & Biradar, S. (2013). Scheduling Virtual Machines for Load balancing in Cloud Computing Platform. [IJSR]. *International Journal of Science and Research*, 2(6), 437–441.

Ullman, J. (1975). NP-complete scheduling problems. *Journal of Computer and System Sciences*, 10(3), 384–393. doi:10.1016/S0022-0000(75)80008-0

Vijindra, S. S. (2012). Survey on Scheduling Issues in Cloud computing. *ICMOC. Elsevier Publications*, 38, 2881–2888.

Villegas, D., Rodero, I., Fong, L., Bobroff, N., Liu, Y., Parashar, M., & Masoud Sadjadi, S. (2010). The Role of Grid Computing Technologies in Cloud Computing. *Handbook of Cloud Computing, Springer Publications*, 183- 218.

Wen, G., Hong, J., Xu, C., Balaji, P., Feng, S., & Jiang, P. (2011). Energy-aware Hierarchical Scheduling of Applications in Large Scale Data Centers. *International Conference on Cloud and Service Computing, IEEE Publications, 158-165*. doi:10.1109/CSC.2011.6138514

Wu, X., Deng, M., Zhang, R., Zeng, B., & Zhou, S. (2013). A task scheduling algorithm based on QoS-driven in Cloud Computing. *Elsevier Publications*, 17, 1162–1169.

Xu, B., Zhao, C., Hu, E., & Hu, B. (2011). Job scheduling algorithm based on Berger model in cloud environment. *Advances in Engineering Software*, 42(7), 419–425. doi:10.1016/j.advengsoft.2011.03.007

Zhu, L., Li, Q., & He, L. (2012). Study on Cloud Computing Resource Scheduling Strategy Based on the Ant Colony Optimization Algorithm. *IJCSI International Journal of Computer Science Issues*, 9(5), 54–58.

Chapter 14
Green, Energy–Efficient Computing and Sustainability Issues in Cloud

Monica Gahlawat
L. J. Institute of Computer Application, India

Priyanka Sharma
Raksha Shakti University, India

ABSTRACT

Sustainability creates and maintains the conditions under which humans and nature can exist in productive accord, that permit fulfilling the social, economic and other requirements of present and future generations. There is a debate that cloud computing is green contributing to sustainability or a risk of climate change. Cloud computing if compared to traditional on-premise computing, is a cost effective, energy-efficient, scalable and on-demand computing. There is no doubt that the expansive power of computing can help us address sustainability challenges, but this technology also draws from the Earth's finite environmental stocks and biosphere which results in risk of climate change.

INTRODUCTION

The emergence of cloud computing has drastically altered everyone's perception of infrastructure architectures, software delivery and development models. It is a paradigm shift from CAPEX model (capital expenditure) to OPEX model (operational expenditure), means the organizations shares cloud infrastructure on pay per use instead of purchasing the costly dedicated hardware and software for satisfying the computing needs of the organization. To support the CAPEX model various cloud service providers came into existence like AMAZON, Google, yahoo and SalesForce.com etc. To handle sudden spikes in the demand requires huge data-centers to be tightly-coupled with the system, the increasing use of which yields heavy consumption of energy and huge emission of carbon footprints. Carbon emission leads to climate change and a health related risk to the society.

DOI: 10.4018/978-1-4666-9767-6.ch014

Copyright © 2016, IGI Global. Copying or distributing in print or electronic forms without written permission of IGI Global is prohibited.

There is no doubt that the expansive power of computing can help us address sustainability challenges, but this technology also draws from the Earth's finite environmental stocks and biosphere. In 2013, U.S. data centers consumed an estimated 91 billion kilowatt-hours of electricity, equivalent to the annual output of 34 large (500-megawatt) coal-fired power plants. According to the Natural Resources Defense Council (NRDC), Data center electricity consumption is projected to increase to roughly 140 billion kilowatt-hours annually by 2020, the equivalent annual output of 50 power plants, costing American businesses $13 billion annually in electricity bills and emitting nearly 100 million metric tons of carbon pollution per year.

There are troubling signs that data center power use will continue to grow substantially. The pros and cons of the cloud computing leads to a debate that cloud computing is a green opportunity or climate change risk. If compared with on-premise computing the cloud computing is a green initiative. Virtualization also played a great role in optimum utilization of the resources to maximize profit and minimizing the energy consumption. The Carbon Disclosure Project (CDP) found in its research that large US companies that use cloud computing will be able to save $12.3bn in energy costs and 85.7 million metric tons of CO2 emissions annually by 2020. But because of random, unpredictable consumer demand, the resource allocation algorithms in the data centers should be dynamic and intelligent enough to utilize the data center capacity at optimum level so that energy consumption can be reduced.

Energy Consumption Patterns

To improve the energy consumption of the data centers, it is first important to understand the energy consumption pattern of the data centers. There are various factors contributing to the total energy consumption of the datacenter. The components can be categorized into 1) Fixed energy consumption components e.g. lighting, networking equipments 2) dynamic energy consumption components e.g. UPS(uninterruptible power supply), PDUs(Power Distribution units), servers etc. The Figure 1 shows the percentage of energy consumed by the components of the data center. The cooling system and the servers are consuming nearly half of the total power consumption. The energy in-efficiencies in the datacenter are because of non-uniformity of the energy consumption of the servers and the traditional cooling and air conditioning units. To attain sustainable energy efficient environment of the data center dynamic energy efficient algorithms are required to be applied on both the components. There are a number of industry initiatives e.g. Climate Savers Computing Initiative (CSCI), Green Computing Impact Organization, Inc. (GCIO), Green Electronics Council, The Green Grid, FIT4Green, ECO2Clouds, Eco4Cloud, International Professional Practice Partnership (IP3) etc. working in the direction of green energy efficient computing.

Taxonomy of Energy Efficient Computing Techniques

Environmental sustainability has been a subject of augmented attention over the last few decades. Natural resources are slowly being depleted, a reason for the issue of sustainable development arising. Virtualization has played a great role to achieve improvement in efficiency and eventually reduction in carbon emissions. The energy management techniques can be broadly categorized into 1) Power Management Techniques and the 2) Thermal Management Techniques. The taxonomy of the energy management techniques is shown in Figure 2.

Figure 1. Components of the datacenter and energy consumption
Source: "Energy Logic: Reducing Data Center Energy Consumption by Creating Savings that Cascade Across Systems"

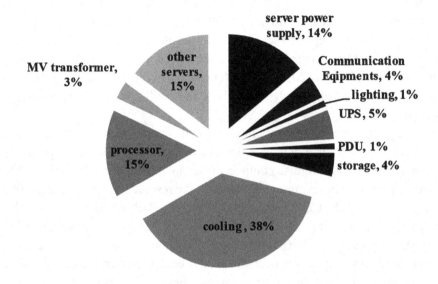

Figure 2. Taxonomy of Energy Management Techniques

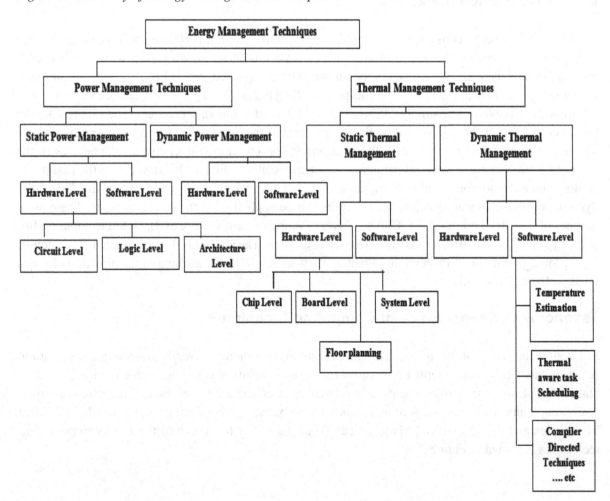

The power management techniques focus on the decreasing the overall power consumption of the datacenter resulting in energy efficient computing. But reducing the power consumption does not always reduce the consumed energy. The relationship between power and energy is: $E = PT$ where E is energy, P is power and T is time. So Energy is the total work completed in a particular time interval. Sometimes reducing the power does not affect the energy e.g. in case of CPU if the power is reduced it will not reduce the energy consumption but delays the application execution.

Power Management Techniques

The energy consumption can be reduced permanently by (SPM) Static Power Management techniques (by optimizing the circuit level design) and temporarily by (DPM) Dynamic Power Management techniques (by optimum utilization of the resources in the data center). Virtualization has also played a very important role in power management. The authors in (Nathuji & Schwan, 2007) have proposed a virtualization based dynamic power management approach named VirtualPower. VirtulPower works on both "soft" and "hard" power scaling. The "soft" power scaling exploits the hypervisor's ability to limit hardware usage by guests and the "hard" power scaling is achieved by processor frequency scaling. VirtualPower approach is suitable for both full and para-virtualized guests. The local managers in individual virtual machines run their independent power management methods termed as VirtualPower Management states-VPM states. The global managers takes the input from the local managers and takes the decision that VM placement in the current datacenter will be feasible or not and the local managers leverages the guest os's power management policies. The authors' have implemented this approach in Xen hypervisor and the results show improvements of up to 31% in the active power consumption.

Virtual machine consolidation approaches have presented a significant opportunity for energy efficiency. The main reason for the energy inefficiency in the cloud data centers is the idle power requirement of the servers to be active all the time. Even at low load (when the CPU utilization is less than 10%), the idle power requirements of the servers are constant. Consolidation is an approach to the efficient usage of computer server resources in order to reduce the total number of servers required to run the active VMs. The authors in (Srikantaiah, Kansal, & Zhao, 2008) applied a heuristics of bin packing on virtual machine allocation and consolidation. The virtual machines are allocated in the servers in such a way that maximum VMs can be packed in the bare minimum servers and the total number of servers can be reduced up to some extent for power conservation. There are many constraints that can affect consolidation e.g. server behavior, security restrictions requiring co-location of the specified application components, workload patterns etc. The authors have done experiments to understand the relationship between the resource utilization and energy consumption. They concluded that energy consumption per transaction of a consolidated workload is influenced by both resource utilization and the performance. The experiment shows that energy per transaction is minimum at 70% CPU utilization and 50% disk utilization (though the percentage depends on the type of machine and the workload used). As the workload in the cloud environment is dynamic so VM placement & consolidation algorithm should be dynamic and online. In paper (Beloglazov & Buyya, 2012) the authors have presented an online algorithm for VM consolidation while ensuring the high level of adherence to the SLA(Service Level Agreements). The authors have solved the consolidation problem by dividing the problem in 4 sub problems 1) Host Underload Detection 2) Host Overload Detection 3) VM selection for migration 4) VM Placement. There are 2 managers at host level called the local managers and one at the data center level called global manager. The local managers continuously monitor the host status that host is overloaded or underloaded and the VM migration takes place for load balancing. At the global level the data center manager takes the input from the local managers to check the feasibility of the VM allocation in the data center. The results derived from the experiments are promising.

Energy efficiency of a data center depends on the optimal VM allocation and online consolidation approaches. Paper (Dhiman, Marchetti, & Rosing, 2010) explain vGreen (a multitiered software system to manage VM scheduling between different physical machines for reducing the overall power consumption and increasing the performance). VGreen is based on client server architecture. The central server is referred as "*vgserv*" and the clients are referred as "*vgnodes*". The *vgnodes* performs online characterization of the VMs running on the physical machines and it regularly updates the *vgserv* with this information. The update allows the *vgserv* to take decisions of VM placement to increase the overall performance & energy efficiency. The experimental results show that vGreen improves the overall performance up to 100% and the energy efficiency up to 55%. Apart from this, vGreen is very lightweight with negligible runtime overhead. The authors in paper(Deng, Liu, Jin, Liao, Liu, & Chen, 2012) tightly constraint the VM allocation and consolidation by SLA as well as reliability constrained and proposed an algorithm called RACE(reliability aware server consolidation strategy). The algorithm is based on an improved grouping of genetic algorithms to search the global optimal solution, which takes advantage of a collection of reliability-aware resource buffering, and virtual machines-to-servers re-mapping heuristics for generating good initial solutions and improving the convergence rate. The simulation is performed in famous cloud simulator, CloudSim. Extensive experiments have demonstrated that RACE can avoid unprofitable reconfigurations under dynamic server consolidation in the long term.

Mostly existing work apply virtual machine consolidation on top of centralized, hierarchical or ring based system topologies which result in poor scalability and/or packing efficiency with increasing no of PMs and VMs. The paper (Feller, Morin, & Esnault, 2012) proposes a fully dynamic decentralized virtual machine consolidation scheme based on an unstructured peer-to-peer network of physical machines. The scheme is validated using the well known virtual machine consolidation algorithms: First-Fit Decreasing, Sercon, and Ant Colony Optimization algorithms. The scheme is well suited for dynamic environment like cloud because the system topology is periodically and randomly modified through the exchange of neighborhood information among the PMs to form random PM neighborhoods. Each physical machine periodically triggers a consolidation process. Before sending a consolidation request it checks that the PM is already under consolidation or not. If yes, then the PM is locked in order to avoid concurrent access to PM resources in case of multiple ongoing consolidations. The virtual machine consolidation starts once all the resource information is received from the locked members. It initiates a migration plan which corresponds to the ordered set of the new PM-VM assignment.

Cloud environment is very dynamic and the load balancing algorithms should be fast enough to take decisions about optimal VM placement. VM placement has been solved as bin packing algorithm in the literature. The authors in paper (Sharma, Viney, & Srivastava, 2013) explained the VM placement and consolidation as online bin packing algorithm constrained by the Server utilization threshold. The authors has done experiments and concluded that the CPU utilization has great impact on the energy consumption. The power consumption grows linearly with the growth of the CPU utilization and the energy consumption increased dramatically when the CPU utilization increases 70%(Threshold). The approach used for the energy efficiency in the data center is that if the CPU utilization of the server is increasing up to the threshold then server consolidation takes place for load balancing so that the energy can be saved. The paper (Anderson, Mayr, & Warmuth, 1989) explains the parallel algorithm for bin packing problems. The authors have proposed First Fit Decreasing (FFD) as a parallel algorithm. The experimental results show that the parallel approximation algorithm is the faster alternative to the sequential bin packing algorithm.

VM Migrations have a great role in the energy efficient VM placement algorithms. VM migrations' pre and post processing stages also require power for initiating and completion of the VM migration. The paper (Bhuiyan, Haugue, & Wang, 2013) is focusing on the VM migrations' pre and post phases energy requirements and the proposed a novel approach to minimize the energy usage in these phases. The approach is implemented in Eucalyptus (an open source) cloud and the results are promising. 16% of the energy is saved by applying a systematic approach to reduce the energy consumption in pre and post migration stages.

Thermal Management Techniques

The cooling systems consume nearly half of the total power consumption. The thermal management techniques focus on the thermal aware energy management techniques. Computer chips like any other manufactured product have a temperature range within which they were designed to operate. When that range is exceeded the materials are stressed beyond their tolerance point and can melt, break, burn, or otherwise stop working resulting in a partial or complete failure of the chip. Both static and dynamic thermal management techniques focus on the reducing the temperature of the datacenter equipments for the smooth functioning. The static thermal management techniques focus on the chip level to board level and then to system level techniques which increases the area over which the heat is distributed so that the heat flux decreases. Thermal management predicts the future thermal level of the device based on the current thermal as the feedback to the system to adjust the thermal levels. Thermal aware task scheduling schedules the tasks in the data center based on the thermal based threshold. If the thermal level of the servers crosses the upper threshold the load is balanced between the servers to reduce the thermal level.

A plenty of thermal based energy efficient techniques are presented in literature. Floorplanning is based on the concept that the placement of the architectural block on the chip can affect the temperature of the disk considerably. The basis of thermal-aware floorplanning is maximizing the distance of two hot units to prevent thermal conduction while improving the performance and reducing the energy/power consumption. Blade server racks should be placed in parallel rows facing each other. In this pattern the cold air is inserted from floor to the front side of the racks and the hot air at back is absorbed by the ceiling and the air flows happens in proper manner to reduce the total power required to keep the data centers cool. The optimum placement of the cooling system also plays a great role in energy efficiency. The centralized placement of the cooling system is more utilized and is energy efficient solution to heat as compare to each room separately. (Gholamhosseinian & Khalifeh, 2012)

Apart from these static techniques, most of the real-time control systems work on dynamic manipulation of the cooling resources throughout the data center according to the need of the servers. One such system, called Dynamic Smart Cooling, uses a network of temperature sensors at the air inlet and exhaust of equipment racks. Data from the sensors is fed to a controller where it is evaluated. The controller can then independently manipulate the supply air temperature and airflow rate of each CRAC (computer room air conditioners) in the data center. In order to accomplish this efficiently, the impact of each CRAC in the data center must be evaluated with respect to each sensor.(Bash & Forman, 2007) thermal aware scheduling algorithm also contribute to energy efficiency. In (Wang, Von Laszewski, Dayal, He, Younge, & Furlani, 2009) the author proposed a thermal aware workload scheduling algorithm. The basic idea of scheduling is to schedule the "hot" jobs on the "cold" compute nodes and tries to reduce the temperature of compute nodes based on temperatures of ambient environment and compute nodes which can be obtained from temperature sensors, on-line job-temperature profiles. The experiment results are prominent.

Conventional cooling infrastructure waste substantial energy. Moreover, the cooling zones of computer room air conditioners (CRACs) frequently overlap, resulting in cooling redundancy. Simply stated, data centers waste substantial power by cooling areas that are already cool, because they lack intelligent thermal-monitoring capabilities. Paper (Mannas & Jones, 2011) proposed the multiple temperature-measurement nodes, combined with appropriate temperature data processing, enable an optimized environmental temperature-control system that saves power and reduces cost. Wired solution can increase the overhead of wires in data center. Wireless solution is easy to install for multiple temperature measurement nodes. The sensor placement should be location based so that the human intervention in the data center is less. Results show that the multipoint temperature monitoring reduces cooling energy by 30%.

Paper (Moore, Chase, & Ranganathan, 2006) proposed a automated, online and predictive thermal mapping so that the preventive actions can be taken in advance. The approach is named as "weatherman". The data about fan speed; air temperature and server utilization is collected. The sensors measure the power profiles and the heat profiles and the data is fed to neural nets. Based on the decision rules the neural net take decisions for thermal load balancing VM consolidations. The authors in (Ramos & Bianchini, 2008) proposed a c-oracle, a software infrastructure for internet services that dynamically predicts the temperature. This policy simply turns off any server in which a component has reached its red-line temperature (the maximum temperature that does not cause significant reliability degradation). When human operators detect an obvious thermal fault, such as the failure of one of the air conditioners, servers may be turned off even earlier than this point. Servers are only turned back on when operators have manually eliminated the source of the emergencies.

VMAP is an innovative proactive thermal-aware virtual machine consolidation technique is proposed in (Lee, Viswanathan, & Pompili, 2012) to maximize computing resource utilization, to minimize data-center energy consumption, and to improve the efficiency of heat extraction. The effectiveness of the proposed technique is verified through experimental evaluations with HPC workload traces under single as well as federated-datacenter scenarios (in the machine rooms at Rutgers University and University of Florida). Vmap divides the datacenter into 4 layers 1) Environment layer 2) Hardware Resources Layer 3) Virtualization Layer 4) Application Layer. The application layer provides information about the application characteristics such as resource requirements and energy consumption. The modern blade servers (hardware resource layer) are equipped with internal sensors to sense servers' fan speed and utilization. The environment layer which comprises of humidity sensors and airflow meters measures the thermal behavior of the data center at any given load. The virtualization layer provisions, allocates and manages VM based on the current knowledge obtained by other layers to perform optimal resource allocation in datacenter. The experiments shows that Vmap is 9% and 35% more energy efficient than best fit & "cool job" respectively.

Efficient thermal management is important in modern data centers as cooling consumes up to 50% of the total energy. The author in (Li, Liang, Liu, Nath, Terzis, & Faloutsos, 2011) has proposed Thermocast, a novel thermal forecasting model to predict the temperatures surrounding the servers in a data center, based on continuous streams of temperature and airflow measurements. Based on the learning results, each server predicts its local temperatures for the near future. The predictor uses a past window of size T_w for training and predicts T_p minutes into the future.

GREEN SUSTAINABILITY ISSUES IN CLOUDS

Energy efficient resource management in cloud is a complex process due to the heterogeneous application workload and external factors like SLA (Service Level Agreement) effecting the energy efficient resource allocation algorithms. In SLA the consumer can list the requirements to the service provider and based on these requirements monetary terms are decided. To fulfill the constraints of the SLA sometime requires reconfiguration of the servers in the datacenter. Meeting performance constraints under uncertainties, dynamic scalability, fault tolerance, debugging, reducing operational cost, reducing carbon emission and ensuring security and privacy is a huge challenge. Some of the challenges and issues are discussed below:

Virtual Machine Communication Topologies

Depending on the application size, the applications can be distributed in different virtual machine and depends on the communication network (following a particular topology) to communicate with each other. If the virtual machines executing shared application exists in different data centers (may be at different geographical location), the network traffic will affect the execution of the application in terms of execution delays. Also, the communication network involves switches, access-points, and routers that also consume power. To eliminate the data transfer delays and reduce power consumption, observing the communication pattern among CPUs is important. Therefore, more work is needed to place CPUs on the same or closely located servers. The cloud providers provide a facility to the consumers to select the datacenter in which they can purchase the virtual appliances, which affects the overall communication topology.

Heterogeneous and Dynamic Workload

Cloud data centers often consist of machines with heterogeneous capacities and the performance characteristics. The heterogeneity of the infrastructure is because of the fact that certain type of workload can only be scheduled on particular type of machines. Predicting the workload type is a challenging task in a dynamic environment of cloud because the arrival rate of the resource requests also varies from time to time depending on the actual service demand. Apart from the energy efficiency measurement, scheduling delay metric is also important in the case of resource allocation in cloud preventing SLA violations.

Trend in Microprocessor Architecture

The trend in the microprocessor architecture is to increase the level of circuit integration to reduce the processor size and increase clock speed to improve the throughput. The result is an increase in raw power as well as the power density on the silicon. Over the past few years Power density has grown with the rate of S0.7 for every generation (Hassan & Asghar, 2010). Power consumption and heat dissipation

Table 1. Energy Monitoring and Metering Metrics

Metric	Explanation	Formula
Power usage Effectiveness (PUE)	It is the fraction of total energy Consumed by the service of a data centre to the total energy consumed by IT equipments.	$PUE = \dfrac{Total\ Facility\ Energy}{Total\ Equipment\ Energy}$
Carbon Usage Effectiveness (CUE)	It is a calculation of green house gases (CO_2, CH_4) release in atmosphere by the data centre	$CUE = \dfrac{Total\ CO_2\ emmision\ from\ total\ energy\ used\ for\ service\ of\ datacenter}{Total\ energy\ consumed\ by\ IT\ equipment}$
Water Usage Effectiveness (WUE)	It is calculation of yearly water used by data centre like for cooling, energy Production.	$WUE = \dfrac{AnnualUsageOfWater}{TotalEnergyUsedByITEquipment}$
Energy Reuse Factor (ERF)	It calculates the reusable energy Like hydro power, solar power etc used by data center.	$ERF = \dfrac{ReusedEnergyUsage}{TotalEnergyUsedByITEquipment}$
Energy Reuse Effectiveness (ERE)	It is a parameter for measuring the profit of reuse energy from a data centre.	$ERF = \dfrac{TotalEnergy - ReusedEnergy}{TotalEnergyUsedByITEquipment}$
Data centre Infrastructure Efficiency (DCiE)	This factor is used to calculate The energy efficiency of a data Centre.	$DCiE = \dfrac{TotalITEquipmentPower}{TotalFacilityPower} * 100$
Data Centre Productivity (DCP)	It calculates the amount of useful work done by data centre.	$DCP = \dfrac{TotalUsefulWork}{Total\ ResourceUsedToDoTheWork}$
Compute Power Efficiency (CPE)	It determines the total amount of power is truly used for computing.	$CPE = \dfrac{ITEquimentUtilizationEnergy}{PUE}$
Energy and SLA violation metric(ESV)	It calculates both energy consumption and levels of SLA(service level agreement) violations.	*ESV = Energy*SLAV(SLA violation Metric)* *SLAV = OTF*PDM* *OTF = Overloading Time Fraction* *PDM=Performance Degradation* *Due to VM Migrations* *OTF= The time fraction during* *Which active hosts* *Experienced the 100%* *CPU Utilization*
Green Energy coefficient (GEC)	It measure the amount of green energy used to provide services to data centre.	$GEC = \dfrac{GreenEnergyConsumed}{TotalEnergyConsumed}$

continued on following page

Table 1. Continued

Metric	Explanation	Formula
Space, Wattage and Performance (SWaP)	It is used for work out the space and energy required by the data centre.	$SWaP = \dfrac{Performance}{Space * power}$
DataCentre Energy Productivity (DCeP)	It calculates the quantity of useful work done by data centre as compare to total energy consumed to make this work.	$DCeP = \dfrac{TotalUsefulWorkDone}{TotalEnergyUsedToDoThisWork}$

is the major drawback of silicon-based chips. Large amount of power consumption boosts up the heat generation, increasing danger that transistors interfere with each other. The heat dissipated contributes to the thermal level of the data center. There should be a tradeoff between the processing power and the energy efficiency to attain sustainability because in high temperature in the data center has adverse affect on the reliability, scalability of the data center hardware.

Carbon nanotubes are evolving to replace the silicon in near future. A research is going on in Standford university on nanotubes and it is the prediction of the researchers that in next 5 to 10 years silicon chips will be replaced by nonotubes.

High Server Consolidation vs. Reliability

Server consolidation has major contribution in the energy efficient algorithms. It is a load balancing process which distributes the load in the active servers from the servers running of low utilization mode, such that the active no. of servers can be reduced. But high server consolidation ratio also affects the reliability of the servers because all the VMs on a single server are sharing the resources of that server only and lack of resource availability results in SLA violation affecting reliability.

Moreover, a server consolidation algorithm uses the previous usage pattern to predict the behavior of the servers in the datacenters which is not an appropriate criterion for cloud having non-stationary workload. Prediction of the future server utilization is a key challenge for server consolidation algorithms.

Dynamic Architecture Selection

Provisioning of resource allocation at run time by evaluating the choice of centralized, federated architecture is also a key challenge to attain energy efficient data centers. VM Allocation algorithms search for the appropriate host in terms of cost, energy efficiency under SLA constraints. In some cases the host providing energy efficient computing is outside of the boundaries of the service provider (in federated environment) but costs more to cloud provider. To save the extra cost the cloud provider select energy inefficient host to run the VM. To use centralized and federated environment is decided at run time which not only increase the scheduling delay but also encourages energy inefficient allocation.

Apart from the above challenges another bigger challenge to the energy efficient data centers is governance. Generally data centers do not publish the complete details about the carbon footprints and also there is not a common law for all the service providers. The data centers follow the rule and regulations of the location at which the data centers exists.

MONITORING AND METERING ENERGY EFFICIENCY

An in-depth description of monitoring and metering energy efficiency can be seen in Table 1.

REFERENCES

Anderson, R. J., Mayr, E. W., & Warmuth, M. K. (1989). Parallel approximation algorithms for Bin packing. *Information and Computation*, *82*(3), 262–277. doi:10.1016/0890-5401(89)90003-5

Bash, C., & Forman, G. (2007, June). Cool Job Allocation: Measuring the Power Savings of Placing Jobs at Cooling-Efficient Locations in the Data Center. In *USENIX Annual Technical Conference* (*Vol. 138*, p. 140). USENIX.

Beloglazov, A., & Buyya, R. (2012). Optimal online deterministic algorithms and adaptive heuristics for energy and performance efficient dynamic consolidation of virtual machines in cloud data centers. *Concurrency and Computation*, *24*(13), 1397–1420. doi:10.1002/cpe.1867

Bhuiyan, M. F. H., & Wang, C. (2013). Energy-Efficient Virtual Machine Management in Heterogeneous Environment: Challenges, Approaches and Opportunities. In *Proceedings of Systems, Man, and Cybernetics (SMC), 2013 IEEE International Conference on*. IEEE. doi:10.1109/SMC.2013.702

Deng, W., Liu, F., Jin, H., Liao, X., Liu, H., & Chen, L. (2012, December). Lifetime or energy: Consolidating servers with reliability control in virtualized cloud datacenters. In *Cloud Computing Technology and Science (CloudCom), 2012 IEEE 4th International Conference on* (pp. 18-25). IEEE.

Dhiman, G., Marchetti, G., & Rosing, T. (2010). vGreen: A System for Energy-Efficient Management of Virtual Machines. *ACM Transactions on Design Automation of Electronic Systems*, *16*(1), 1–27. doi:10.1145/1870109.1870115

Feller, Morin, & Esnault. (2012). *A case for fully decentralized dynamic VM consolidation in clouds*. INRIA.

Gholamhosseinian, A., & Khalifeh, A. (2012). *Cloud computing and sustainability: Energy efficiency aspects*. Academic Press.

Hassan, S., & Asghar, M. (2010, February). Limitation of silicon based computation and future prospects. In *Second international conference on communication software and networks* (pp. 559-561). Singapore: IEEE Computer Society. doi:10.1109/ICCSN.2010.81

Lee, E. K., Viswanathan, H., & Pompili, D. (2012, December). Vmap: Proactive thermal-aware virtual machine allocation in hpc cloud datacenters. In *High Performance Computing (HiPC), 2012 19th International Conference on* (pp. 1-10). IEEE.

Li, L., Liang, C. J. M., Liu, J., Nath, S., Terzis, A., & Faloutsos, C. (2011, August). Thermocast: a cyber-physical forecasting model for datacenters. In *Proceedings of the 17th ACM SIGKDD international conference on Knowledge discovery and data mining* (pp. 1370-1378). ACM. doi:10.1145/2020408.2020611

Moore, J., Chase, J. S., & Ranganathan, P. (2006, June). Weatherman: Automated, online and predictive thermal mapping and management for data centers. In *Autonomic Computing, 2006. ICAC'06. IEEE International Conference on* (pp. 155-164). IEEE.

Nathuji, R., & Schwan, K. (2007). Virtualpower: Coordinated power management in virtualized enterprise systems. *Operating Systems Review*, *41*(6), 265–278. doi:10.1145/1323293.1294287

Ramos, L., & Bianchini, R. (2008, February). C-Oracle: Predictive thermal management for data centers. In *High Performance Computer Architecture, 2008. HPCA 2008. IEEE 14th International Symposium on* (pp. 111-122). IEEE.

Sharma, V., & Gur, M. S. S. (2013). Energy efficient architectural framework for virtual machine management in IaaS clouds. In *Proceedings of Contemporary Computing (IC3), 2013 Sixth International Conference on*. IEEE. doi:10.1109/IC3.2013.6612222

Srikantaiah, S., Kansal, A., & Zhao, F. (2008). Energy aware consolidation for cloud computing. In *Proceedings of the 2008 Conference on Power Aware Computing and Systems*. Academic Press.

Wang, L., Von Laszewski, G., Dayal, J., He, X., Younge, A. J., & Furlani, T. R. (2009, December). Towards thermal aware workload scheduling in a data center. In *Pervasive Systems, Algorithms, and Networks (ISPAN), 2009 10th International Symposium on* (pp. 116-122). IEEE. doi:10.1109/I-SPAN.2009.22

Chapter 15
The Heterogeneity Paradigm in Big Data Architectures

Todor Ivanov
Goethe University Frankfurt, Germany

Sead Izberovic
Goethe University Frankfurt, Germany

Nikolaos Korfiatis
University of East Anglia, UK

ABSTRACT

This chapter introduces the concept of heterogeneity as a perspective in the architecture of big data systems targeted to both vertical and generic workloads and discusses how this can be linked with the existing Hadoop ecosystem (as of 2015). The case of the cost factor of a big data solution and its characteristics can influence its architectural patterns and capabilities and as such an extended model based on the 3V paradigm is introduced (Extended 3V). This is examined on a hierarchical set of four layers (Hardware, Management, Platform and Application). A list of components is provided on each layer as well as a classification of their role in a big data solution.

INTRODUCTION

Undoubtedly the exponential growth of data and its use in supporting business decisions has challenged the processing and storage capabilities of modern information systems especially in the past decade. The ability to handle and manage large volumes of data has gradually turned to a strategic one (Chintagunta et al., 2013). Meanwhile, the term "Big Data" (Diebold, 2012) is rapidly transformed into the new hype, following a path similar to Cloud Computing (Armbrust et al., 2010). A general challenge for both researchers and practitioners on answering this issue and meet tight requirements (e.g. time to process), is what kind of design improvements need to be applied and how can the data system in use "*scale*". This requirement for system scalability is applied both in terms of parallel as well as distributed data processing with major architectural changes and use of new software technologies like Hadoop (Apache, 2013a) being the current trend.

DOI: 10.4018/978-1-4666-9767-6.ch015

Copyright © 2016, IGI Global. Copying or distributing in print or electronic forms without written permission of IGI Global is prohibited.

On the other hand, theoretical definitions of what "Big Data" is and how it can be utilized by organizations and enterprises has been a subject of debates (Jacobs, 2009). On that aspect, the 3V framework has gained considerable attention since it was introduced by Laney (Laney, 2001). In that representation "Big Data" can be defined by three distinctive characteristics, namely: *Volume*, *Variety* and *Velocity*.

The *Volume* represents the ever-growing amount of data, which is generated in today's "Internet of things". On the other hand, the *Variety* of data produced by the multitude of sources like sensors, smart devices and social media in raw, semi-structured, unstructured and rich media formats is further complicating the processing and storage of data. Finally, the *Velocity* aspect describes how fast the data is retrieved, stored and processed. However, dealing with imprecisely defined data formats, growing data sizes, and requirements with varying processing times represent a new challenge to the current systems. From an information processing perspective, the three characteristics together describe accurately what Big Data is. Nonetheless, apart from the 3Vs, which describe the quantitative characteristic of Big Data systems, there are additional qualitative characteristics like *Variability* and *Veracity*. The *Variability* aspect defines the different interpretations that a certain data can have when put in different contexts. It focuses on the semantics of the data, instead of its variety in terms of structure or representation. The *Veracity* aspect defines the data accuracy or how truthful it is. If the data is corrupted, imprecise or uncertain, this has direct impact on the quality of the final results. Both variability and veracity have direct influence on the qualitative value of the processed data. The real value obtained from the data analysis, also called data insights, is another qualitative measure which is not possible to define in precise and deterministic way. A graphical representation of the extended V-Model is given in *Figure 1*.

While the 3V model, shown in Figure 1, provides a simplified framework which is well understood by researchers and practitioners. This representation of the data processes, can lead to major architectural pitfalls on the design of Big Data platforms. A particular issue that should be taken into account, is the cost factor that derives from the utilization of the 3V model in the context of a business scenario. Since the requirements of business operations are not equal in any vertical market, the influence of the 3Vs in a Big Data implementation process is not the same. Taking this into account, the 3V framework will be used to address particular cases of different requirements and how this can be saturated on top of an existing infrastructure considering the cost factors associated with systems operations and maintenance. This chapter introduces an architectural paradigm to address these different requirements for Big Data architectures as the *heterogeneity paradigm*. There are different motivations behind the use of heterogeneous platforms, but recently the following have become very relevant: (a) new hardware capabilities – multi-core CPUs, growing size of main memory and storage, different memory and processing accelerator boards such as GPUs, FPGAs or caches; (b) a growing variety of data-intensive workloads sharing the same host platform; (c) complexity of data structures; (d) geographically distributed server locations and (e) higher requirements in terms of cost, processing and energy efficiency as well as computational speed. Based on the above a discussion is provided on the current technical solutions using the Hadoop ecosystem.

To this end, this chapter is structured as follows. The first section discusses the Big Data characteristics and in particular the inequality of the 3Vs and their influence on the cost factor. A brief overview of Cloud Computing in the context of Big Data is also included. The second section of the chapter focuses on the heterogeneity as a feasible architectural paradigm, starting with brief overview of existing heterogeneous system and discussing the emerging Big Data platforms. The third section motivates

Figure 1. Visualization of the Extended V-Model (adopted from E. G. Caldarola, Sacco, and Terkaj (2014))

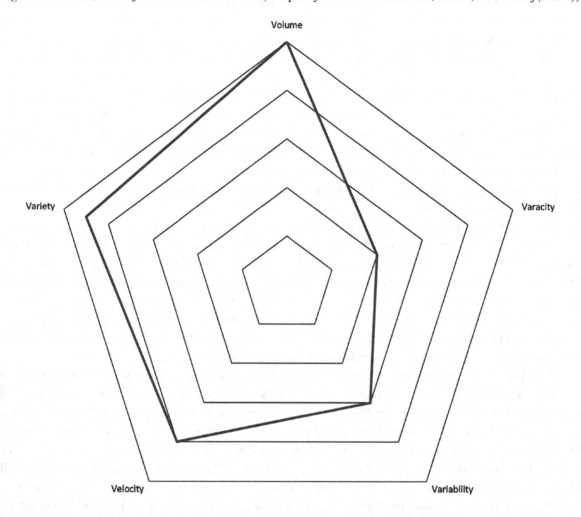

the heterogeneity paradigm in the current Big Data architectures and dives deeper into each of the four heterogeneity levels: hardware, system management, platform and application. The chapter concludes with short summary of perspectives and open issues for future research.

BACKGROUND

Big Data Characteristics and Cost Factor

Depending on the system architecture, the understanding of the 3Vs can be different, especially in the case of Volume (size) and Velocity (speed). For example, in traditional OLAP (Online Analytical Processing) and OLTP (Online Transactional Processing) systems the growing data sizes and the need for quick results are becoming more important. The Variety (structure) of data is of no concern in such systems, as the data format is known in advance and described very precisely in a pre-defined schema. However, in the case of Big Data the emerging data variety is starting to transform the system requirements and question the storage efficiency of existing systems (Huai, Ma, Lee, O'Malley, & Zhang, 2013). Therefore, new architectural approaches like NoSQL (Cattell, 2011), NewSQL, MapReduce-based (Sakr, Liu, & Fayoumi, 2013), Hybrid OLAP-OLTP(Grund et al., 2010; Kemper & Neumann, 2011), In-memory and Column-based (Plattner, 2009) systems are emerging.

A particular architectural requirement is that a system should be capable of handling increasing data volume, high or dynamically changing velocity and high variety of data formats. The exact impact of each of the 3Vs can vary depending on the industry-specific requirements. Therefore, the underlying Big Data infrastructure should be able to deal with any combination of the 3Vs. Furthermore, in this context the Cost-Factor is not a new dimension on the framework but a function that combines the other three, so that a change in each component will affect the value:

$$\text{Cost Factor} = f_c(volume,\ variety,\ velocity,\ v\ldots)$$

The 3Vs combined over the Cost-Factor can be expressed in a *3V Cube Model*. A visualization of this model is given in Figure 2. The Cost-Factor is a very important metric for every Cloud and Big Data service provider (Greenberg, Hamilton, Maltz, & Patel, 2008). It determines how efficient is a platform

Figure 2. Visualization of the 3V Cube Model

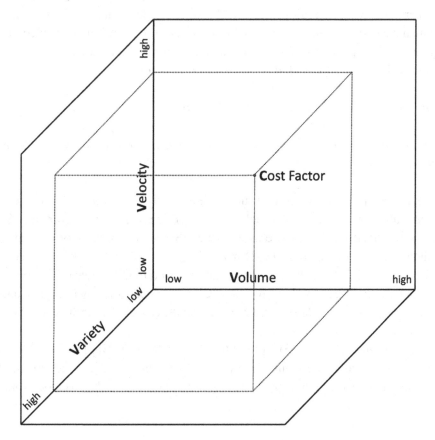

in terms of price per computation unit and how effectively in terms of data storage. This metric includes the costs for hardware, maintenance, administration, electricity, cooling and space. In other words, all essential elements for building Big Data infrastructure are included in the definition of the Cost-Factor characteristics.

For example the parameter *Volume*, should include the costs for the storage hardware, the used electricity to power this hardware and the costs for the hardware maintenance. The *Variety* parameter should include the costs for the needed hardware and the electricity to transform the data into a format that will be used in a specific context. Where the *Velocity* parameter can be seen as multiplication factor. The faster the data should be processed the more the system has to be scaled horizontally.

Clearly the Cost-Factor characteristics are the most complex as they consist of the 3Vs together with additional factors that they influence. Therefore, because of this complexity the Big Data platforms are difficult to benchmark and compare in terms of performance and price. The development of a Big Data benchmark is in progress and should be defined by multiple industry cases as described by Baru *et al.* (Baru et al., 2014; Baru, Bhandarkar, Nambiar, Poess, & Rabl, 2013a, 2013b). Currently as of 2015, there is an urgent need of standardized test workloads against which all software vendors can test their software.

Cloud Computing and Big Data

Cloud Computing has emerged as a major paradigm in the last decade and was quickly adopted by both industry organizations and end users. On the one hand, it offers economic advantages such as a flexible billing model (pay-per-use) as well as potential reductions in infrastructure, administration and license costs. On the other hand, it solves multiple technical challenges, for example, offering optimal resource utilization and management, as well as custom, automated setup and configuration of complex enterprise platforms. A generally accepted definition about Cloud computing is provided by The National Institute of Standards and Technology-NIST (Mell & Grance, 2011) as follows:

Cloud Computing is a model for enabling convenient, on-demand network access to a shared pool of configurable computing resources (e.g., networks, servers, storage, applications and services) that can be rapidly provisioned and released with minimal management effort or service provider interaction. (Mell & Grance, 2011, p. 2)

In such context, cloud providers offer multitude of services starting from the hardware layer and moving up to the application layer. The most widely offered services are Infrastructure as a Service (IaaS), Platform as a Service (PaaS) and Software as a Service (SaaS). The variety of offered cloud services is as wide as their architectural approaches (Rimal, Choi, & Lumb, 2009). In a related work (Ivanov, Petrov, & Buchmann, 2012), the authors surveyed and showed that it is feasible to run data-intensive applications on top of virtualized cloud environment. Cloud services offering relational database storage are called Database as a Service (DaaS) with Amazon RDS, Google CloudSQL and SQL Azure been some major products.

A recent survey (Hashem et al., 2015) looks at the relation between Big Data and Cloud Computing. Both are conjoined, with the Cloud Computing providing facilities and services for the Big Data applications. By leveraging virtualization and using Big Data platforms such as Hadoop for parallel, fault-tolerant data processing, cloud providers are able to address the challenges of the 3Vs characteristics. Intel (Intel, 2014) defines this type of services as Analytics as a Service (AaaS). The report describes the AaaS type as a mix of services based on IaaS, PaaS and SaaS. Similarly, all major cloud providers started offering Big Data services as summarized in Table 1.

Another driver of the Big Data services in the cloud (Wang, Liu, & Soyata, 2014) is the growing number of sensor and mobile devices also known as Internet-of-Things (IoT), which are unable to process the data locally and have to offload it to a more resourceful environment.

CHALLENGES IN BIG DATA ARCHITECTURES

While cloud architectures provide a solid framework for addressing big data challenges a general issue arises in understanding the problem. There are multiple reasons motivating the need for new platform architectures, but recently the following have become very relevant:

- Many new hardware capabilities – multi-core CPUs, growing size of main memory and storage and different memory and processing accelerator boards such as GPUs, FPGAs and caches;
- Growing variety of data-intensive workloads sharing the same host platform;
- Complexity of data structures;
- Geographically distributed server locations and
- Higher requirements in terms of cost, processing and energy efficiency as well as computational speed.

These challenges are gradually becoming relevant for both private and public cloud platforms of any size. Therefore, in this chapter the heterogeneity paradigm is introduced as a feasible technique to better understand and tackle the complexity and challenges of the emerging Big Data architectures. The following subsections provide an introduction to heterogeneous systems and how these are reflected in the emerging Big Data ecosystem.

Heterogeneous Systems

Heterogeneous systems have been the topic of multiple research studies trying to classify them according to their properties and the workloads for which they are best suitable. However, due to the rapidly changing hardware and software system architectures, the concepts of heterogeneity in the platforms have also evolved with the time.

For example, a survey by Khokhar et al. (Khokhar, Prasanna, Shaaban, & Wang, 1993) defines Heterogeneous Computing (HC) as:

A well-orchestrated, coordinated effective use of a suite of diverse high-performance machines (including parallel machines) to provide fast processing for computationally demanding tasks that have diverse computing needs. (Khokhar et al., 1993, p. 19)

In addition, the authors discuss multiple issues and problems stemming from system heterogeneity among which are three very general:

Table 1. Big Data Cloud Providers & Services

Provider	Service	Description
Google Cloud Platform (Google, 2015)	Compute Engine	It offers virtual machines with customizable resources for large-scale workloads hosted on top of the Google's infrastructure.
	App Engine	Google's fully-managed Platform-as-a-Service (PaaS) for running customer applications.
	Cloud Storage	It provides a durable and highly available object storage service for application data from any location.
	Cloud Datastore	It offers automatically scalable storage for non-relational (schemaless) data with support of transactions and SQL-like queries.
	CloudSQL	The service offers relational MySQL database storage, which handles replication, patch management and database management to ensure availability and performance.
	BigQuery	It offers capabilities for analyzing multi-terabyte datasets in real-time by running SQL-live queries on the data.
Amazon (Amazon, 2015)	Amazon Simple Storage Service (Amazon S3)	S3 provides secure, durable, highly-scalable object storage.
	Amazon Elastic Block Store (EBS)	EBS offers consistent, low-latency storage for virtual machines, which can host different big data workloads.
	Amazon DynamoDB	DynamoDB is fast and flexible NoSQL (key-value & document) database service for consistent, large-scale applications.
	Amazon Redshift	Redshift is a fast, fully managed, petabyte-scale data warehouse for cost-effective and efficient analyze of data.
	Amazon Elastic MapReduce (EMR)	EMR provides easy-to-use managed service for creating, managing and running Apache Hadoop clusters on top of high-scalable and secure infrastructure using the Amazon EC2.
	Amazon Glacier	Glacier offers cost-effective, long period (years or decades) archival storage services.
Pivotal (Pivotal, 2015a)	Pivotal Cloud Foundry	It offers relational database (MySQL), Hadoop cluster (Pivotal HD), key-value cache/store (Redis), object store (RiakCS) and NoSQL database (MongoDB) services.
Rackspace (Rackspace, 2015)	Cloud Big Data Platform	It provides Hadoop cluster (Hortonworks Data Platform 2.1) including tools like Hive and Pig.
GoGrid (GoGrid, 2015)	1-Button Deploy Solutions	It offers multiple storage solutions like Apache Cassandra, DataStax Enterprise, Cloudera Enterprise clusters, FoundationDB, Hadoop, HBase, MemSQL, MongoDB and Riak.
Microsoft (Microsoft, 2015)	Hadoop in Azure	HDInsight offers Apache Hadoop cluster services in the cloud.
Infochimps (Infochimps, 2015)	Infochimp Cloud	It offers multiple services: • Cloud::Streams for streaming data and real-time analytics • Cloud::Queries for NoSQL database and ad hoc, query-based analytics • Cloud::Hadoop for Elastic Hadoop clusters and batch analytics
Red Hat (Red Hat, 2015)	OpenShift	OpenShift offers Platform-as-a-Service (PaaS) services for developing, hosting and scaling applications.

- "The types of machines available and their inherent computing characteristics";
- "Alternate solutions to various sub-problems of the applications" and
- "The cost of performing the communication over the network".

In another survey on Heterogeneous Computing by Ekmecic et al. (Ekmecic, Tartalja, & Milutinovic, 1996) the authors discuss the heterogeneous workloads as a major factor behind the need of heterogeneous platforms and divide the heterogeneous computing in three essential phases:

1. Parallelism detection,
2. Parallelism characterization and
3. Resource allocation.

In the *parallelism detection* phase, every task in a heterogeneous application is checked if parallelization is possible. The computation parameters of the tasks are estimated in the *parallelism characterization* phase. Time and place of execution of the tasks is determined in the *resource allocation* phase. Basically, the three phases describe in a more abstract way today's concept of cloud computing.

In a similar study Venugopal et al. (Venugopal, Buyya, & Ramamohanarao, 2006), present a taxonomy of Data Grids, and highlight heterogeneity as an essential characteristic of data grid environments and applications. Furthermore, they briefly mentioned that heterogeneity can be split in multiple levels like hardware, system, protocol and representation heterogeneity, which resemble very much the presented Data Grid layered architecture.

The characteristics of today's Big Data platforms as well as the challenges and problems that they represent are very similar to the one discussed in Heterogeneous Computing and Data Grid environments. Therefore, it is a logical step to look in more detail at the concept of system heterogeneity and investigate how it is coupled with the Big Data characteristics. Lee *et al.* (Lee, Chun, & Katz, 2011) discuss the importance of heterogeneity in cloud environments by suggesting a new architecture, that improves the performance and cost-effectiveness. They propose an architecture consisting of 1) long-living core nodes to host both data and computation as well as 2) accelerator nodes that are added to the cluster temporarily when additional power is needed. Then the resource allocation strategy dynamically adjusts the size of each pool of nodes to reduce the cost and improve utilization. Additionally, they present a scheduling scheme, based on the job progress as a shared metric, which provides resource fairness and improved performance.

In a different study Mars et al. (Mars, Tang, & Hundt, 2011) investigated micro-architectural heterogeneity in warehouse-scale computer (WSC) platforms, in that the authors present a new metric called *opportunity factor* that approximates the application's potential performance improvement opportunity relative to all other applications and given the particular mix of applications and machine types on which is running. They also introduce opportunistic mapping, which solves the optimization problem of finding the optimal resource mapping for heterogeneity-sensitive applications. Using this technique the performance of a real production cluster was reported to improve by 15%, but it could potentially go up to 70%.

The number of studies related to heterogeneity is growing along the conceptual relevance and challenging problems that it brings. The following section investigates the emerging Big Data platforms that are developed to address exactly these challenges.

Emerging Big Data Systems

Monash (Monash, 2013) addresses the problem that there is no single data store that can be efficient for all usage patterns. This issue was previously discussed by Stonebraker *et al.* (Stonebraker et al., 2007), who proposed a taxonomy of database technologies. Interestingly enough, one of the described platforms has MapReduce style architecture (Dean & Ghemawat, 2008) and looks very similar to Apache Hadoop. However, the message here is that the illusion of having one general purpose system that can handle all types of workloads is not realistic. The current systems cannot cope with the dynamic changes in application requirements and the 3Vs characteristics, which opens the opportunity for new kinds of storage systems like: NoSQL, NewSQL, MapReduce-based, Hybrid OLAP-OLTP, In-memory and Column-based systems. Most of the approaches in these new systems are inspired by the inefficiency and complexity of the current storage systems. In addition to that, the advancements in hardware (multi-core processors, faster memory and flash storage devices) brought the prices of enterprise hardware down to the level of commodity machines.

Cattell (Cattell, 2011) identified six key features of the NoSQL data stores namely: "(1) the ability to horizontally scale "simple operation" throughput over many servers; (2) the ability to replicate and to distribute (partition) data over many servers; (3) a simple call level interface or protocol (in contrast to a SQL binding); (4) a weaker concurrency model than the ACID transactions of most relational (SQL) database systems; (5) efficient use of distributed indexes and RAM for data storage; and (6) the ability to dynamically add new attributes to data records".

Similarly, Strauch *et al.* (Strauch, Sites, & Kriha, 2011) summarizes all the motivations behind the emergence of the NoSQL data stores among which are the avoidance of unneeded complexity and expensive object-relational mapping, higher data throughput, ease of horizontal scalability (do not rely on the hardware availability) and offer new functionalities that are more suitable for cloud environments in comparison to the relational databases. Additionally, he presents extensive classification and comparison of the NoSQL databases by looking into their internal architectural differences and functional capabilities.

Industry perspectives such as the one's advocated by Fan (Fan, 2012) view emerging systems as a transformation between the traditional relational database systems working with *CRUD (Create, Read, Update, Delete)* data and the *CRAP (Create, Replicate, Append, Process)* data. His major argument is that the *CRUD* (structured) data is very different from the *CRAP* (unstructured) data because of the new Big Data characteristics. The new semi-structured and unstructured data is stored and processed in near real-time and not really updated. The incoming data streams are appended. Therefore, *CRAP* data has very different characteristics and is not appropriate to be stored in the relational database systems.

Marz (Marz, 2012) discusses the problem of mutability in the existing database architectures, which is caused by the Update and Delete operations. They allow human interaction in the system, which changes the data consistency and leads to undesired data corruption and data loss. To avoid this, Marz suggests a new Big Data architecture called ***Lambda Architecture*** (Marz & Warren, 2012), which major principles are human fault-tolerance, data immutability and recomputation. By removing the U and D from *CRUD* and adding the append functionality similar to Fan (Fan, 2012), the data immutability is assured. The raw data is aggregated as it comes and sorted by timestamp which greatly restricts the possibility of errors and data loss caused by human fault-tolerance. The re-computation or data processing is done simply by applying a function over the raw data (query). In addition to that the architecture supports both batch and real-time data processing.

From an ecosystem perspective, Hadoop-style systems - inspired by Google's MapReduce paper (Dean & Ghemawat, 2008) - have been growing in adoption thanks to their scalability, fault-tolerance and distributed parallel processing capabilities. The fact that such systems can be built on commodity hardware and its licensing model provide an important advantage over commercial vendors. In a similar spirit of innovation, most of the new infrastructure architectures try to solve only a predefined set of problems, bound to specific use case scenarios and ignore the other general system requirements.

Therefore, a typical design approach is to combine two or more system features and build a new hybrid architecture which improves the performance for the targeted use case, but adds an additional complexity. HadoopDB (Abouzeid, Bajda-Pawlikowski, Abadi, Silberschatz, & Rasin, 2009) is such hybrid system, trying to combine the best features of the MapReduce-based systems and the traditional analytical DBMS, by integrating PostgreSQL as the database layer, Hadoop as the distributed communication layer and Hive as a translation layer. Other systems just iteratively improve an existing platform like Haloop (Bu, Howe, Balazinska, & Ernst, 2010, 2012) and Hadoop++ (Dittrich et al., 2010) which further improve the Hadoops' scheduling and caching mechanisms as well as indexing and joining processing. Also Starfish (Herodotou et al., 2011) extends Hadoop by enabling it to automatically adapt and self-tune depending on the user workload and in this way provide better performance. A comprehensive survey by Sakr et al. (Sakr et al., 2013) on the family of MapReduce frameworks provides an overview of approaches and mechanisms for large scale data processing.

In a recent work Qin *et al.* (Qin, Qin, Du, & Wang, 2013) identify the MapReduce computing model as a de-facto standard which addresses the challenges stemming from the 3Vs characteristics. Furthermore, the authors divide the enterprise Big Data platforms in three categories: (1) Co-Exist solutions; (2) SQL with MapReduce Support solutions; and (3) MapReduce with SQL Support solutions. In the first category they put IBM Big Data Platform and Oracle Big Plan as both offer end-to-end solutions consisting of several data management and processing components. In the second category fall systems integrating Hadoop support like PolyBase (DeWitt et al., 2013), EMC Greenplum and TeraData Aster Data. In the last category fall Hadoop systems that integrate SQL support using Drill, Hive, Hortonworks Stinger, Cloudera Impala and similar.

Having provided the case for heterogeneity, the chapter proceeds with highlighting the case of heterogeneity in Big Data Systems by describing the different layers in the sections that follow.

HETEROGENEITY IN BIG DATA SYSTEMS

The growing number of new Big Data technologies as outlined in the previous section, accompanied by their complexity and specific functionality makes it difficult to clearly classify and categorize them. Multiple studies, summarized in Table 2, have investigated and developed different classifications, categorizations and taxonomies in order to make the Big Data field more understandable. The majority of the studies focus on a particular feature or technical functionality and does not depict the system complexity and variety in a general architectural overview. One of the main reasons for this is that the new systems consist of multiple components each with specific functionality, which makes a possible representation hard and unintuitive to illustrate. At the same time, having such Big Data architectural overview will help to deeper understand the different layers and the interconnection between its components. We call this concept the *heterogeneity paradigm*. In its essence the idea is to help the system architects and developers to better understand the various challenges caused by the new Big Data characteristics and the inability to define a unified architecture for all prominent use cases. This work focuses on heterogeneity paradigm in the Hadoop Ecosystem.

The term heterogeneity is often used in the context of Big Data to represent the variety of data sources and data formats (G. G. Caldarola, Picariello, & Castelluccia, 2015; Hashem et al., 2015; Jagadish et al., 2014). To cope with this challenge, the authors of the BigDawg architecture (Duggan et al., 2015) propose a multi-storage reference implementation consisting of streaming, array and relational stores.

Table 2. Classifications of Big Data Systems

Title & Authors	Description
Toward Scalable Systems for Big Data Analytics: A Technology Tutorial (Hu, Wen, Chua, & Li, 2014)	The authors first present the history and definitions of Big Data, then continue with a map of the Big Data technologies dividing them into four phases: Generation, Acquisition, Storage and Analytics. They also suggest a Big Data layered architecture consisting of infrastructure, computing and application layers.
The rise of "big data" on cloud computing: Review and open research issues (Hashem et al., 2015)	The authors motivate the classification of the Big Data technologies with the large-scale data in the cloud. They identify five aspects: i) data source, ii) content format, iii) data stores, iv) data staging, and v) data processing. Additionally, they present case studies, discuss Big Data research challenges and open issues.
Deciphering Big Data Stacks: An Overview of Big Data Tools (Lipic, Skala, & Afgan, 2014)	The authors present a Big Data Application and Libraries classification consisting of six functional categories. Additionally, they provide an abstract Big Data analysis stack consisting of four layers: i) Cloud resources, ii) Processing engines, iii) Applications and iv) Data analysis.
Survey on Large-Scale Data Management Systems for Big Data Applications (Wu, Yuan, & You, 2015)	The authors present a comprehensive taxonomy based on various aspects of the large-scale data management systems covering the data model, the system architecture and the consistency model.
Towards HPC-ABDS: An Initial High-Performance Big Data Stack (Qiu, Jha, & Fox, 2014)	The authors give an extensive overview of the Apache Big Data Stack and propose an integration with High Performance Big Data Stack. The current version of the stack can be found under http://hpc-abds.org/kaleidoscope .

In the same line of thought, the heterogeneity paradigm that we introduced does not only exist on the storage layer, but on each layer of a Big Data system. For example, data, stream or graph processing technologies can be used depending on the use case. They are core components of a Big Data platform and represent the functional heterogeneity in this layer.

Based on the concept of heterogeneity an abstract view of a Big Data architecture was defined and presented in Table 3. The architecture consists of four layers, which are also called levels: *hardware*, *management*, *platform* and *application*. This division in levels is not strict, but represents the major features and functionality of the components in a Big Data platform.

The *hardware* layer represents the server components of the system and the fact that they can vary in storage, memory and processor type and size. The *management* layer is dealing with the system resource management and offers services to the applications running on the upper layers. The *platform* layer represents the main storage and processing services that a Big Data platform provides. Finally, the *application* layer is hosting the variety of Big Data applications running on top of the services provided by the lower layers.

The rest of this section looks deeper into each level by enlisting the respective technology components and their categories.

Hardware Level

Undoubtedly recent advances in the processing and storing capabilities of the current commodity (off-the-shelf) servers have drastically improved while at the same time becoming cheaper (Intel, 2006). This reduces the overall cost of large-scale clusters consisting of thousands of machines and enables the vendors to cope with the exponentially growing data volumes, as well as the velocity with which the data should be processed. However, there have been other components like FPGAs, GPUs, accelerator

Table 3. Abstract Big Data Architecture

Heterogeneity Level	Abstract Big Data Architecture	
Application	Data, Stream & Graph Analytics	Content Analysis
	Machine Learning	Procedural Language
	Application Framework	Search Engine
	SQL-on-Hadoop	Data Modeling
	Data Acquisition	Library Collection
Platform	Data Collection	Data Governance
	Data Serialization	Machine Learning Framework
	Data Layout	Workflow Scheduling
	In-Memory Storage	Execution Framework
	Data & Graph Storage	Data, Stream & Graph Processing
Management	System Interfaces	
	Cloud Application Deployment	Application Management
	Distributed Coordination	Messaging Management
	Cluster Monitoring & Management	
	Virtualization-based & Container-based Resource Management	
Hardware	Memory Type & Size	CPU Type & Number of Cores
	Storage Type & Size	Accelerator Modules

modules and co-processors which have become part of the enterprise-ready servers. They offer numerous new capabilities which can further boost the overall system performance such as:

- Optimal processing of calculation intensive application;
- Offloading part or entire CPU computations to them;
- Faster and energy efficient parallel processing capabilities; and
- Improved price to processing ratio compared to standard CPUs.

Recently, there have been multiple studies investigating how these emerging components can be successfully integrated in the Big Data platforms. In (Shan et al., 2010), the authors present a MapReduce framework (FPMR) implemented on FPGA that achieves 31.8x speedup compared to CPU-based software system. (Kambatla & Chen, 2014) investigate the performance improvements of using Solid State Drives (SSDs) as an alternative to hard-disk drives and conclude that SSDs can achieve up to 70% higher performance for the 2.5x higher cost-per-performance. Similarly, (S.-H. Kang, Koo, Kang, & Lee, 2013) show that sorting in Hadoop with SSDs can be more than 3 times faster and reduce drastically the power consumption compared to hard disks.

Diversifying the core platform components motivates the investigation of the concept of heterogeneity on a hardware level and the new challenges that it introduces. Using the right hardware modules for a particular application can be crucial for obtaining the best price-performance ratio.

Management Level

As seen in Table 3 the management layer is positioned directly above the hardware level. It is responsible for the management and optimal allocation and usage of the underlying hardware components. There are multiple ways to achieve this:

- Directly installing operating system,
- Using a container technology (container-based virtualization),
- Using a virtualization technology (hypervisor-based virtualization) and
- Utilizing a hybrid solution between OS and virtualization.

In the recent years, virtualization has become the standard technology for infrastructure management both for bigger cloud and datacenter providers as well as for smaller private companies (Staten, Yates, Gillett, Saleh, & Dines, 2008). However, along with the multiple benefits that virtualization brings, there are also new challenges. The co-location of virtual machines hosting different application workloads on the same server makes the effective and fair resource allocation problematic. Also the logical division of virtual machines with similar characteristics is not always possible. In the case of Big Data platforms with changing workloads, it is difficult to meet the network and storage I/O guarantees. Therefore, the container-based virtualization, which comes at much smaller overhead as it is directly supported by the operating systems, has become very popular alternative. Virtualization technologies provide better resource sharing and isolation in exchange to a higher overhead, whereas container-based systems achieve near-native performance but offer poor security and isolation (Xavier, Neves, & Rose, 2014).

The Serengeti project (VMware, 2013, 2014) is one of the first initiatives to automate the management, starting, stopping and pre-configuring of Hadoop clusters on the fly. It is an open source project started by VMware and now integrated in vSphere as Big Data Extension, which has the goal to ease the management of virtualized Hadoop clusters. By the implementation of hooks to all major Hadoop modules, it is possible to know the exact cluster topology and make it aware of the hypervisor layer. This open source module is called Hadoop Virtual Extension (HVE) (VMware, 2013). Very interesting is the new ability to define the nodes (virtual machines) as either only compute or data nodes. The above implies that some nodes are storing the data in HDFS, while others are responsible for the computation of MapReduce jobs. Another very similar project, called Sahara (OpenStack, 2014), was developed as part of the OpenStack platform.

At the same time, there are variety of other technologies, which help and improve the management of a Big Data environment, such as monitoring, deployment, coordination, messaging and resource scheduling tools. An extensive list of such tools together with short description is provided in Table 4.

Platform Level

The platform layer represents the actual Big Data platform which is responsible for the provision of general data and processing capabilities. In the last years Apache Hadoop has become the de facto platform for Big Data. It has two core components: HDFS and YARN (MapReduce 2.0). HDFS is responsible for the data storage, whereas YARN is for the processing and resource allocation between the jobs. More recently, Yahoo released the Storm-YARN (Yahoo, 2013) application which combines the advantages of both applications: real-time (low-latency) and batch processing. It enables Storm applications to utilize

Table 4. Management Level Components

Type	Tools	Description
Virtualization-based Resource Management	Serengeti/Big Data Extensions	It is an open-source project, initiated by VMware, to enable the rapid deployment of Hadoop (HDFS, MapReduce, Pig, Hive, and HBase) on a virtual platform (vSphere). (VMware, 2013, 2014)
	Sahara/Savanna	It aims to provide users with simple means to provision a Hadoop cluster at OpenStack by specifying several parameters like Hadoop version, cluster topology, nodes hardware details and a few more. (OpenStack, 2014)
Cluster Resource Management	Mesos	A cluster manager that provides efficient resource isolation and sharing across distributed applications, or frameworks like Hadoop, MPI, Hypertable, Spark, and other applications. (Hindman et al., 2011)
	YARN	YARN (Yet Another Resource Negotiator/MapReduce 2.0) is a framework for job scheduling and cluster resource management. (Vavilapalli et al., 2013)
Container-based Resource Management	Docker	It is an open platform for developers and sysadmins to build, ship, and run distributed applications. Consisting of Docker Engine, a portable, lightweight runtime and packaging tool, and Docker Hub, a cloud service for sharing applications and automating workflows. (Docker, 2014)
	LXC/Linux Containers	LXC provides operating system-level virtualization through a virtual environment that has its own process and network space, instead of creating a full-fledged virtual machine. LXC relies on the Linux kernel cgroups functionality that was released in version 2.6.24.
	CoreOS	CoreOS is an open source lightweight operating system based on the Linux kernel and designed for providing infrastructure to clustered deployments, while focusing on automation, ease of applications deployment, security, reliability and scalability.
Cluster Monitoring & Management	Ambari	It provides an intuitive, easy-to-use Hadoop management web UI backed by its RESTful APIs for provisioning, managing, and monitoring Apache Hadoop clusters
	Helix	Apache Helix is a generic cluster management framework used for the automatic management of partitioned, replicated and distributed resources hosted on a cluster of nodes. Helix automates reassignment of resources in the face of node failure and recovery, cluster expansion, and reconfiguration.
Application Management	Cloudera Manager	Cloudera Manager is application management tool for the Cloudera Hadoop Distribution. It automates the administration, installation, configuration and deployment of cluster applications as well as offers monitoring and diagnostic capabilities.
Cloud Application Deployment	Whirr	Whirr is a set of libraries for running cloud services. It provides a cloud-neutral way to run services, a common service API and can be used as a command line tool for deploying clusters.
	JCloud	Jcloud is an open source multi-cloud toolkit for the Java platform. It provides functionality to create and control portable applications across clouds using their cloud-specific features.
Distributed Coordination	ZooKeeper	A centralized service that enables highly reliable distributed coordination by maintaining configuration information, naming, providing distributed synchronization, and group services. (Hunt, Konar, Junqueira, & Reed, 2010; Junqueira & Reed, 2009)
Messaging Management	Kafka	It is a distributed messaging system for collecting and delivering high volumes of log data with low latency. (Kreps, Narkhede, & Rao, 2011)
System Interfaces	Hue	Hue is a Web interface for analyzing data with Apache Hadoop. It supports a file and job browser, Hive, Pig, Impala, Spark, Oozie editors, Solr Search dashboards, Hbase, Sqoop2, and more.

the Hadoop resources managed by YARN, which will offer new abilities for faster and more optimal data processing. The Spark platform developed by Zaharia *et al.* (Zaharia et al., 2012; Zaharia et al., 2010) is built on top of HDFS and introduces the concept of Resilient Distributed Datasets (RDDs). RDDs are fault-tolerant, parallel data structures that let users explicitly persist intermediate results in memory, control their partitioning to optimize data placement, and manipulate them using a rich set of MapReduce-like parallel operations (iterative machine learning algorithms and interactive data analytics).

The above are just a few examples of the existing platforms for data storage and processing. The question "How to choose the right framework for a specific use case?" is very important, but one needs sufficient background knowledge in order to answer it, as pointed out by Grover (Grover, 2015). In his post, he discusses and categorizes the different frameworks which can be run on top of HDFS. This complies with the chapter's goal, on providing an overview of the variety of frameworks in the platform layer. Table 5 provides a list of components, grouped by their functionality types. In the upper part are the storage components (Data, Graph and In-memory storage), followed by multiple processing frameworks (Data, Stream and Graph processing) and data tools. In addition, there are execution and machine learning frameworks as well as tools for workflow management.

The list of new frameworks and tools is constantly growing as are the new application requirements of the upper layer. Therefore, the importance of understanding the heterogeneity on this platform level is very essential for the successful management and processing of large datasets.

Application Level

Satisfying all the Big Data application characteristics requires the platform to support all types of components starting from the data retrieval, aggregation and processing including data mining and analytics. Moreover, applications with very different characteristics should be able to run effectively co-located on the same platform, which should further guarantee optimal resource and functionality management, fair scheduling and workload isolation. These requirements outline the importance of understanding the heterogeneity on the application level. To achieve these, the variety of existing technologies and their features should be thoroughly investigated and understood. Table 6 summarizes major part of the tools in the Hadoop Ecosystem, grouping them according to their functionality type.

In the first category defined as data acquisition are tools used to move and store data into Hadoop. Sqoop (Ting & Cecho, 2013) and Flume are the most widely used tools for data acquisition.

The second category, called SQL-on-Hadoop, represents the variety of Data Warehousing, Business Intelligence, ETL (Extract-transform-load) (Baer, 2013) and reporting capabilities offered by the applications on top of Hadoop. Hive (A. Thusoo et al., 2010; Ashish Thusoo et al., 2009) is the most popular application in this category. It is a data warehouse infrastructure on top of Hadoop that provides data summarization and ad-hoc querying in SQL-like language, called HiveQL.

Another important category is the application frameworks, which offer ready to use packages, libraries and tools for building custom Big Data applications. The search engine category enlist components for enabling full-text search capabilities on top of Hadoop.

The last categories include different analytics types (Data, Graph and Stream analytics), machine learning and content analysis components, implementing specific use case functionalities.

Table 5. Platform Level Components

Type	Tools	Description
Data Storage	HDFS	Apache HDFS (Hadoop Distributed File System) is a distributed file system that provides high-throughput access to application data. (Borthakur, 2008)
	Hbase	Apache Hbase is the Hadoop database, a distributed, scalable, big data store. It is used for random, realtime read/write access to your Big Data and is modeled after Google's Bigtable (Chang et al., 2008) (George, 2011)
	Accumulo	Apache Accumulo sorted, distributed key/value store is a robust, scalable, high performance data storage and retrieval system. It is based on Google's Bigtable design and is built on top of Apache Hadoop, Zookeeper, and Thrift.
	Hypertable	Hypertable is open source,scalable, distributed key/value store based on Google's Bigtable design, running on top of Hadoop.
	Cassandra	Apache Cassandra's data model offers the convenience of column indexes with the performance of log-structured updates, strong support for denormalization and materialized views, and powerful built-in caching.
	Phoenix	Apache Phoenix is high performance relational database layer over Hbase for low latency applications.
Graph Storage	Titan	Titan is a scalable graph database optimized for storing and querying graphs containing hundreds of billions of vertices and edges distributed across a multi-machine cluster. Titan is a transactional database that can support thousands of concurrent users executing complex graph traversals in real time.
In-Memory Storage	Tachyon	Tachyon is an open source, memory-centric distributed file system enabling reliable file sharing at memory-speed across cluster frameworks, such as Spark and MapReduce. (Li et al., 2013; Li, Ghodsi, Zaharia, Shenker, & Stoica, 2014)
Data Governance	Cloudera Navigator	Cloudera Navigator offers comprehensive auditing across Hadoop cluster by defining and automatically collecting data lifecycle activities such as retention and encryption policies.
	Falcon	Apache Falcon is a data processing and management solution for Hadoop designed for data motion, coordination of data pipelines, lifecycle management, and data discovery. Falcon enables end consumers to quickly onboard their data and its associated processing and management tasks on Hadoop clusters.
Data Collection	Chukwa	Apache Chukwa is a data collection system for managing large distributed systems. It also includes a flexible and powerful toolkit for displaying, monitoring and analyzing results to make the best use of the collected data. (Boulon et al., 2008; Rabkin & Katz, 2010)
Data Serialization	Avro	Apache Avro is a data serialization system. It provides: 1) rich data structures; 2) a compact, fast, binary data format; 3) a container file, to store persistent data; 4) remote procedure call (RPC) and 5) simple integration with dynamic languages.
Data Layout	Parquet	Apache Parquet is a columnar storage format available to any project in the Hadoop ecosystem, regardless of the choice of data processing framework, data model or programming language.
Data Processing	MapReduce	A YARN-based system for parallel processing of large data sets. (Dean & Ghemawat, 2008)
	Spark	Apache Spark is an open source cluster computing system that aims to run programs faster by providing primitives for in-memory cluster computing. Jobs can load data into memory and query it repeatedly much more quickly than with disk-based systems like Hadoop MapReduce. (Zaharia et al., 2012; Zaharia et al., 2010)

continued on following page

Table 5. Continued

Type	Tools	Description
Stream Processing	Storm	An open source distributed real-time computation system. Storm makes it easy to reliably process unbounded streams of data, doing for real-time processing what Hadoop did for batch processing. (Leibiusky, Eisbruch, & Simonassi, 2012)
	Storm-YARN	It enables Storm applications to utilize the computational resources in a Hadoop-YARN cluster along with accessing Hadoop storage resources such as Hbase and HDFS. (Yahoo, 2013)
	Samza	Apache Samza is a distributed stream processing framework. It uses Kafka for messaging, and Hadoop YARN to provide fault tolerance, processor isolation, security, and resource management.
	S4	Apache S4 is a general-purpose, distributed, scalable, fault-tolerant, pluggable platform that allows programmers to easily develop applications for processing continuous unbounded streams of data.
	Spark Streaming	Spark Streaming makes it easy to build scalable fault-tolerant streaming applications by using the Spark's language-integrated API, which supports Java, Scala and Python. (Zaharia et al., 2013)
Workflow Scheduling	Oozie	Apache Oozie is a workflow scheduler system to manage Apache Hadoop jobs. (Islam et al., 2012)
Execution Framework	REEF	REEF (Retainable Evaluator Execution Framework) framework builds on top of YARN to provide crucial features (Retainability, Composability, Cost modeling, Fault handling and Elasticity) to a range of different applications. (Chun et al., 2013)
Graph Processing	Giraph	Apache Giraph is an iterative graph processing system built for high scalability. It originated as the open-source counterpart to Pregel (Malewicz et al., 2010), the graph processing architecture developed at Google.
	GraphX	GraphX is Apache Spark's API for graphs and graph-parallel computation. It unifies ETL, exploratory analysis, and iterative graph computation within a single system. (Gonzalez et al., 2014)
	Dato/ GraphLab	GraphLab is an open source, graph-based, high performance, distributed computation framework written in C++. (Low et al., 2012)
	Pegasus	PEGASUS is a Peta-scale graph mining system, fully written in Java. It runs in parallel, distributed manner on top of Hadoop. (U. Kang, Tsourakakis, & Faloutsos, 2009)
Machine Learning Framework	Oryx	The Oryx open source project provides simple, real-time large-scale machine learning / predictive analytics infrastructure. It implements a few classes of algorithm commonly used in business applications: collaborative filtering / recommendation, classification / regression, and clustering. (Cloudera, 2015)
	MLbase	MLbase is a platform for Implementing and consuming Machine Learning techniques at scale, and consists of three components: MLlib, MLI, ML Optimizer. MLlib is Spark's scalable machine learning library consisting of common learning algorithms and utilities. (Kraska et al., 2013; Talwalkar et al., 2012)
	H2O	H2O is an open source platform, offering machine learning algorithms for classification and regression over BigData. It is extensible and users can build blocks using simple math legos in the core. H2O keeps familiar interfaces like R, Excel & JSON. (0xdata, 2015)

Table 6. Application Level Components

Type	Tool	Description
Data Acquisition	Sqoop	A tool designed for efficiently transferring bulk data between Apache Hadoop and structured data stores such as relational databases. (Ting & Cecho, 2013)
	Flume	A distributed, reliable, and available service for efficiently collecting, aggregating, and moving large amounts of log data.
SQL-on-Hadoop	Hive	A data warehouse infrastructure that provides data summarization and ad hoc querying. (A. Thusoo et al., 2010; Ashish Thusoo et al., 2009)
	HCatalog	A set of interfaces that open up access to Hive's metastore for tools inside and outside of the Hadoop grid. It is now part of Hive. (Capriolo, Wampler, & Rutherglen, 2012)
	Impala	It is an open source Massively Parallel Processing (MPP) query engine that runs natively on Hadoop, enabling users to issue low-latency SQL queries to data stored in HDFS and HBase without requiring data movement or transformation. (Kornacker et al., 2015)
	Big SQL (IBM)	Big SQL is a massively parallel processing (MPP) SQL engine that deploys directly on the physical Hadoop Distributed File System (HDFS) cluster. This SQL engine pushes processing down to the same nodes that hold the data.
	SparkSQL (Shark)	A fully Hive-compatible data warehousing on top of Spark system that can run 100x faster than Hive. (Engle et al., 2012; Xin et al., 2013)
	Drill	Apache Drill is an open-source software framework (inspired by Google's Dremel) that supports data-intensive distributed applications for interactive analysis of large-scale datasets. (Hausenblas & Nadeau, 2013)
	Tajo	A relational and distributed data warehouse system for Hadoop, that is designed for low-latency and scalable ad-hoc queries, online aggregation and ETL on large-data sets by leveraging advanced database techniques.
	Presto (Facebook)	Presto is an open source distributed SQL query engine for running interactive analytic queries against data sources of all sizes ranging from gigabytes to petabytes. (Choi et al., 2013)
	HAWK (Pivotal, 2015b)	HAWQ is a parallel SQL query engine that combines the Pivotal Analytic Database with the scalability and convenience of Hadoop. HAWQ reads data from and writes data to HDFS natively. It delivers performance, linear scalability and provides tools interaction with petabyte range data sets. HAWQ provides users with a complete, standards compliant SQL interface.
	MRQL	Apache MRQL (pronounced miracle) is a query processing and optimization system for large-scale, distributed data analysis, built on top of Apache Hadoop, Hama, and Spark.
	BlinkDB	BlinkDB is a massively parallel, approximate query engine for running interactive SQL queries on large volumes of data. It allows users to trade-off query accuracy for response time, enabling interactive queries over massive data by running queries on data samples and presenting results annotated with meaningful error bars. (Agarwal et al., 2012, 2013)
Library Collection	DataFu	Apache DataFu is a collection of libraries for working with large-scale data in Hadoop. The project was inspired by the need for stable, well-tested libraries for data mining and statistics. (Hayes & Shah, 2013)
Data Modeling	Gora	Apache Gora is an open source framework that provides an in-memory data model and persistence for big data. It supports persisting to column stores, key/value stores, document stores and RDBMSs, and analyzing the data with extensive MapReduce support.
	Kite	Kite is a high-level data layer for Hadoop. It is an API and a set of tools that speed up development by enabling you to configure how Kite stores your data in Hadoop. (Kite, 2015)

continued on following page

Table 6. Continued

Type	Tool	Description
Application Framework	Tez	Apache Tez is a general-purpose resource management framework which allows for a complex processing of directed-acyclic-graph of tasks and is built atop Hadoop YARN. (Apache, 2015)
	Cascading	Cascading is an open source application development platform for building data applications on Hadoop. It is used to create and execute complex data processing workflows on a Hadoop cluster using any JVM-based language (Java, JRuby, Clojure, etc.), hiding the underlying complexity of MapReduce jobs.
	Flink (Stratosphere)	Apache Flink features powerful programming abstractions in Java and Scala, a high-performance runtime, and automatic program optimization. It has native support for iterations, incremental iterations, and programs consisting of large DAGs of operations. (Alexandrov et al., 2014)
	Crunch	Apache Crunch Java library provides a framework for writing, testing, and running MapReduce pipelines. Its goal is to make pipelines that are composed of many user-defined functions simple to write, easy to test, and efficient to run.
Search Engine	Lucene	Apache Lucene is an open source, high-performance, full-featured text search engine library written entirely in Java. It is a technology suitable for nearly any application that requires full-text search, especially cross-platform. (McCandless, Hatcher, & Gospodnetic, 2010)
	Solr	Apache Solr is highly reliable, scalable and fault tolerant, providing distributed indexing, replication and load-balanced querying, automated failover and recovery, centralized configuration and more. It is built on Apache Lucene.
	Nutch	Apache Nutch is an open source web search engine based on Lucene and Java for the search and index component. It has a highly modular architecture, allowing developers to create plug-ins for media-type parsing, data retrieval, querying and clustering. (Khare, Cutting, Sitaker, & Rifkin, 2005)
	Elasticsearch	Elasticsearch is an open source, search server based on Lucene. It provides a distributed, multitenant-capable full-text search engine with a RESTful web interface and schema-free JSON documents.
Machine Learning	Mahout	A scalable machine learning and data mining library. (Owen, Anil, Dunning, & Friedman, 2011)
Data Analytics	Hama	Apache Hama is an open source project, allowing you to do advanced analytics beyond MapReduce.
Stream Analytics	SAMOA	Apache SAMOA is distributed streaming machine learning (ML) framework that contains a programing abstraction for distributed streaming ML algorithms. (De Francisci Morales, 2013)
Procedural Language	Pig	A high-level data-flow language and execution framework for parallel computation. (Gates et al., 2009; Olston, Reed, Srivastava, Kumar, & Tomkins, 2008)
Content Analysis	Tika	Apache Tika is a toolkit that detects and extracts metadata and structured text content from various documents using existing parser libraries. (Mattmann & Zitting, 2011)
Graph Analytics	Faunus	Faunus is a Hadoop-based graph analytics engine for analyzing graphs represented across a multi-machine compute cluster.

SUMMARY AND FUTURE RESEARCH DIRECTIONS

In this chapter the concept of heterogeneity was introduced in relation with the design and implementation of Big Data platforms and discussed how the existing tools comprising the Hadoop ecosystem adapt on these challenges. The emergence of new analytical applications opens new Big Data challenges both for researchers and practitioners (Zicari, 2013). These challenges are not only in relation with Data Characteristics (quality, availability, discovery and comprehensiveness), but also in terms of Data Processing (cleansing, capturing, and modeling) and Data Management (privacy, security and governance). Such an evaluation framework should be able to give the technology guidelines on how to build the best cost-performance Big Data platform for both vertical and generic data processing workloads.

This chapter provided an overview of a generic heterogeneous approach for addressing the above challenges. Nevertheless such as approach also has its limitations since the current perspective on the Hadoop ecosystem is subject to continuous development. However, architectural patterns become more relevant once an overall system architecture has been proven to work. This theoretical overview can provide a solid application especially for the challenges addressed by practitioners in the area where fast and effective processing of data is of strategic importance.

REFERENCES

Abouzeid, A., Bajda-Pawlikowski, K., Abadi, D., Silberschatz, A., & Rasin, A. (2009). HadoopDB: An architectural hybrid of MapReduce and DBMS technologies for analytical workloads. *Proceedings of the VLDB Endowment*, *2*(1), 922–933. doi:10.14778/1687627.1687731

Agarwal, S., Iyer, A. P., Panda, A., Madden, S., Mozafari, B., & Stoica, I. (2012). Blink and it's done: Interactive queries on very large data. *Proceedings of the VLDB Endowment*, *5*(12), 1902–1905. doi:10.14778/2367502.2367533

Agarwal, S., Mozafari, B., Panda, A., Milner, H., Madden, S., & Stoica, I. (2013). BlinkDB: queries with bounded errors and bounded response times on very large data. In *Proceedings of the 8th ACM European Conference on Computer Systems* (pp. 29–42). ACM. doi:10.1145/2465351.2465355

Alexandrov, A., Bergmann, R., Ewen, S., Freytag, J.-C., Hueske, F., Heise, A., & Markl, V. et al. (2014). The Stratosphere platform for big data analytics. *The VLDB Journal*, *23*(6), 939–964. doi:10.1007/s00778-014-0357-y

Amazon. (2015). AWS - Big Data Analytics. Retrieved February 2, 2015, from http://aws.amazon.com/big-data/

Apache. (2015). Apache Tez. Retrieved March 14, 2015, from http://hortonworks.com/hadoop/tez/

Baer, T. (2013). Hadoop as your other data warehouse. Retrieved February 24, 2015, from http://www.onstrategies.com/blog/2013/05/05/hadoop-as-your-other-data-warehouse/

Baru, C., Bhandarkar, M., Curino, C., Danisch, M., Frank, M., & Gowda, B. … Youn, C. (2014). Discussion of BigBench: A Proposed Industry Standard Performance Benchmark for Big Data. In R. Nambiar & M. Poess (Eds.), Performance Characterization and Benchmarking. Traditional to Big Data (pp. 44–63). Springer International Publishing.

Baru, C., Bhandarkar, M., Nambiar, R., Poess, M., & Rabl, T. (2013a). Benchmarking Big Data Systems and the BigData Top100 List. *Big Data*, *1*(1), 60–64. doi:10.1089/big.2013.1509

Baru, C., Bhandarkar, M., Nambiar, R., Poess, M., & Rabl, T. (2013b). Setting the Direction for Big Data Benchmark Standards. In R. Nambiar & M. Poess (Eds.), *Selected Topics in Performance Evaluation and Benchmarking* (pp. 197–208). Springer Berlin Heidelberg; doi:10.1007/978-3-642-36727-4_14

Borthakur, D. (2008). *HDFS architecture guide*. Apache Hadoop.

Boulon, J., Konwinski, A., Qi, R., Rabkin, A., Yang, E., & Yang, M. (2008). Chukwa, a large-scale monitoring system. In *Proceedings of CCA* (Vol. 8).

Bu, Y., Howe, B., Balazinska, M., & Ernst, M. D. (2010). HaLoop: Efficient iterative data processing on large clusters. *Proceedings of the VLDB Endowment*, *3*(1-2), 285–296. doi:10.14778/1920841.1920881

Bu, Y., Howe, B., Balazinska, M., & Ernst, M. D. (2012). The HaLoop approach to large-scale iterative data analysis. *The VLDB Journal*, *21*(2), 169–190. doi:10.1007/s00778-012-0269-7

Caldarola, E. G., Sacco, M., & Terkaj, W. (2014). Big Data: the current wave front of the tsunami. ACS Applied Computer Science, 10(4).

Caldarola, G. G., Picariello, A., & Castelluccia, D. (2015). Modern Enterprises in the Bubble: Why Big Data Matters. *Software Engineering Notes*, *40*(1), 1–4. doi:10.1145/2693208.2693228

Capriolo, E., Wampler, D., & Rutherglen, J. (2012). *Programming Hive*. O'Reilly.

Cattell, R. (2011). Scalable SQL and NoSQL data stores. *SIGMOD Record*, *39*(4), 12–27. doi:10.1145/1978915.1978919

Chang, F., Dean, J., Ghemawat, S., Hsieh, W. C., Wallach, D. A., Burrows, M., & Gruber, R. E. et al. (2008). Bigtable: A distributed storage system for structured data. *ACM Transactions on Computer Systems*, *26*(2), 4. doi:10.1145/1365815.1365816

Choi, H., Son, J., Yang, H., Ryu, H., Lim, B., Kim, S., & Chung, Y. D. (2013). Tajo: A distributed data warehouse system on large clusters. In 2013 IEEE 29th International Conference on Data Engineering (ICDE) (pp. 1320–1323). IEEE.

Chun, B.-G., Condie, T., Curino, C., Douglas, C., Matusevych, S., & Myers, B., … Rosen, J. (2013). REEF: retainable evaluator execution framework. Proceedings of the VLDB Endowment, 6(12), 1370–1373.

Cloudera. (2015). Oryx 2. Retrieved February 20, 2015, from https://github.com/OryxProject/oryx

De Francisci Morales, G. (2013). SAMOA: A platform for mining big data streams. In *Proceedings of the 22nd international conference on World Wide Web companion* (pp. 777–778). International World Wide Web Conferences Steering Committee.

Dean, J., & Ghemawat, S. (2008). MapReduce: Simplified data processing on large clusters. *Communications of the ACM, 51*(1), 107–113. doi:10.1145/1327452.1327492

DeWitt, D. J., Halverson, A., Nehme, R., Shankar, S., Aguilar-Saborit, J., & Avanes, A. (2013). *Gramling, J.* Split Query Processing in Polybase. SIGMOD.

Dittrich, J., Quiané-Ruiz, J.-A., Jindal, A., Kargin, Y., Setty, V., & Schad, J. (2010). Hadoop++: Making a yellow elephant run like a cheetah (without it even noticing). *Proceedings of the VLDB Endowment, 3*(1-2), 515–529. doi:10.14778/1920841.1920908

Docker. (2014). Docker. Retrieved February 23, 2015, from https://www.docker.com/

Duggan, J., Elmore, A., Kraska, T., Madden, S., Mattson, T., & Stonebraker, M. (2015). *The BigDawg Architecture and Reference Implementation.* New England Database Day.

Ekmecic, I., Tartalja, I., & Milutinovic, V. (1996). A survey of heterogeneous computing: Concepts and systems. *Proceedings of the IEEE, 84*(8), 1127–1144. doi:10.1109/5.533958

Engle, C., Lupher, A., Xin, R., Zaharia, M., Franklin, M. J., Shenker, S., & Stoica, I. (2012). Shark: Fast Data Analysis Using Coarse-grained Distributed Memory. In *Proceedings of the 2012 ACM SIGMOD International Conference on Management of Data* (pp. 689–692). New York, NY: ACM. doi:10.1145/2213836.2213934

Fan, C. (2012). CRAP and CRUD: From Database to Datacloud. Retrieved February 11, 2015, from http://reflectionsblog.emc.com/2012/11/crap-and-crud-from-database-to-datacloud.html

Gates, A. F., Natkovich, O., Chopra, S., Kamath, P., Narayanamurthy, S. M., & Olston, C., … Srivastava, U. (2009). Building a high-level dataflow system on top of Map-Reduce: the Pig experience. Proceedings of the VLDB Endowment, 2(2), 1414–1425. doi:10.14778/1687553.1687568

George, L. (2011). *HBase: the definitive guide.* O'Reilly Media, Inc.

GoGrid. (2015). GoGrid Solutions. Retrieved February 2, 2015, from http://www.gogrid.com/solutions

Gonzalez, J. E., Xin, R. S., Dave, A., Crankshaw, D., Franklin, M. J., & Stoica, I. (2014). Graphx: Graph processing in a distributed dataflow framework. In *Proceedings of the 11th USENIX Symposium on Operating Systems Design and Implementation (OSDI).*

Google. (2015). Google Cloud Platform. Retrieved February 2, 2015, from https://cloud.google.com/

Greenberg, A., Hamilton, J., Maltz, D. A., & Patel, P. (2008). The cost of a cloud: Research problems in data center networks. *Computer Communication Review, 39*(1), 68–73. doi:10.1145/1496091.1496103

Grover, M. (2015). Processing frameworks for Hadoop. Retrieved March 8, 2015, from http://radar.oreilly.com/2015/02/processing-frameworks-for-hadoop.html

Grund, M., Krüger, J., Plattner, H., Zeier, A., Cudre-Mauroux, P., & Madden, S. (2010). HYRISE: A main memory hybrid storage engine. *Proceedings of the VLDB Endowment, 4*(2), 105–116. doi:10.14778/1921071.1921077

Hashem, I. A. T., Yaqoob, I., Anuar, N. B., Mokhtar, S., Gani, A., & Khan, S. U. (2015). The rise of "big data" on cloud computing: Review and open research issues. *Information Systems*, *47*, 98–115. doi:10.1016/j.is.2014.07.006

Hausenblas, M., & Nadeau, J. (2013). Apache drill: Interactive ad-hoc analysis at scale. *Big Data*, *1*(2), 100–104. doi:10.1089/big.2013.0011

Hayes, M., & Shah, S. (2013). Hourglass: A library for incremental processing on Hadoop. In Big Data, 2013 IEEE International Conference on (pp. 742–752). IEEE. doi:10.1109/BigData.2013.6691647

Herodotou, H., Lim, H., Luo, G., Borisov, N., Dong, L., Cetin, F. B., & Babu, S. (2011). Starfish: A self-tuning system for big data analytics. In *Proceedings of the Fifth CIDR Conference*.

Hindman, B., Konwinski, A., Zaharia, M., Ghodsi, A., Joseph, A. D., & Katz, R., … Stoica, I. (2011). Mesos: A platform for fine-grained resource sharing in the data center. In Proceedings of the 8th USE-NIX conference on Networked systems design and implementation (pp. 22–22). USENIX Association.

Hu, H., Wen, Y., Chua, T.-S., & Li, X. (2014). Toward Scalable Systems for Big Data Analytics: A Technology Tutorial. *IEEE Access*, *2*, 652–687. doi:10.1109/ACCESS.2014.2332453

Huai, Y., Ma, S., Lee, R., O'Malley, O., & Zhang, X. (2013). Understanding insights into the basic structure and essential issues of table placement methods in clusters. *Proceedings of the VLDB Endowment*, *6*(14), 1750–1761. doi:10.14778/2556549.2556559

Hunt, P., Konar, M., Junqueira, F. P., & Reed, B. (2010). ZooKeeper: wait-free coordination for internet-scale systems. In Proceedings of the 2010 USENIX conference on USENIX annual technical conference (Vol. 8, pp. 11–11). USENIX.

Infochimps. (2015). Big Data Technology Suite of Cloud Services. Retrieved February 2, 2015, from http://www.infochimps.com/infochimps-cloud/overview/

Intel. (2006). Increasing Data Center Density While Driving Down Power and Cooling Costs. Retrieved February 4, 2015, from http://www.intel.com/design/Xeon/whitepaper/313462.htm

Intel. (2014). Big Data Cloud: Converging Technologies. Retrieved February 2, 2015, from http://www.intel.com/content/www/us/en/big-data/big-data-cloud-technologies-brief.html

Islam, M., Huang, A. K., Battisha, M., Chiang, M., Srinivasan, S., & Peters, C., … Abdelnur, A. (2012). Oozie: towards a scalable workflow management system for Hadoop. In Proceedings of the 1st ACM SIGMOD Workshop on Scalable Workflow Execution Engines and Technologies (p. 4). ACM. doi:10.1145/2443416.2443420

Ivanov, T., Petrov, I., & Buchmann, A. (2012). A Survey on Database Performance in Virtualized Cloud Environments. *International Journal of Data Warehousing and Mining*, *8*(3), 1–26. doi:10.4018/jdwm.2012070101

Jagadish, H. V., Gehrke, J., Labrinidis, A., Papakonstantinou, Y., Patel, J. M., Ramakrishnan, R., & Shahabi, C. (2014). Big data and its technical challenges. *Communications of the ACM*, *57*(7), 86–94. doi:10.1145/2611567

Junqueira, F. P., & Reed, B. C. (2009). The life and times of a zookeeper. In *Proceedings of the 28th ACM symposium on Principles of distributed computing* (pp. 4–4). ACM. doi:10.1145/1582716.1582721

Kambatla, K., & Chen, Y. (2014). The truth about MapReduce performance on SSDs. In *Proceedings of the 28th USENIX conference on Large Installation System Administration* (pp. 109–117). USENIX Association.

Kang, S.-H., Koo, D.-H., Kang, W.-H., & Lee, S.-W. (2013). A case for flash memory ssd in hadoop applications. *International Journal of Control and Automation*, *6*(1), 201–210.

Kang, U., Tsourakakis, C. E., & Faloutsos, C. (2009). PEGASUS: A Peta-Scale Graph Mining System Implementation and Observations. In Ninth IEEE International Conference on Data Mining, 2009. ICDM '09 (pp. 229–238). doi:10.1109/ICDM.2009.14

Kemper, A., & Neumann, T. (2011). HyPer: A hybrid OLTP&OLAP main memory database system based on virtual memory snapshots. In Data Engineering (ICDE), 2011 IEEE 27th International Conference on (pp. 195–206). IEEE. doi:10.1109/ICDE.2011.5767867

Khare, R., Cutting, D., Sitaker, K., & Rifkin, A. (2005). Nutch: A flexible and scalable open-source web search engine. In *Proceedings of the 14th international conference on World Wide Web* (Vol. 1, pp. 32–32).

Khokhar, A. A., Prasanna, V. K., Shaaban, M. E., & Wang, C.-L. (1993). Heterogeneous computing: Challenges and opportunities. *Computer*, *26*(6), 18–27. doi:10.1109/2.214439

Kite. (2015). Kite. Retrieved March 6, 2015, from http://kitesdk.org/docs/1.0.0/

Kornacker, M., Behm, A., Bittorf, V., Bobrovytsky, T., Ching, C., & Choi, A., … Yoder, M. (2015). Impala: A Modern, Open-Source SQL Engine for Hadoop. In Proceedings of the Seventh CIDR Conference.

Kraska, T., Talwalkar, A., Duchi, J. C., Griffith, R., Franklin, M. J., & Jordan, M. I. (2013). MLbase: A Distributed Machine-learning System. In *Proceedings of the Sixth CIDR Conference*.

Kreps, J., Narkhede, N., & Rao, J. (2011). Kafka: A distributed messaging system for log processing. In *Proceedings of 6th International Workshop on Networking Meets Databases (NetDB)*.

Lee, G., Chun, B.-G., & Katz, R. H. (2011). Heterogeneity-aware resource allocation and scheduling in the cloud. In Proceedings of the 3rd USENIX Workshop on Hot Topics in Cloud Computing, HotCloud (Vol. 11).

Leibiusky, J., Eisbruch, G., & Simonassi, D. (2012). *Getting started with storm*. O'Reilly Media, Inc.

Li, H., Ghodsi, A., Zaharia, M., Baldeschwieler, E., Shenker, S., & Stoica, I. (2013). Tachyon: Memory Throughput I/O for Cluster Computing Frameworks. *Memory (Hove, England)*, *18*, 1.

Li, H., Ghodsi, A., Zaharia, M., Shenker, S., & Stoica, I. (2014). Tachyon: Reliable, memory speed storage for cluster computing frameworks. In *Proceedings of the ACM Symposium on Cloud Computing* (pp. 1–15). ACM. doi:10.1145/2670979.2670985

Lipic, T., Skala, K., & Afgan, E. (2014). Deciphering Big Data Stacks: An Overview of Big Data Tools. Big Data Analytics: Challenges and Opportunities (BDAC-14).

Low, Y., Bickson, D., Gonzalez, J., Guestrin, C., Kyrola, A., & Hellerstein, J. M. (2012). Distributed GraphLab: A framework for machine learning and data mining in the cloud. *Proceedings of the VLDB Endowment*, *5*(8), 716–727. doi:10.14778/2212351.2212354

Malewicz, G., Austern, M. H., Bik, A. J., Dehnert, J. C., Horn, I., Leiser, N., & Czajkowski, G. (2010). Pregel: a system for large-scale graph processing. In *Proceedings of the 2010 ACM SIGMOD International Conference on Management of data* (pp. 135–146). ACM. doi:10.1145/1807167.1807184

Mars, J., Tang, L., & Hundt, R. (2011). Heterogeneity in "homogeneous" warehouse-scale computers: A performance opportunity. *Computer Architecture Letters*, *10*(2), 29–32. doi:10.1109/L-CA.2011.14

Marz, N. (2012). Runaway complexity in Big Data... And a plan to stop it. Retrieved March 10, 2015, from http://www.slideshare.net/nathanmarz/runaway-complexity-in-big-data-and-a-plan-to-stop-it

Marz, N., & Warren, J. (2012). *Big data: principles and best practices of scalable realtime data systems*. Greenwich: Manning Publications.

Mattmann, C., & Zitting, J. (2011). *Tika in Action*. Manning Publications Co.

McCandless, M., Hatcher, E., & Gospodnetic, O. (2010). *Lucene in Action: Covers Apache Lucene 3.0*. Manning Publications Co.

Mell, P., & Grance, T. (2011). *The NIST definition of cloud computing*. NIST. doi:10.6028/NIST.SP.800-145

Microsoft. (2015). Cloud Services - HDInsight (Hadoop). Retrieved February 2, 2015, from http://azure.microsoft.com/en-us/services/hdinsight/

Monash, C. (2013). One database to rule them all? Retrieved March 4, 2015, from http://www.dbms2.com/2013/02/21/one-database-to-rule-them-all/

Olston, C., Reed, B., Srivastava, U., Kumar, R., & Tomkins, A. (2008). Pig latin: a not-so-foreign language for data processing. In *Proceedings of the 2008 ACM SIGMOD international conference on Management of data* (pp. 1099–1110). ACM. doi:10.1145/1376616.1376726

OpenStack. (2014). Sahara. Retrieved March 7, 2015, from https://wiki.openstack.org/wiki/Sahara

Owen, S., Anil, R., Dunning, T., & Friedman, E. (2011). *Mahout in action*. Manning.

Oxdata. (2015). H2O. Retrieved February 20, 2015, from https://github.com/h2oai/h2o

Pivotal. (2015a). Pivotal Cloud Foundry. Retrieved February 2, 2015, from http://www.pivotal.io/platform-as-a-service/pivotal-cloud-foundry

Pivotal. (2015b). Pivotal HAWQ. Retrieved January 22, 2015, from http://www.pivotal.io/big-data/hadoop/sql-on-hadoop

Plattner, H. (2009). A common database approach for OLTP and OLAP using an in-memory column database. In *Proceedings of the 2009 ACM SIGMOD International Conference on Management of data* (pp. 1–2). ACM. doi:10.1145/1559845.1559846

Qin, X., Qin, B., Du, X., & Wang, S. (2013). Reflection on the Popularity of MapReduce and Observation of Its Position in a Unified Big Data Platform. In Y. Gao, K. Shim, Z. Ding, P. Jin, Z. Ren, Y. Xiao, … S. Qiao (Eds.), Web-Age Information Management (pp. 339–347). Springer Berlin Heidelberg. doi:10.1007/978-3-642-39527-7_33

Qiu, J., Jha, S., & Fox, G. C. (2014). Towards HPC-ABDS: An Initial High-Performance BigData Stack. Building Robust Big Data Ecosystem ISO/IEC JTC 1 Study Group on Big Data.

Rabkin, A., & Katz, R. (2010). Chukwa: A system for reliable large-scale log collection. In *Proceedings of the 24th international conference on Large installation system administration* (pp. 1–15). USENIX Association.

Rackspace. (2015). Rackspace Cloud Big Data Platform. Retrieved February 2, 2015, from http://www.rackspace.com/cloud/big-data/

Red Hat. (2015). OpenShift Platform as a Service. Retrieved February 2, 2015, from https://www.openshift.com/products

Rimal, B. P., Choi, E., & Lumb, I. (2009). A Taxonomy and Survey of Cloud Computing Systems. In Networked Computing and Advanced Information Management, International Conference on (Vol. 0, pp. 44–51). Los Alamitos, CA: IEEE Computer Society. doi:10.1109/NCM.2009.218

Sakr, S., Liu, A., & Fayoumi, A. G. (2013). The Family of Mapreduce and Large-scale Data Processing Systems. ACM Computing Surveys, 46(1), 11:1–11:44.

Shan, Y., Wang, B., Yan, J., Wang, Y., Xu, N., & Yang, H. (2010). FPMR: MapReduce Framework on FPGA. In *Proceedings of the 18th Annual ACM/SIGDA International Symposium on Field Programmable Gate Arrays* (pp. 93–102). New York, NY: ACM. doi:10.1145/1723112.1723129

Staten, J., Yates, S., Gillett, F. E., Saleh, W., & Dines, R. A. (2008). *Is cloud computing ready for the enterprise*. Forrester Research.

Stonebraker, M., Bear, C., Çetintemel, U., Cherniack, M., Ge, T., & Hachem, N., … Zdonik, S. (2007). One size fits all? Part 2: Benchmarking results. In Proceedings of the Third CIDR Conference.

Strauch, C., Sites, U.-L. S., & Kriha, W. (2011). NoSQL databases. Retrieved February 2, 2015, from http://www.christof-strauch.de/nosqldbs.pdf

Talwalkar, A., Kraska, T., Griffith, R., Duchi, J., Gonzalez, J., & Britz, D., … Wibisono, A. (2012). Mlbase: A distributed machine learning wrapper. In NIPS Big Learning Workshop.

Thusoo, A., Sarma, J. S., Jain, N., Shao, Z., Chakka, P., & Anthony, S. (1626–1629). … Murthy, R. (2009). Hive: A Warehousing Solution over a Map-reduce Framework. *Proceedings of the VLDB Endowment*, 2(2).

Thusoo, A., Sarma, J. S., Jain, N., Shao, Z., Chakka, P., & Zhang, N. … Murthy, R. (2010). Hive - a petabyte scale data warehouse using Hadoop. In 2010 IEEE 26th International Conference on Data Engineering (ICDE) (pp. 996–1005).

Ting, K., & Cecho, J. J. (2013). *Apache Sqoop Cookbook*. O'Reilly Media.

Vavilapalli, V. K., Murthy, A. C., Douglas, C., Agarwal, S., Konar, M., & Evans, R., … Baldeschwieler, E. (2013). Apache Hadoop YARN: Yet Another Resource Negotiator. In Proceedings of the 4th Annual Symposium on Cloud Computing (pp. 5:1–5:16). New York: ACM. doi:10.1145/2523616.2523633

Venugopal, S., Buyya, R., & Ramamohanarao, K. (2006). A Taxonomy of Data Grids for Distributed Data Sharing, Management, and Processing. ACM Computing Surveys, 38(1), 3, es. doi:10.1145/1132952.1132955

VMware. (2013). Serengeti. Retrieved March 8, 2015, from http://www.projectserengeti.org

VMware. (2014). VMware vSphere Big Data Extensions. Retrieved February 16, 2015, from http://www.vmware.com/products/big-data-extensions

Wang, H., Liu, W., & Soyata, T. (2014). Accessing big data in the cloud using mobile devices. In P. R. Chelliah & G. Deka (Eds.), *Handbook of Research on Cloud Infrastructures for Big Data Analytics* (pp. 444–470)., doi:10.4018/978-1-4666-5864-6.ch018

Wu, L., Yuan, L., & You, J. (2015). Survey of Large-Scale Data Management Systems for Big Data Applications. *Journal of Computer Science and Technology*, 30(1), 163–183. doi:10.1007/s11390-015-1511-8

Xavier, M. G., Neves, M. V., & Rose, C. A. F. D. (2014). A Performance Comparison of Container-Based Virtualization Systems for MapReduce Clusters. In Parallel, Distributed and Network-Based Processing (PDP), 2014 22nd Euromicro International Conference on (pp. 299–306). IEEE. doi:10.1109/PDP.2014.78

Xin, R. S., Rosen, J., Zaharia, M., Franklin, M. J., Shenker, S., & Stoica, I. (2013). Shark: SQL and Rich Analytics at Scale. In *Proceedings of the 2013 ACM SIGMOD International Conference on Management of Data* (pp. 13–24). New York, NY, USA: ACM. doi:10.1145/2463676.2465288

Yahoo. (2013). Storm-YARN. Retrieved March 14, 2015, from https://github.com/yahoo/storm-yarn

Zaharia, M., Chowdhury, M., Das, T., Dave, A., Ma, J., & McCauley, M., … Stoica, I. (2012). Resilient distributed datasets: A fault-tolerant abstraction for in-memory cluster computing. In Proceedings of the 9th USENIX conference on Networked Systems Design and Implementation (pp. 2–2). USENIX Association.

Zaharia, M., Chowdhury, M., Franklin, M. J., Shenker, S., & Stoica, I. (2010). Spark: cluster computing with working sets. In *Proceedings of the 2nd USENIX conference on Hot topics in cloud computing* (pp. 10–10).

Zaharia, M., Das, T., Li, H., Hunter, T., Shenker, S., & Stoica, I. (2013). Discretized Streams: Fault-tolerant Streaming Computation at Scale. In *Proceedings of the Twenty-Fourth ACM Symposium on Operating Systems Principles* (pp. 423–438). New York, NY: ACM. doi:10.1145/2517349.2522737

Zicari, R. (2013). Big Data: Challenges and Opportunities. In R. Akerkar (Ed.), *Big Data Computing* (p. 564). Chapman and Hall/CRC; doi:10.1201/b16014-5

Related References

To continue our tradition of advancing information science and technology research, we have compiled a list of recommended IGI Global readings. These references will provide additional information and guidance to further enrich your knowledge and assist you with your own research and future publications.

Abramowicz, W., Stolarski, P., & Tomaszewski, T. (2013). Legal ontologies in ICT and law. In *Digital rights management: Concepts, methodologies, tools, and applications* (pp. 34–49). Hershey, PA: Information Science Reference; doi:10.4018/978-1-4666-2136-7.ch003

Adamich, T. (2012). Materials-to-standards alignment: How to "chunk" a whole cake and even use the "crumbs": State standards alignment models, learning objects, and formative assessment – methodologies and metadata for education. In L. Tomei (Ed.), *Advancing education with information communication technologies: Facilitating new trends* (pp. 165–178). Hershey, PA: Information Science Reference; doi:10.4018/978-1-61350-468-0.ch014

Adomi, E. E. (2011). Regulation of internet content. In E. Adomi (Ed.), *Frameworks for ICT policy: Government, social and legal issues* (pp. 233–246). Hershey, PA: Information Science Reference; doi:10.4018/978-1-61692-012-8.ch015

Aggestam, L. (2011). Guidelines for preparing organizations in developing countries for standards-based B2B. In *Global business: Concepts, methodologies, tools and applications* (pp. 206–228). Hershey, PA: Business Science Reference; doi:10.4018/978-1-60960-587-2.ch114

Akowuah, F., Yuan, X., Xu, J., & Wang, H. (2012). A survey of U.S. laws for health information security & privacy. [IJISP]. *International Journal of Information Security and Privacy*, 6(4), 40–54. doi:10.4018/jisp.2012100102

Akowuah, F., Yuan, X., Xu, J., & Wang, H. (2013). A survey of security standards applicable to health information systems. [IJISP]. *International Journal of Information Security and Privacy*, 7(4), 22–36. doi:10.4018/ijisp.2013100103

Al Hadid, I. (2012). Applying the certification's standards to the simulation study steps. In E. Abu-Taieh, A. El Sheikh, & M. Jafari (Eds.), *Technology engineering and management in aviation: Advancements and discoveries* (pp. 294–307). Hershey, PA: Information Science Reference; doi:10.4018/978-1-60960-887-3.ch017

Al Mohannadi, F., Arif, M., Aziz, Z., & Richardson, P. A. (2013). Adopting BIM standards for managing vision 2030 infrastructure development in Qatar. *International Journal of 3-D Information Modeling (IJ3DIM), 2*(3), 64-73. doi:10.4018/ij3dim.2013070105

Al-Nu'aimi, A. A. (2011). Using watermarking techniques to prove rightful ownership of web images. [IJITWE]. *International Journal of Information Technology and Web Engineering, 6*(2), 29–39. doi:10.4018/jitwe.2011040103

Alejandre, G. M. (2013). IT security governance legal issues. In D. Mellado, L. Enrique Sánchez, E. Fernández-Medina, & M. Piattini (Eds.), *IT security governance innovations: Theory and research* (pp. 47–73). Hershey, PA: Information Science Reference; doi:10.4018/978-1-4666-2083-4.ch003

Alexandropoulou-Egyptiadou, E. (2013). The Hellenic framework for computer program copyright protection following the implementation of the relative European Union directives. In *Digital rights management: Concepts, methodologies, tools, and applications* (pp. 738–745). Hershey, PA: Information Science Reference; doi:10.4018/978-1-4666-2136-7.ch033

Ali, S. (2012). Practical web application security audit following industry standards and compliance. In J. Zubairi & A. Mahboob (Eds.), *Cyber security standards, practices and industrial applications: Systems and methodologies* (pp. 259–279). Hershey, PA: Information Science Reference; doi:10.4018/978-1-60960-851-4.ch013

Alirezaee, M., & Afsharian, M. (2011). Measuring the effect of the rules and regulations on global malmquist index. [IJORIS]. *International Journal of Operations Research and Information Systems, 2*(3), 64–78. doi:10.4018/joris.2011070105

Alirezaee, M., & Afsharian, M. (2013). Measuring the effect of the rules and regulations on global malmquist index. In J. Wang (Ed.), *Optimizing, innovating, and capitalizing on information systems for operations* (pp. 215–229). Hershey, PA: Business Science Reference; doi:10.4018/978-1-4666-2925-7.ch011

Alves de Lima, A., Carvalho dos Reis, P., Branco, J. C., Danieli, R., Osawa, C. C., Winter, E., & Santos, D. A. (2013). Scenario-patent protection compared to climate change: The case of green patents. [IJSESD]. *International Journal of Social Ecology and Sustainable Development, 4*(3), 61–70. doi:10.4018/jsesd.2013070105

Amirante, A., Castaldi, T., Miniero, L., & Romano, S. P. (2013). Protocol interactions among user agents, application servers, and media servers: Standardization efforts and open issues. In D. Kanellopoulos (Ed.), *Intelligent multimedia technologies for networking applications: Techniques and tools* (pp. 48–63). Hershey, PA: Information Science Reference; doi:10.4018/978-1-4666-2833-5.ch003

Anker, P. (2013). The impact of regulations on the business case for cognitive radio. In T. Lagkas, P. Sarigiannidis, M. Louta, & P. Chatzimisios (Eds.), *Evolution of cognitive networks and self-adaptive communication systems* (pp. 142–170). Hershey, PA: Information Science Reference; doi:10.4018/978-1-4666-4189-1.ch006

Antunes, A. M., Mendes, F. M., Schumacher, S. D., Quoniam, L., & Lima de Magalhães, J. (2014). The contribution of information science through intellectual property to innovation in the Brazilian health sector. In G. Jamil, A. Malheiro, & F. Ribeiro (Eds.), *Rethinking the conceptual base for new practical applications in information value and quality* (pp. 83–115). Hershey, PA: Information Science Reference; doi:10.4018/978-1-4666-4562-2.ch005

Atiskov, A. Y., Novikov, F. A., Fedorchenko, L. N., Vorobiev, V. I., & Moldovyan, N. A. (2013). Ontology-based analysis of cryptography standards and possibilities of their harmonization. In A. Elçi, J. Pieprzyk, A. Chefranov, M. Orgun, H. Wang, & R. Shankaran (Eds.), *Theory and practice of cryptography solutions for secure information systems* (pp. 1–33). Hershey, PA: Information Science Reference; doi:10.4018/978-1-4666-4030-6.ch001

Ayanso, A., & Herath, T. (2012). Law and technology at crossroads in cyberspace: Where do we go from here? In A. Dudley, J. Braman, & G. Vincenti (Eds.), *Investigating cyber law and cyber ethics: Issues, impacts and practices* (pp. 57–77). Hershey, PA: Information Science Reference; doi:10.4018/978-1-61350-132-0.ch004

Ayanso, A., & Herath, T. (2014). Law and technology at crossroads in cyberspace: Where do we go from here? In *Cyber behavior: Concepts, methodologies, tools, and applications* (pp. 1990–2010). Hershey, PA: Information Science Reference; doi:10.4018/978-1-4666-5942-1.ch105

Aydogan-Duda, N. (2012). Branding innovation: The case study of Turkey. In N. Ekekwe & N. Islam (Eds.), *Disruptive technologies, innovation and global redesign: Emerging implications* (pp. 238–248). Hershey, PA: Information Science Reference; doi:10.4018/978-1-4666-0134-5.ch012

Bagby, J. W. (2011). Environmental standardization for sustainability. In Z. Luo (Ed.), *Green finance and sustainability: Environmentally-aware business models and technologies* (pp. 31–55). Hershey, PA: Business Science Reference; doi:10.4018/978-1-60960-531-5.ch002

Bagby, J. W. (2013). Insights from U.S. experience to guide international reliance on standardization: Achieving supply chain sustainability. [IJAL]. *International Journal of Applied Logistics*, *4*(3), 25–46. doi:10.4018/jal.2013070103

Baggio, B., & Beldarrain, Y. (2011). Intellectual property in an age of open source and anonymity. In *Anonymity and learning in digitally mediated communications: Authenticity and trust in cyber education* (pp. 39–57). Hershey, PA: Information Science Reference; doi:10.4018/978-1-60960-543-8.ch003

Balzli, C. E., & Fragnière, E. (2012). How ERP systems are centralizing and standardizing the accounting function in public organizations for better and worse. In S. Chhabra & M. Kumar (Eds.), *Strategic enterprise resource planning models for e-government: Applications and methodologies* (pp. 55–72). Hershey, PA: Information Science Reference; doi:10.4018/978-1-60960-863-7.ch004

Banas, J. R. (2011). Standardized, flexible design of electronic learning environments to enhance learning efficiency and effectiveness. In A. Kitchenham (Ed.), *Models for interdisciplinary mobile learning: Delivering information to students* (pp. 66–86). Hershey, PA: Information Science Reference; doi:10.4018/978-1-60960-511-7.ch004

Bao, C., & Castresana, J. M. (2011). Interoperability approach in e-learning standardization processes. In F. Lazarinis, S. Green, & E. Pearson (Eds.), *Handbook of research on e-learning standards and interoperability: Frameworks and issues* (pp. 399–418). Hershey, PA: Information Science Reference; doi:10.4018/978-1-61692-789-9.ch020

Bao, C., & Castresana, J. M. (2012). Interoperability approach in e-learning standardization processes. In *Virtual learning environments: Concepts, methodologies, tools and applications* (pp. 542–560). Hershey, PA: Information Science Reference; doi:10.4018/978-1-4666-0011-9.ch307

Barrett, B. (2011). Evaluating and implementing teaching standards: Providing quality online teaching strategies and techniques standards. In F. Lazarinis, S. Green, & E. Pearson (Eds.), *Developing and utilizing e-learning applications* (pp. 66–83). Hershey, PA: Information Science Reference; doi:10.4018/978-1-61692-791-2.ch004

Berleur, J. (2011). Ethical and social issues of the internet governance regulations. In D. Haftor & A. Mirijamdotter (Eds.), *Information and communication technologies, society and human beings: Theory and framework (festschrift in honor of Gunilla Bradley)* (pp. 466–476). Hershey, PA: Information Science Reference; doi:10.4018/978-1-60960-057-0.ch038

Bhattathiripad, V. P. (2014). Software copyright infringement and litigation. In *Judiciary-friendly forensics of software copyright infringement* (pp. 35–55). Hershey, PA: Information Science Reference; doi:10.4018/978-1-4666-5804-2.ch002

Bin, X., & Chuan, T. K. (2011). The effect of business characteristics on the methods of knowledge protections. [IJSESD]. *International Journal of Social Ecology and Sustainable Development, 2*(3), 34–60. doi:10.4018/jsesd.2011070103

Bin, X., & Chuan, T. K. (2013). The effect of business characteristics on the methods of knowledge protections. In E. Carayannis (Ed.), *Creating a sustainable ecology using technology-driven solutions* (pp. 172–200). Hershey, PA: Information Science Reference; doi:10.4018/978-1-4666-3613-2.ch013

Bin, X., & Chuan, T. K. (2013). The effect of business characteristics on the methods of knowledge protections. In *Digital rights management: Concepts, methodologies, tools, and applications* (pp. 1283–1311). Hershey, PA: Information Science Reference; doi:10.4018/978-1-4666-2136-7.ch063

Bogers, M., Bekkers, R., & Granstrand, O. (2012). Intellectual property and licensing strategies in open collaborative innovation. In C. de Pablos Heredero & D. López (Eds.), *Open innovation in firms and public administrations: Technologies for value creation* (pp. 37–58). Hershey, PA: Information Science Reference; doi:10.4018/978-1-61350-341-6.ch003

Bogers, M., Bekkers, R., & Granstrand, O. (2013). Intellectual property and licensing strategies in open collaborative innovation. In *Digital rights management: Concepts, methodologies, tools, and applications* (pp. 1204–1224). Hershey, PA: Information Science Reference; doi:10.4018/978-1-4666-2136-7.ch059

Bourcier, D. (2013). Law and governance: The genesis of the commons. In F. Doridot, P. Duquenoy, P. Goujon, A. Kurt, S. Lavelle, N. Patrignani, & A. Santuccio et al. (Eds.), *Ethical governance of emerging technologies development* (pp. 166–183). Hershey, PA: Information Science Reference; doi:10.4018/978-1-4666-3670-5.ch011

Bousquet, F., Fomin, V. V., & Drillon, D. (2011). Anticipatory standards development and competitive intelligence. [IJBIR]. *International Journal of Business Intelligence Research, 2*(1), 16–30. doi:10.4018/jbir.2011010102

Bousquet, F., Fomin, V. V., & Drillon, D. (2013). Anticipatory standards development and competitive intelligence. In R. Herschel (Ed.), *Principles and applications of business intelligence research* (pp. 17–30). Hershey, PA: Business Science Reference; doi:10.4018/978-1-4666-2650-8.ch002

Brabazon, A. (2013). Optimal patent design: An agent-based modeling approach. In B. Alexandrova-Kabadjova, S. Martinez-Jaramillo, A. Garcia-Almanza, & E. Tsang (Eds.), *Simulation in computational finance and economics: Tools and emerging applications* (pp. 280–302). Hershey, PA: Business Science Reference; doi:10.4018/978-1-4666-2011-7.ch014

Bracci, F., Corradi, A., & Foschini, L. (2014). Cloud standards: Security and interoperability issues. In H. Mouftah & B. Kantarci (Eds.), *Communication infrastructures for cloud computing* (pp. 465–495). Hershey, PA: Information Science Reference; doi:10.4018/978-1-4666-4522-6.ch020

Briscoe, D. R. (2012). Globalization and international labor standards, codes of conduct, and ethics: An International HRM perspective. In C. Wankel & S. Malleck (Eds.), *Ethical models and applications of globalization: Cultural, socio-political and economic perspectives* (pp. 1–22). Hershey, PA: Business Science Reference; doi:10.4018/978-1-61350-332-4.ch001

Briscoe, D. R. (2014). Globalization and international labor standards, codes of conduct, and ethics: An International HRM perspective. In *Cross-cultural interaction: Concepts, methodologies, tools and applications* (pp. 40–62). Hershey, PA: Information Science Reference; doi:10.4018/978-1-4666-4979-8.ch004

Brooks, R. G., & Geradin, D. (2011). Interpreting and enforcing the voluntary FRAND commitment. [IJITSR]. *International Journal of IT Standards and Standardization Research, 9*(1), 1–23. doi:10.4018/jitsr.2011010101

Brown, C. A. (2013). Common core state standards: The promise for college and career ready students in the U.S. In V. Wang (Ed.), *Handbook of research on teaching and learning in K-20 education* (pp. 50–82). Hershey, PA: Information Science Reference; doi:10.4018/978-1-4666-4249-2.ch004

Buyurgan, N., Rardin, R. L., Jayaraman, R., Varghese, V. M., & Burbano, A. (2011). A novel GS1 data standard adoption roadmap for healthcare providers. [IJHISI]. *International Journal of Healthcare Information Systems and Informatics, 6*(4), 42–59. doi:10.4018/jhisi.2011100103

Buyurgan, N., Rardin, R. L., Jayaraman, R., Varghese, V. M., & Burbano, A. (2013). A novel GS1 data standard adoption roadmap for healthcare providers. In J. Tan (Ed.), *Healthcare information technology innovation and sustainability: Frontiers and adoption* (pp. 41–57). Hershey, PA: Medical Information Science Reference; doi:10.4018/978-1-4666-2797-0.ch003

Campolo, C., Cozzetti, H. A., Molinaro, A., & Scopigno, R. M. (2012). PHY/MAC layer design in vehicular ad hoc networks: Challenges, standard approaches, and alternative solutions. In R. Aquino-Santos, A. Edwards, & V. Rangel-Licea (Eds.), *Wireless technologies in vehicular ad hoc networks: Present and future challenges* (pp. 70–100). Hershey, PA: Information Science Reference; doi:10.4018/978-1-4666-0209-0.ch004

Cantatore, F. (2014). Copyright support structures. In *Authors, copyright, and publishing in the digital era* (pp. 81–93). Hershey, PA: Information Science Reference; doi:10.4018/978-1-4666-5214-9.ch005

Cantatore, F. (2014). History and development of copyright. In *Authors, copyright, and publishing in the digital era* (pp. 10–32). Hershey, PA: Information Science Reference; doi:10.4018/978-1-4666-5214-9.ch002

Cantatore, F. (2014). Research findings: Authors' perceptions and the copyright framework. In Authors, copyright, and publishing in the digital era (pp. 147-189). Hershey, PA: Information Science Reference. doi:10.4018/978-1-4666-5214-9.ch008

Cassini, J., Medlin, B. D., & Romaniello, A. (2011). Forty years of federal legislation in the area of data protection and information security. In H. Nemati (Ed.), *Pervasive information security and privacy developments: Trends and advancements* (pp. 14–23). Hershey, PA: Information Science Reference; doi:10.4018/978-1-61692-000-5.ch002

Charlesworth, A. (2012). Addressing legal issues in online research, publication and archiving: A UK perspective. In C. Silva (Ed.), *Online research methods in urban and planning studies: Design and outcomes* (pp. 368–393). Hershey, PA: Information Science Reference; doi:10.4018/978-1-4666-0074-4.ch022

Chaudhary, C., & Kang, I. S. (2011). Pirates of the copyright and cyberspace: Issues involved. In R. Santanam, M. Sethumadhavan, & M. Virendra (Eds.), *Cyber security, cyber crime and cyber forensics: Applications and perspectives* (pp. 59–68). Hershey, PA: Information Science Reference; doi:10.4018/978-1-60960-123-2.ch005

Chen, L., Hu, W., Yang, M., & Zhang, L. (2011). Security and privacy issues in secure e-mail standards and services. In H. Nemati (Ed.), *Security and privacy assurance in advancing technologies: New developments* (pp. 174–185). Hershey, PA: Information Science Reference; doi:10.4018/978-1-60960-200-0.ch013

Ciaghi, A., & Villafiorita, A. (2012). Law modeling and BPR for public administration improvement. In K. Bwalya & S. Zulu (Eds.), *Handbook of research on e-government in emerging economies: Adoption, E-participation, and legal frameworks* (pp. 391–410). Hershey, PA: Information Science Reference; doi:10.4018/978-1-4666-0324-0.ch019

Ciptasari, R. W., & Sakurai, K. (2013). Multimedia copyright protection scheme based on the direct feature-based method. In K. Kondo (Ed.), *Multimedia information hiding technologies and methodologies for controlling data* (pp. 412–439). Hershey, PA: Information Science Reference; doi:10.4018/978-1-4666-2217-3.ch019

Clark, L. A., Jones, D. L., & Clark, W. J. (2012). Technology innovation and the policy vacuum: A call for ethics, norms, and laws to fill the void. [IJT]. *International Journal of Technoethics, 3*(1), 1–13. doi:10.4018/jte.2012010101

Cooklev, T. (2013). The role of standards in engineering education. In K. Jakobs (Ed.), *Innovations in organizational IT specification and standards development* (pp. 129–137). Hershey, PA: Information Science Reference; doi:10.4018/978-1-4666-2160-2.ch007

Cooper, A. R. (2013). Key challenges in the design of learning technology standards: Observations and proposals. In K. Jakobs (Ed.), *Innovations in organizational IT specification and standards development* (pp. 241–249). Hershey, PA: Information Science Reference; doi:10.4018/978-1-4666-2160-2.ch014

Cordella, A. (2011). Emerging standardization. [IJANTTI]. *International Journal of Actor-Network Theory and Technological Innovation, 3*(3), 49–64. doi:10.4018/jantti.2011070104

Cordella, A. (2013). Emerging standardization. In A. Tatnall (Ed.), *Social and professional applications of actor-network theory for technology development* (pp. 221–237). Hershey, PA: Information Science Reference; doi:10.4018/978-1-4666-2166-4.ch017

Curran, K., & Lautman, R. (2011). The problems of jurisdiction on the internet. [IJACI]. *International Journal of Ambient Computing and Intelligence, 3*(3), 36–42. doi:10.4018/jaci.2011070105

Dani, D. E., Salloum, S., Khishfe, R., & BouJaoude, S. (2013). A tool for analyzing science standards and curricula for 21st century science education. In M. Khine, & I. Saleh (Eds.), *Approaches and strategies in next generation science learning* (pp. 265-289). Hershey, PA: Information Science Reference. doi:10.4018/978-1-4666-2809-0.ch014

De Silva, S. (2012). Legal issues with FOS-ERP: A UK law perspective. In R. Atem de Carvalho & B. Johansson (Eds.), *Free and open source enterprise resource planning: Systems and strategies* (pp. 102–115). Hershey, PA: Business Science Reference; doi:10.4018/978-1-61350-486-4.ch007

de Vries, H. J. (2011). Implementing standardization education at the national level. [IJITSR]. *International Journal of IT Standards and Standardization Research, 9*(2), 72–83. doi:10.4018/jitsr.2011070104

de Vries, H. J. (2013). Implementing standardization education at the national level. In K. Jakobs (Ed.), *Innovations in organizational IT specification and standards development* (pp. 116–128). Hershey, PA: Information Science Reference; doi:10.4018/978-1-4666-2160-2.ch006

de Vuyst, B., & Fairchild, A. (2012). Legal and economic justification for software protection. [IJOSSP]. *International Journal of Open Source Software and Processes, 4*(3), 1–12. doi:10.4018/ijossp.2012070101

Dedeke, A. (2012). Politics hinders open standards in the public sector: The Massachusetts open document format decision. In C. Reddick (Ed.), *Cases on public information management and e-government adoption* (pp. 1–23). Hershey, PA: Information Science Reference; doi:10.4018/978-1-4666-0981-5.ch001

Delfmann, P., Herwig, S., Lis, L., & Becker, J. (2012). Supporting conceptual model analysis using semantic standardization and structural pattern matching. In S. Smolnik, F. Teuteberg, & O. Thomas (Eds.), *Semantic technologies for business and information systems engineering: Concepts and applications* (pp. 125–149). Hershey, PA: Business Science Reference; doi:10.4018/978-1-60960-126-3.ch007

den Uijl, S., de Vries, H. J., & Bayramoglu, D. (2013). The rise of MP3 as the market standard: How compressed audio files became the dominant music format. [IJITSR]. *International Journal of IT Standards and Standardization Research, 11*(1), 1–26. doi:10.4018/jitsr.2013010101

Dickerson, J., & Coleman, H. V. (2012). Technology, e-leadership and educational administration in schools: Integrating standards with context and guiding questions. In V. Wang (Ed.), *Encyclopedia of e-leadership, counseling and training* (pp. 408–422). Hershey, PA: Information Science Reference; doi:10.4018/978-1-61350-068-2.ch030

Dindaroglu, B. (2013). R&D productivity and firm size in semiconductors and pharmaceuticals: Evidence from citation yields. In I. Yetkiner, M. Pamukcu, & E. Erdil (Eds.), *Industrial dynamics, innovation policy, and economic growth through technological advancements* (pp. 92–113). Hershey, PA: Information Science Reference; doi:10.4018/978-1-4666-1978-4.ch006

Ding, W. (2011). Development of intellectual property of communications enterprise and analysis of current situation of patents in emerging technology field. [IJAPUC]. *International Journal of Advanced Pervasive and Ubiquitous Computing*, *3*(2), 21–28. doi:10.4018/japuc.2011040103

Ding, W. (2013). Development of intellectual property of communications enterprise and analysis of current situation of patents in emerging technology field. In T. Gao (Ed.), *Global applications of pervasive and ubiquitous computing* (pp. 89–96). Hershey, PA: Information Science Reference; doi:10.4018/978-1-4666-2645-4.ch010

Dorloff, F., & Kajan, E. (2012). Balancing of heterogeneity and interoperability in e-business networks: The role of standards and protocols. [IJEBR]. *International Journal of E-Business Research*, *8*(4), 15–33. doi:10.4018/jebr.2012100102

Dorloff, F., & Kajan, E. (2012). Efficient and interoperable e-business –Based on frameworks, standards and protocols: An introduction. In E. Kajan, F. Dorloff, & I. Bedini (Eds.), *Handbook of research on e-business standards and protocols: Documents, data and advanced web technologies* (pp. 1–20). Hershey, PA: Business Science Reference; doi:10.4018/978-1-4666-0146-8.ch001

Driouchi, A., & Kadiri, M. (2013). Challenges to intellectual property rights from information and communication technologies, nanotechnologies and microelectronics. In *Digital rights management: Concepts, methodologies, tools, and applications* (pp. 1474–1492). Hershey, PA: Information Science Reference; doi:10.4018/978-1-4666-2136-7.ch075

Dubey, M., & Hirwade, M. (2013). Copyright relevancy at stake in libraries of the digital era. In T. Ashraf & P. Gulati (Eds.), *Design, development, and management of resources for digital library services* (pp. 379–384). Hershey, PA: Information Science Reference; doi:10.4018/978-1-4666-2500-6.ch030

Egyedi, T. M. (2011). Between supply and demand: Coping with the impact of standards change. In *Global business: Concepts, methodologies, tools and applications* (pp. 105–120). Hershey, PA: Business Science Reference; doi:10.4018/978-1-60960-587-2.ch108

Egyedi, T. M., & Koppenhol, A. (2013). The standards war between ODF and OOXML: Does competition between overlapping ISO standards lead to innovation? In K. Jakobs (Ed.), *Innovations in organizational IT specification and standards development* (pp. 79–90). Hershey, PA: Information Science Reference; doi:10.4018/978-1-4666-2160-2.ch004

Egyedi, T. M., & Muto, S. (2012). Standards for ICT: A green strategy in a grey sector. [IJITSR]. *International Journal of IT Standards and Standardization Research*, *10*(1), 34–47. doi:10.4018/jitsr.2012010103

El Kharbili, M., & Pulvermueller, E. (2012). Semantic policies for modeling regulatory process compliance. In S. Smolnik, F. Teuteberg, & O. Thomas (Eds.), *Semantic technologies for business and information systems engineering: Concepts and applications* (pp. 311–336). Hershey, PA: Business Science Reference; doi:10.4018/978-1-60960-126-3.ch016

El Kharbili, M., & Pulvermueller, E. (2013). Semantic policies for modeling regulatory process compliance. In *IT policy and ethics: Concepts, methodologies, tools, and applications* (pp. 218–243). Hershey, PA: Information Science Reference; doi:10.4018/978-1-4666-2919-6.ch011

Ervin, K. (2014). Legal and ethical considerations in the implementation of electronic health records. In J. Krueger (Ed.), *Cases on electronic records and resource management implementation in diverse environments* (pp. 193–210). Hershey, PA: Information Science Reference; doi:10.4018/978-1-4666-4466-3.ch012

Escayola, J., Trigo, J., Martínez, I., Martínez-Espronceda, M., Aragüés, A., Sancho, D., & García, J. et al. (2012). Overview of the ISO/ieee11073 family of standards and their applications to health monitoring. In W. Chen, S. Oetomo, & L. Feijs (Eds.), *Neonatal monitoring technologies: Design for integrated solutions* (pp. 148–173). Hershey, PA: Medical Information Science Reference; doi:10.4018/978-1-4666-0975-4.ch007

Escayola, J., Trigo, J., Martínez, I., Martínez-Espronceda, M., Aragüés, A., Sancho, D., . . . García, J. (2013). Overview of the ISO/IEEE11073 family of standards and their applications to health monitoring. In User-driven healthcare: Concepts, methodologies, tools, and applications (pp. 357-381). Hershey, PA: Medical Information Science Reference. doi:10.4018/978-1-4666-2770-3.ch018

Espada, J. P., Martínez, O. S., García-Bustelo, B. C., Lovelle, J. M., & Ordóñez de Pablos, P. (2011). Standardization of virtual objects. In M. Lytras, P. Ordóñez de Pablos, & E. Damiani (Eds.), *Semantic web personalization and context awareness: Management of personal identities and social networking* (pp. 7–21). Hershey, PA: Information Science Reference; doi:10.4018/978-1-61520-921-7.ch002

Falkner, N. J. (2011). Security technologies and policies in organisations. In M. Quigley (Ed.), *ICT ethics and security in the 21st century: New developments and applications* (pp. 196–213). Hershey, PA: Information Science Reference; doi:10.4018/978-1-60960-573-5.ch010

Ferrer-Roca, O. (2011). Standards in telemedicine. In A. Moumtzoglou & A. Kastania (Eds.), *E-health systems quality and reliability: Models and standards* (pp. 220–243). Hershey, PA: Medical Information Science Reference; doi:10.4018/978-1-61692-843-8.ch017

Ferullo, D. L., & Soules, A. (2012). Managing copyright in a digital world. [IJDLS]. *International Journal of Digital Library Systems*, *3*(4), 1–25. doi:10.4018/ijdls.2012100101

Fichtner, J. R., & Simpson, L. A. (2011). Legal issues facing companies with products in a digital format. In T. Strader (Ed.), *Digital product management, technology and practice: Interdisciplinary perspectives* (pp. 32–52). Hershey, PA: Business Science Reference; doi:10.4018/978-1-61692-877-3.ch003

Fichtner, J. R., & Simpson, L. A. (2013). Legal issues facing companies with products in a digital format. In *Digital rights management: Concepts, methodologies, tools, and applications* (pp. 1334–1354). Hershey, PA: Information Science Reference; doi:10.4018/978-1-4666-2136-7.ch066

Folmer, E. (2012). BOMOS: Management and development model for open standards. In E. Kajan, F. Dorloff, & I. Bedini (Eds.), *Handbook of research on e-business standards and protocols: Documents, data and advanced web technologies* (pp. 102–128). Hershey, PA: Business Science Reference; doi:10.4018/978-1-4666-0146-8.ch006

Fomin, V. V. (2012). Standards as hybrids: An essay on tensions and juxtapositions in contemporary standardization. [IJITSR]. *International Journal of IT Standards and Standardization Research*, *10*(2), 59–68. doi:10.4018/jitsr.2012070105

Fomin, V. V., & Matinmikko, M. (2014). The role of standards in the development of new informational infrastructure. In M. Khosrow-Pour (Ed.), *Systems and software development, modeling, and analysis: New perspectives and methodologies* (pp. 149–160). Hershey, PA: Information Science Reference; doi:10.4018/978-1-4666-6098-4.ch006

Fomin, V. V., Medeisis, A., & Vitkute-Adžgauskiene, D. (2012). Pre-standardization of cognitive radio systems. [IJITSR]. *International Journal of IT Standards and Standardization Research*, *10*(1), 1–16. doi:10.4018/jitsr.2012010101

Francia, G., & Hutchinson, F. S. (2012). Regulatory and policy compliance with regard to identity theft prevention, detection, and response. In T. Chou (Ed.), *Information assurance and security technologies for risk assessment and threat management: Advances* (pp. 292–322). Hershey, PA: Information Science Reference; doi:10.4018/978-1-61350-507-6.ch012

Francia, G. A., & Hutchinson, F. S. (2014). Regulatory and policy compliance with regard to identity theft prevention, detection, and response. In *Crisis management: Concepts, methodologies, tools and applications* (pp. 280–310). Hershey, PA: Information Science Reference; doi:10.4018/978-1-4666-4707-7.ch012

Fulkerson, D. M. (2012). Copyright. In D. Fulkerson (Ed.), *Remote access technologies for library collections: Tools for library users and managers* (pp. 33–48). Hershey, PA: Information Science Reference; doi:10.4018/978-1-4666-0234-2.ch003

Galinski, C., & Beckmann, H. (2014). Concepts for enhancing content quality and eaccessibility: In general and in the field of eprocurement. In *Assistive technologies: Concepts, methodologies, tools, and applications* (pp. 180–197). Hershey, PA: Information Science Reference; doi:10.4018/978-1-4666-4422-9.ch010

Gaur, R. (2013). Facilitating access to Indian cultural heritage: Copyright, permission rights and ownership issues vis-à-vis IGNCA collections. In *Digital rights management: Concepts, methodologies, tools, and applications* (pp. 817–833). Hershey, PA: Information Science Reference; doi:10.4018/978-1-4666-2136-7.ch038

Geiger, C. (2011). Copyright and digital libraries: Securing access to information in the digital age. In I. Iglezakis, T. Synodinou, & S. Kapidakis (Eds.), *E-publishing and digital libraries: Legal and organizational issues* (pp. 257–272). Hershey, PA: Information Science Reference; doi:10.4018/978-1-60960-031-0.ch013

Geiger, C. (2013). Copyright and digital libraries: Securing access to information in the digital age. In *Digital rights management: Concepts, methodologies, tools, and applications* (pp. 99–114). Hershey, PA: Information Science Reference; doi:10.4018/978-1-4666-2136-7.ch007

Gencer, M. (2012). The evolution of IETF standards and their production. [IJITSR]. *International Journal of IT Standards and Standardization Research*, *10*(1), 17–33. doi:10.4018/jitsr.2012010102

Gillam, L., & Vartapetiance, A. (2014). Gambling with laws and ethics in cyberspace. In R. Luppicini (Ed.), *Evolving issues surrounding technoethics and society in the digital age* (pp. 149–170). Hershey, PA: Information Science Reference; doi:10.4018/978-1-4666-6122-6.ch010

Grandinetti, L., Pisacane, O., & Sheikhalishahi, M. (2014). Standardization. In *Pervasive cloud computing technologies: Future outlooks and interdisciplinary perspectives* (pp. 75–96). Hershey, PA: Information Science Reference; doi:10.4018/978-1-4666-4683-4.ch004

Grant, S., & Young, R. (2013). Concepts and standardization in areas relating to competence. In K. Jakobs (Ed.), *Innovations in organizational IT specification and standards development* (pp. 264–280). Hershey, PA: Information Science Reference; doi:10.4018/978-1-4666-2160-2.ch016

Grassetti, M., & Brookby, S. (2013). Using the iPad to develop preservice teachers' understanding of the common core state standards for mathematical practice. In D. Polly (Ed.), *Common core mathematics standards and implementing digital technologies* (pp. 370–386). Hershey, PA: Information Science Reference; doi:10.4018/978-1-4666-4086-3.ch025

Gray, P. J. (2012). CDIO Standards and quality assurance: From application to accreditation. [IJQA-ETE]. *International Journal of Quality Assurance in Engineering and Technology Education, 2*(2), 1–8. doi:10.4018/ijqaete.2012040101

Graz, J., & Hauert, C. (2011). The INTERNORM project: Bridging two worlds of expert- and lay-knowledge in standardization. [IJITSR]. *International Journal of IT Standards and Standardization Research, 9*(1), 52–62. doi:10.4018/jitsr.2011010103

Graz, J., & Hauert, C. (2013). The INTERNORM project: Bridging two worlds of expert- and lay-knowledge in standardization. In K. Jakobs (Ed.), *Innovations in organizational IT specification and standards development* (pp. 154–164). Hershey, PA: Information Science Reference; doi:10.4018/978-1-4666-2160-2.ch009

Grobler, M. (2012). The need for digital evidence standardisation. [IJDCF]. *International Journal of Digital Crime and Forensics, 4*(2), 1–12. doi:10.4018/jdcf.2012040101

Grobler, M. (2013). The need for digital evidence standardisation. In C. Li (Ed.), *Emerging digital forensics applications for crime detection, prevention, and security* (pp. 234–245). Hershey, PA: Information Science Reference; doi:10.4018/978-1-4666-4006-1.ch016

Guest, C. L., & Guest, J. M. (2011). Legal issues in the use of technology in higher education: Copyright and privacy in the academy. In D. Surry, R. Gray Jr, & J. Stefurak (Eds.), *Technology integration in higher education: Social and organizational aspects* (pp. 72–85). Hershey, PA: Information Science Reference; doi:10.4018/978-1-60960-147-8.ch006

Gupta, A., Gantz, D. A., Sreecharana, D., & Kreyling, J. (2012). The interplay of offshoring of professional services, law, intellectual property, and international organizations. [IJSITA]. *International Journal of Strategic Information Technology and Applications, 3*(2), 47–71. doi:10.4018/jsita.2012040104

Hai-Jew, S. (2011). Staying legal and ethical in global e-learning course and training developments: An exploration. In V. Wang (Ed.), *Encyclopedia of information communication technologies and adult education integration* (pp. 958–970). Hershey, PA: Information Science Reference; doi:10.4018/978-1-61692-906-0.ch058

Halder, D., & Jaishankar, K. (2012). Cyber space regulations for protecting women in UK. In *Cyber crime and the victimization of women: Laws, rights and regulations* (pp. 95–104). Hershey, PA: Information Science Reference; doi:10.4018/978-1-60960-830-9.ch007

Han, M., & Cho, C. (2013). XML in library cataloging workflows: Working with diverse sources and metadata standards. In J. Tramullas & P. Garrido (Eds.), *Library automation and OPAC 2.0: Information access and services in the 2.0 landscape* (pp. 59–72). Hershey, PA: Information Science Reference; doi:10.4018/978-1-4666-1912-8.ch003

Hanseth, O., & Nielsen, P. (2013). Infrastructural innovation: Flexibility, generativity and the mobile internet. [IJITSR]. *International Journal of IT Standards and Standardization Research, 11*(1), 27–45. doi:10.4018/jitsr.2013010102

Hartong, M., & Wijesekera, D. (2012). U.S. regulatory requirements for positive train control systems. In F. Flammini (Ed.), *Railway safety, reliability, and security: Technologies and systems engineering* (pp. 1–21). Hershey, PA: Information Science Reference; doi:10.4018/978-1-4666-1643-1.ch001

Hasan, H. (2011). Formal and emergent standards in KM. In D. Schwartz & D. Te'eni (Eds.), *Encyclopedia of knowledge management* (2nd ed., pp. 331–342). Hershey, PA: Information Science Reference; doi:10.4018/978-1-59904-931-1.ch032

Hatzimihail, N. (2011). Copyright infringement of digital libraries and private international law: Jurisdiction issues. In I. Iglezakis, T. Synodinou, & S. Kapidakis (Eds.), *E-publishing and digital libraries: Legal and organizational issues* (pp. 447–460). Hershey, PA: Information Science Reference; doi:10.4018/978-1-60960-031-0.ch021

Hauert, C. (2013). Where are you? Consumers' associations in standardization: A case study on Switzerland. In K. Jakobs (Ed.), *Innovations in organizational IT specification and standards development* (pp. 139–153). Hershey, PA: Information Science Reference; doi:10.4018/978-1-4666-2160-2.ch008

Hawks, V. D., & Ekstrom, J. J. (2011). Balancing policies, principles, and philosophy in information assurance. In M. Dark (Ed.), *Information assurance and security ethics in complex systems: Interdisciplinary perspectives* (pp. 32–54). Hershey, PA: Information Science Reference; doi:10.4018/978-1-61692-245-0.ch003

Henningsson, S. (2012). International e-customs standardization from the perspective of a global company. [IJITSR]. *International Journal of IT Standards and Standardization Research, 10*(2), 45–58. doi:10.4018/jitsr.2012070104

Hensberry, K. K., Paul, A. J., Moore, E. B., Podolefsky, N. S., & Perkins, K. K. (2013). PhET interactive simulations: New tools to achieve common core mathematics standards. In D. Polly (Ed.), *Common core mathematics standards and implementing digital technologies* (pp. 147–167). Hershey, PA: Information Science Reference; doi:10.4018/978-1-4666-4086-3.ch010

Heravi, B. R., & Lycett, M. (2012). Semantically enriched e-business standards development: The case of ebXML business process specification schema. In E. Kajan, F. Dorloff, & I. Bedini (Eds.), *Handbook of research on e-business standards and protocols: Documents, data and advanced web technologies* (pp. 655–675). Hershey, PA: Business Science Reference; doi:10.4018/978-1-4666-0146-8.ch030

Higuera, J., & Polo, J. (2012). Interoperability in wireless sensor networks based on IEEE 1451 standard. In N. Zaman, K. Ragab, & A. Abdullah (Eds.), *Wireless sensor networks and energy efficiency: Protocols, routing and management* (pp. 47–69). Hershey, PA: Information Science Reference; doi:10.4018/978-1-4666-0101-7.ch004

Hill, D. S. (2012). An examination of standardized product identification and business benefit. In E. Kajan, F. Dorloff, & I. Bedini (Eds.), *Handbook of research on e-business standards and protocols: Documents, data and advanced web technologies* (pp. 387–411). Hershey, PA: Business Science Reference; doi:10.4018/978-1-4666-0146-8.ch018

Hill, D. S. (2013). An examination of standardized product identification and business benefit. In *Supply chain management: Concepts, methodologies, tools, and applications* (pp. 171–195). Hershey, PA: Business Science Reference; doi:10.4018/978-1-4666-2625-6.ch011

Holloway, K. (2012). Fair use, copyright, and academic integrity in an online academic environment. In V. Wang (Ed.), *Encyclopedia of e-leadership, counseling and training* (pp. 298–309). Hershey, PA: Information Science Reference; doi:10.4018/978-1-61350-068-2.ch022

Hoops, D. S. (2011). Legal issues in the virtual world and e-commerce. In B. Ciaramitaro (Ed.), *Virtual worlds and e-commerce: Technologies and applications for building customer relationships* (pp. 186–204). Hershey, PA: Business Science Reference; doi:10.4018/978-1-61692-808-7.ch010

Hoops, D. S. (2012). Lost in cyberspace: Navigating the legal issues of e-commerce. [JECO]. *Journal of Electronic Commerce in Organizations, 10*(1), 33–51. doi:10.4018/jeco.2012010103

Hopkinson, A. (2012). Establishing the digital library: Don't ignore the library standards and don't forget the training needed. In A. Tella & A. Issa (Eds.), *Library and information science in developing countries: Contemporary issues* (pp. 195–204). Hershey, PA: Information Science Reference; doi:10.4018/978-1-61350-335-5.ch014

Hua, G. B. (2013). The construction industry and standardization of information. In *Implementing IT business strategy in the construction industry* (pp. 47–66). Hershey, PA: Business Science Reference; doi:10.4018/978-1-4666-4185-3.ch003

Huang, C., & Lin, H. (2011). Patent infringement risk analysis using rough set theory. In Q. Zhang, R. Segall, & M. Cao (Eds.), *Visual analytics and interactive technologies: Data, text and web mining applications* (pp. 123–150). Hershey, PA: Information Science Reference; doi:10.4018/978-1-60960-102-7.ch008

Huang, C., Tseng, T. B., & Lin, H. (2013). Patent infringement risk analysis using rough set theory. In *Digital rights management: Concepts, methodologies, tools, and applications* (pp. 1225–1251). Hershey, PA: Information Science Reference; doi:10.4018/978-1-4666-2136-7.ch060

Iyamu, T. (2013). The impact of organisational politics on the implementation of IT strategy: South African case in context. In J. Abdelnour-Nocera (Ed.), *Knowledge and technological development effects on organizational and social structures* (pp. 167–193). Hershey, PA: Information Science Reference; doi:10.4018/978-1-4666-2151-0.ch011

Jacinto, K., Neto, F. M., Leite, C. R., & Jacinto, K. (2014). Accessibility in u-learning: Standards, legislation, and future visions. In F. Neto (Ed.), *Technology platform innovations and forthcoming trends in ubiquitous learning* (pp. 215–236). Hershey, PA: Information Science Reference; doi:10.4018/978-1-4666-4542-4.ch012

Jakobs, K., Wagner, T., & Reimers, K. (2011). Standardising the internet of things: What the experts think. [IJITSR]. *International Journal of IT Standards and Standardization Research, 9*(1), 63–67. doi:10.4018/jitsr.2011010104

Juzoji, H. (2012). Legal bases for medical supervision via mobile telecommunications in Japan. [IJEHMC]. *International Journal of E-Health and Medical Communications, 3*(1), 33–45. doi:10.4018/jehmc.2012010103

Kallinikou, D., Papadopoulos, M., Kaponi, A., & Strakantouna, V. (2011). Intellectual property issues for digital libraries at the intersection of law, technology, and the public interest. In I. Iglezakis, T. Synodinou, & S. Kapidakis (Eds.), *E-publishing and digital libraries: Legal and organizational issues* (pp. 294–341). Hershey, PA: Information Science Reference; doi:10.4018/978-1-60960-031-0.ch015

Kallinikou, D., Papadopoulos, M., Kaponi, A., & Strakantouna, V. (2013). Intellectual property issues for digital libraries at the intersection of law, technology, and the public interest. In *Digital rights management: Concepts, methodologies, tools, and applications* (pp. 1043–1090). Hershey, PA: Information Science Reference; doi:10.4018/978-1-4666-2136-7.ch052

Kaupins, G. (2012). Laws associated with mobile computing in the cloud. [IJWNBT]. *International Journal of Wireless Networks and Broadband Technologies, 2*(3), 1–9. doi:10.4018/ijwnbt.2012070101

Kaur, P., & Singh, H. (2013). Component certification process and standards. In H. Singh & K. Kaur (Eds.), *Designing, engineering, and analyzing reliable and efficient software* (pp. 22–39). Hershey, PA: Information Science Reference; doi:10.4018/978-1-4666-2958-5.ch002

Kayem, A. V. (2013). Security in service oriented architectures: Standards and challenges. In *Digital rights management: Concepts, methodologies, tools, and applications* (pp. 50–73). Hershey, PA: Information Science Reference; doi:10.4018/978-1-4666-2136-7.ch004

Kemp, M. L., Robb, S., & Deans, P. C. (2013). The legal implications of cloud computing. In A. Bento & A. Aggarwal (Eds.), *Cloud computing service and deployment models: Layers and management* (pp. 257–272). Hershey, PA: Business Science Reference; doi:10.4018/978-1-4666-2187-9.ch014

Khansa, L., & Liginlal, D. (2012). Regulatory influence and the imperative of innovation in identity and access management. [IRMJ]. *Information Resources Management Journal, 25*(3), 78–97. doi:10.4018/irmj.2012070104

Kim, E. (2012). Government policies to promote production and consumption of renewable electricity in the US. In M. Tortora (Ed.), *Sustainable systems and energy management at the regional level: Comparative approaches* (pp. 1–18). Hershey, PA: Information Science Reference; doi:10.4018/978-1-61350-344-7.ch001

Kinsell, C. (2014). Technology and disability laws, regulations, and rights. In B. DaCosta & S. Seok (Eds.), *Assistive technology research, practice, and theory* (pp. 75–87). Hershey, PA: Medical Information Science Reference; doi:10.4018/978-1-4666-5015-2.ch006

Kitsiou, S. (2010). Overview and analysis of electronic health record standards. In J. Rodrigues (Ed.), *Health information systems: Concepts, methodologies, tools, and applications* (pp. 374–392). Hershey, PA: Medical Information Science Reference; doi:10.4018/978-1-60566-988-5.ch025

Kloss, J. H., & Schickel, P. (2011). X3D: A secure ISO standard for virtual worlds. In A. Rea (Ed.), *Security in virtual worlds, 3D webs, and immersive environments: Models for development, interaction, and management* (pp. 208–220). Hershey, PA: Information Science Reference; doi:10.4018/978-1-61520-891-3.ch010

Kotsonis, E., & Eliakis, S. (2011). Information security standards for health information systems: The implementer's approach. In A. Chryssanthou, I. Apostolakis, & I. Varlamis (Eds.), *Certification and security in health-related web applications: Concepts and solutions* (pp. 113–145). Hershey, PA: Medical Information Science Reference; doi:10.4018/978-1-61692-895-7.ch006

Kotsonis, E., & Eliakis, S. (2013). Information security standards for health information systems: The implementer's approach. In *User-driven healthcare: Concepts, methodologies, tools, and applications* (pp. 225–257). Hershey, PA: Medical Information Science Reference; doi:10.4018/978-1-4666-2770-3.ch013

Koumaras, H., & Kourtis, M. (2013). A survey on video coding principles and standards. In R. Farrugia & C. Debono (Eds.), *Multimedia networking and coding* (pp. 1–27). Hershey, PA: Information Science Reference; doi:10.4018/978-1-4666-2660-7.ch001

Krupinski, E. A., Antoniotti, N., & Burdick, A. (2011). Standards and guidelines development in the american telemedicine association. In A. Moumtzoglou & A. Kastania (Eds.), *E-health systems quality and reliability: Models and standards* (pp. 244–252). Hershey, PA: Medical Information Science Reference; doi:10.4018/978-1-61692-843-8.ch018

Kuanpoth, J. (2011). Biotechnological patents and morality: A critical view from a developing country. In S. Hongladarom (Ed.), *Genomics and bioethics: Interdisciplinary perspectives, technologies and advancements* (pp. 141–151). Hershey, PA: Medical Information Science Reference; doi:10.4018/978-1-61692-883-4.ch010

Kuanpoth, J. (2013). Biotechnological patents and morality: A critical view from a developing country. In *Digital rights management: Concepts, methodologies, tools, and applications* (pp. 1417–1427). Hershey, PA: Information Science Reference; doi:10.4018/978-1-4666-2136-7.ch071

Kulmala, R., & Kettunen, J. (2012). Intellectual property protection and process modeling in small knowledge intensive enterprises. In *Organizational learning and knowledge: Concepts, methodologies, tools and applications* (pp. 2963–2980). Hershey, PA: Business Science Reference; doi:10.4018/978-1-60960-783-8.ch809

Kulmala, R., & Kettunen, J. (2013). Intellectual property protection in small knowledge intensive enterprises. [IJCWT]. *International Journal of Cyber Warfare & Terrorism*, 3(1), 29–45. doi:10.4018/ ijcwt.2013010103

Küster, M. W. (2012). Standards for achieving interoperability of egovernment in Europe. In E. Kajan, F. Dorloff, & I. Bedini (Eds.), *Handbook of research on e-business standards and protocols: Documents, data and advanced web technologies* (pp. 249–268). Hershey, PA: Business Science Reference; doi:10.4018/978-1-4666-0146-8.ch012

Kyobe, M. (2011). Factors influencing SME compliance with government regulation on use of IT: The case of South Africa. In F. Tan (Ed.), *International enterprises and global information technologies: Advancing management practices* (pp. 85–116). Hershey, PA: Information Science Reference; doi:10.4018/978-1-60960-605-3.ch005

Lam, J. C., & Hills, P. (2011). Promoting technological environmental innovations: What is the role of environmental regulation? In Z. Luo (Ed.), *Green finance and sustainability: Environmentally-aware business models and technologies* (pp. 56–73). Hershey, PA: Business Science Reference; doi:10.4018/978-1-60960-531-5.ch003

Lam, J. C., & Hills, P. (2013). Promoting technological environmental innovations: The role of environmental regulation. In Z. Luo (Ed.), *Technological solutions for modern logistics and supply chain management* (pp. 230–247). Hershey, PA: Business Science Reference; doi:10.4018/978-1-4666-2773-4.ch015

Laporte, C., & Vargas, E. P. (2012). The development of international standards to facilitate process improvements for very small entities. In S. Fauzi, M. Nasir, N. Ramli, & S. Sahibuddin (Eds.), *Software process improvement and management: Approaches and tools for practical development* (pp. 34–61). Hershey, PA: Information Science Reference; doi:10.4018/978-1-61350-141-2.ch003

Laporte, C., & Vargas, E. P. (2014). The development of international standards to facilitate process improvements for very small entities. In *Software design and development: Concepts, methodologies, tools, and applications* (pp. 1335–1361). Hershey, PA: Information Science Reference; doi:10.4018/978-1-4666-4301-7.ch065

Lautman, R., & Curran, K. (2013). The problems of jurisdiction on the internet. In K. Curran (Ed.), *Pervasive and ubiquitous technology innovations for ambient intelligence environments* (pp. 164–170). Hershey, PA: Information Science Reference; doi:10.4018/978-1-4666-2041-4.ch016

Layne-Farrar, A. (2011). Innovative or indefensible? An empirical assessment of patenting within standard setting. [IJITSR]. *International Journal of IT Standards and Standardization Research*, 9(2), 1–18. doi:10.4018/jitsr.2011070101

Layne-Farrar, A. (2013). Innovative or indefensible? An empirical assessment of patenting within standard setting. In K. Jakobs (Ed.), *Innovations in organizational IT specification and standards development* (pp. 1–18). Hershey, PA: Information Science Reference; doi:10.4018/978-1-4666-2160-2.ch001

Layne-Farrar, A., & Padilla, A. J. (2011). Assessing the link between standards and patents. [IJITSR]. *International Journal of IT Standards and Standardization Research*, 9(2), 19–49. doi:10.4018/ jitsr.2011070102

Layne-Farrar, A., & Padilla, A. J. (2013). Assessing the link between standards and patents. In K. Jakobs (Ed.), *Innovations in organizational IT specification and standards development* (pp. 19–51). Hershey, PA: Information Science Reference; doi:10.4018/978-1-4666-2160-2.ch002

Lee, H., & Huh, J. C. (2012). Korea's strategies for ICT standards internationalisation: A comparison with China's. [IJITSR]. *International Journal of IT Standards and Standardization Research, 10*(2), 1–13. doi:10.4018/jitsr.2012070101

Li, Y., & Wei, C. (2011). Digital image authentication: A review. [IJDLS]. *International Journal of Digital Library Systems, 2*(2), 55–78. doi:10.4018/jdls.2011040104

Li, Y., Xiao, X., Feng, X., & Yan, H. (2012). Adaptation and localization: Metadata research and development for Chinese digital resources. [IJDLS]. *International Journal of Digital Library Systems, 3*(1), 1–21. doi:10.4018/jdls.2012010101

Lim, W., & Kim, D. (2013). Do technologies support the implementation of the common core state standards in mathematics of high school probability and statistics? In D. Polly (Ed.), *Common core mathematics standards and implementing digital technologies* (pp. 168–183). Hershey, PA: Information Science Reference; doi:10.4018/978-1-4666-4086-3.ch011

Linton, J., & Stegall, D. (2013). Common core standards for mathematical practice and TPACK: An integrated approach to instruction. In D. Polly (Ed.), *Common core mathematics standards and implementing digital technologies* (pp. 234–249). Hershey, PA: Information Science Reference; doi:10.4018/978-1-4666-4086-3.ch016

Liotta, A., & Liotta, A. (2011). Privacy in pervasive systems: Legal framework and regulatory challenges. In A. Malatras (Ed.), *Pervasive computing and communications design and deployment: Technologies, trends and applications* (pp. 263–277). Hershey, PA: Information Science Reference; doi:10.4018/978-1-60960-611-4.ch012

Lissoni, F. (2013). Academic patenting in Europe: Recent research and new perspectives. In I. Yetkiner, M. Pamukcu, & E. Erdil (Eds.), *Industrial dynamics, innovation policy, and economic growth through technological advancements* (pp. 75–91). Hershey, PA: Information Science Reference; doi:10.4018/978-1-4666-1978-4.ch005

Litaay, T., Prananingrum, D. H., & Krisanto, Y. A. (2011). Indonesian legal perspectives on biotechnology and intellectual property rights. In S. Hongladarom (Ed.), *Genomics and bioethics: Interdisciplinary perspectives, technologies and advancements* (pp. 171–183). Hershey, PA: Medical Information Science Reference; doi:10.4018/978-1-61692-883-4.ch012

Litaay, T., Prananingrum, D. H., & Krisanto, Y. A. (2013). Indonesian legal perspectives on biotechnology and intellectual property rights. In *Digital rights management: Concepts, methodologies, tools, and applications* (pp. 834–845). Hershey, PA: Information Science Reference; doi:10.4018/978-1-4666-2136-7.ch039

Losavio, M., Pastukhov, P., & Polyakova, S. (2014). Regulatory aspects of cloud computing in business environments. In S. Srinivasan (Ed.), *Security, trust, and regulatory aspects of cloud computing in business environments* (pp. 156–169). Hershey, PA: Information Science Reference; doi:10.4018/978-1-4666-5788-5.ch009

Lu, B., Tsou, B. K., Jiang, T., Zhu, J., & Kwong, O. Y. (2011). Mining parallel knowledge from comparable patents. In W. Wong, W. Liu, & M. Bennamoun (Eds.), *Ontology learning and knowledge discovery using the web: Challenges and recent advances* (pp. 247–271). Hershey, PA: Information Science Reference; doi:10.4018/978-1-60960-625-1.ch013

Lucas-Schloetter, A. (2011). Digital libraries and copyright issues: Digitization of contents and the economic rights of the authors. In I. Iglezakis, T. Synodinou, & S. Kapidakis (Eds.), *E-publishing and digital libraries: Legal and organizational issues* (pp. 159–179). Hershey, PA: Information Science Reference; doi:10.4018/978-1-60960-031-0.ch009

Lyytinen, K., Keil, T., & Fomin, V. (2010). A framework to build process theories of anticipatory information and communication technology (ICT) standardizing. In K. Jakobs (Ed.), *New applications in IT standards: Developments and progress* (pp. 147–186). Hershey, PA: Information Science Reference; doi:10.4018/978-1-60566-946-5.ch008

Macedo, M., & Isaías, P. (2013). Standards related to interoperability in EHR & HS. In M. Sicilia & P. Balazote (Eds.), *Interoperability in healthcare information systems: Standards, management, and technology* (pp. 19–44). Hershey, PA: Medical Information Science Reference; doi:10.4018/978-1-4666-3000-0.ch002

Madden, P. (2011). Greater accountability, less red tape: The Australian standard business reporting experience. [IJEBR]. *International Journal of E-Business Research, 7*(2), 1–10. doi:10.4018/jebr.2011040101

Maravilhas, S. (2014). Quality improves the value of patent information to promote innovation. In G. Jamil, A. Malheiro, & F. Ribeiro (Eds.), *Rethinking the conceptual base for new practical applications in information value and quality* (pp. 61–82). Hershey, PA: Information Science Reference; doi:10.4018/978-1-4666-4562-2.ch004

Marshall, S. (2011). E-learning standards: Beyond technical standards to guides for professional practice. In F. Lazarinis, S. Green, & E. Pearson (Eds.), *Handbook of research on e-learning standards and interoperability: Frameworks and issues* (pp. 170–192). Hershey, PA: Information Science Reference; doi:10.4018/978-1-61692-789-9.ch008

Martino, L., & Bertino, E. (2012). Security for web services: Standards and research issues. In L. Jie-Zhang (Ed.), *Innovations, standards and practices of web services: Emerging research topics* (pp. 336–362). Hershey, PA: Information Science Reference; doi:10.4018/978-1-61350-104-7.ch015

McCarthy, V., & Hulsart, R. (2012). Management education for integrity: Raising ethical standards in online management classes. In C. Wankel & A. Stachowicz-Stanusch (Eds.), *Handbook of research on teaching ethics in business and management education* (pp. 413–425). Hershey, PA: Information Science Reference; doi:10.4018/978-1-61350-510-6.ch024

McGrath, T. (2012). The reality of using standards for electronic business document formats. In E. Kajan, F. Dorloff, & I. Bedini (Eds.), *Handbook of research on e-business standards and protocols: Documents, data and advanced web technologies* (pp. 21–32). Hershey, PA: Business Science Reference; doi:10.4018/978-1-4666-0146-8.ch002

Medlin, B. D., & Chen, C. C. (2012). A global perspective of laws and regulations dealing with information security and privacy. In *Cyber crime: Concepts, methodologies, tools and applications* (pp. 1349–1363). Hershey, PA: Information Science Reference; doi:10.4018/978-1-61350-323-2.ch609

Mehrfard, H., & Hamou-Lhadj, A. (2011). The impact of regulatory compliance on agile software processes with a focus on the FDA guidelines for medical device software. [IJISMD]. *International Journal of Information System Modeling and Design*, 2(2), 67–81. doi:10.4018/jismd.2011040104

Mehrfard, H., & Hamou-Lhadj, A. (2013). The impact of regulatory compliance on agile software processes with a focus on the FDA guidelines for medical device software. In J. Krogstie (Ed.), *Frameworks for developing efficient information systems: Models, theory, and practice* (pp. 298–314). Hershey, PA: Engineering Science Reference; doi:10.4018/978-1-4666-4161-7.ch013

Mendoza, R. A., & Ravichandran, T. (2011). An exploratory analysis of the relationship between organizational and institutional factors shaping the assimilation of vertical standards. [IJITSR]. *International Journal of IT Standards and Standardization Research*, 9(1), 24–51. doi:10.4018/jitsr.2011010102

Mendoza, R. A., & Ravichandran, T. (2012). An empirical evaluation of the assimilation of industry-specific data standards using firm-level and community-level constructs. In M. Tavana (Ed.), *Enterprise information systems and advancing business solutions: Emerging models* (pp. 287–312). Hershey, PA: Business Science Reference; doi:10.4018/978-1-4666-1761-2.ch017

Mendoza, R. A., & Ravichandran, T. (2012). Drivers of organizational participation in XML-based industry standardization efforts. In M. Tavana (Ed.), *Enterprise information systems and advancing business solutions: Emerging models* (pp. 268–286). Hershey, PA: Business Science Reference; doi:10.4018/978-1-4666-1761-2.ch016

Mendoza, R. A., & Ravichandran, T. (2013). An exploratory analysis of the relationship between organizational and institutional factors shaping the assimilation of vertical standards. In K. Jakobs (Ed.), *Innovations in organizational IT specification and standards development* (pp. 193–221). Hershey, PA: Information Science Reference; doi:10.4018/978-1-4666-2160-2.ch012

Mense, E. G., Fulwiler, J. H., Richardson, M. D., & Lane, K. E. (2011). Standardization, hybridization, or individualization: Marketing IT to a diverse clientele. In U. Demiray & S. Sever (Eds.), *Marketing online education programs: Frameworks for promotion and communication* (pp. 291–299). Hershey, PA: Information Science Reference; doi:10.4018/978-1-60960-074-7.ch019

Metaxa, E., Sarigiannidis, M., & Folinas, D. (2012). Legal issues of the French law on creation and internet (Hadopi 1 and 2). [IJT]. *International Journal of Technoethics*, 3(3), 21–36. doi:10.4018/jte.2012070102

Meyer, N. (2012). Standardization as governance without government: A critical reassessment of the digital video broadcasting project's success story. [IJITSR]. *International Journal of IT Standards and Standardization Research*, 10(2), 14–28. doi:10.4018/jitsr.2012070102

Miguel da Silva, F., Neto, F. M., Burlamaqui, A. M., Pinto, J. P., Fernandes, C. E., & Castro de Souza, R. (2014). T-SCORM: An extension of the SCORM standard to support the project of educational contents for t-learning. In F. Neto (Ed.), *Technology platform innovations and forthcoming trends in ubiquitous learning* (pp. 94–119). Hershey, PA: Information Science Reference; doi:10.4018/978-1-4666-4542-4.ch006

Moon, A. (2014). Copyright and licensing essentials for librarians and copyright owners in the digital age. In N. Patra, B. Kumar, & A. Pani (Eds.), *Progressive trends in electronic resource management in libraries* (pp. 106–117). Hershey, PA: Information Science Reference; doi:10.4018/978-1-4666-4761-9. ch006

Moralis, A., Pouli, V., Grammatikou, M., Kalogeras, D., & Maglaris, V. (2012). Security standards and issues for grid computing. In *Grid and cloud computing: Concepts, methodologies, tools and applications* (pp. 1656–1671). Hershey, PA: Information Science Reference; doi:10.4018/978-1-4666-0879-5.ch708

Moreno, L., Iglesias, A., Calvo, R., Delgado, S., & Zaragoza, L. (2012). Disability standards and guidelines for learning management systems: Evaluating accessibility. In R. Babo & A. Azevedo (Eds.), *Higher education institutions and learning management systems: Adoption and standardization* (pp. 199–218). Hershey, PA: Information Science Reference; doi:10.4018/978-1-60960-884-2.ch010

Moro, N. (2013). Digital rights management and corporate hegemony: Avenues for reform. In H. Rahman & I. Ramos (Eds.), *Ethical data mining applications for socio-economic development* (pp. 281–299). Hershey, PA: Information Science Reference; doi:10.4018/978-1-4666-4078-8.ch013

Mula, D., & Lobina, M. L. (2012). Legal protection of the web page. In H. Sasaki (Ed.), *Information technology for intellectual property protection: Interdisciplinary advancements* (pp. 213–236). Hershey, PA: Information Science Reference; doi:10.4018/978-1-61350-135-1.ch008

Mula, D., & Lobina, M. L. (2013). Legal protection of the web page. In *Digital rights management: Concepts, methodologies, tools, and applications* (pp. 1–18). Hershey, PA: Information Science Reference; doi:10.4018/978-1-4666-2136-7.ch001

Mulcahy, D. (2011). Performativity in practice: An actor-network account of professional teaching standards. [IJANTTI]. *International Journal of Actor-Network Theory and Technological Innovation*, *3*(2), 1–16. doi:10.4018/jantti.2011040101

Mulcahy, D. (2013). Performativity in practice: An actor-network account of professional teaching standards. In A. Tatnall (Ed.), *Social and professional applications of actor-network theory for technology development* (pp. 1–16). Hershey, PA: Information Science Reference; doi:10.4018/978-1-4666-2166-4. ch001

Mustaffa, M. T. (2012). Multi-standard multi-band reconfigurable LNA. In A. Marzuki, A. Rahim, & M. Loulou (Eds.), *Advances in monolithic microwave integrated circuits for wireless systems: Modeling and design technologies* (pp. 1–23). Hershey, PA: Engineering Science Reference; doi:10.4018/978-1-60566-886-4.ch001

Nabi, S. I., Al-Ghmlas, G. S., & Alghathbar, K. (2012). Enterprise information security policies, standards, and procedures: A survey of available standards and guidelines. In M. Gupta, J. Walp, & R. Sharman (Eds.), *Strategic and practical approaches for information security governance: Technologies and applied solutions* (pp. 67–89). Hershey, PA: Information Science Reference; doi:10.4018/978-1-4666-0197-0.ch005

Nabi, S. I., Al-Ghmlas, G. S., & Alghathbar, K. (2014). Enterprise information security policies, standards, and procedures: A survey of available standards and guidelines. In *Crisis management: Concepts, methodologies, tools and applications* (pp. 750–773). Hershey, PA: Information Science Reference; doi:10.4018/978-1-4666-4707-7.ch036

Naixiao, Z., & Chunhua, H. (2012). Research on open innovation in China: Focus on intellectual property rights and their operation in Chinese enterprises. [IJABIM]. *International Journal of Asian Business and Information Management, 3*(1), 65–71. doi:10.4018/jabim.2012010106

Naixiao, Z., & Chunhua, H. (2013). Research on open innovation in China: Focus on intellectual property rights and their operation in Chinese enterprises. In *Digital rights management: Concepts, methodologies, tools, and applications* (pp. 714–720). Hershey, PA: Information Science Reference; doi:10.4018/978-1-4666-2136-7.ch031

Ndjetcheu, L. (2013). Social responsibility and legal financial communication in African companies in the south of the Sahara: Glance from the OHADA accounting law viewpoint. [IJIDE]. *International Journal of Innovation in the Digital Economy, 4*(4), 1–17. doi:10.4018/ijide.2013100101

Ng, W. L. (2013). Improving long-term financial risk forecasts using high-frequency data and scaling laws. In B. Alexandrova-Kabadjova, S. Martinez-Jaramillo, A. Garcia-Almanza, & E. Tsang (Eds.), *Simulation in computational finance and economics: Tools and emerging applications* (pp. 255–278). Hershey, PA: Business Science Reference; doi:10.4018/978-1-4666-2011-7.ch013

Noury, N., Bourquard, K., Bergognon, D., & Schroeder, J. (2013). Regulations initiatives in France for the interoperability of communicating medical devices. [IJEHMC]. *International Journal of E-Health and Medical Communications, 4*(2), 50–64. doi:10.4018/jehmc.2013040104

Null, E. (2013). Legal and political barriers to municipal networks in the United States. In A. Abdelaal (Ed.), *Social and economic effects of community wireless networks and infrastructures* (pp. 27–56). Hershey, PA: Information Science Reference; doi:10.4018/978-1-4666-2997-4.ch003

O'Connor, R. V., & Laporte, C. Y. (2014). An innovative approach to the development of an international software process lifecycle standard for very small entities. [IJITSA]. *International Journal of Information Technologies and Systems Approach, 7*(1), 1–22. doi:10.4018/ijitsa.2014010101

Onat, I., & Miri, A. (2013). RFID standards. In A. Miri (Ed.), *Advanced security and privacy for RFID technologies* (pp. 14–22). Hershey, PA: Information Science Reference; doi:10.4018/978-1-4666-3685-9.ch002

Orton, I., Alva, A., & Endicott-Popovsky, B. (2013). Legal process and requirements for cloud forensic investigations. In K. Ruan (Ed.), *Cybercrime and cloud forensics: Applications for investigation processes* (pp. 186–229). Hershey, PA: Information Science Reference; doi:10.4018/978-1-4666-2662-1.ch008

Ortt, J. R., & Egyedi, T. M. (2014). The effect of pre-existing standards and regulations on the development and diffusion of radically new innovations. [IJITSR]. *International Journal of IT Standards and Standardization Research, 12*(1), 17–37. doi:10.4018/ijitsr.2014010102

Ozturk, Y., & Sharma, J. (2011). mVITAL: A standards compliant vital sign monitor. In C. Röcker, & M. Ziefle (Eds.), Smart healthcare applications and services: Developments and practices (pp. 174-196). Hershey, PA: Medical Information Science Reference. doi:10.4018/978-1-60960-180-5.ch008

Ozturk, Y., & Sharma, J. (2013). mVITAL: A standards compliant vital sign monitor. In IT policy and ethics: Concepts, methodologies, tools, and applications (pp. 515-538). Hershey, PA: Information Science Reference. doi:10.4018/978-1-4666-2919-6.ch024

Parsons, T. D. (2011). Affect-sensitive virtual standardized patient interface system. In D. Surry, R. Gray Jr, & J. Stefurak (Eds.), *Technology integration in higher education: Social and organizational aspects* (pp. 201–221). Hershey, PA: Information Science Reference; doi:10.4018/978-1-60960-147-8.ch015

Parveen, S., & Pater, C. (2012). Utilizing innovative video chat technology to meet national standards: A Case study on a STARTALK Hindi language program. [IJVPLE]. *International Journal of Virtual and Personal Learning Environments*, *3*(3), 1–20. doi:10.4018/jvple.2012070101

Pawlowski, J. M., & Kozlov, D. (2013). Analysis and validation of learning technology models, standards and specifications: The reference model analysis grid (RMAG). In K. Jakobs (Ed.), *Innovations in organizational IT specification and standards development* (pp. 223–240). Hershey, PA: Information Science Reference; doi:10.4018/978-1-4666-2160-2.ch013

Pina, P. (2011). The private copy issue: Piracy, copyright and consumers' rights. In T. Strader (Ed.), *Digital product management, technology and practice: Interdisciplinary perspectives* (pp. 193–205). Hershey, PA: Business Science Reference; doi:10.4018/978-1-61692-877-3.ch011

Pina, P. (2013). Between Scylla and Charybdis: The balance between copyright, digital rights management and freedom of expression. In Digital rights management: Concepts, methodologies, tools, and applications (pp. 1355-1367). Hershey, PA: Information Science Reference. doi:10.4018/978-1-4666-2136-7.ch067

Pina, P. (2013). Computer games and intellectual property law: Derivative works, copyright and copyleft. In *Digital rights management: Concepts, methodologies, tools, and applications* (pp. 777–788). Hershey, PA: Information Science Reference; doi:10.4018/978-1-4666-2136-7.ch035

Pina, P. (2013). The private copy issue: Piracy, copyright and consumers' rights. In *Digital rights management: Concepts, methodologies, tools, and applications* (pp. 1546–1558). Hershey, PA: Information Science Reference; doi:10.4018/978-1-4666-2136-7.ch078

Piotrowski, M. (2011). QTI: A failed e-learning standard? In F. Lazarinis, S. Green, & E. Pearson (Eds.), *Handbook of research on e-learning standards and interoperability: Frameworks and issues* (pp. 59–82). Hershey, PA: Information Science Reference; doi:10.4018/978-1-61692-789-9.ch004

Ponte, D., & Camussone, P. F. (2013). Neither heroes nor chaos: The victory of VHS against Betamax. [IJANTTI]. *International Journal of Actor-Network Theory and Technological Innovation*, *5*(1), 40–54. doi:10.4018/jantti.2013010103

Pradhan, A. (2011). Pivotal role of the ISO 14001 standard in the carbon economy. [IJGC]. *International Journal of Green Computing*, *2*(1), 38–46. doi:10.4018/jgc.2011010104

Pradhan, A. (2011). Standards and legislation for the carbon economy. In B. Unhelkar (Ed.), *Handbook of research on green ICT: Technology, business and social perspectives* (pp. 592–606). Hershey, PA: Information Science Reference; doi:10.4018/978-1-61692-834-6.ch043

Pradhan, A. (2013). Pivotal role of the ISO 14001 standard in the carbon economy. In K. Ganesh & S. Anbuudayasankar (Eds.), *International and interdisciplinary studies in green computing* (pp. 38–46). Hershey, PA: Information Science Reference; doi:10.4018/978-1-4666-2646-1.ch004

Prentzas, J., & Hatzilygeroudis, I. (2011). Techniques, technologies and patents related to intelligent educational systems. In G. Magoulas (Ed.), *E-infrastructures and technologies for lifelong learning: Next generation environments* (pp. 1–28). Hershey, PA: Information Science Reference; doi:10.4018/978-1-61520-983-5.ch001

Ramos, I., & Fernandes, J. (2011). Web-based intellectual property marketplace: A survey of current practices. [IJICTHD]. *International Journal of Information Communication Technologies and Human Development*, *3*(3), 58–68. doi:10.4018/jicthd.2011070105

Ramos, I., & Fernandes, J. (2013). Web-based intellectual property marketplace: A survey of current practices. In S. Chhabra (Ed.), *ICT influences on human development, interaction, and collaboration* (pp. 203–213). Hershey, PA: Information Science Reference; doi:10.4018/978-1-4666-1957-9.ch012

Rashmi, R. (2011). Biopharma drugs innovation in India and foreign investment and technology transfer in the changed patent regime. In P. Ordóñez de Pablos, W. Lee, & J. Zhao (Eds.), *Regional innovation systems and sustainable development: Emerging technologies* (pp. 210–225). Hershey, PA: Information Science Reference; doi:10.4018/978-1-61692-846-9.ch016

Rashmi, R. (2011). Optimal policy for biopharmaceutical drugs innovation and access in India. In P. Ordóñez de Pablos, W. Lee, & J. Zhao (Eds.), *Regional innovation systems and sustainable development: Emerging technologies* (pp. 74–114). Hershey, PA: Information Science Reference; doi:10.4018/978-1-61692-846-9.ch007

Rashmi, R. (2013). Biopharma drugs innovation in India and foreign investment and technology transfer in the changed patent regime. In *Digital rights management: Concepts, methodologies, tools, and applications* (pp. 846–859). Hershey, PA: Information Science Reference; doi:10.4018/978-1-4666-2136-7.ch040

Reed, C. N. (2011). The open geospatial consortium and web services standards. In P. Zhao & L. Di (Eds.), *Geospatial web services: Advances in information interoperability* (pp. 1–16). Hershey, PA: Information Science Reference; doi:10.4018/978-1-60960-192-8.ch001

Rejas-Muslera, R., Davara, E., Abran, A., & Buglione, L. (2013). Intellectual property systems in software. [IJCWT]. *International Journal of Cyber Warfare & Terrorism*, *3*(1), 1–14. doi:10.4018/ijcwt.2013010101

Rejas-Muslera, R. J., García-Tejedor, A. J., & Rodriguez, O. P. (2011). Open educational resources in e-learning: standards and environment. In F. Lazarinis, S. Green, & E. Pearson (Eds.), *Handbook of research on e-learning standards and interoperability: Frameworks and issues* (pp. 346–359). Hershey, PA: Information Science Reference; doi:10.4018/978-1-61692-789-9.ch017

Ries, N. M. (2011). Legal issues in health information and electronic health records. In *Clinical technologies: Concepts, methodologies, tools and applications* (pp. 1948–1961). Hershey, PA: Medical Information Science Reference; doi:10.4018/978-1-60960-561-2.ch708

Riillo, C. A. (2013). Profiles and motivations of standardization players. [IJITSR]. *International Journal of IT Standards and Standardization Research, 11*(2), 17–33. doi:10.4018/jitsr.2013070102

Rodriguez, E., & Lolas, F. (2011). Social issues related to gene patenting in Latin America: A bioethical reflection. In S. Hongladarom (Ed.), *Genomics and bioethics: Interdisciplinary perspectives, technologies and advancements* (pp. 152–170). Hershey, PA: Medical Information Science Reference; doi:10.4018/978-1-61692-883-4.ch011

Rutherford, M. (2013). Implementing common core state standards using digital curriculum. In D. Polly (Ed.), *Common core mathematics standards and implementing digital technologies* (pp. 38–44). Hershey, PA: Information Science Reference; doi:10.4018/978-1-4666-4086-3.ch003

Rutherford, M. (2014). Implementing common core state standards using digital curriculum. In *K-12 education: Concepts, methodologies, tools, and applications* (pp. 383–389). Hershey, PA: Information Science Reference; doi:10.4018/978-1-4666-4502-8.ch022

Ryan, G., & Shinnick, E. (2011). Knowledge and intellectual property rights: An economics perspective. In D. Schwartz & D. Te'eni (Eds.), *Encyclopedia of knowledge management* (2nd ed., pp. 489–496). Hershey, PA: Information Science Reference; doi:10.4018/978-1-59904-931-1.ch047

Ryoo, J., & Choi, Y. (2011). A taxonomy of green information and communication protocols and standards. In B. Unhelkar (Ed.), *Handbook of research on green ICT: Technology, business and social perspectives* (pp. 364–376). Hershey, PA: Information Science Reference; doi:10.4018/978-1-61692-834-6.ch026

Saeed, K., Ziegler, G., & Yaqoob, M. K. (2013). Management practices in exploration and production industry. In S. Saeed, M. Khan, & R. Ahmad (Eds.), *Business strategies and approaches for effective engineering management* (pp. 151–187). Hershey, PA: Business Science Reference; doi:10.4018/978-1-4666-3658-3.ch010

Saiki, T. (2014). Intellectual property in mergers & acquisitions. In J. Wang (Ed.), *Encyclopedia of business analytics and optimization* (pp. 1275–1283). Hershey, PA: Business Science Reference; doi:10.4018/978-1-4666-5202-6.ch117

Santos, O., & Boticario, J. (2011). A general framework for inclusive lifelong learning in higher education institutions with adaptive web-based services that support standards. In G. Magoulas (Ed.), *E-infrastructures and technologies for lifelong learning: Next generation environments* (pp. 29–58). Hershey, PA: Information Science Reference; doi:10.4018/978-1-61520-983-5.ch002

Santos, O., Boticario, J., Raffenne, E., Granado, J., Rodriguez-Ascaso, A., & Gutierrez y Restrepo, E. (2011). A standard-based framework to support personalisation, adaptation, and interoperability in inclusive learning scenarios. In F. Lazarinis, S. Green, & E. Pearson (Eds.), *Handbook of research on e-learning standards and interoperability: Frameworks and issues* (pp. 126–169). Hershey, PA: Information Science Reference; doi:10.4018/978-1-61692-789-9.ch007

Sarabdeen, J. (2012). Legal issues in e-healthcare systems. In M. Watfa (Ed.), *E-healthcare systems and wireless communications: Current and future challenges* (pp. 23–48). Hershey, PA: Medical Information Science Reference; doi:10.4018/978-1-61350-123-8.ch002

Scheg, A. G. (2014). Common standards for online education found in accrediting organizations. In *Reforming teacher education for online pedagogy development* (pp. 50–76). Hershey, PA: Information Science Reference; doi:10.4018/978-1-4666-5055-8.ch003

Sclater, N. (2012). Legal and contractual issues of cloud computing for educational institutions. In L. Chao (Ed.), *Cloud computing for teaching and learning: Strategies for design and implementation* (pp. 186–199). Hershey, PA: Information Science Reference; doi:10.4018/978-1-4666-0957-0.ch013

Selwyn, L., & Eldridge, V. (2013). Governance and organizational structures. In *Public law librarianship: Objectives, challenges, and solutions* (pp. 41–71). Hershey, PA: Information Science Reference; doi:10.4018/978-1-4666-2184-8.ch003

Seo, D. (2012). The significance of government's role in technology standardization: Two cases in the wireless communications industry. In C. Reddick (Ed.), *Cases on public information management and e-government adoption* (pp. 219–231). Hershey, PA: Information Science Reference; doi:10.4018/978-1-4666-0981-5.ch009

Seo, D. (2013). Analysis of various structures of standards setting organizations (SSOs) that impact tension among members. [IJITSR]. *International Journal of IT Standards and Standardization Research, 11*(2), 46–60. doi:10.4018/jitsr.2013070104

Seo, D. (2013). Background of standards strategy. In *Evolution and standardization of mobile communications technology* (pp. 1–17). Hershey, PA: Information Science Reference; doi:10.4018/978-1-4666-4074-0.ch001

Seo, D. (2013). Developing a theoretical model. In *Evolution and standardization of mobile communications technology* (pp. 18–42). Hershey, PA: Information Science Reference; doi:10.4018/978-1-4666-4074-0.ch002

Seo, D. (2013). The 1G (first generation) mobile communications technology standards. In *Evolution and standardization of mobile communications technology* (pp. 54–75). Hershey, PA: Information Science Reference; doi:10.4018/978-1-4666-4074-0.ch005

Seo, D. (2013). The 2G (second generation) mobile communications technology standards. In *Evolution and standardization of mobile communications technology* (pp. 76–114). Hershey, PA: Information Science Reference; doi:10.4018/978-1-4666-4074-0.ch006

Seo, D. (2013). The 3G (third generation) of mobile communications technology standards. In *Evolution and standardization of mobile communications technology* (pp. 115–161). Hershey, PA: Information Science Reference; doi:10.4018/978-1-4666-4074-0.ch007

Seo, D. (2013). The significance of government's role in technology standardization: Two cases in the wireless communications industry. In K. Jakobs (Ed.), *Innovations in organizational IT specification and standards development* (pp. 183–192). Hershey, PA: Information Science Reference; doi:10.4018/978-1-4666-2160-2.ch011

Seo, D., & Koek, J. W. (2012). Are Asian countries ready to lead a global ICT standardization? [IJITSR]. *International Journal of IT Standards and Standardization Research, 10*(2), 29–44. doi:10.4018/jitsr.2012070103

Sharp, R. J., Ewald, J. A., & Kenward, R. (2013). Central information flows and decision-making requirements. In J. Papathanasiou, B. Manos, S. Arampatzis, & R. Kenward (Eds.), *Transactional environmental support system design: Global solutions* (pp. 7–32). Hershey, PA: Information Science Reference; doi:10.4018/978-1-4666-2824-3.ch002

Shen, X., Graham, I., Stewart, J., & Williams, R. (2013). Standards development as hybridization. [IJITSR]. *International Journal of IT Standards and Standardization Research, 11*(2), 34–45. doi:10.4018/jitsr.2013070103

Sherman, M. (2013). Using technology to engage students with the standards for mathematical practice: The case of DGS. In D. Polly (Ed.), *Common core mathematics standards and implementing digital technologies* (pp. 78–101). Hershey, PA: Information Science Reference; doi:10.4018/978-1-4666-4086-3.ch006

Singh, J., & Kumar, V. (2013). Compliance and regulatory standards for cloud computing. In R. Khurana & R. Aggarwal (Eds.), *Interdisciplinary perspectives on business convergence, computing, and legality* (pp. 54–64). Hershey, PA: Business Science Reference; doi:10.4018/978-1-4666-4209-6.ch006

Singh, S., & Paliwal, M. (2014). Exploring a sense of intellectual property valuation for Indian SMEs. [IJABIM]. *International Journal of Asian Business and Information Management, 5*(1), 15–36. doi:10.4018/ijabim.2014010102

Singh, S., & Siddiqui, T. J. (2013). Robust image data hiding technique for copyright protection. [IJISP]. *International Journal of Information Security and Privacy, 7*(2), 44–56. doi:10.4018/jisp.2013040103

Spies, M., & Tabet, S. (2012). Emerging standards and protocols for governance, risk, and compliance management. In E. Kajan, F. Dorloff, & I. Bedini (Eds.), *Handbook of research on e-business standards and protocols: Documents, data and advanced web technologies* (pp. 768–790). Hershey, PA: Business Science Reference; doi:10.4018/978-1-4666-0146-8.ch035

Spinello, R. A., & Tavani, H. T. (2008). Intellectual property rights: From theory to practical implementation. In H. Sasaki (Ed.), *Intellectual property protection for multimedia information technology* (pp. 25–69). Hershey, PA: Information Science Reference; doi:10.4018/978-1-59904-762-1.ch002

Spyrou, S., Bamidis, P., & Maglaveras, N. (2010). Health information standards: Towards integrated health information networks. In J. Rodrigues (Ed.), *Health information systems: Concepts, methodologies, tools, and applications* (pp. 2145–2159). Hershey, PA: Medical Information Science Reference; doi:10.4018/978-1-60566-988-5.ch136

Stanfill, D. (2012). Standards-based educational technology professional development. In V. Wang (Ed.), *Encyclopedia of e-leadership, counseling and training* (pp. 819–834). Hershey, PA: Information Science Reference; doi:10.4018/978-1-61350-068-2.ch060

Steen, H. U. (2011). The battle within: An analysis of internal fragmentation in networked technologies based on a comparison of the DVB-H and T-DMB mobile digital multimedia broadcasting standards. [IJITSR]. *International Journal of IT Standards and Standardization Research, 9*(2), 50–71. doi:10.4018/jitsr.2011070103

Steen, H. U. (2013). The battle within: An analysis of internal fragmentation in networked technologies based on a comparison of the DVB-H and T-DMB mobile digital multimedia broadcasting standards. In K. Jakobs (Ed.), *Innovations in organizational IT specification and standards development* (pp. 91–114). Hershey, PA: Information Science Reference; doi:10.4018/978-1-4666-2160-2.ch005

Stoll, M., & Breu, R. (2012). Information security governance and standard based management systems. In M. Gupta, J. Walp, & R. Sharman (Eds.), *Strategic and practical approaches for information security governance: Technologies and applied solutions* (pp. 261–282). Hershey, PA: Information Science Reference; doi:10.4018/978-1-4666-0197-0.ch015

Suzuki, O. (2013). Search efforts, selective appropriation, and the usefulness of new knowledge: Evidence from a comparison across U.S. and non-U.S. patent applicants. *International Journal of Knowledge Management (IJKM), 9*(1), 42-59. doi:10.4018/jkm.2013010103

Tajima, M. (2012). The role of technology standardization in RFID adoption: The pharmaceutical context. [IJITSR]. *International Journal of IT Standards and Standardization Research, 10*(1), 48–67. doi:10.4018/jitsr.2012010104

Talevi, A., Castro, E. A., & Bruno-Blanch, L. E. (2012). Virtual screening: An emergent, key methodology for drug development in an emergent continent: A bridge towards patentability. In E. Castro & A. Haghi (Eds.), *Advanced methods and applications in chemoinformatics: Research progress and new applications* (pp. 229–245). Hershey, PA: Engineering Science Reference; doi:10.4018/978-1-60960-860-6.ch011

Tauber, A. (2012). Requirements and properties of qualified electronic delivery systems in egovernment: An Austrian experience. In S. Sharma (Ed.), *E-adoption and technologies for empowering developing countries: Global advances* (pp. 115–128). Hershey, PA: Information Science Reference; doi:10.4018/978-1-4666-0041-6.ch009

Telesko, R., & Nikles, S. (2012). Semantic-enabled compliance management. In S. Smolnik, F. Teuteberg, & O. Thomas (Eds.), *Semantic technologies for business and information systems engineering: Concepts and applications* (pp. 292–310). Hershey, PA: Business Science Reference; doi:10.4018/978-1-60960-126-3.ch015

Tella, A., & Afolabi, A. K. (2013). Internet policy issues and digital libraries' management of intellectual property. In S. Thanuskodi (Ed.), *Challenges of academic library management in developing countries* (pp. 272–284). Hershey, PA: Information Science Reference; doi:10.4018/978-1-4666-4070-2.ch019

Tiwari, S. C., Gupta, M., Khan, M. A., & Ansari, A. Q. (2013). Intellectual property rights in semiconductor industries: An Indian perspective. In S. Saeed, M. Khan, & R. Ahmad (Eds.), *Business strategies and approaches for effective engineering management* (pp. 97–110). Hershey, PA: Business Science Reference; doi:10.4018/978-1-4666-3658-3.ch006

Truyen, F., & Buekens, F. (2013). Professional ICT knowledge, epistemic standards, and social epistemology. In T. Takševa (Ed.), *Social software and the evolution of user expertise: Future trends in knowledge creation and dissemination* (pp. 274–294). Hershey, PA: Information Science Reference; doi:10.4018/978-1-4666-2178-7.ch016

Tummons, J. (2011). Deconstructing professionalism: An actor-network critique of professional standards for teachers in the UK lifelong learning sector. [IJANTTI]. *International Journal of Actor-Network Theory and Technological Innovation*, 3(4), 22–31. doi:10.4018/jantti.2011100103

Tummons, J. (2013). Deconstructing professionalism: An actor-network critique of professional standards for teachers in the UK lifelong learning sector. In A. Tatnall (Ed.), *Social and professional applications of actor-network theory for technology development* (pp. 78–87). Hershey, PA: Information Science Reference; doi:10.4018/978-1-4666-2166-4.ch007

Tuohey, W. G. (2014). Lessons from practices and standards in safety-critical and regulated sectors. In I. Ghani, W. Kadir, & M. Ahmad (Eds.), *Handbook of research on emerging advancements and technologies in software engineering* (pp. 369–391). Hershey, PA: Engineering Science Reference; doi:10.4018/978-1-4666-6026-7.ch016

Tzoulia, E. (2013). Legal issues to be considered before setting in force consumer-centric marketing strategies within the European Union. In H. Kaufmann & M. Panni (Eds.), *Customer-centric marketing strategies: Tools for building organizational performance* (pp. 36–56). Hershey, PA: Business Science Reference; doi:10.4018/978-1-4666-2524-2.ch003

Unland, R. (2012). Interoperability support for e-business applications through standards, services, and multi-agent systems. In E. Kajan, F. Dorloff, & I. Bedini (Eds.), *Handbook of research on e-business standards and protocols: Documents, data and advanced web technologies* (pp. 129–153). Hershey, PA: Business Science Reference; doi:10.4018/978-1-4666-0146-8.ch007

Uslar, M., Grüning, F., & Rohjans, S. (2013). A use case for ontology evolution and interoperability: The IEC utility standards reference framework 62357. In M. Khosrow-Pour (Ed.), *Cases on performance measurement and productivity improvement: Technology integration and maturity* (pp. 387–415). Hershey, PA: Business Science Reference; doi:10.4018/978-1-4666-2618-8.ch018

van de Kaa, G. (2013). Responsible innovation and standardization: A new research approach? [IJITSR]. *International Journal of IT Standards and Standardization Research*, 11(2), 61–65. doi:10.4018/jitsr.2013070105

van de Kaa, G., Blind, K., & de Vries, H. J. (2013). The challenge of establishing a recognized interdisciplinary journal: A citation analysis of the international journal of IT standards and standardization research. [IJITSR]. *International Journal of IT Standards and Standardization Research*, 11(2), 1–16. doi:10.4018/jitsr.2013070101

Venkataraman, H., Ciubotaru, B., & Muntean, G. (2012). System design perspective: WiMAX standards and IEEE 802.16j based multihop WiMAX. In G. Cornetta, D. Santos, & J. Vazquez (Eds.), *Wireless radio-frequency standards and system design: Advanced techniques* (pp. 287–309). Hershey, PA: Engineering Science Reference; doi:10.4018/978-1-4666-0083-6.ch012

Vishwakarma, P., & Mukherjee, B. (2014). Knowing protection of intellectual contents in digital era. In N. Patra, B. Kumar, & A. Pani (Eds.), *Progressive trends in electronic resource management in libraries* (pp. 147–165). Hershey, PA: Information Science Reference; doi:10.4018/978-1-4666-4761-9.ch008

Wasilko, P. J. (2011). Law, architecture, gameplay, and marketing. In M. Cruz-Cunha, V. Varvalho, & P. Tavares (Eds.), *Business, technological, and social dimensions of computer games: Multidisciplinary developments* (pp. 476–493). Hershey, PA: Information Science Reference; doi:10.4018/978-1-60960-567-4.ch029

Wasilko, P. J. (2012). Law, architecture, gameplay, and marketing. In *Computer engineering: concepts, methodologies, tools and applications* (pp. 1660–1677). Hershey, PA: Engineering Science Reference; doi:10.4018/978-1-61350-456-7.ch703

Wasilko, P. J. (2014). Beyond compliance: Understanding the legal aspects of information system administration. In I. Portela & F. Almeida (Eds.), *Organizational, legal, and technological dimensions of information system administration* (pp. 57–75). Hershey, PA: Information Science Reference; doi:10.4018/978-1-4666-4526-4.ch004

White, G. L., Mediavilla, F. A., & Shah, J. R. (2011). Information privacy: Implementation and perception of laws and corporate policies by CEOs and managers. [IJISP]. *International Journal of Information Security and Privacy*, 5(1), 50–66. doi:10.4018/jisp.2011010104

White, G. L., Mediavilla, F. A., & Shah, J. R. (2013). Information privacy: Implementation and perception of laws and corporate policies by CEOs and managers. In H. Nemati (Ed.), *Privacy solutions and security frameworks in information protection* (pp. 52–69). Hershey, PA: Information Science Reference; doi:10.4018/978-1-4666-2050-6.ch004

Whyte, K. P., List, M., Stone, J. V., Grooms, D., Gasteyer, S., Thompson, P. B., & Bouri, H. et al. (2014). Uberveillance, standards, and anticipation: A case study on nanobiosensors in U.S. cattle. In M. Michael & K. Michael (Eds.), *Uberveillance and the social implications of microchip implants: Emerging technologies* (pp. 260–279). Hershey, PA: Information Science Reference; doi:10.4018/978-1-4666-4582-0.ch012

Wilkes, W., Reusch, P. J., & Moreno, L. E. (2012). Flexible classification standards for product data exchange. In E. Kajan, F. Dorloff, & I. Bedini (Eds.), *Handbook of research on e-business standards and protocols: Documents, data and advanced web technologies* (pp. 448–466). Hershey, PA: Business Science Reference; doi:10.4018/978-1-4666-0146-8.ch021

Wittkower, D. E. (2011). Against strong copyright in e-business. In *Global business: Concepts, methodologies, tools and applications* (pp. 2157–2176). Hershey, PA: Business Science Reference; doi:10.4018/978-1-60960-587-2.ch720

Wright, D. (2012). Evolution of standards for smart grid communications. [IJITN]. *International Journal of Interdisciplinary Telecommunications and Networking*, 4(1), 47–55. doi:10.4018/jitn.2012010103

Wurster, S. (2013). Development of a specification for data interchange between information systems in public hazard prevention: Dimensions of success and related activities identified by case study research. [IJITSR]. *International Journal of IT Standards and Standardization Research*, 11(1), 46–66. doi:10.4018/jitsr.2013010103

Wyburn, M. (2011). Copyright and ethical issues in emerging models for the digital media reporting of sports news in Australia. In M. Quigley (Ed.), *ICT ethics and security in the 21st century: New developments and applications* (pp. 66–85). Hershey, PA: Information Science Reference; doi:10.4018/978-1-60960-573-5.ch004

Wyburn, M. (2013). Copyright and ethical issues in emerging models for the digital media reporting of sports news in Australia. In *Digital rights management: Concepts, methodologies, tools, and applications* (pp. 290–309). Hershey, PA: Information Science Reference; doi:10.4018/978-1-4666-2136-7.ch014

Xiaohui, T., Yaohui, Z., & Yi, Z. (2012). The management system of enterprises' intellectual property rights: A case study from China. [IJABIM]. *International Journal of Asian Business and Information Management*, 3(1), 50–64. doi:10.4018/jabim.2012010105

Xiaohui, T., Yaohui, Z., & Yi, Z. (2013). The management system of enterprises' intellectual property rights: A case study from China. In *Digital rights management: Concepts, methodologies, tools, and applications* (pp. 1092–1106). Hershey, PA: Information Science Reference; doi:10.4018/978-1-4666-2136-7.ch053

Xuan, X., & Xiaowei, Z. (2012). The dilemma and resolution: The patentability of traditional Chinese medicine. [IJABIM]. *International Journal of Asian Business and Information Management*, 3(3), 1–8. doi:10.4018/jabim.2012070101

Yang, C., & Lu, Z. (2011). A blind image watermarking scheme utilizing BTC bitplanes. [IJDCF]. *International Journal of Digital Crime and Forensics*, 3(4), 42–53. doi:10.4018/jdcf.2011100104

Yastrebenetsky, M., & Gromov, G. (2014). International standard bases and safety classification. In M. Yastrebenetsky & V. Kharchenko (Eds.), *Nuclear power plant instrumentation and control systems for safety and security* (pp. 31–60). Hershey, PA: Engineering Science Reference; doi:10.4018/978-1-4666-5133-3.ch002

Zouag, N., & Kadiri, M. (2014). Intellectual property rights, innovation, and knowledge economy in Arab countries. In A. Driouchi (Ed.), *Knowledge-based economic policy development in the Arab world* (pp. 245–272). Hershey, PA: Business Science Reference; doi:10.4018/978-1-4666-5210-1.ch010

Compilation of References

Abouzeid, A., Bajda-Pawlikowski, K., Abadi, D., Silberschatz, A., & Rasin, A. (2009). HadoopDB: An architectural hybrid of MapReduce and DBMS technologies for analytical workloads. *Proceedings of the VLDB Endowment*, *2*(1), 922–933. doi:10.14778/1687627.1687731

Agarwal, S., Iyer, A. P., Panda, A., Madden, S., Mozafari, B., & Stoica, I. (2012). Blink and it's done: Interactive queries on very large data. *Proceedings of the VLDB Endowment*, *5*(12), 1902–1905. doi:10.14778/2367502.2367533

Agarwal, S., Mozafari, B., Panda, A., Milner, H., Madden, S., & Stoica, I. (2013). BlinkDB: queries with bounded errors and bounded response times on very large data. In *Proceedings of the 8th ACM European Conference on Computer Systems* (pp. 29–42). ACM. doi:10.1145/2465351.2465355

Aha, D. W., Kibler, D., & Albert, M. K. (1991). Instance-based learning algorithms. *Machine Learning*, *6*(1), 37–66. doi:10.1007/BF00153759

Aiello, L. M., Milanesio, M., Ruffo, G., & Schifanella, R. (2008, September). Tempering Kademlia with a robust identity based system. In *Peer-to-Peer Computing, 2008. P2P'08. Eighth International Conference on* (pp. 30-39). IEEE. doi:10.1109/P2P.2008.40

Aiello, L. M., & Ruffo, G. (2012). LotusNet: Tunable privacy for distributed online social network services. *Computer Communications*, *35*(1), 75–88. doi:10.1016/j.comcom.2010.12.006

Alexandrov, A., Bergmann, R., Ewen, S., Freytag, J.-C., Hueske, F., Heise, A., & Markl, V. et al. (2014). The Stratosphere platform for big data analytics. *The VLDB Journal*, *23*(6), 939–964. doi:10.1007/s00778-014-0357-y

Ali, S., Veltri, R., Epstein, J. I., Christudass, C., & Madabhushi, A. (2011). Adaptive energy selective active contour with shape priors for nuclear segmentation and gleason grading of prostate cancer. In *Proceedings of Medical Image Computing and Computer-Assisted Intervention–MICCAI 2011*. Toronto, Canada: Springer. doi:10.1007/978-3-642-23623-5_83

Al-Kadi, O. S. (2010). Texture measures combination for improved meningioma classification of histopathological images. *Pattern Recognition*, *43*(6), 2043–2053. doi:10.1016/j.patcog.2010.01.005

Al-Kadi, O. S. (2015). A multiresolution clinical decision support system based on fractal model design for classification of histological brain tumours. *Computerized Medical Imaging and Graphics*, *41*, 67–79. doi:10.1016/j.compmedimag.2014.05.013 PMID:24962336

Amanatullah, Y., Lim, C., Ipung, H. P., & Juliandri, A. (2013). *Toward Cloud Computing Reference Architecture: Cloud Service Management Perspective*. Paper presented at the International Conference on ICT for Smart Society (ICISS), Jakarta, Indonesia.

Amazon simple storage service (2011). Available: www.aws.amazon.com/s3/

Amazon. (2015). AWS - Big Data Analytics. Retrieved February 2, 2015, from http://aws.amazon.com/big-data/

Ananthanarayanan, G., Agarwal, S., Kandula, S., Greenberg, A., Stoica, I., Harlan, D., ... (2011). Scarlett: coping with skewed content popularity in mapreduce clusters. In Proceedings of the sixth conference on computer systems (pp. 287–300). New York, NY, USA: ACM; Available from http://doi.acm.org/10.1145/1966445.1966472 doi:10.1145/1966445.1966472

Ananthanarayanan, G., Ghodsi, A., Shenker, S., & Stoica, I. (2013). Effective straggler mitigation: Attack of the clones. In Proceedings of the 10th usenix conference on networked systems design and implementation (pp. 185–198). Berkeley, CA, USA: USENIX Association; Available from http://dl.acm.org/citation.cfm?id=2482626.2482645

Ananthanarayanan, G., Kandula, S., Greenberg, A., Stoica, I., Lu, Y., Saha, B., ... (2010). Reining in the outliers in map-reduce clusters using Mantri. In Proceedings of the 9th usenix conference on operating systems design and implementation (pp. 1–16). Berkeley, CA, USA: USENIX Association; Available from http://dl.acm.org/ citation. cfm?id=1924943.1924962

Anderson, R. J., Mayr, E. W., & Warmuth, M. K. (1989). Parallel approximation algorithms for Bin packing. *Information and Computation*, *82*(3), 262–277. doi:10.1016/0890-5401(89)90003-5

Anjan, Srinath, Sharma, Kumar, Madhu, & Shanbag. (2012). Map Reduce Design and Implementation of a Priori Algorithm for Handling Voluminous data-sets. Advanced Computing: An International Journal, 3(6).

Apache Hadoop NextGen MapReduce (YARN). (2015). http://hadoop.apache.org/docs/ current/hadoop-yarn/hadoop-yarn-site/YARN.html

Apache Hadoop Project. (2015). http://hadoop.apache.org/

Apache Zookeeper. (2015). http://zookeeper.apache.org/

Apache. (2015). Apache Tez. Retrieved March 14, 2015, from http://hortonworks.com/hadoop/tez/

Armbrust, et al. (2009). Above the Clouds: A Berkeley View of Cloud Computing. Berkeley Technical Report. University of California.

Armbrust, M., Fox, A., Griffith, R., Anthony, D. J., Randy, H. K., Konwinski, A., . . . Zaharia, M. (2009). *Above the Clouds: A Berkeley View of Cloud Computing.* University of California at Berkley, USA. Technical Rep UCB/EECS-2009-28.

Atupelage, C., Nagahashi, H., Yamaguchi, M., Abe, T., Hashiguchi, A., & Sakamoto, M. (2013). Computational grading of hepatocellular carcinoma using multifractal feature description. *Computerized Medical Imaging and Graphics*, *37*(1), 61–71. doi:10.1016/j.compmedimag.2012.10.001 PMID:23141965

Baden, R., Bender, A., Spring, N., Bhattacharjee, B., & Starin, D. (2009, August). Persona: An online social network with user-defined privacy.[). ACM.]. *Computer Communication Review*, *39*(4), 135–146. doi:10.1145/1594977.1592585

Baer, T. (2013). Hadoop as your other data warehouse. Retrieved February 24, 2015, from http://www.onstrategies.com/ blog/2013/05/05/hadoop-as-your-other-data-warehouse/

Bandyopadhyay, D., & Sen, J. (2011). Internet of things: Applications and challenges in technology and standardization. *Wireless Personal Communications*, *58*(1), 49–69. doi:10.1007/s11277-011-0288-5

Barrachina & O'Driscoll. (2014). A big data methodology for categorizing technical support requests using Hadoop and Mahout. *Journal of Big Data.*

Baru, C., Bhandarkar, M., Curino, C., Danisch, M., Frank, M., & Gowda, B. … Youn, C. (2014). Discussion of BigBench: A Proposed Industry Standard Performance Benchmark for Big Data. In R. Nambiar & M. Poess (Eds.), Performance Characterization and Benchmarking. Traditional to Big Data (pp. 44–63). Springer International Publishing.

Baru, C., Bhandarkar, M., Nambiar, R., Poess, M., & Rabl, T. (2013a). Benchmarking Big Data Systems and the BigData Top100 List. *Big Data*, *1*(1), 60–64. doi:10.1089/big.2013.1509

Baru, C., Bhandarkar, M., Nambiar, R., Poess, M., & Rabl, T. (2013b). Setting the Direction for Big Data Benchmark Standards. In R. Nambiar & M. Poess (Eds.), *Selected Topics in Performance Evaluation and Benchmarking* (pp. 197–208). Springer Berlin Heidelberg; doi:10.1007/978-3-642-36727-4_14

Bash, C., & Forman, G. (2007, June). Cool Job Allocation: Measuring the Power Savings of Placing Jobs at Cooling-Efficient Locations in the Data Center. In *USENIX Annual Technical Conference* (*Vol. 138*, p. 140). USENIX.

Beloglazov, A., & Buyya, R. (2012). Optimal online deterministic algorithms and adaptive heuristics for energy and performance efficient dynamic consolidation of virtual machines in cloud data centers. *Concurrency and Computation*, *24*(13), 1397–1420. doi:10.1002/cpe.1867

Bhuiyan, M. F. H., & Wang, C. (2013). Energy-Efficient Virtual Machine Management in Heterogeneous Environment: Challenges, Approaches and Opportunities. In *Proceedings of Systems, Man, and Cybernetics (SMC), 2013 IEEE International Conference on*. IEEE. doi:10.1109/SMC.2013.702

Bodriagov, O., Kreitz, G., & Buchegger, S. (2014, March). Access control in decentralized online social networks: Applying a policy-hiding cryptographic scheme and evaluating its performance. In *Pervasive Computing and Communications Workshops (PERCOM Workshops), 2014 IEEE International Conference on* (pp. 622-628). IEEE.

Bodriagov, O., & Buchegger, S. (2013). *Encryption for peer-to-peer social networks* (pp. 47–65). Springer New York.

Borthakur, D., Gray, J., Sarma, J. S., Muthukkaruppan, K., Spiegelberg, N., Kuang, H., ... (2011). Apache Hadoop goes realtime at Facebook. In Proceedings of the 2011 acm sigmod international conference on management of data (pp. 1071–1080). New York, NY, USA: ACM; Available from http://doi.acm.org/10.1145/1989323.1989438 doi:10.1145/1989323.1989438

Borthakur, D. (2008). *HDFS architecture guide*. Apache Hadoop.

Boulon, J., Konwinski, A., Qi, R., Rabkin, A., Yang, E., & Yang, M. (2008). Chukwa, a large-scale monitoring system. In *Proceedings of CCA* (Vol. 8).

Breiman, L. (2001). Random forests. *Machine Learning*, *45*(1), 5–32. doi:10.1023/A:1010933404324

Bressoud, T. C., & Kozuch, M. A. (2009). Cluster fault-tolerance: An experimental evaluation of checkpointing and MapReduce through simulation. In Proceedings of the 2009 IEEE International Conference on Cluster Computing and Workshops (CLUSTER'09) (pp. 1–10). New York, NY, USA: IEEE. Available from doi:10.1109/CLUSTR.2009.5289185

Broch, J. (1998). A performance comparison of multi-hop wireless ad hoc network routing protocols. In *Proceedings of the 4th annual ACM/IEEE international conference on Mobile computing and networking*. ACM. doi:10.1145/288235.288256

Bryant, R., Katz, R. H., & Lazowska, E. D. (2008). *Big-data computing: creating revolutionary breakthroughs in commerce, science and society*. Academic Press.

Buchegger, S., & Datta, A. (2009, February). A case for P2P infrastructure for social networks-opportunities & challenges. In *Wireless On-Demand Network Systems and Services, 2009. WONS 2009. Sixth International Conference on* (pp. 161-168). IEEE. doi:10.1109/WONS.2009.4801862

Buchegger, S., Schiöberg, D., Vu, L. H., & Datta, A. (2009, March). PeerSoN: P2P social networking: early experiences and insights. In *Proceedings of the Second ACM EuroSys Workshop on Social Network Systems* (pp. 46-52). ACM.

Bu, Y., Howe, B., Balazinska, M., & Ernst, M. D. (2010). HaLoop: Efficient iterative data processing on large clusters. *Proceedings of the VLDB Endowment, 3*(1-2), 285–296. doi:10.14778/1920841.1920881

Bu, Y., Howe, B., Balazinska, M., & Ernst, M. D. (2012). The HaLoop approach to large-scale iterative data analysis. *The VLDB Journal, 21*(2), 169–190. doi:10.1007/s00778-012-0269-7

Buyya, R., Yeo, C., Venugopal, S., Broberg, J., & Brandic, I. (2009). Cloud Computing and Emerging IT Platforms: Vision, Hype, and Reality for Delivering Computing as the 5th Utility. *Future Generation Computer Systems, 25*(6), 599–616. doi:10.1016/j.future.2008.12.001

Cachin, C., Guerraoui, R., & Rodrigues, L. (2011). Introduction to Reliable and Secure Distributed Programming (2. ed.). Springer.

Caldarola, E. G., Sacco, M., & Terkaj, W. (2014). Big Data: the current wave front of the tsunami. ACS Applied Computer Science, 10(4).

Caldarola, G. G., Picariello, A., & Castelluccia, D. (2015). Modern Enterprises in the Bubble: Why Big Data Matters. *Software Engineering Notes, 40*(1), 1–4. doi:10.1145/2693208.2693228

Capriolo, E., Wampler, D., & Rutherglen, J. (2012). *Programming Hive.* O'Reilly.

Cattell, R. (2011). Scalable SQL and NoSQL data stores. *SIGMOD Record, 39*(4), 12–27. doi:10.1145/1978915.1978919

Chandra, A., Prinja, R., Jain, S., & Zhang, Z. (2008, August). Co-designing the failure analysis and monitoring of large-scale systems. SIGMETRICS Perform. Eval. Rev., 36, 10–15. Available from http://doi.acm.org/10.1145/1453175.1453178

Chang, F., Dean, J., Ghemawat, S., Hsieh, W. C., Wallach, D. A., Burrows, M., & Gruber, R. E. et al. (2008). Bigtable: A distributed storage system for structured data. *ACM Transactions on Computer Systems, 26*(2), 4. doi:10.1145/1365815.1365816

Cheng, B., Stein, L., Jin, H., & Zheng, Z. (2008). Towards Cinematic Internet Video-On-Demand. In *Proceedings of the 3rd ACM SIGOPS/EuroSys European Conference on Computer Systems.* ACM.

Chen, Q., Liu, C., & Xiao, Z. (2014, April). Improving mapreduce performance using smart speculative execution strategy. Computers. *IEEE Transactions on, 63*(4), 954–967.

Chen, Y., Alspaugh, S., & Katz, R. H. (2012). Interactive analytical processing in big data systems: A cross-industry study of mapreduce workloads. *Proceedings of VLDB Endowment, 5*(12), 1802–1813. doi:10.14778/2367502.2367519

Chiluka, N., Andrade, N., Pouwelse, J., & Sips, H. (2015, April). Social Networks Meet Distributed Systems: Towards a Robust Sybil Defense under Churn. In *Proceedings of the 10th ACM Symposium on Information, Computer and Communications Security* (pp. 507-518). ACM. doi:10.1145/2714576.2714606

Chohan, N., Castillo, C., Spreitzer, M., Steinder, M., Tantawi, A., & Krintz, C. (2010). See Spot Run: Using Spot Instances for MapReduce Workflows. In Proceedings of the 2nd usenix conference on hot topics in cloud computing (pp. 7–7). Berkeley, CA, USA: USENIX Association. Available from http://dl.acm.org/citation.cfm?id= 1863103.1863110

Choi, H., Son, J., Yang, H., Ryu, H., Lim, B., Kim, S., & Chung, Y. D. (2013). Tajo: A distributed data warehouse system on large clusters. In 2013 IEEE 29th International Conference on Data Engineering (ICDE) (pp. 1320–1323). IEEE.

Choi, B., & Yao, Z. (2005). Web Page Classification.[Springer.]. *Studies in Fuzziness and Soft Computing., 180,* 221–274. doi:10.1007/11362197_9

Choi, H.-J., & Choi, H.-K. (2007). Grading of renal cell carcinoma by 3d morphological analysis of cell nuclei. *Computers in Biology and Medicine, 37*(9), 1334–1341. doi:10.1016/j.compbiomed.2006.12.008 PMID:17331492

Chun, B.-G., Condie, T., Curino, C., Douglas, C., Matusevych, S., & Myers, B., ... Rosen, J. (2013). REEF: retainable evaluator execution framework. Proceedings of the VLDB Endowment, 6(12), 1370–1373.

Chun, S. I. B.-G., Maniatis, P., & Naik, M. (2010). Clonecloud: boosting mobile device applications through cloud clone execution. *arXiv preprint arXiv:1009.3088*,

Cloudera. (2015). Oryx 2. Retrieved February 20, 2015, from https://github.com/OryxProject/oryx

Cocking, L. (2012). *The Future of Mobile Cloud Infrastructure*. Available: http://www.guardtime.com/2012/08/13/the-future-of mobile cloud- infrastructure/

Cooper, B. F., Ramakrishnan, R., Srivastava, U., Silberstein, A., Bohannon, P., Jacobsen, H.-A., & Yerneni, R. et al. (2008). PNUTS:Yahoo!'s hosted data serving platform. *Proceedings of the VLDB Endowment, 1*(2), 1277–1288. doi:10.14778/1454159.1454167

Correia, M., Costa, P., Pasin, M., Bessani, A., Ramos, F., & Verissimo, P. (2012, Oct). On the feasibility of byzantine fault-tolerant mapreduce in clouds-of-clouds. In Reliable distributed systems (srds), 2012 ieee 31st symposium on (p. 448-453). doi:10.1109/SRDS.2012.46

Costa, P., Pasin, M., Bessani, A., & Correia, M. (2010). Byzantine Fault-Tolerant MapReduce: Faults are Not Just Crashes. In Proceedings of the 3rd ieee second international conference on cloud computing technology and science (pp. 17–24). Washington, DC, USA: IEEE Computer Society. Available from doi:10.1109/CloudCom.2010.25

Cuervo, A. B. E., Cho, D.-k., Wolman, A., Saroiu, S., Chandra, R., & Bahl, P. (2010). Maui: making smartphones last longer with code offload. *8th international conference on Mobile systems, applications, and services,* pp. 49–62. doi:10.1145/1814433.1814441

Cuervo, A. B. E., Cho, D.-k., Wolman, A., Saroiu, S., Chandra, R., & Bahl, P. (2010).Making smartphones last longer with code offload. In *8th international conference on Mobile systems, applications, and services,* pp. 49–62.

Cutillo, L. A., Molva, R., & Strufe, T. (2009, February). Privacy preserving social networking through decentralization. In *Wireless On-Demand Network Systems and Services, 2009. WONS 2009. Sixth International Conference on*(pp. 145-152). IEEE. doi:10.1109/WONS.2009.4801860

Cutillo, L. A., Molva, R., & Strufe, T. (2009). Safebook: A privacy-preserving online social network leveraging on real-life trust. *Communications Magazine, IEEE, 47*(12), 94–101. doi:10.1109/MCOM.2009.5350374

Dai, J., Huang, J., Huang, S., Huang, B., & Liu, Y. (2011). HiTune: dataflow-based performance analysis for big data cloud. In Proc. of the 2011 USENIX ATC, (pp. 87-100). USENIX.

Dawei, L., & Rui, W. (2013). *Large-Scale IP Network Testbed Based on OS-level Virtualization*. Paper presented at the International Conference on Cloud Computing and Big Data (CloudCom-Asia), Fuzhou, China.

De Cristofaro, E., Manulis, M., & Poettering, B. (2011, January). Private discovery of common social contacts. In *Applied Cryptography and Network Security* (pp. 147–165). Springer Berlin Heidelberg. doi:10.1007/978-3-642-21554-4_9

De Cristofaro, E., Manulis, M., & Poettering, B. (2013). Private discovery of common social contacts. *International Journal of Information Security, 12*(1), 49–65. doi:10.1007/s10207-012-0183-4

De Francisci Morales, G. (2013). SAMOA: A platform for mining big data streams. In *Proceedings of the 22nd international conference on World Wide Web companion* (pp. 777–778). International World Wide Web Conferences Steering Committee.

Dean, J. (2006). Experiences with MapReduce, an abstraction for large-scale computation. In Proceedings of the 15th international conference on parallel architectures and compilation techniques (pp. 1–1). New York, NY, USA: ACM; Available from http://doi.acm.org/10.1145/1152154.1152155 doi:10.1145/1152154.1152155

Dean, J. (2010). Building Software Systems at Google and Lessons Learned. (Stanford EE Computer Systems Colloquium. Available at http://www.stanford.edu/class/ ee380/Abstracts/101110-slides.pdf)

Dean, J., & Ghemawat, S. (2004). MapReduce: simplified data processing on large clusters. In Proceedings of the 6th conference on symposium on operating systems design & implementation. USENIX Association. doi:10.1145/1327452.1327492

Dejan Kovachev, Y. C. R. K. (2009). *Mobile Cloud Computing: A Comparison of Application Models.* Middleware Springer.

Demirkan, H., & Delen, D. (2013). Leveraging the capabilities of service-oriented decision support systems: Putting analytics and big data in cloud. *Decision Support Systems, 55*(1), 412–421. doi:10.1016/j.dss.2012.05.048

Deng, W., Liu, F., Jin, H., Liao, X., Liu, H., & Chen, L. (2012, December). Lifetime or energy: Consolidating servers with reliability control in virtualized cloud datacenters. In *Cloud Computing Technology and Science (CloudCom), 2012 IEEE 4th International Conference on* (pp. 18-25). IEEE.

Design, H. D. F. S. (2015). Retrieved from http://hadoop.apache.org/docs/r1.2.1/hdfs design.html

Devi, M. I., Rajaram, R., & Selvakuberan, K. (2008, March 1). *Generating best features for web page classification.* Retrieved Jul 15, 2015, from Generating best features for web page classification: http://www.webology.org/2008/v5n1/a52.html

DeWitt, D. J., Halverson, A., Nehme, R., Shankar, S., Aguilar-Saborit, J., & Avanes, A. (2013). *Gramling, J.* Split Query Processing in Polybase. SIGMOD.

Dhiman, G., Marchetti, G., & Rosing, T. (2010). vGreen: A System for Energy-Efficient Management of Virtual Machines. *ACM Transactions on Design Automation of Electronic Systems, 16*(1), 1–27. doi:10.1145/1870109.1870115

Dinh, C. L. H. T., Niyato, D., & Wang, P. (2011). *A survey of mobile cloud computing: architecture, applications, and approaches.* Wireless Communications and Mobile Computing.

Dinu, F., & Ng, T. E. (2012). Understanding the effects and implications of compute node related failures in Hadoop. In Hpdc '12: Proceedings of the 21st international symposium on high-performance parallel and distributed computing (pp. 187–198). New York, NY, USA: ACM.

Dinu, F., & Ng, T. S. E. (2011). Hadoop's Overload Tolerant Design Exacerbates Failure Detection and Recovery. In *Proceedings of the 9th usenix conference on operating systems design and implementation* (pp. 1–7). New York, NY, USA: ACM.

Dittrich, J., Quiané-Ruiz, J.-A., Jindal, A., Kargin, Y., Setty, V., & Schad, J. (2010). Hadoop++: Making a yellow elephant run like a cheetah (without it even noticing). *Proceedings of the VLDB Endowment, 3*(1-2), 515–529. doi:10.14778/1920841.1920908

Docker. (2014). Docker. Retrieved February 23, 2015, from https://www.docker.com/

Dong, F., Irshad, H., Oh, E.-Y., Lerwill, M. F., Brachtel, E. F., Jones, N. C., … Beck, A. H. (2014). Computational pathology to discriminate benign from malignant intraductal proliferations of the breast. *PLoS ONE, 9*(12).

Doukas, T. P. I. M. C. (2010). Mobile healthcare information management utilizing cloud computing and Android OS. In *Engineering in Medicine and Biology Society (EMBC), Annual International Conference of the IEEE.*, pp. 1037–1040, Aug. 31-Sept. 4 2010.

Duggan, J., Elmore, A., Kraska, T., Madden, S., Mattson, T., & Stonebraker, M. (2015). *The BigDawg Architecture and Reference Implementation*. New England Database Day.

Dundar, M. M., Badve, S., Bilgin, G., Raykar, V., Jain, R., Sertel, O., & Gurcan, M. N. (2011). Computerized classification of intraductal breast lesions using histopathological images. *IEEE Transactions on Bio-Medical Engineering, 58*(7), 1977–1984. doi:10.1109/TBME.2011.2110648 PMID:21296703

Durr, M., Maier, M., & Dorfmeister, F. (2012, September). Vegas--A Secure and Privacy-Preserving Peer-to-Peer Online Social Network. In *Privacy, Security, Risk and Trust (PASSAT), 2012 International Conference on and 2012 International Confernece on Social Computing (SocialCom)* (pp. 868-874). IEEE.

Ekmecic, I., Tartalja, I., & Milutinovic, V. (1996). A survey of heterogeneous computing: Concepts and systems. *Proceedings of the IEEE, 84*(8), 1127–1144. doi:10.1109/5.533958

Engle, C., Lupher, A., Xin, R., Zaharia, M., Franklin, M. J., Shenker, S., & Stoica, I. (2012). Shark: Fast Data Analysis Using Coarse-grained Distributed Memory. In *Proceedings of the 2012 ACM SIGMOD International Conference on Management of Data* (pp. 689–692). New York, NY: ACM. doi:10.1145/2213836.2213934

Epstein, A., Lorenz, D. H., Silvera, E., & Shapira, I. (2010). *Virtual Appliance Content Distribution for a Global Infrastructure Cloud Service*. San Diego, CA: INFOCOM IEEE. doi:10.1109/INFCOM.2010.5462176

Facebook, Inc. (2015). https://www.facebook.com/

Fan, C. (2012). CRAP and CRUD: From Database to Datacloud. Retrieved February 11, 2015, from http://reflectionsblog.emc.com/2012/11/crap-and-crud-from-database-to-datacloud.html

Fan, W., & Bifet, A. (2012). Mining Big Data: Current Status and Forecast to the Future. *SIGKDD Explorations Newsletter, 14*.

Fatima, K., Arooj, A., & Majeed, H. (2014). A new texture and shape based technique for improving meningioma classification. *Microscopy Research and Technique, 77*(11), 862–873. doi:10.1002/jemt.22409 PMID:25060536

Feller, Morin, & Esnault. (2012). *A case for fully decentralized dynamic VM consolidation in clouds*. INRIA.

Fisher, D., DeLine, R., Czerwinski, M., & Drucker, S. (2012). Interactions with big data analytics. *Interaction, 19*(3), 50–59. doi:10.1145/2168931.2168943

Forsyth, S., & Daudjee, K. (2013, July). Update Management in Decentralized Social Networks. In *2013 IEEE 33rd International Conference on Distributed Computing Systems Workshops* (pp. 196-201). IEEE. doi:10.1109/ICDCSW.2013.54

Frey, D., Kermarrec, A. M., & Leroy, V. (2009). PAPEER: Bringing Social Networks into Research.

Galloway, M. (1975). Texture analysis using gray level run lengths. *Computer Graphics and Image Processing, 4*(2), 172–179. doi:10.1016/S0146-664X(75)80008-6

Garfinkel, T., & Rosenblum, M. (2003). A Virtual Machine Introspection Based Architecture For Intrusion Detection, San Diego, California. In *Proceedings of The Internet Society's 2003 Symposium on Network and Distributed Systems Security IEEE*. IEEE.

Gartner. (2014). *Gartner Says 4.9 Billion Connected "Things" Will Be in Use in 2015*. Retrieved July 5, 2015, from http://www.gartner.com/newsroom/id/2905717

Gartner. Available: http://www.gartner.com/newsroom/id/1529214

Gates, A. F., Natkovich, O., Chopra, S., Kamath, P., Narayanamurthy, S. M., & Olston, C., ... Srivastava, U. (2009). Building a high-level dataflow system on top of Map-Reduce: the Pig experience. Proceedings of the VLDB Endowment, 2(2), 1414–1425. doi:10.14778/1687553.1687568

George, L. (2011). *HBase: the definitive guide*. O'Reilly Media, Inc.

Gesbert, D., Bölcskei, H., Gore, D., & Paulraj, A. J. (2002). Outdoor MIMO wireless channels: Models and performance prediction. *Communications. IEEE Transactions on, 50*(12), 1926–1934. doi:10.1109/TCOMM.2002.806555

Gholamhosseinian, A., & Khalifeh, A. (2012). *Cloud computing and sustainability: Energy efficiency aspects*. Academic Press.

Glotsos, D., Kalatzis, I., Spyridonos, P., Kostopoulos, S., Daskalakis, A., Athanasiadis, E., & Cavouras, D. et al. (2008). Improving accuracy in astrocytomas grading by integrating a robust least squares mapping driven support vector machine classifier into a two level grade classification scheme. *Computer Methods and Programs in Biomedicine, 90*(3), 251–261. doi:10.1016/j.cmpb.2008.01.006 PMID:18343526

Gluster, F. S. (2015). Retrieved from http://en.wikipedia.org/wiki/GlusterFS

GoGrid. (2015). GoGrid Solutions. Retrieved February 2, 2015, from http://www.gogrid.com/solutions

Gonzalez, J. E., Xin, R. S., Dave, A., Crankshaw, D., Franklin, M. J., & Stoica, I. (2014). Graphx: Graph processing in a distributed dataflow framework. In *Proceedings of the 11th USENIX Symposium on Operating Systems Design and Implementation (OSDI)*.

Gonzalez, R. C., & Woods, R. E. (2009). *Digital Image Processing* (3rd ed.). India: Pearson Education Inc.

Google. (2015). Google Cloud Platform. Retrieved February 2, 2015, from https://cloud.google.com/

Graffi, K., Podrajanski, S., Mukherjee, P., Kovacevic, A., & Steinmetz, R. (2008, December). A distributed platform for multimedia communities. In*Multimedia, 2008. ISM 2008. Tenth IEEE International Symposium on* (pp. 208-213). IEEE. doi:10.1109/ISM.2008.11

Greenberg, A., Hamilton, J., Maltz, D. A., & Patel, P. (2008). The cost of a cloud: Research problems in data center networks. *Computer Communication Review, 39*(1), 68–73. doi:10.1145/1496091.1496103

Greschbach, B., Kreitz, G., & Buchegger, S. (2012, March). The devil is in the metadata—New privacy challenges in Decentralised Online Social Networks. In*Pervasive Computing and Communications Workshops (PERCOM Workshops), 2012 IEEE International Conference on* (pp. 333-339). IEEE.

Grid5000:Home. (2015). https://www.grid5000.fr/

Grover, M. (2015). Processing frameworks for Hadoop. Retrieved March 8, 2015, from http://radar.oreilly.com/2015/02/processing-frameworks-for-hadoop.html

Grund, M., Krüger, J., Plattner, H., Zeier, A., Cudre-Mauroux, P., & Madden, S. (2010). HYRISE: A main memory hybrid storage engine. *Proceedings of the VLDB Endowment, 4*(2), 105–116. doi:10.14778/1921071.1921077

Guan, X. K. L., Song, M., & Song, J. (2011), A survey of research on mobile cloud computing. In*Computer and Information Science (ICIS) IEEE/ACIS 10th International Conference on. IEEE*, pp. 387– 392. doi:10.1109/ICIS.2011.67

Gubbi, J., Buyya, R., Marusic, S., & Palaniswami, M. (2013). Internet of things (iot): A vision, architectural elements, and future directions. *Future Generation Computer Systems, 29*(7), 1645–1660. doi:10.1016/j.future.2013.01.010

Guha, S., Tang, K., & Francis, P. (2008, August). NOYB: privacy in online social networks. In *Proceedings of the first workshop on Online social networks*(pp. 49-54). ACM. doi:10.1145/1397735.1397747

Gurcan, M., Boucheron, L., Can, A., Madabhushi, A., Rajpoot, N., & Yener, B. (2009). Histopathological image analysis: A review. *IEEE Reviews in Biomedical Engineering, 2,* 147–171. doi:10.1109/RBME.2009.2034865 PMID:20671804

H. yu, J. H., & Chuan, K. (2002). PEBL: positive example based Learning for web page classification using SVM . *ACM SIGKDD international conference on knowledge discovery and data mining* (pp. 239-248). ACM.

Hadoop Ambari. (2015). Retrieved from http://hadoop.apache.org/

Hadoop Transform. (2015). Retrieved from http://opensource.com/business/15/3/three-open-source-projects-transform-hado

Han Qi, A. G. (2012). Research on Mobile Cloud Computing: Review, Trend and Perspectives. In *Proceedings of the Second International Conference on Digital Information and Communication Technology and its Applications (DICTAP), IEEE*, pp. 195-202.

Hashem, I., Yaqoob, I., Anuar, N. B., Mokhtar, S., Gani, A., & Khan, S. U. (2015). The rise of "big data" on cloud computing: Review and open research issues. *Information Systems, 47,* 98–115. doi:10.1016/j.is.2014.07.006

Hassan, S., & Asghar, M. (2010, February). Limitation of silicon based computation and future prospects. In *Second international conference on communication software and networks* (pp. 559-561). Singapore: IEEE Computer Society. doi:10.1109/ICCSN.2010.81

Hausenblas, M., & Nadeau, J. (2013). Apache drill: Interactive ad-hoc analysis at scale. *Big Data, 1*(2), 100–104. doi:10.1089/big.2013.0011

Hayes, M., & Shah, S. (2013). Hourglass: A library for incremental processing on Hadoop. In Big Data, 2013 IEEE International Conference on (pp. 742–752). IEEE. doi:10.1109/BigData.2013.6691647

He, B., Fang, W., Luo, Q., Govindaraju, N. K., & Wang, T. (2008). Mars: a MapReduce framework on graphics processors. In Proceedings of the 17th international conference on Parallel architectures and compilation techniques (PACT'08) (pp. 260–269). New York, NY, USA: ACM; Available from http://doi.acm.org/10.1145/1454115.1454152 doi:10.1145/1454115.1454152

Herodotou, H., Lim, H., Luo, G., Borisov, N., Dong, L., Cetin, F. B., & Babu, S. (2011, January). Starfish: A Self-tuning System for Big Data Analytics. In CIDR (Vol. 11, pp. 261-272). Academic Press.

Herodotou, H., Lim, H., Luo, G., Borisov, N., Dong, L., Cetin, F. B., & Babu, S. (2011). Starfish: A self-tuning system for big data analytics. In *Proceedings of the Fifth CIDR Conference.*

Hindman, B., Konwinski, A., Zaharia, M., Ghodsi, A., Joseph, A. D., & Katz, R., … Stoica, I. (2011). Mesos: A platform for fine-grained resource sharing in the data center. In Proceedings of the 8th USENIX conference on Networked systems design and implementation (pp. 22–22). USENIX Association.

Hu, Wen, Chua, & Li. (n.d.). Toward Scalable Systems for Big Data Analytics: A Technology Tutorial. *IEEE Access.*

Huai, Y., Ma, S., Lee, R., O'Malley, O., & Zhang, X. (2013). Understanding insights into the basic structure and essential issues of table placement methods in clusters. *Proceedings of the VLDB Endowment, 6*(14), 1750–1761. doi:10.14778/2556549.2556559

Huang, D., Shi, X., Ibrahim, S., Lu, L., Liu, H., Wu, S., ... (2010). MR-scope: a real-time tracing tool for MapReduce. In Proceedings of the 19th ACM International Symposium on High Performance Distributed Computing (HPDC'10) (pp. 849–855). New York, NY, USA: ACM; Available from http://doi.acm.org/10.1145/1851476.1851598 doi:10.1145/1851476.1851598

Huang, P.-W., & Lai, Y.-H. (2010). Effective segmentation and classification for hcc biopsy images. *Pattern Recognition*, *43*(4), 1550–1563. doi:10.1016/j.patcog.2009.10.014

Hu, H., Wen, Y., Chua, T.-S., & Li, X. (2014). Toward Scalable Systems for Big Data Analytics: A Technology Tutorial. *IEEE Access*, *2*, 652–687. doi:10.1109/ACCESS.2014.2332453

Hunt, P., Konar, M., Junqueira, F. P., & Reed, B. (2010). ZooKeeper: wait-free coordination for internet-scale systems. In Proceedings of the 2010 USENIX conference on USENIX annual technical conference (Vol. 8, pp. 11–11). USENIX.

Hurwitz, J., Nugent, A., Halper, & Kaufman. (2013). Big Data For Dummies. John Wiley & Sons.

IBM. (2012). *IBM What Is Big Data: Bring Big Data to the Enterprise*. Retrieved from http:// www-01.ibm.com/software/data/bigdata/

Ibrahim, S., Jin, H., Lu, L., He, B., & Wu, S. (2011). Adaptive Disk I/O Scheduling for MapReduce in Virtualized Environment. In Proceedings of the 2011 International Conference on Parallel Processing (ICPP 2011) (pp.335–344). Washington, DC, USA: IEEE Computer Society. Available from doi:10.1109/ICPP.2011.86

Ibrahim, S., Jin, H., Lu, L., He, B., Antoniu, G., & Wu, S. (2012). Maestro: Replica-Aware Map Scheduling for MapReduce. In Proceedings of the 2012 12th ieee/acm international symposium on cluster, cloud and grid computing (ccgrid 2012) (pp. 435– 442). Washington, DC, USA: IEEE Computer Society. Available from doi:<ALIGNMENT.qj></ALIGNMENT>10.1109/CCGrid.2012.122

Ibrahim, S., Jin, H., Lu, L., Qi, L., Wu, S., & Shi, X. (2009). Evaluating mapreduce on virtual machines: The hadoop case. In Proceedings of the 1st International Conference on Cloud Computing (cloudcom'09) (pp. 519–528). Springer Berlin Heidelberg: Springer Berlin Heidelberg. Available from doi:10.1007/978-3-642-10665-1_47

Ibrahim, S., Jin, H., Lu, L., He, B., Antoniu, G., & Wu, S. (2013). Handling partitioning skew in MapReduce using LEEN. *Peer-to-Peer Networking and Applications*, *6*(4), 409–424. doi:10.1007/s12083-013-0213-7

Infochimps. (2015). Big Data Technology Suite of Cloud Services. Retrieved February 2, 2015, from http://www.infochimps.com/infochimps-cloud/overview/

Intel. (2006). Increasing Data Center Density While Driving Down Power and Cooling Costs. Retrieved February 4, 2015, from http://www.intel.com/design/Xeon/whitepaper/313462.htm

Intel. (2014). Big Data Cloud: Converging Technologies. Retrieved February 2, 2015, from http://www.intel.com/content/www/us/en/big-data/big-data-cloud-technologies-brief.html

Irshad, H., Gouaillard, A., Roux, L., & Racoceanu, D. (2014). Multispectral band selection and spatial characterization: Application to mitosis detection in breast cancer histopathology. *Computerized Medical Imaging and Graphics*, *38*(5), 390–402. doi:10.1016/j.compmedimag.2014.04.003 PMID:24831181

Irshad, H., Veillard, A., Roux, L., & Racoceanu, D. (2014). Methods for nuclei detection, segmentation, and classification in digital histopathology: A review, current status and future potential. *IEEE Reviews in Biomedical Engineering*, *7*, 97–114. doi:10.1109/RBME.2013.2295804 PMID:24802905

Isard, M., Budiu, M., Yu, Y., Birrell, A., & Fetterly, D. (2007). Dryad: distributed data-parallel programs from sequential building blocks. In Proceedings of the 2nd acm sigops/eurosys 2007 (pp. 59–72). New York, NY, USA: ACM; Available from http://doi.acm.org/10.1145/1272996.1273005 doi:10.1145/1272996.1273005

Islam, M., Huang, A. K., Battisha, M., Chiang, M., Srinivasan, S., & Peters, C., ... Abdelnur, A. (2012). Oozie: towards a scalable workflow management system for Hadoop. In Proceedings of the 1st ACM SIGMOD Workshop on Scalable Workflow Execution Engines and Technologies (p. 4). ACM. doi:10.1145/2443416.2443420

Ivanov, T., Petrov, I., & Buchmann, A. (2012). A Survey on Database Performance in Virtualized Cloud Environments. *International Journal of Data Warehousing and Mining, 8*(3), 1–26. doi:10.4018/jdwm.2012070101

J'egou, Y., Lant'eri, S., Leduc, J., Melab, N., Mornet, G., & Namyst, R. et al.. (2006, November). Grid'5000: A large scale and highly reconfigurable experimental Grid testbed. *International Journal of High Performance Computing Applications, 20*(4), 481–494. doi:10.1177/1094342006070078

M. G. Jaatun, G. Zhao, & C. Rong (Eds.). (2009). Parallel K-Means Clustering Based on MapReduce. In *Proceedings of CloudCom 2009* (LNCS), (vol. 5931, pp. 674–679). Springer-Verlag.

Jagadish, H. V., Gehrke, J., Labrinidis, A., Papakonstantinou, Y., Patel, J. M., Ramakrishnan, R., & Shahabi, C. (2014). Big data and its technical challenges. *Communications of the ACM, 57*(7), 86–94. doi:10.1145/2611567

Jahid, S., Nilizadeh, S., Mittal, P., Borisov, N., & Kapadia, A. (2012, March). DECENT: A decentralized architecture for enforcing privacy in online social networks. In *Pervasive Computing and Communications Workshops (PERCOM Workshops), 2012 IEEE International Conference on* (pp. 326-332). IEEE. doi:10.1109/PerComW.2012.6197504

Javed, B., Bloodsworth, P., Rasool, R., Munir, K., & Rana, O. (2015). *Cloud Market Maker: An automated dynamic pricing marketplace for cloud users, 2015.* .10.1016/j.future.2015.06.004

Ji, C., Li, Y., Qiu, W., Awada, U., & Li, K. (2012). Big data processing in cloud computing environments. In Proceedings of the International Symposium on Parallel Architectures, Algorithms and Networks, I-SPAN. doi:10.1109/I-SPAN.2012.9

Jian, D., Ooi, B. C., Shi, L., & Wu, S. (2010). The performance of mapreduce: An in-depth study. *Proceedings of VLDB Endowment, 3*(1-2), 472–483. doi:10.14778/1920841.1920903

Jin, H., Ibrahim, S., Li, Q., Cao, H., Wu, S., & Shi, X. (2011). *The mapreduce programming model and implementations. Cloud computing: Principles and Paradigms* (pp. 373–390). John Wiley & Sons, Inc. doi:10.1002/9780470940105.ch14

Jin, H., & Sun, X.-H. (2013). Performance comparison under failures of MPI and MapReduce: An analytical approach. In *Future Generation Computer Systems 29 (7)* (pp. 1808–1815). Available from; doi:10.1016/j.future.2013.01.013

Joseph, J., Sharif, O., & Kumar, A. (2014). *Using Big Data for Machine Learning Analytics in Manufacturing.* Tata Consultancy Services Limited White Paper.

Junqueira, F. P., & Reed, B. C. (2009). The life and times of a zookeeper. In *Proceedings of the 28th ACM symposium on Principles of distributed computing* (pp. 4–4). ACM. doi:10.1145/1582716.1582721

Kambatla, K., & Chen, Y. (2014). The truth about MapReduce performance on SSDs. In *Proceedings of the 28th USENIX conference on Large Installation System Administration* (pp. 109–117). USENIX Association.

Kambatla, K., Kollias, G., Kumar, V., & Grama, A. (2014). Trends in big data analytics. *Journal of Parallel and Distributed Computing, 74*(7), 2561–2573. doi:10.1016/j.jpdc.2014.01.003

Kang & Faloutsos. (n.d.). Big Graph Mining: Algorithms and Discoveries. *SIGKDD Explorations, 14*(2).

Kang & Faloutsos. (n.d.). Big Graph Mining: Algorithms and Discoveries. *SIGKDD Explorations, 14*(2).

Kang, U., Tsourakakis, C. E., & Faloutsos, C. (2009). PEGASUS: A Peta-Scale Graph Mining System Implementation and Observations. In Ninth IEEE International Conference on Data Mining, 2009. ICDM '09 (pp. 229–238). doi:10.1109/ICDM.2009.14

Kang, S.-H., Koo, D.-H., Kang, W.-H., & Lee, S.-W. (2013). A case for flash memory ssd in hadoop applications. *International Journal of Control and Automation, 6*(1), 201–210.

Kecskemeti, G., Terstyanszky, G., Kacsuk, P., & Nemeth, Z. (2013). Towards Efficient Virtual Appliance Delivery with Minimal Manageable Virtual Appliances. IEEE Transaction on Services Computing, 7(2), 279-292.

Kemp, N. P. R., Kielmann, T., & Bal, H. (2012). Cuckoo: a computation offloading framework for smartphones. Mobile Computing, Applications, and Services (Vol. 76, pp. 59–79). Springer. doi:10.1007/978-3-642-29336-8_4

Kemper, A., & Neumann, T. (2011). HyPer: A hybrid OLTP&OLAP main memory database system based on virtual memory snapshots. In Data Engineering (ICDE), 2011 IEEE 27th International Conference on (pp. 195–206). IEEE. doi:10.1109/ICDE.2011.5767867

Khalife, R. F. I. (2011). Mobile cloud computing educational tool for image/video processing algorithms.In Digital Signal Processing Workshop and IEEE Signal Processing Education Workshop (DSP/SPE), pp. 529–533, 4-7 Jan 2011.

Khare, R., Cutting, D., Sitaker, K., & Rifkin, A. (2005). Nutch: A flexible and scalable open-source web search engine. In *Proceedings of the 14th international conference on World Wide Web* (Vol. 1, pp. 32–32).

Khokhar, A. A., Prasanna, V. K., Shaaban, M. E., & Wang, C.-L. (1993). Heterogeneous computing: Challenges and opportunities. *Computer, 26*(6), 18–27. doi:10.1109/2.214439

Kite. (2015). Kite. Retrieved March 6, 2015, from http://kitesdk.org/docs/1.0.0/

Ko, S. Y., Hoque, I., Cho, B., & Gupta, I. (2010). Making cloud intermediate data fault-tolerant. In Proceedings of the 1st acm symposium on cloud computing (pp. 181– 192). New York, NY, USA: ACM. Available from http://doi.acm.org/10.1145/ 1807128.1807160

Koll, D., Li, J., & Fu, X. (2013). *With a Little help from my friends: replica placement in decentralized online social networks*. Technical Report IFI-TB-2013-01, Institute of Computer Science, University of Goettingen, Germany.

Kornacker, M., Behm, A., Bittorf, V., Bobrovytsky, T., Ching, C., & Choi, A., … Yoder, M. (2015). Impala: A Modern, Open-Source SQL Engine for Hadoop. In Proceedings of the Seventh CIDR Conference.

Kosta, A. A. S., Hui P., Mortier, R., & Zhang, X. (2011). Unleashing the Power of Mobile Cloud Computing using ThinkAir. *Computing Research Repository.*

Koundinya, Srinath, Sharma, Kumar, Madhu, & Shanbag. (2012). Map Reduce Design and Implementation of apriori Algorithm for Handling Voluminous Data. *Advanced Computing: An International Journal, 3*(6).

Kraska, T., Talwalkar, A., Duchi, J. C., Griffith, R., Franklin, M. J., & Jordan, M. I. (2013). MLbase: A Distributed Machine-learning System. In *Proceedings of the Sixth CIDR Conference.*

Kreps, J., Narkhede, N., & Rao, J. (2011). Kafka: A distributed messaging system for log processing. In *Proceedings of 6th International Workshop on Networking Meets Databases (NetDB).*

Kryczka, M., Cuevas, R., Guerrero, C., Yoneki, E., & Azcorra, A. (2010, April). A first step towards user assisted online social networks. In *Proceedings of the 3rd workshop on social network systems* (p. 6). ACM. doi:10.1145/1852658.1852664

Kumar, R., Bhushan, B., Gupta, S., Sharma, Y., & Gupta, N. (2014). Apache Hadoop, NoSQL and NewSQL Solutions of Big Data. *International Journal of Modern Computer Science, 3.*

Kwak, J. T., Hewitt, S. M., Sinha, S., & Bhargava, R. (2011). Multimodal microscopy for automated histologic analysis of prostate cancer. *BMC Cancer*, *11*(1), 62. doi:10.1186/1471-2407-11-62 PMID:21303560

Kwon, Y. C., Balazinska, M., Howe, B., & Rolia, J. (2012). SkewTune: mitigating skew in mapreduce applications. In Proceedings of the 2012 ACM SIGMOD International Conference on Management of Data (SIGMOD'12) (pp. 25–36). New York, NY, USA: ACM; Available from http://doi.acm.org/10.1145/2213836.2213840 doi:10.1145/2213836.2213840

Lee, E. K., Viswanathan, H., & Pompili, D. (2012, December). Vmap: Proactive thermal-aware virtual machine allocation in hpc cloud datacenters. In *High Performance Computing (HiPC), 2012 19th International Conference on* (pp. 1-10). IEEE.

Lee, G., Chun, B.-G., & Katz, R. H. (2011). Heterogeneity-aware resource allocation and scheduling in the cloud. In Proceedings of the 3rd USENIX Workshop on Hot Topics in Cloud Computing, HotCloud (Vol. 11).

Leibiusky, J., Eisbruch, G., & Simonassi, D. (2012). *Getting started with storm*. O'Reilly Media, Inc.

Li, L., Liang, C. J. M., Liu, J., Nath, S., Terzis, A., & Faloutsos, C. (2011, August). Thermocast: a cyber-physical forecasting model for datacenters. In *Proceedings of the 17th ACM SIGKDD international conference on Knowledge discovery and data mining* (pp. 1370-1378). ACM. doi:10.1145/2020408.2020611

Li, H., Ghodsi, A., Zaharia, M., Baldeschwieler, E., Shenker, S., & Stoica, I. (2013). Tachyon: Memory Throughput I/O for Cluster Computing Frameworks. *Memory (Hove, England)*, *18*, 1.

Li, H., Ghodsi, A., Zaharia, M., Shenker, S., & Stoica, I. (2014). Tachyon: Reliable, memory speed storage for cluster computing frameworks. In *Proceedings of the ACM Symposium on Cloud Computing* (pp. 1–15). ACM. doi:10.1145/2670979.2670985

Lin & Dyer. (2010). *Data-Intensive Text Processing with MapReduce*. Academic Press.

Lin, H., Ma, X., & Feng, W.-C. (2012, June). Reliable MapReduce Computing on Opportunistic Resources. Cluster Computing, 15 (2), 145–161. Available from 10.1007/s10586-011-0158-7

Lin, H., Ma, X., Archuleta, J., Feng, W.-c., Gardner, M., & Zhang, Z. (2010). MOON: MapReduce On Opportunistic eNvironments. In Proceedings of the 19th acm international symposium on high performance distributed computing (pp. 95–106). New York, NY, USA: ACM; Available from http://doi.acm.org/10.1145/1851476.1851489

Lin, J., & Dyer, C. (2010). *Data-Intensive Text Processing with MapReduce*. Academic Press.

Lipic, T., Skala, K., & Afgan, E. (2014). Deciphering Big Data Stacks: An Overview of Big Data Tools. Big Data Analytics: Challenges and Opportunities (BDAC-14).

Liu, H. (2011). Cutting MapReduce Cost with Spot Market. In Proceedings of the 3rd usenix conference on hot topics in cloud computing (pp. 5–5). Berkeley, CA, USA: USENIX Association. Available from http://dl.acm.org/citation.cfm?id= 1863103.1863110

Low, Y., Bickson, D., Gonzalez, J., Guestrin, C., Kyrola, A., & Hellerstein, J. M. (2012). Distributed GraphLab: A framework for machine learning and data mining in the cloud. *Proceedings of the VLDB Endowment*, *5*(8), 716–727. doi:10.14778/2212351.2212354

Lyon, L. (2014). *Integrating Big Data into the Enterprise Data Warehouse*. Retrieved July 2, 2015, from http://www.databasejournal.com/features/db2/integrating-big-data-into-the-enterprise-data-warehouse/

Mahdian, A., Han, R., Lv, Q., & Mishra, S. (2013). Results from a Practical Deployment of the MyZone Decentralized P2P Social Network. *arXiv preprint arXiv:1305.0606.*

Malewicz, G., Austern, M. H., Bik, A. J., Dehnert, J. C., Horn, I., Leiser, N., & Czajkowski, G. (2010). Pregel: a system for large-scale graph processing. In *Proceedings of the 2010 ACM SIGMOD International Conference on Management of data* (pp. 135–146). ACM. doi:10.1145/1807167.1807184

Mangai, J., Kothari, D., & Kumar, V. (2012). *A supervised discretization algorithm for web page classification. Innovations in Information Technology (IIT)* (pp. 226–231). Dubai: IEEE.

MapReduce Tutorial. (2015). Retrieved from http://hadoop.apache.org/docs/r1.2.1/mapred tutorial.html

March, Y. G. V., Leonardi, E., Goh, G., Kirchberg, M., & Lee, B. S. (2011). μcloud: Towards a new paradigm of rich mobile applications. *Procedia Computer Science*, *5*, 618–624. doi:10.1016/j.procs.2011.07.080

Marinelli, E. (2009). *Cloud Computing on Mobile Devices using MapReduce* (Master Thesis Draft). Computer Science Dept., Carnegie Mellon University (CMU).

Mars, J., Tang, L., & Hundt, R. (2011). Heterogeneity in "homogeneous" warehouse-scale computers: A performance opportunity. *Computer Architecture Letters*, *10*(2), 29–32. doi:10.1109/L-CA.2011.14

Marx, V. (2013). Biology: The big challenges of big data.[PubMed]. *Nature*, *498*(7453), 255–260. doi:10.1038/498255a PMID:23765498

Marz, N. (2012). Runaway complexity in Big Data... And a plan to stop it. Retrieved March 10, 2015, from http://www.slideshare.net/nathanmarz/runaway-complexity-in-big-data-and-a-plan-to-stop-it

Marz, N., & Warren, J. (2012). *Big data: principles and best practices of scalable realtime data systems*. Greenwich: Manning Publications.

Mascolo, C. (2010). The power of mobile computing in a social era. *IEEE Internet Computing*, *14*(6), 76–79. doi:10.1109/MIC.2010.150

Mattmann, C., & Zitting, J. (2011). *Tika in Action*. Manning Publications Co.

Maymounkov, P., & Mazieres, D. (2002). Kademlia: A peer-to-peer information system based on the xor metric. In Peer-to-Peer Systems (pp. 53-65). Springer Berlin Heidelberg. doi:10.1007/3-540-45748-8_5

Maziku, H., & Shetty, S. (2014). *Towards a Network Aware Virtual Machine Migration: Evaluating the Cost of Virtual Machine Migration in Cloud Data Centers*. Paper presented at the 3rd International Conference on Cloud Networking (CloudNet), Luxembourg.

McCandless, M., Hatcher, E., & Gospodnetic, O. (2010). *Lucene in Action: Covers Apache Lucene 3.0*. Manning Publications Co.

Mega, G., Montresor, A., & Picco, G. P. (2011, August). Efficient dissemination in decentralized social networks. In *Peer-to-Peer Computing (P2P), 2011 IEEE International Conference on* (pp. 338-347). IEEE. doi:10.1109/P2P.2011.6038753

Mell, P., & Grance, T. (2011). *The NIST definition of cloud computing*. NIST. doi:10.6028/NIST.SP.800-145

Memishi, B., Perez, M. S., & Antoniu, G. (2015). Diarchy: An optimized management approach for mapreduce masters. Procedia Computer Science, 51, 9 - 18. Available from http://www.sciencedirect.com/science/article/pii/S1877050915009874 (International Conference on Computational Science, {ICCS} 2015 Computational Science at the Gates of Nature)

Michel, F. (2015). *How Many Photos Are Uploaded to Flickr Every Day and Month?* Retrieved from https://www.flickr.com/photos/franckmichel/6855169886/

Microsoft, Inc. (2015). http://www.microsoft.com/

Microsoft. (2015). Cloud Services - HDInsight (Hadoop). Retrieved February 2, 2015, from http://azure.microsoft.com/en-us/services/hdinsight/

Miller, R. (2013, October 13). Facebook Now Has 30,000 Servers [article]. Retrieved August 6, 2015 from http://www.datacenterknowledge.com/archives/2009/10/13/facebook-now-has-30000-servers/

Monash, C. (2013). One database to rule them all? Retrieved March 4, 2015, from http://www.dbms2.com/2013/02/21/one-database-to-rule-them-all/

Mone, G. (2013, January). Beyond Hadoop. *Communications of the ACM, 56*(1), 22–24. http://doi.acm.org/10.1145/2398356.2398364 doi:10.1145/2398356.2398364

Moniruzzaman, A., & Hossain, S. (2013). Nosql database: New era of databases for big data analytics-classification, characteristics and comparison. *International Journal of Database Theory & Application, 6*(4), 1–14.

Moore, J., Chase, J. S., & Ranganathan, P. (2006, June). Weatherman: Automated, online and predictive thermal mapping and management for data centers. In *Autonomic Computing, 2006. ICAC'06. IEEE International Conference on* (pp. 155-164). IEEE.

Nandakumar & Yambem. (2014). A Survey on Data Mining Algorithms on Apache Hadoop Platform. *International Journal of Emerging Technology and Advanced Engineering, 4*(1).

Nandakumar, & Yambem. (2014). A Survey on Data Mining Algorithms on Apache Hadoop Platform. *International Journal of Emerging Technology and Advanced Engineering, 4*(1).

Naphade, M., Banavar, G., Harrison, C., Paraszczak, J., & Morris, R. (2011). Smarter cities and their innovation challenges. Computer, 44, 32–39.

Narendula, R., Papaioannou, T. G., & Aberer, K. (2012, June). Towards the realization of decentralized online social networks: an empirical study. In*Distributed Computing Systems Workshops (ICDCSW), 2012 32nd International Conference on* (pp. 155-162). IEEE. doi:10.1109/ICDCSW.2012.62

Narendula, R., Papaioannou, T. G., & Aberer, K. "A decentralized online social network with efficient user-driven replication."*Privacy, Security, Risk and Trust (PASSAT),2012International Conference on and 2012 International Confernece on Social Computing (SocialCom).* IEEE, 2012. doi:10.1109/SocialCom-PASSAT.2012.127

Nasim, R., & Buchegger, S. (2014, December). XACML-Based Access Control for Decentralized Online Social Networks. In *Proceedings of the 2014 IEEE/ACM 7th International Conference on Utility and Cloud Computing* (pp. 671-676). IEEE Computer Society. doi:10.1109/UCC.2014.108

Nathuji, R., & Schwan, K. (2007). Virtualpower: Coordinated power management in virtualized enterprise systems. *Operating Systems Review, 41*(6), 265–278. doi:10.1145/1323293.1294287

Nilizadeh, S., Jahid, S., Mittal, P., Borisov, N., & Kapadia, A. (2012, December). Cachet: a decentralized architecture for privacy preserving social networking with caching. In *Proceedings of the 8th international conference on Emerging networking experiments and technologies* (pp. 337-348). ACM. doi:10.1145/2413176.2413215

Niroshinie Fernando, S. W. L., & Rahayu, W. (2013). Mobile cloud computing: A survey. *Future Generation Computer Systems, 29*, 84–106.

Niwas, S. I., Palanisamy, P., Chibbar, R., & Zhang, W. (2012). An expert support system for breast cancer diagnosis using color wavelet features. *Journal of Medical Systems, 36*(5), 3091–3102. doi:10.1007/s10916-011-9788-9 PMID:22005900

Nolle, T. (n.d.). *How to choose the best cloud big data platform. A vendor cloud platform comparison guide.* Retrieved July 4, 2015, from http://searchcloudapplications.techtarget.com/tip/How-to-choose-the-best-cloud-big-data-platform

O'Driscoll, A., Daugelaite, J., & Sleator, R. D. (2013). 'Big data', Hadoop and cloud computing in genomics.[PubMed]. *Journal of Biomedical Informatics, 46*(5), 774–781. doi:10.1016/j.jbi.2013.07.001 PMID:23872175

Okorafor, E., & Patrick, M. K. (2012, May). Availability of JobTracker machine in Hadoop/MapReduce Zookeeper coordinated clusters. Advanced Computing: An International Journal, 3 (3), 19–30. Available from http://www.chinacloud.cn/upload/ 2012-07/12072600543782.pdf

Olston, C., Reed, B., Srivastava, U., Kumar, R., & Tomkins, A. (2008). Pig latin: a not-so-foreign language for data processing. In *Proceedings of the 2008 ACM SIGMOD international conference on Management of data* (pp. 1099–1110). ACM. doi:10.1145/1376616.1376726

OpenStack. (2014). Sahara. Retrieved March 7, 2015, from https://wiki.openstack.org/wiki/Sahara

OpenStack. (2015). Retrieved from http://en.wikipedia.org/wiki/OpenStack

OpenWRT website: http://openwrt.org/

Oppenheimer, D., Ganapathi, A., & Patterson, D. A. (2003). Why do Internet services fail, and what can be done about it? In Proceedings of the 4th conference on usenix symposium on internet technologies and systems -volume 4 (pp. 1–1). Berkeley, CA, USA: USENIX Association. Available from http://dl.acm.org/citation.cfm?id= 1251460.1251461

Ortiz, J., De Almeida, V. T., & Balazinska, M. (2013, June). A vision for personalized service level agreements in the cloud. In *Proceedings of the Second Workshop on Data Analytics in the Cloud* (pp. 21-25). ACM. doi:10.1145/2486767.2486772

Owen, S., Anil, R., Dunning, T., & Friedman, E. (2011). *Mahout in action.* Manning.

Oxdata. (2015). H2O. Retrieved February 20, 2015, from https://github.com/h2oai/h2o

Ozel, S. A. (2011a). A web page classification system based on a genetic algorithm using tagged-terms as features. *Expert Systems with Applications, 38*(4), 3407–3415. doi:10.1016/j.eswa.2010.08.126

Ozel, S. A. (2011b). *A genetic algorithm based optimal feature selection for Web page classification. Innovations in Intelligent Systems and Applications (INISTA)* (pp. 1–5). Istanbul: IEEE.

Oztan, B., Kong, H., Gurcan, M. N., & Yener, B. (2012). Follicular lymphoma grading using cell-graphs and multi-scale feature analysis. In Proceedings of SPIE 8315, Medical Imaging 2012: Computer-Aided Diagnosis. doi:10.1117/12.911360

Pääkkönen, P., & Pakkala, D. (2015). *Reference Architecture and Classification of Technologies, Products and Services for Big Data Systems.* Academic Press.

Papageorgiou, E., Spyridonos, P., Glotsos, D. T., Stylios, C. D., Ravazoula, P., Nikiforidis, G., & Groumpos, P. P. (2008). Brain tumor characterization using the soft computing technique of fuzzy cognitive maps. *Applied Soft Computing, 8*(1), 820–828. doi:10.1016/j.asoc.2007.06.006

Paul, T., Famulari, A., & Strufe, T. (2014). A survey on decentralized Online Social Networks. *Computer Networks, 75*, 437–452. doi:10.1016/j.comnet.2014.10.005

Pavlo, A., Paulson, E., Rasin, A., Abadi, D. J., DeWitt, D. J., Madden, S., & Stonebraker, M. (2009). A comparison of approaches to large-scale data analysis. In *Proc. ACM International Conference on Management of Data (SIGMOD'09).* New York: ACM.

Philip, N. (2014). *Cluster Computing Comparisons: MapReduce vs. Apache Spark*. Retrieved July 5, 2015, from http://www.qubole.com/blog/big-data/spark-vs-mapreduce/

Pinheiro, E., Weber, W.-D., & Barroso, L. A. (2007). Failure trends in a large disk drive population. In Proceedings of the 5th usenix conference on file and storage technologies (pp. 2–2). Berkeley, CA, USA: USENIX Association; Available from http://dl.acm.org/citation.cfm?id=1267903.1267905

Pivotal. (2015a). Pivotal Cloud Foundry. Retrieved February 2, 2015, from http://www.pivotal.io/platform-as-a-service/pivotal-cloud-foundry

Pivotal. (2015b). Pivotal HAWQ. Retrieved January 22, 2015, from http://www.pivotal.io/big-data/hadoop/sql-on-hadoop

Plank, J. S., Allen, M., & Wolski, R. (2001). The Effect of Timeout Prediction and Selection on Wide Area Collective Operations. In Proceedings of the ieee international symposium on network computing and applications (nca'01) (pp. 320–329). Washington, DC, USA: IEEE Computer Society; Available from http://dl.acm.org/citation.cfm?id=580585.883098

Plattner, H. (2009). A common database approach for OLTP and OLAP using an in-memory column database. In *Proceedings of the 2009 ACM SIGMOD International Conference on Management of data* (pp. 1–2). ACM. doi:10.1145/1559845.1559846

Porter, M. (2006). An algorithm for suffix stripping. *Program*, *40*(3), 211–218. doi:10.1108/00330330610681286

PoweredBy Hadoop. (2015). http://wiki.apache.org/hadoop/PoweredBy

Prajapati, V. (2013). *Big Data Analytics with R and Hadoop*. Packet Publishing.

Prerez, S. (2009). *Why cloud computing is the future of mobile*. Available: http://www.readwriteweb.com

Princeton University. (2010, January 1). *About WordNet. Princeton University. 2010*. Retrieved July 14, 2015, from http://wordnet.princeton.edu

Qin, X., Qin, B., Du, X., & Wang, S. (2013). Reflection on the Popularity of MapReduce and Observation of Its Position in a Unified Big Data Platform. In Y. Gao, K. Shim, Z. Ding, P. Jin, Z. Ren, Y. Xiao, … S. Qiao (Eds.), Web-Age Information Management (pp. 339–347). Springer Berlin Heidelberg. doi:10.1007/978-3-642-39527-7_33

Qiu, J., Jha, S., & Fox, G. C. (2014). Towards HPC-ABDS: An Initial High-Performance BigData Stack. Building Robust Big Data Ecosystem ISO/IEC JTC 1 Study Group on Big Data.

Qureshi, H., Rajpoot, N., Nattkemper, T., & Hans, V. (2009). A robust adaptive wavelet-based method for classification of meningioma histology images. In *Proceedings of MICCAI'2009 Workshop on Optical Tissue Image Analysis in Microscopy, Histology, and Endoscopy (OPTIMHisE)*. Academic Press.

Qureshi, H., Sertel, O., Rajpoot, N., Wilson, R., & Gurcan, M. (2008). Adaptive discriminant wavelet packet transform and local binary patterns for meningioma subtype classification. In *Proceedings of Medical Image Computing and Computer-Assisted Intervention–MICCAI 2008*. New York: Springer. doi:10.1007/978-3-540-85990-1_24

Rabkin, A., & Katz, R. (2010). Chukwa: A system for reliable large-scale log collection. In *Proceedings of the 24th international conference on Large installation system administration* (pp. 1–15). USENIX Association.

Rackspace. (2015). Rackspace Cloud Big Data Platform. Retrieved February 2, 2015, from http://www.rackspace.com/cloud/big-data/

Rajaraman, A., & Ullman, J. (2011). *Mining of Massive Data Sets*. Cambridge Univ. Press. doi:10.1017/CBO9781139058452

Ramos, L., & Bianchini, R. (2008, February). C-Oracle: Predictive thermal management for data centers. In *High Performance Computer Architecture, 2008. HPCA 2008. IEEE 14th International Symposium on* (pp. 111-122). IEEE.

Red Hat. (2015). OpenShift Platform as a Service. Retrieved February 2, 2015, from https://www.openshift.com/products

Ren, K., López, J., & Gibson, G. (2011). Otus: Resource Attribution in Data-intensive Clusters. In *Proceedings of the second international workshop on MapReduce and its applications*. doi:10.1145/1996092.1996094

Rimal, B. P., Choi, E., & Lumb, I. (2009). A Taxonomy and Survey of Cloud Computing Systems. In Networked Computing and Advanced Information Management, International Conference on (Vol. 0, pp. 44–51). Los Alamitos, CA: IEEE Computer Society. doi:10.1109/NCM.2009.218

Ronk, J. (2014). *Structured, Semi-Structured and Unstructured Data*. Retrieved July 2, 2015, from https://jeremyronk. wordpress.com/2014/09/01/structured-semi-structured-and-unstructured-data/

Roy, I., Setty, S. T. V., Kilzer, A., Shmatikov, V., & Witchel, E. (2010). Airavat: security and privacy for MapReduce. In Proceedings of the 7th USENIX conference on Networked systems design and implementation (pp. 20–20). Berkeley, CA, USA: USENIX Association. Available from http://dl.acm.org/citation.cfm?id= 1855711.1855731

Royer, E. M., & Toh, C. K. (1999). A review of current routing protocols for ad hoc mobile wireless networks. *Personal Communications, IEEE, 6*(2), 46–55. doi:10.1109/98.760423

Ruay-Shiung Chang, J. G., & Gao, V. Jingsha He; Roussos, G.; Wei-Tek Tsai, "Mobile Cloud Computing Research - Issues, Challenges and Needs," *Service Oriented System Engineering (SOSE),2013IEEE 7th International Symposium on* pp. 442, 453, 25-28 March 2013.

Rutman, N. (2011). Map/Reduce on Lustre -Hadoop Performance in HPC Environments (Tech. Rep.). Langstone Road, Havant, Hampshire, PO9 1SA, England. Available from http://doi.acm.org/10.1145/1629175.1629197

Rzadca, K., Datta, A., & Buchegger, S. (2010, June). Replica placement in p2p storage: Complexity and game theoretic analyses. In *Distributed Computing Systems (ICDCS), 2010 IEEE 30th International Conference on* (pp. 599-609). IEEE.

Sakr, S., Liu, A., & Fayoumi, A. G. (2013). The Family of Mapreduce and Large-scale Data Processing Systems. ACM Computing Surveys, 46(1), 11:1–11:44.

Salfner, F., Lenk, M., & Malek, M. (2010). A survey of online failure prediction methods. *ACM Computing Surveys, 42*(3), 1–42. doi:10.1145/1670679.1670680

Sanaei, S. A. Z., Gani, A., & Khokhar, R. H. (2012) "Tripod of requirements in horizontal heterogeneous mobile cloud computing," *Proceedings of the 1st International Conference on Computing, Information Systems, and Communications*.

Sap_Analytics. (2015). Big Data Research. Retrieved from www.sap.com/solution/big-data/software/hadoop/index.html

Satyanarayanan, M. A. K. M., Helfrich, C. J., & Hallaron, D. R. O. (2005). Towards seamless mobility on pervasive hardware. Pervasive and Mobile Computing, 1, 157–189.

Satyanarayanan, P. B. M., Caceres, R., & Davies, N. (2009). The case for VM-based cloudlets in mobile computing. *IEEE Pervasive Computing / IEEE Computer Society [and] IEEE Communications Society, 8*(4), 14–23. doi:10.1109/MPRV.2009.82

Scaling Hadoop to 4000 nodes at Yahoo! (2014). http://developer.yahoo.com/blogs/ hadoop/posts/2008/09/scaling\ hadoop\ to\ 4000 nodes\ a/.

Schulz, S., & Strufe, T. (2013, June). d 2 Deleting Diaspora: Practical attacks for profile discovery and deletion. In *Communications (ICC), 2013 IEEE International Conference on* (pp. 2042-2046). IEEE.

Schwittmann, L., Boelmann, C., Wander, M., & Weis, T. (2013, July). SoNet--Privacy and Replication in Federated Online Social Networks. In *Distributed Computing Systems Workshops (ICDCSW), 2013 IEEE 33rd International Conference on* (pp. 51-57). IEEE.

Seong, S. W., Seo, J., Nasielski, M., Sengupta, D., Hangal, S., Teh, S. K., & Lam, M. S. et al. (2010, June). PrPl: a decentralized social networking infrastructure. In *Proceedings of the 1st ACM Workshop on Mobile Cloud Computing & Services: Social Networks and Beyond* (p. 8). ACM.

Sertel, O., Lozanski, G., Shana'ah, A., & Gurcan, M. N. (2010). Computer-aided detection of centroblasts for follicular lymphoma grading using adaptive likelihood-based cell segmentation. *IEEE Transactions on Bio-Medical Engineering, 57*(10), 2613–2616. doi:10.1109/TBME.2010.2055058 PMID:20595077

Shahriar, N., Chowdhury, S. R., Sharmin, M., Ahmed, R., Boutaba, R., & Mathieu, B. (2013, July). Ensuring Beta-Availability in P2P Social Networks. In*Distributed Computing Systems Workshops (ICDCSW), 2013 IEEE 33rd International Conference on* (pp. 150-155). IEEE. doi:10.1109/ICDCSW.2013.91

Shakimov, A., Lim, H., Ćaceres, R., Cox, L. P., Li, K., Liu, D., & Varshavsky, A. (2011, January). Vis-a-vis: Privacy-preserving online social networking via virtual individual servers. In *Communication Systems and Networks (COMSNETS), 2011 Third International Conference on* (pp. 1-10). IEEE.

Shakimov, A., Varshavsky, A., Cox, L. P., & Cáceres, R. (2009, August). Privacy, cost, and availability tradeoffs in decentralized OSNs. In *Proceedings of the 2nd ACM workshop on Online social networks* (pp. 13-18). ACM. doi:10.1145/1592665.1592669

Shan, Y., Wang, B., Yan, J., Wang, Y., Xu, N., & Yang, H. (2010). FPMR: MapReduce Framework on FPGA. In *Proceedings of the 18th Annual ACM/SIGDA International Symposium on Field Programmable Gate Arrays* (pp. 93–102). New York, NY: ACM. doi:10.1145/1723112.1723129

Sharma, R., & Datta, A. (2012, January). Supernova: Super-peers based architecture for decentralized online social networks. In *Communication Systems and Networks (COMSNETS), 2012 Fourth International Conference on*(pp. 1-10). IEEE.

Sharma, V., & Gur, M. S. S. (2013). Energy efficient architectural framework for virtual machine management in IaaS clouds. In *Proceedings of Contemporary Computing (IC3),2013Sixth International Conference on*. IEEE. doi:10.1109/IC3.2013.6612222

Shekhar, S., Gunturi, V., Evans, M. R., & Yang, K. (2012, May). Spatial big-data challenges intersecting mobility and cloud computing. In *Proceedings of the Eleventh ACM International Workshop on Data Engineering for Wireless and Mobile Access* (pp. 1-6). ACM. doi:10.1145/2258056.2258058

Shi, L., Banikazemi, M., & Wang, Q. B. (2008). *Iceberg: An Image Streamer For Space And Time Efficient Provisioning Of Virtual Machines*. Paper presented at the International Conference on Parallel Processing – Workshops, Portland, OR.

Shinjo, Y., Guo, F., Kaneko, N., Matsuyama, T., Taniuchi, T., & Sato, A. (2011, October). A distributed web browser as a platform for running collaborative applications. In *Collaborative Computing: Networking, Applications and Worksharing (CollaborateCom), 2011 7th International Conference on* (pp. 278-286). IEEE. doi:10.4108/icst.collaboratecom.2011.247088

Simpson, T., & Dao, T. (2010, Feb 8). *WordNet-based semantic similarity measurement*. Retrieved July 14, 2015, from http://www.codeproject.com/Articles/11835/WordNet-based-semantic-similarity-measurement

Singh. (2014). Big Data Analytic and Mining with Machine Learning Algorithm. *International Journal of Information and Computation Technology, 4*.

Srikantaiah, S., Kansal, A., & Zhao, F. (2008). Energy aware consolidation for cloud computing. In *Proceedings of the 2008 Conference on Power Aware Computing and Systems*. Academic Press.

Staten, J., Yates, S., Gillett, F. E., Saleh, W., & Dines, R. A. (2008). *Is cloud computing ready for the enterprise*. Forrester Research.

Stonebraker, M., Bear, C., Çetintemel, U., Cherniack, M., Ge, T., & Hachem, N., ... Zdonik, S. (2007). One size fits all? Part 2: Benchmarking results. In Proceedings of the Third CIDR Conference.

Stonebraker, M., Abadi, D., DeWitt, D. J., Madden, S., Paulson, E., Pavlo, A., & Rasin, A. (2010, January). MapReduce and parallel DBMSs: Friends or foes? *Communications of the ACM*, *53*(1), 64–71. http://doi.acm.org/10.1145/1629175.1629197 doi:10.1145/1629175.1629197

Strauch, C., Sites, U.-L. S., & Kriha, W. (2011). NoSQL databases. Retrieved February 2, 2015, from http://www.christof-strauch.de/nosqldbs.pdf

Sun, Z. (2012). Study on Parallel SVM Based on MapReduce. Paper presented at Conference on Worldcomp.

Su, S., Li, J., Huang, Q., Huang, X., Shuang, K., & Wang, J. (2013). Cost-efficient task scheduling for executing large programs in the cloud. *Parallel Computing Elsevier Publications*, *39*(4-5), 177–188. doi:10.1016/j.parco.2013.03.002

Suykens, J., & Vandewalle, J. (1999). Least squares support vector machine classifiers. *Neural Processing Letters*, *9*(3), 293–300. doi:10.1023/A:1018628609742

Talia, D. (2013). Toward cloud-based big data analytics. Retrieved from http://xa.yimg.com/kq/groups/16253916/1476905727/name/06515548.pdf

Talwalkar, A., Kraska, T., Griffith, R., Duchi, J., Gonzalez, J., & Britz, D., ... Wibisono, A. (2012). Mlbase: A distributed machine learning wrapper. In NIPS Big Learning Workshop.

Tandukar, U., & Vassileva, J. (2012). Selective propagation of social data in decentralized online social network. In *Advances in User Modeling* (pp. 213–224). Springer Berlin Heidelberg. doi:10.1007/978-3-642-28509-7_20

Tang, X. (1998). Texture information in run-length matrices. *IEEE Transactions on Image Processing*, *7*(11), 1602–1609. doi:10.1109/83.725367 PMID:18276225

Tan, K. H., Zhan, Y., Ji, G., Ye, F., & Chang, C. (2015). Harvesting Big Data to Enhance Supply Chain Innovation Capabilities: An Analytic Infrastructure Based on Deduction Graph. *International Journal of Production Economics*, *165*, 223–233. doi:10.1016/j.ijpe.2014.12.034

Ternberg, S. R. S. (1986). Grayscale morphology. *Computer Vision Graphics and Image Processing*, *35*(3), 333–355. doi:10.1016/0734-189X(86)90004-6

Thilakarathna, K., Petander, H., Mestre, J., & Seneviratne, A. (2012, October). Enabling mobile distributed social networking on smartphones. In *Proceedings of the 15th ACM international conference on Modeling, analysis and simulation of wireless and mobile systems* (pp. 357-366). ACM. doi:10.1145/2387238.2387299

Thusoo, A., Sarma, J. S., Jain, N., Shao, Z., Chakka, P., & Zhang, N. ... Murthy, R. (2010). Hive - a petabyte scale data warehouse using Hadoop. In 2010 IEEE 26th International Conference on Data Engineering (ICDE) (pp. 996–1005).

Thusoo, A., Sarma, J. S., Jain, N., Shao, Z., Chakka, P., & Anthony, S. (1626–1629). ... Murthy, R. (2009). Hive: A Warehousing Solution over a Map-reduce Framework. *Proceedings of the VLDB Endowment*, *2*(2).

Ting, K., & Cecho, J. J. (2013). *Apache Sqoop Cookbook*. O'Reilly Media.

Tirumala, A., Dunigan, T., & Cottrell, L. (2003). Measuring end-to-end bandwidth with Iperf using Web100. No. SLAC-PUB-9733.

Twitter. (2012). *Twitter Blog, Dispatch from the Denver Debate*. Retrieved from http://blog.twitter.com/2012/10/dispatch-from-denver-debate.html

US Mobile Data Market Updates. (2010). Chetan Sharma Consulting. Retrieved from http://www.chetansharma.com/usmarketupdateq32010.html

Vafopoulos, M. (2006). Information Society: the two faces of Janus. In Artificial Intelligence Applications and Innovations (pp. 643-648). Springer US. doi:10.1007/0-387-34224-9_75

Vaquero, L. M., Merino, L. R., Caceres, J., & Lindner, M. (2009). A break in the clouds: Towards a cloud definition, *ACM Computer Communication. RE:view*, *39*, 50–55.

Vavilapalli, V. K., Murthy, A. C., Douglas, C., Agarwal, S., Konar, M., & Evans, R., ... Baldeschwieler, E. (2013). Apache Hadoop YARN: Yet Another Resource Negotiator. In Proceedings of the 4th Annual Symposium on Cloud Computing (pp. 5:1–5:16). New York: ACM. doi:10.1145/2523616.2523633

Vavilapalli, V. K., Murthy, A. C., Douglas, C., Agarwal, S., Konar, M., Evans, R., ... (2013). Apache Hadoop YARN: Yet Another Resource Negotiator. In Proceedings of the 4th annual symposium on cloud computing (pp. 5:1–5:16). New York, NY, USA: ACM. Available from http://doi.acm.org/10.1145/2523616.2523633

Venugopal, S., Buyya, R., & Ramamohanarao, K. (2006). A Taxonomy of Data Grids for Distributed Data Sharing, Management, and Processing. ACM Computing Surveys, 38(1), 3, es. doi:10.1145/1132952.1132955

VMware. (2013). Serengeti. Retrieved March 8, 2015, from http://www.projectserengeti.org

VMware. (2014). VMware vSphere Big Data Extensions. Retrieved February 16, 2015, from http://www.vmware.com/products/big-data-extensions

Wang et al. (Eds.). (2010). Parallel K-Means Clustering of Remote Sensing Images Based on MapReduce. In *Proceedings of WISM 2010* (LNCS), (vol. 6318, pp. 162–170). Springer-Verlag.

Wang, F., Qiu, J., Yang, J., Dong, B., Li, X., & Li, Y. (2009). Hadoop high availability through metadata replication. In Proceedings of the first international workshop on cloud data management (pp. 37–44). New York, NY, USA: ACM; Available from http://doi.acm.org/10.1145/1651263.1651271 doi:10.1145/1651263.1651271

Wang, L., Von Laszewski, G., Dayal, J., He, X., Younge, A. J., & Furlani, T. R. (2009, December). Towards thermal aware workload scheduling in a data center. In *Pervasive Systems, Algorithms, and Networks (ISPAN), 2009 10th International Symposium on* (pp. 116-122). IEEE. doi:10.1109/I-SPAN.2009.22

Wang, H., Liu, W., & Soyata, T. (2014). Accessing big data in the cloud using mobile devices. In P. R. Chelliah & G. Deka (Eds.), *Handbook of Research on Cloud Infrastructures for Big Data Analytics* (pp. 444–470)., doi:10.4018/978-1-4666-5864-6.ch018

Ward, J. S., & Barker, A. (2013). *Undefined By Data: A Survey of Big Data Definitions*. arXiv:1309.5821v1 (cs.DB)

White, T. (2012). Hadoop -The Definitive Guide: Storage and Analysis at Internet Scale (3. ed., revised and updated). O'Reilly.

Wikipedia. _BigData. (2015). Visualization of daily Wikipedia edits created by IBM. Retrieved from http://en.wikipedia.org/wiki/Big_data

Wikipedia. _R. (2015). Retrieved from http://en.wikipedia.org/wiki/R_(programming_language

Wikipedia. _SpotFire. (2015). Retrieved from http://en.wikipedia.org/wiki/Spotfire

Wu, C., Li, B., & Zhao, S. (2009). Diagnosing Network-wide P2P Live Streaming Inefficiencies. In Proceedings of INFOCOM IEEE. IEEE.

Wu. (2009). *MReC4.5: C4.5 Ensemble Classification with MapReduce*. China Grid.

Wu. (2009). MReC4.5: C4.5 Ensemble Classification with MapReduce. *chinagrid*.

Wu, L., Yuan, L., & You, J. (2015). Survey of Large-Scale Data Management Systems for Big Data Applications. *Journal of Computer Science and Technology, 30*(1), 163–183. doi:10.1007/s11390-015-1511-8

Wu, X., Zhu, X., Wu, G. Q., & Ding, W. (2014). Data mining with big data. *Transactions on Knowledge and Data Engineering: IEEE, 26*(1), 97–107. doi:10.1109/TKDE.2013.109

Wu, X., Zhu, X., Wu, G.-Q., & Ding, W. (2014). Data Mining with Big Data. *IEEE Transactions on Knowledge and Data Engineering, 26*(1).

Xavier, M. G., Neves, M. V., & Rose, C. A. F. D. (2014). A Performance Comparison of Container-Based Virtualization Systems for MapReduce Clusters. In Parallel, Distributed and Network-Based Processing (PDP), 2014 22nd Euromicro International Conference on (pp. 299–306). IEEE. doi:10.1109/PDP.2014.78

Xin, R. S., Rosen, J., Zaharia, M., Franklin, M. J., Shenker, S., & Stoica, I. (2013). Shark: SQL and Rich Analytics at Scale. In *Proceedings of the 2013 ACM SIGMOD International Conference on Management of Data* (pp. 13–24). New York, NY, USA: ACM. doi:10.1145/2463676.2465288

Xu, H., & Lau, W. C. (2014, June). Speculative execution for a single job in a mapreducelike system. In Cloud computing (cloud), 2014 ieee 7th international conference on (p. 586-593).

Xu, T., Chen, Y., Zhao, J., & Fu, X. (2010, June). Cuckoo: towards decentralized, socio-aware online microblogging services and data measurements. In *Proceedings of the 2nd ACM International Workshop on Hot Topics in Planet-scale Measurement* (p. 4). ACM. doi:10.1145/1834616.1834622

Yahoo. (2013). Storm-YARN. Retrieved March 14, 2015, from https://github.com/yahoo/storm-yarn

Yahoo. Inc. (2015). http://www.yahoo.com/

Yang, T. P. X., & Shen, J. (2010). On 3g mobile e- commerce platform based on cloud computing. In *Ubi- media Computing (U-Media), 3rd IEEE International Conference on. IEEE,* pp. 198–201, 5-6 July 2010.

Yin. (2012). Accelerating Expectation-Maximization Algorithms with Frequent Updates. In *Proceedings of 2012 IEEE International Conference on Cluster Computing*. IEEE.

Zaharia, M., Borthakur, D., Sarma, J. S., Elmeleegy, K., Shenker, S., ... (2010). Delay scheduling: a simple technique for achieving locality and fairness in cluster scheduling. In Proceedings of the 5th European conference on Computer systems (EuroSys' 10) (pp. 265–278). New York, NY, USA: ACM; Available from http://doi.acm.org/10.1145/1755913.1755940 doi:10.1145/1755913.1755940

Zaharia, M., Chowdhury, M., Das, T., Dave, A., Ma, J., & McCauley, M., ... Stoica, I. (2012). Resilient distributed datasets: A fault-tolerant abstraction for in-memory cluster computing. In Proceedings of the 9th USENIX conference on Networked Systems Design and Implementation (pp. 2–2). USENIX Association.

Zaharia, M., Konwinski, A., Joseph, A. D., Katz, R., & Stoica, I. (2008). Improving MapReduce performance in heterogeneous environments. In Proceedings of the 8th USENIX conference on Operating systems design and implementation (pp. 29–42). Berkeley, CA, USA: USENIX Association; Available from http://dl.acm.org/ citation.cfm?id=1855741.185574

Zaharia, M., Chowdhury, M., Franklin, M. J., Shenker, S., & Stoica, I. (2010). Spark: cluster computing with working sets. In *Proceedings of the 2nd USENIX conference on Hot topics in cloud computing* (pp. 10–10).

Zaharia, M., Das, T., Li, H., Hunter, T., Shenker, S., & Stoica, I. (2013). Discretized Streams: Fault-tolerant Streaming Computation at Scale. In *Proceedings of the Twenty-Fourth ACM Symposium on Operating Systems Principles* (pp. 423–438). New York, NY: ACM. doi:10.1145/2517349.2522737

Zhang, L., Wu, C., Li, Z., Guo, C., Chen, M., & Lau, F. C. M. (2013). Moving big data to the cloud. In INFOCOM (pp. 405–409). IEEE. Retrieved from doi:10.1109/INFCOM.2013.6566804

Zhao, Y., & Wu, J. (2013). Dache: A Data Aware Caching for Big-Data Applications Using the MapReduce Framework. In *Proc. 32nd IEEE Conference on Computer Communications, INFOCOM 2013*. IEEE Press. doi:10.1109/INFCOM.2013.6566730

Zhong, B. W. L., & Wei, H. (2012). Cloud Computing Applied in the Mobile Internet. In *7th International Conference on Computer Science & Education (ICCSE)*, pp. 218-221. doi:10.1109/ICCSE.2012.6295061

Zhu, H., & Chen, H. (2011). Adaptive failure detection via heartbeat under Hadoop. In Proceedings of the 2011 IEEE Asia-Pacific Services Computing Conference (ApSCC'11) (pp. 231–238). New York, NY, USA: IEEE. Available from doi:10.1109/APSCC.2011.46

Zicari, R. (2013). Big Data: Challenges and Opportunities. In R. Akerkar (Ed.), *Big Data Computing* (p. 564). Chapman and Hall/CRC; doi:10.1201/b16014-5

About the Contributors

Rajkumar Kannan received the B.Sc and M.Sc degrees in Computer Science from Bharathidasan University – Tiruchirappalli, India in 1991 and 1993 respectively and the PhD degree in Computer Applications from National Institute of Technology – Tiruchirappalli, India in 2007. Rajkumar works for King Faisal University, Saudi Arabia in the College of Computer Science and Information Technology. His research activities primarily lie at the confluence of multimedia, information retrieval, semantic web, social informatics and collective intelligence. Rajkumar is a member of ACM and life member of CSI-India and ISTE-India.

Raihan ur Rasool is currently serving at King Faisal University (KFU) as Assistant Professor –where he is leading the effort of building CCSIT Innovation and Research Showcase (CIRS). Prior to joining CCSIT-KFU he was Fulbright post-doctorate fellow at the University of Chicago. He has over 8 years of post-PhD research, teaching and administration experience. After earning PhD from Wuhan University of Technology, China in 2007 he joined National University of Sciences and Technology (NUST) Pakistan; where he fulfilled duties at different levels. He worked as a knowledge group head, head of department and Associate Dean. Under his leadership NUST Pakistan won the ACM global award of 'Best School Services' consecutively for 3 years. His research interests include computer architecture, virtualization technology, cluster and cloud computing, peer-to-peer computing and big data analysis with pattern matching. His research work, comprising over 35 articles is published in various international conferences and journals. He has published in leading avenues of research like ISCA, HiPEC, CCGrid, ACM SIGARCH, IEEE Transactions in Cloud Computing & FGFS.

Hai Jin is a Professor of Computer Science and Engineering at the Huazhong University of Science and Technology (HUST) in China. He is now the Dean of School of Computer Science and Technology at HUST. He received his Ph.D. in computer engineering from HUST in 1994. In 1996, he was awarded German Academic Exchange Service (DAAD) fellowship for visiting the Technical University of Chemnitz in Germany. He worked for the University of Hong Kong between 1998 and 2000 and participated in the HKU Cluster project. He worked as a visiting scholar at the University of Southern California between 1999 and 2000. He is the chief scientist of the largest grid computing project, ChinaGrid, in China. Dr. Jin is a senior member of IEEE and member of ACM. He is the member of Grid Forum Steering Group (GFSG). His research interests include computer architecture, cluster computing and grid computing, virtualization technology, peer-to-peer computing, network storage, network security.

S. R. Balasundaram has been working since 1987 at National Institute of Technology (formerly known as Regional Engineering College) Tiruchirappalli After completing M.C.A. from PSG College of Technology, Coimbatore, he joined REC Trichy during 1987 as Computer Programmer. He completed M.E. in Computer Science & Engineering during 1992. Currently he is working as Associate Professor in the Department of Computer Applications, earned his doctorate in "E-Learning and Assessment" from NIT, Trichy. Has more than 40 papers in reputed Journals and Proceedings of International conferences. His areas of interest are: Web & Mobile Technologies, Cognitive Sciences and e-Learning Technologies.

* * *

Muhammad Adeel is an Assistant Professor at Department of Computer Science and Software Engineering, International Islamic University, Islamabad.

S. ZerAfshan Goher has done her MS in information technology from School of Electrical Engineering and Computer Science (SEECS) a constituent college of National University of Sciences and Technology (NUST). Her area of interest lies in Grid and cloud computing. She has been teaching in a private university for last three years and has supervised many students of different research areas.

Farid Ahmad was born in Baghpat, Uttar Pradesh (India). He received the Ph.D. degree in Computer Science from Indian university in 2012. He has sound experience of academic as well as industry. He is currently working as Assistant Professor in the Department of Computing, Adama Science and Technology University, Adama (Ethiopia), Africa. He started his career by IT Industry and earlier worked in many renowned companies like HCL Infosystems Ltd, Tata Consultancy Services Ltd (TCS) and BirlaSoft Ltd., etc. His research interest fields are database systems and wireless networking.

Gabriel Antoniu is a Senior Research Scientist at Inria Rennes, where he founded and is now leading the KerData team focusing on scalable distributed storage. His current research activities include data management for large scale distributed infrastructures including clouds and post-petascale HPC machines. In this area, he has served a lead for the MapReduce ANR project, the A-Brain and Z-CloudFlow projects on scalable storage for Azure clouds in partnership with Microsoft Research. He also leads the Data@Exascale associated team with the Argonne National Laboratory and University of Chicago. He served as a Program Chair for IEEE Cluster 2014, he has been involved in the organization of several international conferences in the area of distributed computing (HPDC, Euro-Par, Cluster) and regularly participates to Program Committees of the major international conferences in this area. He has acted for advisor of 17 PhD theses and has co- authored over 100 international scientific publications.

Usman Ashraf is currently an Assistant Professor at the department of Computer Networks in the College of Computer Sciences and Information Technology at King Faisal University Al-Ahsa. He was previously the chair of the department of Computer Science at Air University, Pakistan where he headed the Network Research Lab (NRL). He was also the Principal Investigator for the $125,000 WiMesh project in which Wi-Fi based communication is being explored for emergency communication in disaster scenarios. He holds a BS (Honors) degree in Computer Science from the National University of Computer and Emerging Sciences (NUCES), Lahore, Pakistan, an M.S. degree in Computer Science from University of Toulouse, France and a PhD degree in Computer Science from INSA Toulouse, France (2010). He has several international journal publications to his credit. His research interests include QoS and Routing Solutions for Wireless Networks.

Mohammad Faisal Azeem completed his Bachelors of Computer Science degree from Air University Islamabad. His research interests include wireless routing protocols and performance evaluation of wireless mesh networks.

Saadia Batool is a MSCS (Computer Science) Finalist Software Engineer at Elixir Technologies. She has teaching experience as well.

Peter Bloodsworth joined NUST-SEECS (DoC) as a Foreign Professor in autumn 2011. He has a PhD in Multi-agent Systems from Oxford Brookes University in the UK. Dr. Bloodsworth has more than ten years of experience in academia with a special interest in multi-agent systems, semantic technologies and cloud computing. His current research group is around twenty strong and contains a vibrant mixture of PhD, Masters and Undergraduate students. Before joining SEECS, he worked as a Research Fellow in the Centre for Complex Cooperative Systems at UWE, Bristol and at CERN in Geneva. He has participated in several European projects and was a work package leader in the FP7 funded neuGRID project. His research work is published in various international journals and conferences. He is a full member of IEEE and served in the program committees of major IEEE conferences. He is also a Chartered Member of the British Computing Society (BCS) and continues to act as a reviewer for several IEEE and other international journals.

A. Channabasamma currently works as an assistant professor in the department of Computer Science & Engineering at Acharya Institute of technology, Bangalore. Her Research interest is in the field of Cloud Computing, Data Mining, and Big Data.

M. K. Kavitha Devi received her Degree and Master Degree in Computer Science and Engineering with Distinction and PhD in 1994, 2004 and 2011 respectively. Her area of interest is application of machine learning techniques in recommender systems, data mining and security. She has published more than 10 papers in referred International Journals and Conferences. She is recognized supervisor in Anna University, Chennai and guiding 10 PhD scholars in the field of Computer Science.

Firoza Erum is an MS student at NUCES and is actively working on the classification of text corpus using semantics.

Kiran Fatima has received the MS degree in Computer Science from National University of Computer and Emerging Sciences (NUCES), Islamabad, Pakistan in 2008. She is currently working toward the Ph.D. degree at NUCES, Islamabad. Her research interests include medical image processing, texture and shape analysis, segmentation, feature extraction and classification.

Monica Gahlawat obtained her MCA degree in 2005 from Kurukshetra University. She is pursuing PhD in Computer Science from Gujarat Technological University. She is working as an Assistant Professor in L.J Institute of computer application affiliated to Gujarat Technological University. Her area of interest includes Web Technologies, Distributed Computing specifically cloud computing.

Syed Salman Haider graduated with a Bachelors degree in Computer Science from Air University Islamabad. He has active interests in Wireless Mesh Networking and also works as a freelancer.

R. S. Hegadi obtained MCA in 1995, M.Phil. in 2003 and PhD in Computer Science in 2007 from Gulbarga University, India. He is currently working as Associate Professor and I/c. Director of School of Computational Sciences at Solapur University, Solapur, India. He has more than 18 years of experience teaching and 2 years of industrial experience. His area of interest are Medical image processing, document image analysis, Biometrics. He has published more than 100 research articles in reputed journals and conference proceedings.

Shadi Ibrahim is a permanent Inria Research Scientist within the KerData research team. He obtained his Ph.D. in Computer Science from Huazhong University of Science and Technology in Wuhan of China in 2011. From November 2011 to September 2013, he was a postdoc researcher within the KerData research team working on scalable Big Data managements on clouds. His research interests are in cloud computing, big data management, data-intensive computing, virtualization technology, and file and storage systems. He has published several research papers in recognized Big Data and cloud computing research conferences and journals including TPDS, FGCS, PPNA, SC, IPDPS, Mascots, CCGrid, ICPP, SCC, Cluster, and Cloudcom.

Todor Ivanov is a Ph.D. Student in Computer Science at the Databases and Information Systems (DBIS) Department in Goethe University Frankfurt am Main, Germany.

Barkha Javed did her M.Sc. degree in Information Technology from NUST School of Electrical Engineering and Computer Science (NUST-SEECS), Pakistan. Her main research interests are Distributed Computing, Artificial Intelligence, and Data Management.

Nikolaos Korfiatis is an Assistant Professor in Business Analytics at the Norwich Business School, University of East Anglia (UEA). Prior to his appointment to UEA he cofounded the Frankfurt Big Data Lab at the Goethe University Frankfurt and acted as co-director for Data Science and Analytics. He has solid industrial experience in Analytics and Data Management working both as an educator and consultant. He holds a PhD in Information Management from Copenhagen Business School and a Diploma in Engineering from Royal Institute of Technology, Stockholm Sweden. His research work has been published in international journals and proceedings such as International Journal of Electronic Commerce, Expert Systems with Applications, Journal of the American Society for Information Science and Technology etc. as well as at the International Conference on Information Systems.

Hammad Majeed is currently working as an Assistant Professor at National University of Computer and Emerging Sciences (NUCES), Islamabad, Pakistan. He received the B.E (Software Engineering) degree from NUST, Islamabad, Pakistan in 1999 and the Ph.D. (Computer Science) degree from the University of Limerick, Ireland in 2007. He has research interests in the areas of Artificial Intelligence, Computational Intelligence, Machine Learning, Data Mining and Knowledge Discovery, Evolutionary Gaming, Machine Vision and Robotics.

Asad W. Malik is an assistant professor at NUST School of Electrical Engineering and Computer Science, Islamabad Pakistan. Asad's research interests include optimization, cloud computing and parallel and distributed simulations.

Mehwish Malik is a MS student starting thesis at Department of Computing, National University of Sciences and Technology-SEECS, Islamabad, Pakistan.

T. N. Manjunath received his M. Tech in Computer Science and Engineering from JNNCE, Shimoga during the year 2004. He received his PhD degree in the Area of Effective Data Quality Models for Data Migration Business Enterprises from Bharathiar University, Coimbatore, Tamil Nadu, India. He is currently working as a Professor in the department of CSE at BMS Institute of Technology Bangalore. He is having around 14 years of Professional and Industry experience. He has published and presented around 20 papers in journals, international and national level conferences. His areas of interests are Data Warehouse & Business Intelligence, multimedia and Databases.

Bunjamin Memishi is a PhD student at Universidad Politecnica de Madrid (UPM). Since 2010, he is a member of the Operating Systems Laboratory in UPM, working on fault-tolerant storage systems. Before this, he got his MSc. degree in Computer Engineering from Sapienza University of Rome in 2010, his BSc. degree in Computer Science from South East European University in 2007, where he worked as a teaching assistant for a year. His research interests concern dependability and security in large-scale distributed systems and databases.

Manjunath Thimmasandra Narayanapppa received his M. Tech in Computer Science and Engineering from JNNCE, Shimoga during the year 2004. He received his PhD degree in the Area of Effective Data Quality Models for Data Migration Business Enterprises from Bharathiar University, Coimbatore, Tamil Nadu, India. He is currently working as a Professor in the department of CSE at BMS Institute of Technology Bangalore. He is having around 14 years of Professional and Industry experience. He has published and presented around 20 papers in journals, international and national level conferences. His areas of interests are Data Warehouse & Business Intelligence, multimedia and Databases.

Shahid Nawaz is a Visiting Lecturer at PMAS Arid Agriculture University, Rawaplind, Pakistan.

Maria S. Perez received her Ph.D. in Computer Science in 2003 and an Extraordinary Ph.D. Award from the same university. Since 1998 she has been an associate professor at the Universidad Politecnica de Madrid. Her research interest includes high-performance and large-scale computing, parallel I/O, Big Data and Data Science. She is coauthor of 4 books, 7 book chapters and she has published more than 80 articles in international journals and conferences. She has been involved in the organization of several workshops and conferences, and she has edited several proceedings, books and special issues. She has served as a program committee member of many international conferences (IEEE Cluster, CCGrid, ICPP, SC). She has participated in several international projects funded by European Commission, coordinating the H2020 BigStorage project.

Kumar T. P. Puneeth received his M.Tech in Computer Science and Engineering from Acharya Institute of Technology, Bengaluru during the year 2013.He is having 2 years of experience in Teaching. His areas of interests are Data Warehouse, Business Intelligence and Big Data.

Maryam Qamar is a gold medalist in BS computer science, currently enrolled in MS computer science at Department of Computing, National University of Sciences and Technology-SEECS, Islamabad, Pakistan and her MS thesis research field is saliency modeling.

Anis ur Rahman received his Master's degree in Parallel and Distributed Systems from the Joseph Fourier University, France, and Ph.D. degree in Computer Science in 2013 from Grenoble University, France. He is now an Assistant Professor at NUST. His main research interests comprise modeling of visual attention by assessing the different mechanisms guiding it, and efficient implementations of large-scale scientific problems on commodity graphical processing units (GPUs). More details about Anis can be seen at http://seecs.nust.edu.pk/faculty/anisrahman.html.

Priyanka Sharma has more than 16 years of Teaching & Research experience at Master level in Computer Science and currently working as Professor (IT) in Raksha Shakti University. She has published books and presented and published more than 150 various journal and research papers. She had completed various research projects under UGC grant and guiding Ph.D. Scholars. Her area of interest is Knowledge based systems, Cyber Security, Expert Systems, etc.

K. Indira Suthakar works as Assistant Professor, Information Technology department, in Thiagarajar College of Engineering, Madurai and is doing her research in cloud computing scheduling issues under the guidance of Dr. M. K. Kavitha Devi, Associate Professor, Computer Science Department, Thiagarajar College of Engineering.

Sajid Umair was born in Nowshera KPK, Pakistan in 1992. He received the B.S. degree in computer science from University of Agriculture Peshawar, Pakistan, in 2013, and got a silver medal in his B.S. degree, and is currently pursuing M.S. in computer science from School of Electrical Engineering and Computer Science (SEECS), National University of Sciences and Technology (NUST), Islamabad, Pakistan. His current research work includes Computer vision and Digital image processing. He is also a member of High Performance Computing (HPC) Lab. He is also a chief commissioner award holder in scouting.

Muhammad Nauman Zahoor was born in Islamabad, Pakistan. He received the B.S. degree in Computer Engineering from the Comsats Institute of Information Technology, Islamabad, Pakistan, in 2012, and is currently pursuing Masters of Sciences in Computer Science degree from School of Electrical Engineering and Computer Science, National University of Sciences and Technology, Islamabad, Pakistan.

Index

Become an IRMA Member

Members of the **Information Resources Management Association (IRMA)** understand the importance of community within their field of study. The Information Resources Management Association is an ideal venue through which professionals, students, and academicians can convene and share the latest industry innovations and scholarly research that is changing the field of information science and technology. Become a member today and enjoy the benefits of membership as well as the opportunity to collaborate and network with fellow experts in the field.

IRMA Membership Benefits:

- **One FREE Journal Subscription**

- **30% Off Additional Journal Subscriptions**

- **20% Off Book Purchases**

- Updates on the latest events and research on Information Resources Management through the IRMA-L listserv.

- Updates on new open access and downloadable content added to Research IRM.

- A copy of the Information Technology Management Newsletter twice a year.

- A certificate of membership.

IRMA Membership $195

Scan code to visit irma-international.org and begin by selecting your free journal subscription.

Membership is good for one full year.

www.irma-international.org

Printed in the United States
By Bookmasters